Praise for

100 POEMS TO BREAK YOUR HEART

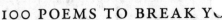

"I was really amazed by Edward Hirsch's *100 Poems to Break Your Heart*. This is really a beautiful book." **—YUSEF KOMUNYAKAA,** *BOSTON GLOBE*

"Who will reach for this assemblage of poems meant to break our hearts? Those who know that solace can be found in poetry and its assurance that one is not alone in facing heartbreak and loss, which is visited upon us in new and crushing ways in the time of COVID-19. Another draw is Hirsch himself, of course, a consummate poet all too fluent in grief, whose radiant books about poetry have guided readers to a deeper appreciation for this endlessly surprising and affecting literary form. Each profoundly arresting poem is accompanied by a succinct yet passionate essay masterfully combining biography and commentary. Hirsch has selected lyrics confronting sorrow engendered by the death of a loved one, war, genocide, exile, violence, racism, and other crimes against humanity.... Darkly illuminating." **—*BOOKLIST* (STARRED REVIEW)**

"Teacher and poet Edward Hirsch explores the ennobling powers of poetry in his compendium of masterful works from around the world." **—CBS NEWS**

Praise for

A POET'S GLOSSARY

"Absorbing.... Full of Hirsch's passion." **—*THE NEW YORKER***

"Edward Hirsch's *A Poet's Glossary* is an instant classic that belongs on the bookshelf of every serious poet and literature student. . . . Hirsch explains them all with the ease of a tour guide who has spent a lifetime learning the territory.... The more you read in this insightful book, the more you'll feel a part of a communal journey that has continued for thousands of years." **—*WASHINGTON POST***

"A glossary is useful, welcome, sometimes fun, but rarely, if ever, a catalyst for astonishment. Leave it to revered poet, poetry apostle, and glossator extraordinaire Hirsch (*The Living Fire*, 2010) to turn this humble resource into a vibrant, polyglot, world-circling, century-spanning, mind-expanding work of profound scholarship and literary art. . . . A thrilling 'repertoire of poetic secrets,' this radiant compendium is shaped by Hirsch's abiding gratitude for the demands and power, illumination, and solace of poetry, 'a human fundamental.'"
—*BOOKLIST* (STARRED REVIEW)

"Offering definitions, a discussion of poetic techniques, and an unalloyed spiritual quality to his work. . . . This compilation of stimulating information and of beautiful writing by a master of expression is for all who love language, not just poets."
—*LIBRARY JOURNAL* (STARRED REVIEW)

Praise for

HOW TO READ A POEM

—◆—

"A lovely book, full of joy and wisdom."
—*BALTIMORE SUN*

"Hirsch's contribution is significant, [grounded] in the obvious pleasure he has experienced through words. . . . Who could resist the wiles of this poetry broker—a writer rapidly becoming the baby boomers' preeminent man of letters?"
—*DETROIT FREE PRESS*

"Laudable. . . . The answer Hirsch gives to the question of how to read a poem is: ecstatically."
—*BOSTON BOOK REVIEW*

100 Poems to Break Your Heart

100 Poems

to

Break

Your Heart

—

Edward Hirsch

ecco

An Imprint of HarperCollins*Publishers*

HarperCollins books may be purchased for educational, business, or sales promotional use. For information, please email the Special Markets Department at SPsales@harpercollins.com.

Ecco® and HarperCollins® are trademarks of HarperCollins Publishers.

A hardcover edition of this book was published in 2021 by Houghton Mifflin Harcourt.

FIRST ECCO PAPERBACK EDITION PUBLISHED 2023

Excerpt from *The Witness of Poetry* by Czesław Miłosz. Copyright © 1983 by the President and Fellows of Harvard College. Used by permission of Harvard University Press. Excerpt from the essay "The Real and the Paradigms" by Czesław Miłosz published in *Poetry Australia*. Copyright © 1979 by Czesław Miłosz. Used by permission of The Wylie Agency LLC.

Credits for poems are listed on pages 483 to 492.

Designed by Greta Sibley

The Library of Congress has cataloged the hardcover edition as follows:

Names: Hirsch, Edward, editor.
Title: 100 poems to break your heart / Edward Hirsch.
Other titles: One hundred poems to break your heart
Description: Boston : Houghton Mifflin Harcourt, 2021. | Includes bibliographical references.
Identifiers: LCCN 2020033839 (print) | LCCN 2020033840 (ebook) | ISBN 9780544931886 (hardcover) | ISBN 9780544931800 (ebook)
Subjects: LCSH: Poetry—Collections. | Poetry—Translations into English. | Poetry—History and criticism.
Classification: LCC PN6101 .A1638 2021 (print) | LCC PN6101 (ebook) | DDC 808.81—dc23
LC record available at https://lccn.loc.gov/2020033839
LC ebook record available at https://lccn.loc.gov/2020033840

ISBN 978-0-358-69935-4 (pbk.)

23 24 25 26 27 LBC 7 6 5 4 3

In memory of

Irma Hirsch (1928–2019)

CONTENTS

Introduction | xv

WILLIAM WORDSWORTH
"Surprised by joy — impatient as the Wind" (1815, 1820) | 1

JOHN KEATS
"This living hand" (1819) | 5

JOHN CLARE
"I am" (c. 1847) | 8

ALFRED, LORD TENNYSON
In Memoriam, VII (c. 1848) | 12

GERARD MANLEY HOPKINS
"Thou art indeed just, Lord, if I contend" (1889) | 16

CONSTANTINE CAVAFY
"The God Abandons Antony" (1910) | 21

THOMAS HARDY
"The Voice" (1912) | 25

EDWARD THOMAS
"The Owl" (1915) | 29

GUILLAUME APOLLINAIRE
 "The Pretty Redhead" (1918) | 33

EDNA ST. VINCENT MILLAY
 "What lips my lips have kissed, and where, and why" (1920) | 39

LANGSTON HUGHES
 "Song for a Dark Girl" (1927) | 44

CHARLOTTE MEW
 "Rooms" (c. 1929) | 49

CÉSAR VALLEJO
 "Black Stone Lying on a White Stone" (1930) | 53

ALFONSINA STORNI
 "I'm Going to Sleep" (1938) | 58

JULIA DE BURGOS
 "To Julia de Burgos" (1938) | 62

ANNA AKHMATOVA
 "In Memory of M. B." (1940) | 67

MIKLÓS RADNÓTI
 "The Fifth Eclogue" (1943) | 71

CZESŁAW MIŁOSZ
 "Café" (1944) | 76

KADYA MOLODOWSKY
 "Merciful God" (1945) | 81

PRIMO LEVI
 "Shemà" (1946) | 86

NÂZIM HIKMET
 "On Living" (1948) | 91

WELDON KEES
 "Aspects of Robinson" (1948) | 97

GWENDOLYN BROOKS
 "The rites for Cousin Vit" (1949) | 102

STEVIE SMITH
 "Not Waving but Drowning" (1953, 1957) | 105

TADEUSZ RÓŻEWICZ
 "In the Midst of Life" (1955) | 109

DAHLIA RAVIKOVITCH
 "On the road at night there stands the man" (1959) | 115

JORGE LUIS BORGES
 "Poem of the Gifts" (1960) | 119

GWEN HARWOOD
    "In the Park" (1961) | 124

ROBERT HAYDEN
    "The Whipping" (1962) | 128

ROBERT LOWELL
    "Night Sweat" (1963) | 133

ANNE SEXTON
    "Wanting to Die" (1964) | 137

ROSE AUSLÄNDER
    "My Nightingale" (1965) | 142

RANDALL JARRELL
    "Next Day" (1965) | 146

J. V. CUNNINGHAM
    "Montana Fifty Years Ago" (1967) | 151

W. S. MERWIN
    "For the Anniversary of My Death" (1967) | 155

MURIEL RUKEYSER
    "Poem" (1968) | 158

ETHERIDGE KNIGHT
    "The Idea of Ancestry" (1968) | 163

JOHN BERRYMAN
    "Henry's Understanding" (1969) | 169

L. E. SISSMAN
    "A Deathplace" (1969) | 173

PHILIP LEVINE
    "They Feed They Lion" (1969) | 178

SOPHIA DE MELLO BREYNER ANDRESEN
    "The Small Square" (1972) | 185

WISŁAWA SZYMBORSKA
    "Under One Small Star" (1972) | 189

RICHARD HUGO
    "Degrees of Gray in Philipsburg" (1973) | 193

STEPHEN BERG
    "On This Side of the River" (1975) | 199

PHILIP LARKIN
    "Aubade" (1977) | 204

WILLIAM MEREDITH
    "Parents" (1978) | 210

HAYDEN CARRUTH
"Essay" (1978) | 214

JAMES SCHUYLER
"Arches" (1978) | 218

NAOMI SHIHAB NYE
"Kindness" (1978, 1994) | 222

ALLEN GROSSMAN
"The Woman on the Bridge over the Chicago River" (1979) | 228

ANTHONY HECHT
"The Book of Yolek" (1981) | 234

ZBIGNIEW HERBERT
"Mr Cogito and the Imagination" (1983) | 240

C. K. WILLIAMS
"From My Window" (1983) | 247

LOUISE GLÜCK
"Night Song" (1983) | 253

SHARON OLDS
"The Race" (1983) | 259

DONALD JUSTICE
"In Memory of the Unknown Poet, Robert Boardman Vaughn"
(1984) | 264

GERALD STERN
"The Dancing" (1984) | 269

JOY HARJO
"For Anna Mae Pictou Aquash, Whose Spirit Is Present Here
and in the Dappled Stars (for we remember the story and
must tell it again so we may all live)" (1985) | 272

GARRETT HONGO
"Mendocino Rose" (1987) | 279

ADRIENNE RICH
"(Dedications)" (1990–91) | 284

THOM GUNN
"The Gas-poker" (1991) | 289

HEATHER MCHUGH
"What He Thought" (1991) | 295

LES MURRAY
"It Allows a Portrait in Line-Scan at Fifteen" (1993) | 301

THOMAS LUX
"The People of the Other Village" (1993) | 306

LINDA GREGERSON
    "For the Taking" (1993) | 310
NICHOLAS CHRISTOPHER
    "Terminus" (1993) | 316
MARIE HOWE
    "What the Living Do" (1994) | 322
DUNYA MIKHAIL
    "The War Works Hard" (1994) | 327
STANLEY KUNITZ
    "Halley's Comet" (1995) | 332
BRIGIT PEGEEN KELLY
    "Song" (1995) | 336
ROSANNA WARREN
    "Simile" (1996) | 341
FRANK BIDART
    "In Memory of Joe Brainard" (1997) | 345
LUCILLE CLIFTON
    "jasper   texas   1998" (1998) | 350
CYNTHIA HUNTINGTON
    "The Rapture" (2000) | 354
RICHARD HOWARD
    "Elementary Principles at Seventy-Two" (2001) | 359
EAVAN BOLAND
    "Quarantine" (2001) | 363
AGI MISHOL
    "Woman Martyr" (2002) | 369
HARRYETTE MULLEN
    "We Are Not Responsible" (2002) | 373
GALWAY KINNELL
    "Shelley" (2004) | 377
VIJAY SESHADRI
    "Aphasia" (2004) | 381
MARY SZYBIST
    "On Wanting to Tell [ ] About a Girl Eating Fish
    Eyes" (2004) | 385
MARY OLIVER
    "Lead" (2005) | 389
ANYA KRUGOVOY SILVER
    "Persimmon" (2005) | 393

PATRICIA SMITH
    "Ethel's Sestina" (2006) | 398

CAROLYN CREEDON
    "Woman, Mined" (2006) | 403

NATASHA TRETHEWEY
    "Graveyard Blues" (2006) | 407

CAMILLE DUNGY
    "Requiem" (2006) | 412

PETER EVERWINE
    "Aubade in Autumn" (2007) | 417

TONY HOAGLAND
    "Barton Springs" (2007) | 421

PHILIP SCHULTZ
    "Failure" (2007) | 425

MICHAEL COLLIER
    "An Individual History" (2007) | 429

LUCIA PERILLO
    "The Second Slaughter" (2008) | 434

MICHAEL WATERS
    "Old School" (2010) | 439

LUCIE BROCK-BROIDO
    "Infinite Riches in the Smallest Room" (2013) | 442

YUSEF KOMUNYAKAA
    "The African Burial Ground" (2014) | 448

KATE DANIELS
    "The Addict's Mother: Birth Story" (2014–15) | 454

AFAA MICHAEL WEAVER
    "Spirit Boxing" (2015) | 458

VICTORIA CHANG
    "Obit [The Blue Dress]" (2016) | 463

TOI DERRICOTTE
    "Pantoum for the Broken" (2017) | 466

MEENA ALEXANDER
    "Krishna, 3:29 A.M." (2018) | 471

Acknowledgments | 479

Credits | 483

In a murderous time
        the heart breaks and breaks
            and lives by breaking.

— Stanley Kunitz, "The Testing-Tree"

INTRODUCTION

We live in distracting times. Our superficial, materialistic, media-driven culture often seems uncomfortable with true depths of feeling. It's as if the culture as a whole has become increasingly intolerant of that acute sorrow, that intense mental anguish and remorse that can be defined as grief. We want to medicate such sorrow away. We want to divide it into recognizable stages so that grief can be tamed, labeled, and put behind us. But poets have always celebrated grief as one of the strongest human emotions, one of our signature feelings.

Implicit in poetry is the notion that we are deepened by heartbreaks, by the recognition and understanding of suffering — not just our own suffering but also the suffering of others. We are not so much diminished as enlarged by grief, by our refusal to vanish, or to let others vanish, without leaving a verbal record. The poet is one who will not be reconciled, who is determined to leave a trace in words, to transform oceanic depths of feeling into the faithful nuances of art.

Poetry companions us. Poems are written in solitude, but they reach out to others, which makes poetry a social act. It rises out of one solitude to meet another. Poems of terrible sadness and loss trouble and challenge us, but they also make us feel less alone and more connected. Our own desolations become more recognizable to us, more articulate, something shared. We become less isolated in our sorrow, and thus are befriended by the words of another. There is something ennobling in grief that is compacted, expressed, and transfigured into poetry.

I know that I have brought my own griefs and sympathies to bear in the reading and writing of poetry. Over the course of my life, I have been vastly enriched by heartbreaking poems from many different eras and languages. In this book, I have chosen poems from the nineteenth, twentieth, and twenty-first centuries. I have selected poems that have been especially meaningful to me, and I have tried to illuminate them — for myself as well as for others. My goal is to create a dramatic, sometimes biographical, often historical context for the poems, explaining their references, teasing out their meanings, unpacking them. I have tried to show how poems work, how their techniques operate in the service of their subjects. My desire is not to explain poems away, but to enable the reader to experience them more completely and more humanly.

A word about nomenclature. The poems in this book are extreme human documents, but they are also poems, made things. Many of them deal with intensely personal experiences that have been transformed into art. In writing about each poem, I've tried to honor the life experience of the poet who wrote it while also paying close attention to the art of the maker. That's why I tend to use the phrase "the poet" when I'm discussing an author's craft and intention. I use the phrase "the speaker," the constructed "I," for the figure who narrates the poem. This is complicated by the fact that, either intentionally or unintentionally, many of these poems blur the distinction. In such cases it's accurate to say that the speaker serves as a stand-in for the poet. I've tried to be responsive to the personhood of individual works while also heeding Emily Dickinson's warning to Thomas Higginson: "When I state myself, as the Representative of the Verse — it does not mean — Me — but a supposed person."

In discussing these poems, I've avoided technical language whenever possible, but sometimes, especially in nineteenth- and early-twentieth-century metrical poems, I have resorted to formal terms and metrical analysis. Many of these earlier poems were written in blank verse, unrhymed iambic pentameter, the five-beat, ten-syllable line that has characterized so much of English-language poetry. It has been estimated that three-fourths of all English poetry up until the twentieth century is written in blank verse, which suggests that it is the modal pattern in English, the pattern closest to natural speech, and therefore it has often been used to evoke the spoken word, to create a speaker in a dramatic situation.

This book includes sonnets and sestinas, aubades and elegies, an eclogue, a villanelle, a blues poem, a night song or nocturne, a pantoum, prose poems, lyrics that rhyme and lyrics that don't, intentional and unintentional fragments, poems pitched at the level of speech, others that sing. There are prayers and anti-prayers. There are many nonce forms — that is, poetic forms invented for a single purpose; "for the nonce" means "for the occasion." Each one has a discernible pattern. Throughout this book, I've explained the forms and tried to find a vocabulary to describe each poem on its own terms. I hope this language isn't intimidating.

So too certain formal elements recur throughout, such as the difference between end-stopped and enjambed lines; understanding this distinction is crucial to the reading of lyric poems. In an end-stopped line, a natural grammatical pause, such as the end of a phrase, clause, or sentence, coincides with the end of a line. It slows or halts the movement of the verse and creates the sense of the line as a whole syntactical unit, which gives it rhetorical weight and authority, a meaning unto itself. The alternative is an enjambed, or run-over, line. Enjambment is the carryover of one line of poetry to the next without a grammatical break. It creates a dialectical motion of hesitation and flow. The lineation bids the reader to pause at the end of each line, yet the syntax pulls the reader forward. This creates a sensation of hovering expectation. In 1668 John Milton called enjambment "the sense variously drawn out from one verse into another." It breaks the sense of the line as a terminus.

I have included a wide range of poems that have been translated into English from many different languages. It is ideal, of course, to read such a poem in the original. But it's also unlikely that any one reader would know all these languages, since this book includes poems from Greek, French, Spanish, Russian, Hungarian, Polish, Yiddish, Hebrew, Turkish, German, Portuguese, and Arabic. I have spoken to poets and translators working in these languages whenever possible. I've read the criticism available in English, but I'm aware that my formal analysis is necessarily limited by my own linguistic constraints. There is always something untranslatable about a poem. Yet these poems also bring us a sensibility, a range of tones and feelings, that aren't otherwise available in English. They add to the sum of our human experience.

These one hundred poems include a wide range of poets. There are varieties of grief, and I recognize that I have identified only some of them. This book isn't meant to be definitive — there are hundreds of other poets writing in many disparate languages whose work has moved me over the years. I wish I had the space to include them all. I encourage you to put together your own personal anthology. In the meantime, I hope you'll find the poems I've chosen as moving as I have found them. No one escapes unscathed — we all have our hearts broken. And yet, as Czesław Miłosz puts it in his "Elegy for N. N.," "the heart does not die when one thinks it should." Despite everything, we go on. We might even say that we live to have our hearts broken — and restored.

Here are one hundred poems to break your heart.

WILLIAM WORDSWORTH

—

"Surprised by joy
— impatient as the Wind"

(1815, 1820)

On the night of June 4, 1812, William Wordsworth's daughter Catherine died suddenly after a series of convulsions. She was not quite four years old. To make matters worse, both her parents were away, and Wordsworth did not even learn about his daughter's death until a week later, when she was already buried in Grasmere. In December the parents were struck again when their son Thomas died of measles and was buried next to his sister. He was six years old.

"Surprised by joy" was, as Wordsworth recollected, "Suggested by my daughter Catherine, long after her death." It was the only piece he wrote for her. The poet is clearly the speaker of this poem, which commemorates the two worst "pangs" of his life.

> Surprised by joy — impatient as the Wind
> I turned to share the transport — Oh! With whom
> But Thee, deep buried in the silent tomb,
> That spot which no vicissitude can find?
> Love, faithful love recalled thee to my mind —

But how could I forget thee? — Through what power,
Even for the least division of an hour,
Have I been so beguiled as to be blind
To my most grievous loss? — That thought's return
Was the worst pang that sorrow ever bore,
Save one, one only, when I stood forlorn,
Knowing my heart's best treasure was no more;
That neither present time, nor years unborn
Could to my sight that heavenly face restore.

Wordsworth's sonnet unfolds in fourteen regular iambic pentameter lines. Inspired by the Petrarchan sonnet form, the rhyme scheme is tight: *abbaac-cadedede.* Many of Wordsworth's sonnets are grandly rhetorical, fit for public declamation, but this poem is different, tender and filled with self-reproach. It begins emphatically with an indelible phrase, "Surprised by joy," which carries a sense of radical unexpectedness. Wordsworth's poems are filled with seren-dipitous moments, and here the poet is startled into delight over something he has just seen, which leads him to turn toward his companion in order to share that delight.

"Joy" was one of Wordsworth's favorite words. For example, he used it nearly fifty times in *The Prelude,* where joy almost always expresses a feeling of infinity revealed through nature, a spot of time. Wordsworth's pantheistic spirit, which usually came to him in solitude, is all the more poignant here be-cause he so naturally wants to share it with his daughter and cannot. Thus, the shock of loss replaces the feeling of joy. In *The Story of Joy* the scholar Adam Potkay recognizes that "Wordsworth's sonnet of joy is his great poem of sor-row."

The poem's combination of intensity and formal control reflects both Wordsworth's character and his behavior, which were, as his friend Henry Crabb Robinson put it, "that which became a man both of feeling and strength of mind." As a thinker, Wordsworth was composed and confidently declared: "Poetry is the spontaneous overflow of powerful feelings; it takes its origins from emotion recollected in tranquility." This statement is so definitive and forceful that it is easy to forget what he went on to say — that "the emotion is contemplated till, by a species of reaction, the tranquility gradually disap-pears." From a vantage point achieved by the passage of time, the poet can contemplate past emotion, examine and articulate it. By reliving it in memory, the poet can also express the rawness of the feeling as if experiencing it anew, thereby combining the immediacy of emotion with the perspective of intellect.

Wordsworth's editing choices show how his intellect focused his emotions. For example, in the first version of this sonnet he wrote, "I wished to share the transport," but later amended it to "I turned to share the transport," which changes an aspiration into an action, an abrupt pivot toward the missing companion, the lost daughter. I see the speaker physically turn to where he thinks she is, and then realize that she has no vital physical being anymore.

Wordsworth also changed "long" to "deep" in the third line. To be "long buried" is a more abstract temporal description; however, to be "deep buried" brings the burial into the realm of the concrete, which creates the greater shock of a subterranean or bottomless finality. He contrasts his intense responses, his surprise and impatience, with the impenetrability of the tomb, "That spot which no vicissitude can find." *The American Heritage Dictionary* defines *vicissitude* as "a change or variation; mutability."

The poem's first two lines accelerate with an enjambment that pushes the poem forward. The dashes create a feeling both of rapidity and spontaneity, only to be broken off by a sudden exclamation, the hollowness of "Oh! With whom . . ." The exclamatory "Oh!" suggests the O-shape of the speaker's open mouth when he realizes his daughter is not standing next to him. The word "whom" ends the second line and seems to pose a question, soon answered in the third line, with "But Thee, deep buried in the silent tomb," which also indicates that he is addressing an absence. Read retrospectively then, "whom" seems ordained to rhyme with "tomb." Because Wordsworth wrote this poem a few years after Catherine's death, he had started to move on, forgetting his enormous sadness, but then got wrenched back into it.

Wordsworth was not characteristically a self-questioning poet, but here, three questions appear in the poem's first eight lines. The first two are directed to the daughter, but the third one the speaker turns on himself, wondering "Through what power" he could have been "so beguiled as to be blind / To my most grievous loss?" Notice how he makes the short but mortifying leap from "beguiled" to "be blind," with the subtle repetitions of *b, l,* and *d* sounds, the assonance of the long *e* and long *i,* and the lopping off of *be* from "beguiled" to form two words, "be blind." So too the turn toward Catherine is enacted through three words timed to recur at key points in the sonnet: "recalled," "return," "restore." This repetition of the prefix *re-,* which means "back" or "again," drives home the poem's shattering realization that the speaker can never go back nor see his beloved daughter ever again.

After eight and a half lines roiled by dashes and questions, the final sestet unrolls in a single sentence, the pace calmer, more meditative:

> That thought's return
> Was the worst pang that sorrow ever bore,
> Save one, one only, when I stood forlorn,
> Knowing my heart's best treasure was no more;
> That neither present time, nor years unborn
> Could to my sight that heavenly face restore.

We hear the steep echo chamber of triple rhymes: "return" / "forlorn" / "unborn" and "bore" / "more" / "restore," as well as the close assonant rhyming of all six final lines. This relentless sonic repetition — hear the drumbeat of similar *o* and *n* sounds in "Save one, one only, when I stood forlorn" — seems to enact the speaker's denial about the loss of his daughter, so that in these last lines he must repeat what he cannot accept. Neither the present nor the future can "restore" his daughter's "heavenly face." There is a hint of Christianity in the word "heavenly" without any real sense of redemption.

In the end, after Wordsworth turns to speak to his daughter and instead must address her absence, he is forced to face the oppressive silence of death. The heartbreak of the poem is also the answer to its final question and its last pang — that time has the power to make the living forget their griefs, that time consigns the dead to the past and drags the living back to life, where they can be surprised by joy.

JOHN KEATS

——

"This living hand"
(1819)

It was December 1819, and John Keats's health was perilous. The wastage of his body was becoming apparent. The poet Leigh Hunt remembered that his friend, who was just twenty-five years old, often looked at his hand, "which was faded, and swollen in the veins, and say it was the hand of a man of fifty." Keats had received his death warrant from tuberculosis, and the great poems were behind him — the sonnets and the odes, including "To Autumn," which may be the most perfect poem in English. He was working on a comic poem to be called "The Cap and Bells; or, The Jealousies." He never finished this fairy tale, the weakest of his mature poems, whose Spenserian stanzas he churned out with remarkable fluency to earn some money for his publisher; but at some point while he was writing it, he broke off and jotted down some lines in a blank space on the manuscript. He turned from stanza 51 — "*Cupid, I / Do thee defy!*" — and marked this untitled eight-line fragment where there was room on the page:

This living hand, now warm and capable
Of earnest grasping, would, if it were cold
And in the icy silence of the tomb,
So haunt thy days and chill thy dreaming nights
That thou would wish thine own heart dry of blood
So in my veins red life might stream again,
And thou be conscience-calm'd — see, here it is —
I hold it towards you.

It was once thought that these lines were addressed to Keats's great love, his fiancée, Fanny Brawne, but most scholars now agree that Keats meant them for use in a later poem or play. They weren't published until 1898, when they appeared in the sixth edition of H. B. Forman's one-volume edition of Keats's work. Once encountered, though, this fragment of consciousness can't be ignored or forgotten.

The poem begins with an arresting image of a "warm and capable" hand that seems somehow detached from the rest of the body. This image is so vivid that the poem feels straightforward, utterly direct, though the verb tenses are a little tricky. In the middle of the second line Keats introduces the conditional tense with the word "would," set off by commas, indicating a proposition or a hypothetical statement about the hand. The poet imagines the warm hand "cold" and ends the line on this enjambment. The third line elaborates on the hand's coldness: "And in the icy silence of the tomb." In "The Fall of Hyperion" Keats had already foreseen a similar moment: "When this warm scribe my hand is in the grave." Here he makes explicit that the warm detached hand is also a scribe, the instrument by which the poet's thoughts get transposed to the page in the form of a poem.

The detached "hand" of the poem can refer both to the physical hand depicted in it and to the handwriting, the written material that constitutes the poem. The mystery and eeriness of the detached hand are represented by the mystery and eeriness of the poem itself. The hand seems disconnected from the body even as it is memorializing itself in the poem; in an essay on Keats and the uncanny, the scholar Brooke Hopkins points out that, likewise, "the poem gives the appearance of being detached from some larger text."

The dark mortal fantasy of this fragment continues by bringing in an addressee, perhaps a specific person or some future reader. Whichever one Keats imagined, the fourth line lays out this person's hypothetical condition: to be haunted by the cold hand, which would "chill thy dreaming nights" with night-mares of death. This recalls the "cold" hand and the "icy silence of the tomb."

In the fifth and sixth lines, which proceed without punctuation and with increasing fury, the speaker of the poem further elaborates on this strange fan-tasy. He suggests that the reader will be so haunted and chilled by the cold, dead hand "That thou would wish thine own heart dry of blood / So in my veins red life might stream again." Understanding that he would be dead by the time this reader encountered these lines, the speaker is enraged in advance by the fact of his mortality. Therefore, he proposes this impossible bargain: that the reader trade places with him, life for death, a last desperate gesture as he confronts his imminent demise. He even indicates in the following line that the person who takes him up on this bargain will be "conscience-calm'd," as if the imagined future reader will share the speaker's outrage that death will soon rob the hand of its warmth. Surely, as the poet Mary Ruefle puts it, "there is no greater accusatory poem in existence."

At the end of this penultimate line the poem's single sentence breaks off from the conditional with a simple statement in the present tense, set off by dashes — "see, here it is" — a declaration that the hand is still alive, still warm. The sentence continues in the last line with another simple statement in the present tense: "I hold it towards you." It is as if the speaker is reaching out with the hand, alive and warm, to prove that it can still grasp. He is almost challeng-ing the reader to shake that hand and make contact. After seven lines of regu-lar blank verse (unrhymed iambic pentameter) the last line is cut in half, the way the speaker's life will be cut short; it ends on the word "you," signifying the reader, the only one who remains to see the poem. This "you," an intentional change from the formal "thou" used earlier, lends intimacy to this final plea.

Keats's fragment begins with writing and ends with reading. He suggests that he would like to cheat death by haunting you, the reader, troubling your waking hours and your dreams at night, devastating you so thoroughly that you will sacrifice yourself by trading places with him. The impossible black-mail is a last desperate gesture. He once lifted a living hand. It reaches out to us still, but now through words. Here it is — this made work, this living thing. Look, he is holding out his hand. He is daring you, whoever you are, to grasp it.

JOHN CLARE

——

"I am"

(c. 1847)

J ohn Clare was one of the great originals of nineteenth-century rural England, an agricultural laborer and lower-class poet who wrote poems in what he called a "language that is ever green." I am focusing on his anguished asylum poem "I am," but it's worthwhile to recall that it was written by a local poet who found his poetry in the woods and fields, in the wilds and waste places of nature. He wrote some thirty-five hundred poems, and most of them chronicle a world he loved. "Poets love nature and themselves are love," he wrote in a late sonnet.

Clare was a prodigious walker, a solitary who rambled through the countryside with a notebook in his pocket. Socially, he didn't really fit in anywhere. In London, he was taken up and condescended to as "the Northamptonshire Peasant Poet." At home, his neighbors considered him peculiar. He empathized with outsiders, such as the Romani, and identified with shy, vulnerable creatures, such as the snipe, the marten, the badger, the field mouse. I've always been heartened by his lyric determination, the precision and exuberance with which he chronicled a world that was rapidly disappearing because of industrialization, as well as the privatization, and subsequent fencing off, of formerly open public lands.

Clare suffered from debilitating physical and mental troubles, which eventually got the better of him. His biographer Jonathan Bate suggests that Clare "conforms to the classic pattern ... of manic depression or 'bipolar affective disorder.'" He was most likely schizophrenic. He had periods of lucidity mixed with bouts of depression and episodes of mania. He also suffered from hallucinations, as well as aberrant behavior related to his illness.

In 1837, Clare was certified insane and taken to Dr. Matthew Allen's private asylum at High Beach in Epping Forest, Essex, on the northeast edge of London. In July 1841, he escaped from the asylum and headed on foot for his home in Northborough. Lonely and broke, sleeping in the rough and sometimes eating grass, he walked more than eighty miles in four days. He left an extraordinary prose account of this nightmarish trip, "Journey out of Essex." "Having only honest courage and myself in my army," he said, "I led the way and my troops soon followed."

Later that year Clare was again certified insane and committed to the Northampton General Lunatic Asylum. Some of his most enduring works were asylum poems: "A Vision"; a sonnet addressed to his son and namesake; and two disconcerting self-revelations that begin with the words "I am," one a sonnet ("I feel I am — I only know I am"), the other a lyric that stands as his most haunting memorial. It was transcribed and preserved by William Knight, the asylum steward who befriended him. Thomas Inskip, a watch- and clockmaker who sometimes advised Clare, arranged for its publication in the *Bedford Times*. I like to think of local readers opening the newspaper on New Year's Day, 1848, and finding this poem.

I am

> I am — yet what I am none cares or knows;
>   My friends forsake me like a memory lost:
> I am the self-consumer of my woes —
>   They rise and vanish in oblivion's host,
> Like shadows in love-frenzied stifled throes —
>   And yet I am and live — like vapours tossed

> Into the nothingness of scorn and noise,
>   Into the living sea of waking dreams
> Where there is neither sense of life or joys
>   But the vast shipwreck of my life's esteems;
> Even the dearest that I love the best
>   Are strange — nay, rather, stranger than the rest.
>
> I long for scenes where man hath never trod,
>   A place where woman never smiled or wept,
> There to abide with my Creator, God,
>   And sleep as I in childhood sweetly slept,
> Untroubling and untroubled where I lie,
>   The grass below — above, the vaulted sky.

This well-designed eighteen-line lyric consists of three six-line stanzas in a steady iambic pentameter. The first stanza hinges on two rhymes: *ababab*. The second two stanzas alternate rhymes in the first four lines, as in the first stanza, but end with a rhyming couplet. All but one of the rhyme-words ("esteems") are one-syllable words, which gives an emphatic rhythm to the rhymes. For example, in the first stanza there is special insistence in rhyming the words "knows," "woes," and "throes." In the second stanza, the word "noise" clangs with "joys."

The feeling of desolation in this poem is overwhelming. The first line opens with a taut assertion — "I am" — which is followed by a dash, a pause, and then a plaintive logical claim: "I am — yet what I am none cares or knows." The line is especially forceful because it is end-stopped. This declaration has the rhetoric of argumentation: I am — *yet*. The speaker of the poem exists, he reminds himself (and us), though his friends have ostracized him, and he is left to console himself in his loneliness. He thus simultaneously declares his existence, his visibility to himself, and his nonexistence, his invisibility to others.

The poem's first two stanzas comprise one long sentence, a series of images and abstractions that dramatizes the speaker's feeling of death in life. At the end of the first stanza he declares that he lives, but "like vapours tossed" — an enjambed line that then breaks to the second stanza:

> Into the nothingness of scorn and noise,
>   Into the living sea of waking dreams,

> Where there is neither sense of life or joys,
> But the vast shipwreck of my life's esteems . . .

There is an agitated, confusing, almost hallucinatory quality to these lines as he tries to explain his mental anguish, his sense of being completely unmoored. The abstractions pile up and the language almost falls apart under the weight of alienation.

It's worth mentioning that Clare's sensibility here is decidedly Romantic and pre-modern. He is doing precisely what Ezra Pound argues against in his modernist credo "A Few Don'ts" (1913). "Don't use such an expression as 'dim lands of peace,'" Pound declares. "It dulls the image. It mixes an abstraction with the concrete. It comes from the writer's not realizing that the natural object is always the *adequate* symbol." John Clare certainly knew the natural world, the natural object, but he is not trying to portray it here. By pairing a concrete image (a "vast shipwreck") with an abstraction ("my life's esteems") he is summarizing a situation, a general state, a cast of mind. The sense of doom and disorientation is not something we are meant to visualize, as in an Imagist poem, but to feel and understand.

There is a sense of radical alienation in the concluding two lines of the second stanza: "Even the dearest that I love the best / Are strange — nay, rather, stranger than the rest." Note the correction here, the argumentative precision. It's not just that the people close to the speaker are now "strange" — it's that they are now "stranger," as in both "peculiar" and "more remote" than everyone else. Such is the depth of his human disconnection.

The writing calms down in the final stanza, the poem's second sentence, woven across six lines. There's calculated force in pairing "trod" and "God," "wept" and "slept"; there's finality in the closing couplet's rhyme of "lie" and "sky." The agitation gives way to a language that is totally transparent, un-antagonized. The desire for relief and repose from the inevitable pain and rejection of being in a social world becomes palpable. In the end, Clare's speaker longs for some lost Eden-like garden where he can recapture the innocence of childhood, a place where he can rest, alone with God, under "the vaulted sky," a cathedral-shaped heaven. He longs for an almost womblike space, free from the taint of the human, a world outside of time.

ALFRED, LORD TENNYSON

In Memoriam, VII

(c. 1848)

In the introduction to *The Oxford Book of Modern Verse, 1892–1935* (1936), the poet W. B. Yeats declares that "Victorianism has been defeated." Yeats uses Tennyson's *In Memoriam* to illustrate the shortcomings of that era's poetry, citing the critical response of the French poet Paul Verlaine: "The revolt against Victorianism meant to the young poet a revolt against irrelevant descriptions of nature, the scientific and moral discursiveness of *In Memoriam* — 'When he should have been broken-hearted,' says Verlaine, 'he had many reminiscences.'"

I don't much care for the pat sentimentalism that creeps in toward the end of *In Memoriam,* which is part of what makes it a representative Victorian poem, but I disagree with Verlaine's characterization because I believe that Tennyson's elegy for his friend Arthur Hallam is profoundly heartfelt. It is not all "reminiscences"; much of it expresses genuine grief. Hallam died of a cerebral hemorrhage in 1833, and Tennyson's mournfulness was ongoing. He wrote *In Memoriam* over a period of many years and, given its intensity of feeling, worried about making it public.

Canto VII — *In Memoriam* consists of 133 cantos — depicts Tennyson's distress over his friend's death in an especially acute way. He most likely wrote this section sometime between 1848 and 1850 — in other words, at least fifteen years after Hallam's death. He then placed it near the beginning of the sequence.

VII

Dark house, by which once more I stand
    Here in the long unlovely street,
    Doors, where my heart was used to beat
So quickly, waiting for a hand,

A hand that can be clasp'd no more —
    Behold me, for I cannot sleep,
    And like a guilty thing I creep
At earliest morning to the door.

He is not here; but far away
    The noise of life begins again,
    And ghastly thro' the drizzling rain
On the bald street breaks the blank day.

This poem, which consists of just two sentences, three quatrains, a mere twelve lines, uses a clever stanzaic pattern that Tennyson employed for all the poems that comprise *In Memoriam*. The pattern is a quatrain in iambic tetrameter: ˘ / | ˘ / | ˘ / | ˘ /. Its envelope rhyme scheme, *abba*, begins with an expectation and concludes by looking back. This makes it self-enfolding. Tennyson didn't invent this stanza, as he thought — Ben Jonson used it in his 1640 poem "An Elegy" ("Though beauty be the mark of praise") — but Tennyson turned it to such powerful use that it is now referred to as the "In Memoriam stanza."

Tennyson uses it here to great effect. He also varies the meter. Notice, for example, how he starts the first three lines of the poem with heavy stresses, a spondee or a trochee instead of an iamb, to emphasize four significant words, "Dárk hóuse," "Hére," and "Dóors." That the speaker has returned to a "Dark house" indicates that where once he found a welcoming light, he now encounters a somber threshold and is barred from entering. The "Here" of the second line refers to 67 Wimpole Street (the "long unlovely street") in London, where Hallam had lived. The speaker remembers how he once waited in that street, at those "Doors," his heart beating in anticipation. The stanza's last line, in regular iambic tetrameter, explains that his heart beats "So quickly, waiting for a hand." One might interpret this "waiting for a hand" to mean "waiting for help."

However, the second stanza clarifies that he waits for "A hand that can be clasp'd no more." This absent physical hand recalls the disembodied hand in Keats's "This living hand," a hand once "capable / Of earnest grasping," which Keats then envisions as lifeless. Though Keats's poem was not a direct influence — the fragment was published after Tennyson died — it's not surprising that both poets use the hand as a powerful metonym, or stand-in, for the whole person. In the clasp or grasp of a handshake two people feel the intimacies of each other's skin, each other's warmth, strength, pulse. The dead or missing hand just as powerfully represents the absence of the other, the permanent losses of death.

The second line of the second stanza begins with an imperative: "Behold me . . ." Now we see that the intentionally stressed "Dark house" and "Doors" of the first stanza serve not just as details of the setting but also as objects the speaker is addressing. This apostrophe to the house, the doors themselves, seems like a displacement of the speaker's grief. He is asking them to look at him precisely because his friend cannot. He tells the house that he cannot sleep, "And like a guilty thing I creep / At the earliest morning to the door." He returns like the ghost in *Hamlet* ("And then it started like a guilty thing," act 1, scene 1, line 148). Given that Hallam was just twenty-two years old when he died, the speaker's experience of grief is complicated by the guilt felt by a survivor. He understands that, now that his friend is gone, he has become a sort of trespasser in the neighborhood where he was once a familiar presence.

In the first line of the last stanza ("He is not here; but far away") one scholar finds an allusion to Luke 24:6, where the angel stands before Jesus's empty sepulcher ("He is not here, but is risen"). Tennyson's use of a semicolon after "here," rather than a comma as in Luke, is the clue that "far away" doesn't refer to where "He" is, that the hope of a resurrection will not be fulfilled. Indeed, the enjambment between lines 1 and 2 of this stanza joins "far away" to "The noise of life begins again." The word "noise" suggests something ugly and irritating, something hard to take. That "noise of life," the new day, inevitably excludes his friend.

The poem turns in the final stanza from the darkness of early morning to the "ghastly" light of a new day. The predawn hour, a liminal space between night and day, darkness and light, serves as the setting for a type of poem called the aubade, which comes from the Spanish *alba,* meaning "dawn." The aubade is traditionally a dawn song expressing the regret of lovers parting at daybreak, as in the famous balcony scene in *Romeo and Juliet.* It remembers the ecstasy of their union and describes their sadness at separating. Given the quickly beating heart of the speaker standing in his friend's street, his intense longing to clasp that absent hand, his guilty creeping to the darkened door — all of which point to a homoerotic undercurrent that runs through the entire sequence — combined with his desolation at the new day, the canto can be read as a sort of aubade, in which dawn reminds the poet that death has parted the deeply bonded friends forever.

Tennyson's speaker sees the despised signs of life returning to the street through a veil of rain. Everything is obscured by the loss of his friend. The aggressive and almost numbing drumbeat of the alliterative *b* sound, as well as the consonance of *l, d, k,* and *s* sounds in the last line — "On the *bald* *s*treet *b*reaks the *bl*an*k* *d*ay" — sonically reflect the bleakness of both the speaker's state of mind and the city scene at daybreak. The poet literally breaks the word "daybreak" into "breaks" and "day" and reverses their order, inserting "the blank" between them. There is a feeling of utter desolation, exposure, and emptiness. As a new day begins, the speaker is left not with "reminiscences," but with a broken heart.

GERARD MANLEY HOPKINS

—◆—

"Thou art indeed just, Lord, if I contend"

(1889)

By 1885, Gerard Manley Hopkins had written his great poems of praise and exultation, such as "God's Grandeur" ("The world is charged with the grandeur of God"), "The Windhover" ("I caught this morning morning's minion"), and "Pied Beauty" ("Glory be to God for dappled things"). Behind him too were the six so-called terrible sonnets, time capsules of spiritual sterility and religious anguish, such as "Carrion Comfort" and "I wake and feel the fell of dark, not day." After five years of teaching Greek to desultory students at University College in Dublin, which Hopkins considered wasted years, the Jesuit priest took a retreat at the Irish novitiate at Tullabeg. He was forty-four years old and did not waver in his allegiance to the church. But he was desolate. On New Year's Day, 1889, he wrote in a notebook: "I began to enter on that course of loathing and helplessness which I have often felt before, which made me fear madness and led me to give up the practice of meditation except, as now, in retreat and here it is again. I could therefore do no more than repeat *Justus es, Domine, et rectum judicium tuum* . . ."

To console himself he was reciting Psalm 119, verse 137 — "Righteous art thou, O Lord, and upright are thy judgments" — from the Vulgate, the late-fourth-century translation of the Bible, which he dearly loved.

Three months later Hopkins used a similar statement as the title and epi-graph of a sonnet: "*Justus quidem tu es, Domine, si disputem tecum*"; he sent it in a letter to his friend Robert Bridges. This time the poet cites the prophet Jeremiah, who echoes Psalm 119 in his indignant cry. The first three lines are thus Hopkins's literal translation of Jeremiah 12:1, which the King James Ver-sion renders as "Righteous thou art, O LORD, when I plead with thee: yet let me talk with thee of thy judgments: Wherefore doth the way of the wicked prosper? Wherefore are all they happy that deal very treacherously?"

This is one of the last three poems Hopkins completed before he died of typhoid fever in June 1889. He dated it March 17 and informed Bridges that it should be read "*adagio molto* [very slowly] and with great stress."

> *Justus quidem tu es, Domine, si disputem tecum; verumtamen*
> *justa loquar ad te: Quare via impiorum prosperatur? &c.*

Thou art indeed just, Lord, if I contend
With thee; but, sir, so what I plead is just.
Why do sinners' ways prosper? and why must
Disappointment all I endeavour end?
  Wert thou my enemy, O thou my friend,
How wouldst thou worse, I wonder, than thou dost
Defeat, thwart me? Oh, the sots and thralls of lust
Do in spare hours more thrive than I that spend,
Sir, life upon thy cause. See, banks and brakes
Now, leavèd how thick! lacèd they are again
With fretty chervil, look, and fresh wind shakes
Them; birds build — but not I build; no, but strain,
Time's eunuch, and not breed one work that wakes.
Mine, O thou lord of life, send my roots rain.

Hopkins utilizes the argumentative form of a Petrarchan, or Italian, son-net for his anguished quarrel with God. The poem rhymes *abbaabbacdcdcd*. Like Jeremiah, the weeping prophet, the speaker of the poem acknowledges the Lord as "just" but begins with a mournful complaint. Unlike the King

James Version, which translates the word *disputem* as "plead," Hopkins chose the word "contend," which suggests a quarrel, a rivalry, as well as an appeal. Notice how he employs an honorific, "sir," in directing his complaint, though no such title appears in the Bible verse. It's a respectful term one might use with a colleague or an elder, and it's notable that the poet doesn't capitalize it here, bringing his divine addressee down to the level of the human. Theirs is a thwarted intimacy — a gulf has opened between a frustrated petitioner and an unresponsive deity.

The reader is put in the position of overhearing this argument, and its gist is encapsulated in the third and fourth lines: "Why do sinners' ways prosper? and why must / Disappointment all I endeavour end?" In the end-rhyme for the fourth line Hopkins ingeniously contracts the word "endeavour" into the word "end," enacting in language the curtailment the speaker feels and foreshadowing the sonnet's repressed main subject, his inability to write. He follows this question with another more pointed one, a grievance even more personal, essentially accusing God of opposing and obstructing him in his desires. "Wert thou my enemy, O thou my friend, / How wouldst thou worse, I wonder, than thou dost / Defeat, thwart me?" The change in address from "sir" to "thou my friend" has a tinge of sarcasm, since God seems to treat the supplicant just as badly as an enemy would. A quiet alliteration ("*d*ost / *D*efeat") crosses enjambed lines, as does another two lines later, with "*s*pend / *S*ir."

The poem dramatizes this argument two more times, first to end the octave and then to begin the sestet. The speaker bitterly observes that those who indulge their desires for alcohol and sex — "the sots and thralls of lust" — flourish more than he does, with his vow of sterile celibacy. This version of the poem's complaint uses a temporal comparison to make its point; that is, the debauched "Do in spare hours more thrive" than "I that spend, / Sir, life upon thy cause." Notice how he uses "spend instead of give," emphasizing the price of his enormous sacrifice.

Hopkins dramatically begins the volta, or structural turn in the poem, with a sudden halt halfway through the ninth line, a Miltonic move. Reminiscent of Keats's "see, here it is" in "This living hand," the poem comes alive with imperatives — *See, look* — indicating that this iteration of the argument will be more active, visual, concrete in its desire to engage the addressee. It is spring and everything bursts to life in the natural world. The very sound and rhythm of the poem become more frenzied and excited:

> See, banks and brakes
> Now, leavèd how thick! lacèd they are again
> With fretty chervil, look, and fresh wind shakes
> Them; birds build—

So too Hopkins repetitively layers sounds and dislocates the syntax—"*leavèd* how thick! *lacèd* they"—to mimic the fecundity of nature, the aromatic herbs, the nesting birds. This sonorous and lively visual description culminates in the twelfth line with the dash after "birds build." Both words are stressed; both share *b* and *d* sounds. After the dash the argument comes to its final point of comparison, wherein the fecundity of nature mocks the speaker's sterility: "—but not I build; no, but strain." Stresses on most of these crucial one-syllable words create an emphatic rhythm that enacts the very strain he is feeling. Repeated *n* sounds in "not," "no," and "strain" stress his fruitless efforts.

This section of the poem recalls Coleridge's precursor sonnet, "Work without Hope," which the Romantic poet composed on February 21, 1825. It begins:

> All Nature seems at work. Slugs leave their lair—
> The bees are stirring—birds are on the wing—
> And Winter slumbering in the open air,
> Wears on his smiling face a dream of Spring!
> And I the while, the sole unbusy thing,
> Nor honey make, nor pair, nor build, nor sing.

Both Coleridge and Hopkins contrast the busy productivity of nature, specifically in spring, with the "unbusy" nonproductivity of the poet. Unlike the birds, Hopkins's frustrated speaker does not "pair," "build," or "sing." Indeed, the entire poem has a feeling of sexual impotence and confusion, of thwarted desire. In the penultimate line, Hopkins employs the memorable phrase "Time's eunuch," which he borrowed from a letter that he had earlier sent to Bridges: "It kills me to be time's eunuch and never to beget." The *n* sounds in the words "not," "no," and "strain" repeat in "eunuch," as well as in the desolate "*not* breed *one* work that wakes." The fact that the speaker does "not breed" reemphasizes his lack of fecundity. The alliterative *w* sounds of "*one work* that *wakes*" create a sonic echoing that drives this frustration home.

Hopkins's last line is a prayer unto itself. It is also a single sentence, consisting of ten one-syllable words, with six stresses for emphasis: "Míne, O thou lórd of lífe, sénd my róots ráin." This petition begins with the self-asserting "Mine," a contrast to the "sir" and "thou" of previous appeals, and the phrase "my roots" near the end of the line echoes "Mine." The speaker here is claiming the Lord as his intimate. The pattern of *n* sounds starts with the word "not," continues in "mine" and "send," and completes the poem in "rain." The alliteration of "roots" and "rain" links these two key words in the poem's final plea. Like a plant that needs water to grow, the speaker needs, and begs God for, the life-giving grace of inspiration.

Ironically, failed inspiration, this sonnet's repressed complaint and true subject, became the inspiration for one of Hopkins's most enduring works, his last great poem, a skillfully argued and movingly written late devotional.

CONSTANTINE CAVAFY

——

"The God Abandons Antony"

(1910)

Constantine Cavafy, a Greek poet who was born in Alexandria, Egypt, spent his early childhood and most of his adulthood there. His rich inner life combined an exquisitely refined intelligence and a highly sensuous nature with a profound historical sensibility. He was galvanized by the past and fascinated by historical figures, which often served as the inspiration and subject of his poetry. His work therefore unites a historical broadness of scope with a honed emotional intensity, articulated in a direct, understated use of his native Greek. As the novelist Marguerite Yourcenar declares, "Each poem by Cavafy is a memorial poem: historical or personal."

With the same scrupulous eye, disinterested intensity, and conscious poetic austerity that he employed in thinking about Alexandrian kings and Roman emperors, Cavafy probed his own erotic past. He wrote unapologetically and with unusual directness and tenderness about his casual homosexual encounters, which, in retrospect, he deemed sacred. Rather than risk condemnation or compromise his commitment to an honest accounting of his personal experience, however subterranean and unconventional, he circulated his poetry among a small group of intimates without seeking wider publication.

"The God Abandons Antony" is one of seven poems Cavafy wrote about Marcus Antonius (Mark Antony), the Roman soldier, statesmen, and doomed husband of Cleopatra. Mark Antony loved Alexandria, the Greek-speaking metropolis of the Roman east. Before his rival, Octavian, marched into Alexandria to take the city, Antony stabbed himself and died in Cleopatra's arms. Antony's story riveted Cavafy, who considered the bold general a compelling precursor. The poem, which takes place as Antony faces his final moments, sets up a triadic relationship between the poet, an anonymous speaker who is Antony's contemporary, and Antony himself.

The God Abandons Antony

When suddenly, at midnight, you hear
an invisible procession going by
with exquisite music, voices,
don't mourn your luck that's failing now,
work gone wrong, your plans
all proving deceptive — don't mourn them uselessly.
As one long prepared, and graced with courage,
say goodbye to her, the Alexandria that is leaving.
Above all, don't fool yourself, don't say
it was a dream, your ears deceived you:
don't degrade yourself with empty hopes like these.
As one long prepared, and graced with courage,
as is right for you who were given this kind of city,
go firmly to the window
and listen with deep emotion, but not
with the whining, the pleas of a coward;
listen — your final delectation — to the voices,
to the exquisite music of that strange procession,
and say goodbye to her, to the Alexandria you are losing.

(Translated by Edmund Keeley and Philip Sherrard)

Cavafy took his title from Plutarch's *Life of Antony* (chapter 75) and built the poem out of Plutarch's historical narration. Once Antony's troops deserted him for Octavian, his cause was lost. Here is how Plutarch describes Antony's final night:

It is said that, about halfway through this night, while inside the city all was quiet and dejected because of the fear and the anticipation of what was yet to come, suddenly there was heard the combined sounds of all sorts of instruments, and the shouting of a crowd, along with merrymaking and festive acrobats, as if a procession were leaving the city with no little tumult . . . To those interpreting this sign it seemed as though the god to whom Antony once most likened himself and to whom he was most dedicated, was now abandoning him.

Plutarch is referring to Dionysus, the Greek god of wine, fertility, and religious ecstasy. As Antony rose to power, he cast himself as Dionysus born anew and publicly took on the god's attributes. In addition to his reading of Plutarch, Cavafy views the story of Antony's approaching death through the lens of Shakespeare's *Antony and Cleopatra* (act 4, scene 3), where a group of anxious soldiers hears a strange music coming out of the air or the earth and takes it as a tragic omen: "'Tis the god Hercules, whom Antony loved, / Now leaves him." In his play, Shakespeare changes the god to Hercules, the divine hero known for the twelve labors that tested his prodigious strength. Cavafy for his part chooses not to name the god, who isn't mentioned again after the title.

From the start Cavafy conjures an otherworldly scene. The poem begins abruptly, with the phrase "When suddenly." This immediacy continues with the indication that the events take place "at midnight," a time of day that in poetry almost always signals an epiphany, an hour of revelation. The first line ends with the clause "you hear," which both describes what happens suddenly at midnight and introduces someone the speaker is addressing. The next lines specify that the addressee at midnight will suddenly hear "an invisible procession going by / with exquisite music, voices." This is the sound and sign of the god's abandonment; the Dionysian revelry recedes, leaving Antony to his mortal fate.

The following lines are directive: the speaker instructs Antony not to "mourn your luck that's failing now, / work gone wrong, your plans / all proving deceptive — don't mourn them uselessly." Instead the speaker advises him to "say goodbye" to Alexandria "As one long prepared, and graced with courage." Daniel Mendelsohn translates this as "Like one who's long prepared, like someone brave"; both translations use a simile here, indicated by "like" or "as," and both suggest an aspiration, an ideal way to behave. The poem counsels

Antony to adopt a stoicism he may not be feeling when confronting his final moments.

The next eleven lines repeat the structure of the first eight: one sentence on what not to do ("don't") followed by another on what to do instead. The advice ranges from variations on "don't mourn" to "don't fool yourself." Here the speaker urges Antony not to deny what the noise of the invisible procession is telling him — "don't say / it was a dream, your ears deceived you" — that the god is leaving, the city is leaving, the fight is over, not just the military struggle but life itself. The second sentence of the poem's latter portion repeats the aspirational model: "As one long prepared, and graced with courage." The next line expands and personalizes the conceit by exchanging "one" for "you": "as is right for you who were given this kind of city." The speaker then tells Antony what he should do rather than deceive himself: "go firmly to the window / and listen with deep emotion." This directive operates on both physical and metaphorical levels. Just as midnight is a transition point between day and night, a window is a transition point between inside and outside. In *The Poetics of Space,* the philosopher Gaston Bachelard describes the window as a borderline surface between here and the beyond. For Cavafy, the exhortation to listen "not / with the whining, the pleas of a coward" but as a "final delectation" is another way of urging the hero to confront the final ebbing beauty of life with a calm, courageous joy. "The Alexandria that is *leaving*" has turned into "the Alexandria you are *losing.*"

By the end the poem's major elements have taken on multiple valences. The speaker can be read not only as a fictive contemporary speaking to Mark Antony about bidding farewell to Alexandria, but also as the poet talking to himself about leaving that beloved city at the end of his own life. At the same time the poem is advising the reader to face the music, as it were, to leave a treasured place with the serene bravery of a hero. This historical poem is thus also deeply interpersonal, a call for each of us to confront death nobly, to go to the window and listen with deep pleasure to the exquisite procession of life as it passes by for the last time.

THOMAS HARDY

———

"The Voice"

(1912)

The sudden death in November 1912 of Emma Hardy, Thomas Hardy's first wife, loosed a flood of unsuspected feelings in her husband. The two had been long estranged — they hadn't shared a bedroom for years — but the shock of her death undid him. Suddenly it was too late to repair what had happened between them ("All's past amend / Unchangeable"). He mourned her desperately — after she died, he had her coffin placed at the foot of his bed until the funeral — and began to write poems about her almost immediately.

Hardy's vivid, surprising, and metrically resourceful elegies for Emma, "Poems of 1912–1913," appeared as part of his book *Satires of Circumstance* (1914). This sequence of twenty-one poems is ruthlessly truthful and wrenchingly clear, tender, strange, and grief-stricken, filled with nostalgia and remorse. It took him two years to complete, and he would write about Emma intermittently for the rest of his life.

The sequence begins with the traumatic shock of her death. The finality of her swift unforeseen departure ("Never to bid good-bye, / Or lip me the softest call, / Or utter a wish for a word") leaves Hardy's speaker alone with his feelings, and the sequence turns, as if naturally, from loss to the memory of the time when the two first met and courted, some thirty years before, in the west, near Cornwall. "The Voice," dated December 1912, is the ninth poem, the turning point, in the sequence. This haunted poem marks the divergence between the past and the present, between what the couple had been to each other and what they became. That separation now turns out to be more final than the man had ever imagined.

The Voice

Woman much missed, how you call to me, call to me,
Saying that now you are not as you were
When you had changed from the one who was all to me,
But as at first, when our day was fair.

Can it be you that I hear? Let me view you, then,
Standing as when I drew near to the town
Where you would wait for me: yes, as I knew you then,
Even to the original air-blue gown!

Or is it only the breeze, in its listlessness
Travelling across the wet mead to me here,
You being ever dissolved to wan wistlessness
Heard no more again far or near?

    Thus I; faltering forward,
    Leaves around me falling,
Wind oozing thin through the thorn from norward.
    And the woman calling.

Hardy was so spooked by the apparition of Emma's voice that, in an early draft of the poem, he addressed her as "O woman weird." This agitation, as well as the obvious sense of guilt, can be felt in the tortured syntax of the first stanza: "Saying that now you are not as you were / When you had changed from the one who was all to me, / But as at first, when our day was fair." The phantom voice is forcing the speaker to consider three different moments in the couple's life together, all of which are interwoven: the remote past, "when our day was fair" and they were in love; the recent past, "When you had changed from the one who was all to me" and she became estranged from him; and the current moment, "now," when she returns "as at first," so that the remote past has circled back to the present.

The second stanza begins, "Can it be you that I hear?" If the sound the speaker hears is indeed the voice of his late wife, he wants her to reveal herself as she was in the remote past — "as I knew you then" — when she waited for him to come into town. This remembered vision ends the stanza with a strikingly memorable detail, her "original air-blue gown." Hardy puns on the word "original," which means both "inventive" and "from the beginning," and thus emphasizes the uniqueness of the initial besotted phase of the love affair.

This lovely image, the memory itself, dissolves in the third stanza, when the "air" drifts away from the gown and becomes the "breeze." Whereas the second stanza poses the question "Can it be you that I hear?" the third stanza proposes an alternative: "Or is it only the breeze . . . You being . . . Heard no more again . . . ?" Notice how throughout stanzas 1 and 2, as the speaker hears the voice and sees the vision of his late wife, "you" and "me" occur frequently on the same line. When in the third stanza he contemplates the possibility that he's hearing the wind rather than a voice, he formally separates "you" and "me." A single "me" occurs at the end of line 2, while line 3 begins with a single "You," who is "ever dissolved to wan wistlessness."

Hardy was particularly adept at using various poetic devices to enact drama and suspense. He composed each poem in his elegiac sequence with a different stanzaic pattern, as if continually searching for the right form to hold his sorrow. "The Voice" has four quatrains with a ballad rhyme scheme: *abab*. For anyone interested in meter this poem displays complicated and subtle rhythmic effects, which reflect its eerie, tortured subject matter. It employs a baseline of four dactyls (dactylic tetrameter). The dactyl is a metrical foot with three syllables, one accented syllable followed by two unaccented ones (/ ⌣ ⌣), as in a waltz. The tetrameter line consists of four feet. Hardy uses this meter to create a slightly dizzying rhythm of lament: "Wómăn mŭch | míssed, hŏw yŏu | cáll tŏ mě, | cáll tŏ mě."

Notice, though, how he varies the meter within the stanza. Though lines 1 and 3 are regular twelve-syllable, four-beat lines, in line 2 Hardy cuts off the last two syllables of the final foot, truncating the four-beat line to ten syllables. He does the same in line 4, where he shortens the syllable count even further by making significant stressed words last for two beats, such as "day" (line 4), "air" (line 8), and "Heard" and "far" (line 12). Hardy also uses punctuation to pause midfoot on a stressed word, such as "Wómăn mŭch | míssed," which highlights "missed." In a similar fashion he pauses on "hear" and "breeze" in lines 5 and 11: "Can it be | you that I | hear?" and "Or is it | only the | breeze," rhythmically emphasizing the poem's two questions, its central conflict. As the speaker lurches between the hope that his wife is near and the fear that he is imagining things, it is only fitting that the meter also lurches between waltzing longer lines and stuttering truncated ones.

The poem also has a terrific density of sound. Hardy uses triple rhymes (such as "call to me" / "all to me") in each of the regular dactylic tetrameter lines and single rhymes in the shorter lines. The alliteration of significant word pairings, such as "*m*uch *m*issed," "*w*ould *w*ait," "*w*an *w*istlessness," and "*falter-ing f*orward"; the hissing *s* sounds in "li*s*tle*ssn*e*ss*" and "wi*s*tle*ssn*e*ss*"; and the re-peated long *e* sounds blowing through "breeze," "mead," "me," "here," "being," and "near" enact the obsessive nature of the speaker's gloomy ruminations.

Like the speaker's sense of hope, the last stanza dramatically collapses, breaking many of the formal patterns established in the first three stanzas. The indentation and shortening of three of the lines create an immediate visual rupture in the poem, which echoes the rupture caused by Emma's death. The first line of the stanza — "Thus I; faltering forward" — is the only line in the poem that begins with an unstressed syllable; instead, stress falls on "I," which is further emphasized and isolated by a semicolon. These two words, "Thus I," are a stark assessment of the speaker's predicament, that he is utterly alone. Reflecting this devastating revelation, the meter in the first two lines of the stanza becomes irregular, these shorter three-beat lines stumble and falter, and the triple and single rhymes become double rhymes. Consonant sounds relent-lessly echo ("*f*altering *f*orward . . . *f*alling," "*th*in *th*rough the *th*orn") through the bleak landscape where the speaker finds himself faltering and bereft.

Although he knows that he is alone and suspects that he is hearing only the wind, the speaker also can't help but continue to hear the voice, the projec-tion of his guilt and regret. Therefore, the voice returns to the poem in a fur-ther shortened two-beat line, a single haunting last phrase: "And the woman calling." Listen to the way that Hardy cleverly employs shared consonant and vowel sounds to migrate from "W*ind*" to "*th*in," "*thin*" to "*th*orn," "*th*orn" to "*nor*ward," and finally "*norwar*d" to "*wo*man." In this final uncanny line, which is pierced by what Seamus Heaney calls "a banshee note," Hardy's speaker un-derstands that the woman in the wind will continue to reproach him, forever calling to him from the other side.

EDWARD THOMAS

———

"The Owl"

(1915)

E dward Thomas wrote 142 poems, his collected verse, in the short span between December 1914, just months after Britain entered World War I, and April 1917. Here is his poem "The Owl," which he composed in February 1915:

The Owl

Downhill I came, hungry, and yet not starved;
Cold, yet had heat within me that was proof
Against the North wind; tired, yet so that rest
Had seemed the sweetest thing under a roof.

Then at the inn I had food, fire, and rest,
Knowing how hungry, cold, and tired was I.
All of the night was quite barred out except
An owl's cry, a most melancholy cry

Shaken out long and clear upon the hill,
No merry note, nor cause of merriment,
But one telling me plain what I escaped
And others could not, that night, as in I went.

And salted was my food, and my repose,
Salted and sobered, too, by the bird's voice
Speaking for all who lay under the stars,
Soldiers and poor, unable to rejoice.

Thomas first published this poem under the title "Those Others." Later he decided the title was too editorial and changed it to "The Owl." This bird is the trigger to the lyric, which begins outdoors, like almost all of Thomas's poems. Thomas was a peripatetic poet, a walker in the country who loved the mysteries of nature. Here, the speaker comes to a place of rest after a winter tramp in the countryside. The poem begins emphatically and immediately captures the rhythm and feeling of hurrying to the end of a long walk — "Downhill I came . . ." The wanderer is careful to explain his state with some exactitude: how he is hungry but not starved, cold but not frozen, tired but not so exhausted that rest was impossible.

The second stanza moves from the cold, windy outdoors to the refuge of an inn, where the speaker feels lucky to find lodging. Now that he is inside, he can enjoy the sweetness of "food, fire, and rest"; they are the antidote to his condition: "hungry, cold, and tired." The speaker feels relieved that the walls and roof of the inn keep the dangers of night outside — "All of the night was quite barred out except" — though the word "except" at the end of this enjambed line indicates that something of the night will penetrate this shelter. What the inn cannot keep out is "An owl's cry," which completes the stanza and the first half of this sixteen-line poem. Thomas decided to rhyme the second and fourth lines of each stanza (*abcb*), as in many ballads, and here he gets special effect from pairing the words "I" and "cry." It is this cry that unsettles the speaker.

Notice how that cry is "Shaken out long and clear" not only "upon the hill" but also across a line and stanza break, which prolongs and emphasizes its poignancy. Thomas is specifically distinguishing this owl's "most melancholy cry" from the owl in Shakespeare's *Love's Labour Lost* (act 5, scene 2): "Then nightly sings the staring owl 'Tu-whit, to-who!' — / A merry note." Thomas's owl is "No merry note, nor cause of merriment." Rather, it is a note that, in another dramatic enjambment, reminds the speaker of "what I escaped / And others could not, that night, as in I went."

This final line of the third stanza serves as an important hinge in the poem. Not only is it the only eleven-syllable line in a poem composed entirely of ten-syllable lines; it is also the first reference to "those others" of Thomas's original title, and the poem's true, underlying subject. Though Thomas does not yet reveal who the "others" are or what, exactly, he "escaped / And others could not," the line continues with "that night, as in I went." In this context, "that night" can be read not only as an element of the setting but also as the very thing the others could not escape. Recall that what was not "quite barred out" by the inn was "the night," which in the poem embodies the perils of being outdoors, exposed, unprotected. This distinction between inside and outside, which occurs from the poem's outset, opposes "that night" to "in I went," punning on the words "in" and "inn."

The first line of the poem's final, powerful stanza, like the preceding line, begins with the word "And," which creates a correspondence between the two lines, the two stanzas. Because the speaker has escaped what others couldn't, not only is his food "salted," but so is his sleep. The word *salted* means "flavored" or "seasoned" but also carries connotations of tears, of salt poured on open wounds, so that we understand that his rest is disturbed. We hear the emphatic repetition of *s* and *z* sounds, which solemnly whisper through the last stanza, binding many of the key words to one another.

> And *s*alted wa*s* my food, and my repo*s*e,
> *S*alted and *s*obered, too, by the bird'*s* voi*c*e
> *S*peaking for all who lay under the *s*tar*s*,
> *S*oldier*s* and poor, unable to rejoi*c*e.

Now "the owl's cry" has been transformed into "the bird's voice," which speaks for those who "lay under the stars" rather than "under a roof."

The final line blows open and clinches the poem by revealing those for whom the bird's voice speaks: "Soldiers and poor." Thomas doesn't condescend to a class of people by referring to "the poor"; thus, "poor" can be read both as an adjective modifying the word "soldiers" (poor soldiers) and as a noun (poor people). The final rhyme emphasizes that the bird's *voice* does not sing but speaks for all those unable to *rejoice*. The word "unable" also underscores the stark truth that anyone living outdoors deprived of shelter is not necessarily able, as the speaker is, to procure "food, fire, and rest" when "hungry, cold, and tired."

It is not until this sobering last line that we finally recognize "The Owl" as a war poem, a lyric that connects, and opposes, military and civilian life. What Thomas had thus far "escaped" was enlistment in World War I, the historical reality that others could not evade, which the poem represents as the uncomfortable world outside, the night. Like the voice of Hardy's late wife in "The Voice," the voice of the owl speaks as the poet's restless conscience.

Edward Thomas enlisted three months after he wrote "The Owl," an early war poem that refuses to sound a triumphant or patriotic note. His decision to serve reflected what Walter de la Mare called his "compassionate and suffering heart," but it would also lead to his undoing. On April 9, 1917, he died by shell blast in the Battle of Arras on the western front, at the age of thirty-five.

GUILLAUME APOLLINAIRE

—

"The Pretty Redhead"

(1918)

Guillaume Apollinaire was a bohemian poet and critic at the artistic center of Paris, which was the artistic center of Europe, but he was also an outsider, a Roman-born foreigner who desperately wanted to become a French citizen. He volunteered for World War I in 1914 and fought on the front lines — first as part of the artillery, then as an infantry officer. He was badly hurt in 1916, sustaining a shrapnel wound to the temple, and was invalided out of active service. He returned to Paris, where he continued his charmed battles in art, drama, and poetry, but he never fully recovered his health. Apollinaire died of influenza two days before the Armistice of 1918.

He was thirty-eight years old.

The pretty redhead of the poem's title refers to Jacqueline Kolb, whom Apollinaire married in 1918. She also appears in his novel *The Seated Woman* as "pretty Coral, a redhead with nut-brown eyes, who altogether resembled a drop of blood on the tip of a sword." However, "La Jolie Rousse" is not a love poem addressed to his beloved but a condensed memoir about World War I, a meditation on tradition and innovation in art, and a poet's last testimony. It is the final poem in Apollinaire's second and final book of poems, *Calligrammes* (1918), which was subtitled *Poems of Peace and War*.

The Pretty Redhead

I stand here in the sight of everyone a man full of sense
Knowing life and knowing of death what a living man can know
Having gone through the griefs and happinesses of love
Having known sometimes how to impose his ideas
Knowing several languages
Having travelled more than a little
Having seen war in the artillery and the infantry
Wounded in the head trepanned under chloroform
Having lost his best friends in the horror of battle

I know as much as one man alone can know
Of the ancient and the new
And without troubling myself about this war today
Between us and for us my friends
I judge this long quarrel between tradition and imagination
Between order and adventure

You whose mouth is made in the image of God's mouth
Mouth which is order itself
Judge kindly when you compare us
With those who were the very perfection of order
We who are seeking everywhere for adventure

We are not your enemies
Who want to give ourselves vast domains
Where mystery flowers into any hands that long for it
Where there are new fires colors never seen
A thousand fantasies difficult to make sense out of
They must be made real
All we want is to explore kindness the enormous country where everything is
   silent
And there is time which somebody can banish or welcome home

Pity for us who fight always on the frontiers
Of the illimitable and the future
Pity our mistakes pity our sins

Here summer is coming the violent season
And so my youth is as dead as spring
Oh Sun it is the time of reason grown passionate
And I am still waiting
To follow the forms she takes noble and gentle
So I may love her alone
She comes and draws me as a magnet draws filaments of iron
She has the lovely appearance
Of an adorable redhead
Her hair turns golden you would say
A beautiful lightning flash that goes on and on
Or the flames that spread out their feathers
In wilting tea roses

But laugh laugh at me
Men everywhere especially people from here
For there are so many things that I don't dare to tell you
So many things that you would not let me say
Have pity on me

(Translated by James Wright)

"The Pretty Redhead" is an unpunctuated lyric in *vers libre,* free verse. It follows no preexistent pattern, and the absence of punctuation gives it a liberated and spacious feeling. The night before he published his first book, *Alcools* (1913), Apollinaire impulsively decided to drop all punctuation from his poems. The effect was electrifying. As Tony Hoagland points out, "The relationship between beginnings, endings and middles, between poetic fragments and poetic wholes, might be said to have changed that night." Apollinaire's last-minute impulse to undertake this radical formal experiment helped position his work at the forefront of the new modern poetry.

The speaker of "The Pretty Redhead" begins grandly: "I stand here in the sight of everyone a man full of sense," as if he is standing up on the witness stand, giving a deposition to the entire world. He summarizes his experiences in love, intellectual pursuits, travel and languages, battle, and pain and grief, using the third person ("Having lost *his* best friends") to describe himself. It's as if he's reciting the qualifications of a "man full of sense" in order to prove that he has lived and suffered enough to be trustworthy. After a line stating that the speaker lost his best friends in the horror of war, the translator, the poet James Wright, adds a stanza break for emphasis; however, in the French, the poem continues without a break. The speaker returns to the first person ("I know as much as one man alone can know / Of the ancient and the new"). This additional qualification links the literal "war in the artillery and the infantry" to a figurative war via a clever enjambment: "this war today / Between us and for us my friends." The metaphorical war waged between different artistic camps is the poem's principle subject.

Given his knowledge of the old and the new, Apollinaire feels confident to judge "this long quarrel between tradition and imagination / Between order and adventure." In the French text he indents and capitalizes the nouns for emphasis: "De l'Ordre et de l'Aventure." The speaker advocates for a new spirit of innovation against the French classical tradition — *The Oxford English Dictionary* lists the late date of 1877 as the first recorded use of the term *neoclassicism*. Apollinaire took a more polemical, embattled tone in his 1917 lecture "L'esprit nouveau et les poètes" ("The New Spirit and the Poets"), where he argues that poetry needs constant experimentation and innovation to remain relevant in an ever-changing modern world. It is no accident that the aesthetic category known as the avant-garde derives from a French military term, which literally means "the advance-guard," the scouts who forge ahead of the rest of the troops.

Rather than attack those who don't share his experimental aesthetic, Apollinaire employs a range of rhetorical strategies in "The Pretty Redhead" to disarm his skeptics and persuade them to listen to his line of reasoning. He addresses them as "my friends" and later assures them that "We are not your enemies." He good-naturedly cedes "God," "order," and "perfection" to the other side, the old order, and asks them to "judge kindly" when they compare the new ways to the old. For his side he claims the earthly disorder and imperfection of "adventure." He repeatedly asks for understanding, urging them to "Pity our mistakes pity our sins."

The poem passionately makes the case for a new spirit in art. Notice how the "I" switches to "we," the first-person plural speaking not just for the poet but for an entire new generation ("We who are seeking everywhere for adventure"):

> We are not your enemies
> Who want to give ourselves vast domains
> Where mystery flowers into any hands that long for it
> Where there are new fires colors never seen
> A thousand fantasies difficult to make sense out of
> They must be made real

In 1917, Apollinaire coined the term *surréaliste* to suggest a dramatic attempt to go beyond the limits of an agreed-upon reality. He hungered for the marvelous and put his faith in the unconscious, in dreams, fantasies, and hallucinations. This revolutionary set of values anticipates the ideas of André Breton, who used the term *Surrealism* (meaning "superrealism" or "above reality") in 1924 in the first of three manifestos: "I believe in the future resolution of these two states, dream and reality, which are seemingly so contradictory, into a kind of absolute reality, a *surreality*."

In a movingly simple example of Apollinaire's efforts to bring the dream world into a new experience of reality, the poem continues with this key line: "All we want is to explore kindness the enormous country where everything is silent." "Explore kindness" seamlessly joins an action with an abstraction, which is then characterized in evocative concrete terms, "the enormous country where everything is silent." Apollinaire declared that "a work of art must be at the same time clear and mysterious," a statement that especially applies to this compelling line, which inspired James Wright to translate the poem. The writer Charles Baxter heard Wright read "The Pretty Redhead" at SUNY Brockport in 1970 and recalls that Wright paused after he recited the line and whispered, "Christ, I'd rather have written that than to go to heaven."

Apollinaire then returns to one of the poem's main subjects, the past versus the future, with an oddly personalized depiction of future time as a sort of family member or intimate: "And there is time which somebody can banish or welcome home." When he declares, "Pity for us who always fight on the frontiers / Of the illimitable and the future," he once more alludes to war, breaking the line and punning on the literal and metaphorical meanings of the word *frontiers* (*frontières*).

In the penultimate stanza the speaker finds himself on the verge of summer, "the violent season," a season of heat and burning, a ripe season, when his "youth is as dead as spring." He invokes the sun — Frank O'Hara explicitly imitates him in "A True Account of Talking to the Sun at Fire Island" — as the symbol of summer, "the time of reason grown passionate." Rather than worship the God of order and perfection, the speaker chooses to follow and love the sun, as well as "the forms she takes," a reference not just to aspects of the sun but to poetic forms. Here the lovely redhead of the title makes her appearance as a personification of the sun, her hair described in a dynamic series of rapturous images evoking the fire and heat of the sun, moving from "golden" to "A beautiful lightning flash that goes on and on" — note the temporal impossibility of a flash that goes on continuously — to "flames that spread out their feathers / In wilting tea roses."

The poem might have ended here, on an uplifted note, but instead takes a turn in the last stanza. Apollinaire's translator Anne Hyde Greet points out that the last five lines were written in a different ink on the manuscript and thus presumably were added later. The mood of ecstasy is relinquished. Notice the language of argumentation:

> *But* laugh laugh at me
> Men everywhere especially people from here
> *For* there are so many things that I don't dare to tell you
> So many things that you would not let me say
> Have pity on me

Anticipating mockery from skeptics, the speaker encourages them to go ahead and laugh at him. Somewhat grandly, he addresses "Men everywhere" but particularly speaks to his local contemporaries, "people from here." Despite his zeal for a new experimental aesthetic, Apollinaire's image of the future is permeated by bleak forebodings. As the poet Adam Zagajewski suggests, it is as if Apollinaire "knew something about the future, about the terror this century was about to produce, something that his comrades (poets and painters flourishing at the beginning of the century) didn't have a hint of." He ends the poem by asking again for pity. In the end, Apollinaire silently bears the burden of the visionary who perceives things that he doesn't dare to tell, the impending horrors that others, who are stuck in the past, simply refuse to see.

EDNA ST. VINCENT MILLAY

"What lips my lips have kissed, and where, and why"

(1920)

Edna St. Vincent Millay radicalized the love poem. Writing as an openly bisexual woman, she reversed a long tradition of entrenched gender roles in poetry, which posed the male lover as the speaker, the desiring subject, and the artistic creator, while positioning the woman as the object of male desire, a voiceless muse for male artistic inspiration. In Millay's skillful and embattled romantic sonnets, the woman becomes the lover, the desiring subject, the artist. The speaker in her poems is a self-assertive and self-revealing woman who expresses and explores the conflicts between her own physical passions, her sensuality, and the emotional connections and disconnections that arise from erotic entanglements.

Millay is one of five compelling American female lyricists of the 1920s — the others are Elinor Wylie, Sara Teasdale, Léonie Adams, and Louise Bogan (in her first two books) — who have been mostly written out of literary history. These poets, skilled metricists, created a body of work that was essentially romantic at a time when Romanticism itself was in disrepute. Ignoring the stylistic revolution in American poetry inaugurated by Pound and Eliot, they generally observed the formal conventions of the traditional nineteenth-century Anglo-American short poem. Their carefully wrought poems have the quality, as Marianne Moore said about Bogan, of "compactness compacted."

The work of these poets belongs to an alternative tradition of women's poetry. Their poems — many of them comparable to Elizabethan songs — assert the authority of the female self through musical lyrics of personal experience. They are poets of an uncompromising subjectivity committed to emotion. In Bogan's words, emotion is "the kernel which builds outward from inward intensity." Their neo-Romantic aesthetic, through which they sought to capture the nuances and vagaries of female subjectivity with frank accuracy, was also a revolt against Victorian sentimentality, against pat emotion and conventional posturing, against excessive ornamentation. There is also a tension in their work between exuberant desire and the limitations imposed by writing in forms, the demands of clarity and precision. Millay was the most florid and expansive of these poets, Bogan the most clipped and austere, but each expressed a longing for escape within the confines of formal poetry. Love is the circumscribed subject in most of their poetry, partly because the love poem was a form of discourse that included women in a way that the poetry of history did not.

Millay wrote "What lips my lips have kissed, and where, and why" (the title is the first line) in May 1920 and published it as the nineteenth sonnet in her book *The Harp-Weaver and Other Poems* (1923).

> What lips my lips have kissed, and where, and why,
> I have forgotten, and what arms have lain
> Under my head till morning; but the rain
> Is full of ghosts tonight, that tap and sigh
> Upon the glass and listen for reply,
> And in my heart there stirs a quiet pain
> For unremembered lads that not again
> Will turn to me at midnight with a cry.
> Thus in the winter stands the lonely tree,
> Nor knows what birds have vanished one by one,
> Yet knows its boughs more silent than before:
> I cannot say what loves have come and gone,
> I only know that summer sang in me
> A little while, that in me sings no more.

Millay employs the classical model of the Petrarchan or Italian sonnet, which divides into two asymmetrical parts, an octave and a sestet. The longer octave traditionally sets the terms of a sonnet's argument. A volta, or turn in the argument, usually introduces the shorter sestet, which brings the poem, and the argument, to a close. Like Petrarch, Millay builds an obsessive feeling in the octet that is let loose in the sestet. Her poem also has a strict Petrarchan rhyme scheme: *abbaabba cdedce*. Millay marshals her argument in two winding sentences that correspond exactly to the octave/sestet structure.

"What lips my lips have kissed" is driven by a self-dramatizing sense of loss. The opening spondee ("Whát líps") seems to extol a lover's adored physical features, as in "What remarkable lips." The poem thus begins like a blazon, a form popularized by Petrarch and traditionally the domain of male writers, which catalogs the physical attributes of the beloved. But that is not the case. Millay intentionally begins the poem with a direct object, "lips," rather than the subject, to create narrative suspense. She emphasizes three alliterative interrogative pronouns ("what," "where," and "why"), which allude to the mystery of the speaker's sexual encounters. After the firmly end-stopped first line she brutally undercuts the expectation of praise for a lover: "What lips my lips have kissed, and where, and why, / *I have forgotten*." Now the reader understands "What lips" very differently, as in "Whatever lips." Millay then adds a second forgotten object ("what arms have lain"), which dangles at the end of the main clause and the second line.

The sentence shifts after the semicolon in the third line: "*but* the rain / Is full of ghosts tonight." This startling enjambment moves the poem from details remembered in the present perfect tense ("what arms *have lain*") to the scene unfolding in the present tense ("the rain / *Is* full of ghosts"). Just as Hardy's and Thomas's poems feature voices in the wind and in the owl's cry, this speaker hears ghosts in the sound of the rain. She imagines that they "tap and sigh / Upon the glass and listen for reply." But because these ghosts are "unremembered lads," the speaker has no reply, just "a quiet pain," which beautifully rhymes with "not again." The octave closes "at midnight" — recall from Cavafy's "The God Abandons Antony" that in poetry midnight is traditionally a time of revelation — "with a cry." The lover's cry could be a cry of recognition, of sadness, of orgasm. "One of the emotional archetypes of the Petrarchan sonnet structure," the scholar Paul Fussell dryly observes, "is the pattern of sexual pressure and release."

Millay's sonnet turns on the argumentative term "Thus," which associates the "quiet pain" of the solitary speaker with the image of a tree in winter. Notice also how the sestet starts with a trochee, stressing "Thus," which breaks the poem's somewhat strict iambic pentameter. Unaware of the birds that have gradually disappeared, "the lonely tree" still somehow "knows" that its branches are "more silent than before." Here Millay is referencing Shakespeare's Sonnet 73, which famously opens:

> That time of year thou mayst in me behold
> When yellow leaves, or none, or few, do hang
> Upon those boughs which shake against the cold,
> Bare ruin'd choirs, where late the sweet birds sang.

In his love poem Shakespeare uses the metaphor of the season turning to winter (along with day turning to night and fire turning to ash) to characterize the speaker's aging and to praise a beloved "thou" for loving someone who will soon be gone.

Given that Millay was twenty-eight when she wrote her sonnet, she appropriates Shakespeare's image of aging to express a sense of world-weariness, the loneliness and sorrow of feeling spent at a young age. After all, two years before, the sexually adventurous poet notably penned the four-line "First Fig," which begins, "My candle burns at both ends; / It will not last the night." Millay's somewhat antiquated diction, which also harkens back to Shakespeare, adds to the sense that the poet feels old for her age. As the poet Eavan Boland points out, "Her diction reached back to an invented past." But unlike Shakespeare's loyal "thou," no adored addressee appears in this poem, only the "unremembered lads," an absence that makes Millay's reimagining a sort of anti–love sonnet, a sonnet of vanished intimacies.

After the description of the tree in winter the sestet divides neatly into two parts separated by a colon. The "I" returns to the poem, and the speaker equates the tree's silent, bare boughs with her own loneliness:

> I cannot say what loves have come and gone,
> I only know that summer sang in me
> A little while, that in me sings no more.

The speaker once again reminds us that she can't remember any specific loves. However, she reveals what she does "know" in a heartbreaking enjambment: "that summer sang in me / A little while." Notice that it is summer that sings, rather than the birds, a lovely alliterative substitution, which emphasizes the young speaker's awareness that a season of her life has passed. As in the beginning of the first line, the last line ends emphatically with a spondee, the agonizing "no more," which echoes "not again" and stresses the poem's measured sense of finality.

For Millay, the ripeness and burning of Apollinaire's summer is behind her. A sense of treasured things lost — emotional intimacy, physical contact, companionship, youthful innocence — pervades this sonnet, which stands, like the lonely tree, as a powerful testimony to one woman's unflinching look at her own solitude.

LANGSTON HUGHES

—•—

"Song for a Dark Girl"

(1927)

Langston Hughes wrote "Song for a Dark Girl" in 1927. It is one of his nearly three dozen poems that speak out against the violent lynching of African Americans, a notorious grotesquerie of US history. The tradition of lynching poems probably began with Paul Laurence Dunbar's mock-Romantic ballad "The Haunted Oak" (1900), which takes the point of view of the tree where a lynching takes place. Black poets of the early twentieth century, such as Claude McKay and Lesley Pinckney Hill, continued the tradition, followed by an imposing array of poets from the 1920s to the present, including Richard Wright, Robert Hayden, Lucille Clifton, Gwendolyn Brooks, Audre Lord, Elizabeth Alexander, and Patricia Smith, among many others. Langston Hughes's lynching poems stand out in a subgenre of outraged elegiac responses to this sickening barbarism and racist spectacle.

Song for a Dark Girl

Way Down South in Dixie
   (Break the heart of me)
They hung my black young lover
   To a cross roads tree.

Way Down South in Dixie
   (Bruised body high in air)
I asked the white Lord Jesus
   What was the use of prayer.

Way Down South in Dixie
   (Break the heart of me)
Love is a naked shadow
   On a gnarled and naked tree.

The title "Song for a Dark Girl" is ambiguous, especially as concerns the identity of the speaker. Is the poem a song for the dark girl to sing so that she can mourn her murdered lover? Is it a song written to memorialize a "dark girl" who has been lynched? Or is the poem, as a few critics have suggested, a song the speaker is singing to a young Black woman? Most read the poem as a song for a heartbroken girl to sing, but since the pronouns are indeterminate, there is no conclusive way to ascertain the gender or identity of the speaker, relative to the dark girl of the title.

No matter how one reads the title, Hughes brilliantly combines in just three quatrains a soulful elegy, a spiritual reckoning, a critique of racism, a scathing commentary on the South, and a stark vision of a lynching. Hughes indents the second and fourth lines of each stanza, as in a hymn or a short ballad. He also uses a pattern of end-rhymes, *aaba* in the first and last stanzas, *abcb* in the middle stanza. The rhythm and rhymes of the poem's bluesy three-beat lines have a kind of lilt that is hauntingly undermined by the poem's subject matter, the scene of a mourner looking up at the body of a dead lover.

Though the poem on its own is a formidable and horrifying testimony to the cruelty of lynching, it is all the more powerful when read in dialogue with the infamous Confederate anthem "Dixie." Purportedly written by a white Ohio-born minstrel-show composer, the lyrics of "Dixie" recount, in exaggerated African American dialect, the longing of a freed slave to return to the South and the plantation life there. This falsely nostalgic, sentimental racist fantasy was an immediate hit, performed at minstrel shows by singers in blackface, and it became so popular throughout the 1860s that it was eventually adopted by Southern secessionists. Here is the song's refrain:

> I wish I was in Dixie, Hoo-ray! Hoo-ray!
> In Dixie Land I'll take my stand to live and die in Dixie;
> Away, away, away down south in Dixie,
> Away, away, away down south in Dixie.

Hughes takes the final lines of this refrain and uses a shortened version — "Way Down South in Dixie" — as the refrain in his poem. He capitalizes the four main refrain words for emphasis, as a reminder of the song's racist origins. Though a refrain line typically closes each stanza in a poem, Hughes begins his stanzas with the refrain. This way the refrain sets up the subsequent lines in each stanza as a response to the source song, so that the twisted sentiment of "Dixie" echoes through, and is undermined by, each stanza. With every repetition the refrain becomes more and more ironic, more and more damning.

Hughes follows each refrain with a line in parentheses, which acts as a personal commentary, a slyly defiant answer to, and qualifying of, the refrain. Notice how Hughes doesn't say "(break my heart)" but rather "(Break the heart of me)." At this early point in the poem lynching hasn't been mentioned, so the odd diction of "Break *the heart* of me" signals a broader definition of "heart," meaning not only a lover's feelings, but also "the heart" of a person, their very core, which is broken by being "Way Down South." Lynching comes to the poem in the third line, a simple, shocking statement — "They hung my black young lover" — with three beats hammering on "hung," "black," "love," and the perpetrators of this violence an eerie unnamed "They." The fourth line locates this hanging at "a cross roads tree," an image that immediately conjures the cross of the crucifixion.

In the second stanza the refrain is followed by "(Bruised body high in air)," a description that emphasizes the harshly battered physicality of this corpse. As opposed to "Way *Down* South" the body hangs "*high* in air," which also implicitly contrasts with the place where a corpse should rest, below, in the ground. The word "high" also suggests "on high" or "in heaven" — the African America poet Phillis Wheatley writes, for example, of "heav'n's unmeasur'd height," where redeemed souls go, according to Christian belief. This poem's body, however, remains paradoxically "high in air" rather than in heaven, and bound to earth, a lifeless reproach.

The lover asks "the white Lord Jesus / What was the use of prayer." Hughes deliberately places "white Lord Jesus" in exactly the same position in the second stanza as "black young lover" in the first stanza; both phrases have the same number of syllables, with accents falling in the same places, thus creating a direct formal and symbolic parallel between the two. The Black body sacrificed at the crossroads becomes more Christ-like than the white Jesus, who seems to condone brutal racial injustice. These lines are also an indictment of white Christian Southerners, the "They" of the previous stanza, who used scripture and Christian theology to try to convince antislavery proponents that the cruelty of human bondage was ordained by God, to try to convince enslaved people themselves to accept their servitude as part of God's natural order, and later to justify thousands of post–Civil War lynchings. The speaker poses what looks like the first part of a prayer, "I asked the white Lord Jesus," and then ironically points out the futility of praying to a white Jesus by asking, "What was the use of prayer." There is no question mark at the end of this rhetorical question, which makes it a statement.

When the refrain and parenthetical words of the first stanza return in the final stanza, they carry the full weight of the poem's devastating denunciation of the sentiment of "Dixie." The poem concludes that in a violent and racist South, "Love is a naked shadow." This line can be read as the mourner's bleak description of the lover's hanging body, as in "My lover is now just a naked corpse, a shadow or a ghost." It can also be interpreted as a metaphorical statement about a lack of human compassion, as in "In the racist South, love itself is a ghost, a shadow with no object to cast it." The "naked shadow" hangs "On a gnarled and naked tree," the repetition of the word "naked" emphasizing the exposure of this Black body, and the bodies of all African Americans, to the cruelty of racism. The alliterative "*gn*arled and *n*aked tree" calls to mind a tree that bears no fruit, the opposite of the apple tree in the original garden. This is the bare or fruitless apple tree that will appear at the crossroads of the Robert Johnson legend, the place where he supposedly sold his soul to the devil.

Hughes's iconic poem makes its case against racial hatred by using a series of categorical reversals. As the scholar Jahan Ramazani astutely puts it, "Crossing white and black, up and down, mortal and divine, good and bad, deity and demon, the poem adopts the bewildered perspective of the melancholic mourner who gains no consolation from her prayer to a compromised God, but who edges toward finding 'Love' in her dead lover, divinity in the mortal love she feels for him." In the ultimate reversal Hughes takes an offensive minstrel standard, a comic white song form composed of false racist sentiments about Southern plantation life and sung by an actor in blackface, and uses lines from its refrain as a starting point for a heart-wrenching elegy based on the blues, an innovative Black song form.

CHARLOTTE MEW

—◆—

"Rooms"

(c. 1929)

The English poet Charlotte Mew was a writer of smoldering intensities. Like Thomas Hardy, who considered her "far and away the best living woman poet," Mew was metrically adventurous and outwardly traditional, partly a Victorian, partly a modernist. She is usually associated with the early-twentieth-century Georgian poets, whose name alludes to the reign of George V. However, since that group consisted almost exclusively of male poets, Mew is something of an outlier. Her irregular rhythms and rhyming free-verse experiments give her poems a different kind of offbeat energy. Her romantic focus on women also lends it a proto-feminist perspective. She wrote two books of poems, *The Farmer's Bride* (1916) and *The Rambling Sailor* (1929), which appeared posthumously. She often used the dramatic monologue to give voice to her own feelings and experience under the guise of an assumed persona. Here is her poem "Rooms," which is undated and may have been too revealing to publish in her lifetime.

Rooms

I remember rooms that have had their part
    In the steady slowing down of the heart.
The room in Paris, the room at Geneva,
The little damp room with the seaweed smell,
And that ceaseless maddening sound of the tide —
    Rooms where for good or ill — things died.
But there is the room where we two lie dead,
Though every morning we seem to wake and might just as well seem to
    sleep again
        As we shall somewhere in the other quieter, dustier bed
        Out there in the sun — in the rain.

Mew's memorial, consisting of one stanza, is like a room in itself. It has a compact feeling of restrained sorrow. Made up of ten lines, a stanza known as a décima, it divides neatly into three sentences. The first begins the poem with a fluctuating beat in two four-stress lines:

I remémber róoms that have hád their párt
    In the stéady slówing dówn of the héart.

Mew's metrical variations are strategic. In the first line anapests ($\smallsmile\smallsmile$ /) alternate with iambs ($\smallsmile$ /); however, in the second line Mew puts the anapests at either end of the line and the iambs in the middle, so that the stresses fall on "stéady slówing dówn" and literally enact a steady slowing down in the line's rhythm. The alliteration of "*r*emember *r*ooms" and "*s*teady *s*lowing" implicates the rooms, which "have had their part" in this slowing of the heart. Though so far there is no mention of another person in the rooms, "the heart" here, as in Langston Hughes's "Song for a Black Girl," suggests both feelings for a lover and the core of a person. Because the heart in Mew's poem is slowing down, a reader begins to detect the makings of an anti–love poem, or a frustrated love poem, as well as the breakdown of a person's spirits.

The poem's second sentence (actually a fragment consisting of several phrases) catalogs three remembered rooms — one in Paris, one in Geneva, a third at an unnamed seaside resort. Mew rhymes the first two lines ("part" / "heart"), but purposely drops the rhymes in the next two lines ("Geneva" /

"smell"). This change right away undercuts the rhyming pattern established in the first sentence and signals an atmosphere in these rooms that is far from harmonious. Recalling the third room, the speaker goes on to describe the "ceaseless maddening sound of the tide" coming in and going out. That she finds this sound "maddening," rather than calming, connects with Mew's personal feelings. She had a lifelong terror of madness, which afflicted many members of her family and prompted her to swear off marrying and having children.

As she did in line 2, with "stéady slówing dówn," Mew strategically places the iambs in the middle of line 5 so that the stresses fall on "céaseless mádden-ing sóund," which mimics the pounding of the tide. The two phrases formally and thematically parallel each other, and their last words are close half-rhymes. This sentence fragment comes to a stark conclusion with the only past-tense verb in the poem: "Rooms where for good or ill — things died." This devastating line is also the only one without anapests; instead, the line begins with the poem's sole trochee so that the stress falls on the word "Rooms." Notice as well that after the initial "I," Mew hasn't brought in the speaker again, or any other person, and she avoids specific attributions, using "the heart" instead of "my heart" and "things died" instead of identifying what or who died.

Mew's short lyric then turns, in the seventh line, with the logic of a Shakespearean sonnet. The conjunction "But" signals a shift, a change in direction, and the poem returns to the present tense in a final sentence, a fourth room: "But there is the room where we two lie dead." With "we two" the speaker reappears, along with another person, with whom she lies dead, and the undercurrent of frustrated love becomes more explicit. Breaking the four-beat pattern, the following eight-beat line combines a long string of anapests and iambs: "Though év | ery mórn | ing we séem | to wáke | and míght | just as wéll | seem to sléep | agáin." This line visually bursts out of the poem, as if a beam in the room's ceiling has collapsed and punctured a wall. The word "Though" contradicts "we two lie dead"; therefore, the two dead people "seem to wake" each morning and "just as well seem to sleep," as though they were wandering dazed, like zombies, through their days. The speaker then subtly compares the couple's death-in-life sleep to the sleep "we shall" do "in the other quieter, dustier bed." The future tense, as well as the powerful rhyme of "bed" with "dead," pinpoints this bed as the final resting place of coffins. This six-beat line hovers between the preceding eight-beat line and the poem's final and sole three-beat line, which hones the image of the pair in their coffins as "Out there," exposed to the elements.

Mew's concise account of these rooms, which have slowed the speaker's heart to death, throbs with rage, frustration, and longing. One of the most pressing but unspoken subjects in Mew's work is thwarted desire, her closeted lesbianism. Given the criminalization of homosexuality in England at the time — Oscar Wilde was convicted of gross indecency under these laws and served two years of hard labor — Mew was unwilling and unable to acknowledge openly her passion for women. She also seemed incapable of achieving a successful relationship with a woman. As Penelope Fitzgerald points out in her book *Charlotte Mew and Her Friends,* Mew had an unhealthy tendency to be drawn to women who did not reciprocate her feelings.

Read through the lens of these repressed and thwarted desires, the poem's surface reticence yields a rich and poignant portrait of a woman denied the pleasures of sexual intimacy. The "steady slowing down of the heart" evokes the long and gradual death of the speaker's homosexual aspirations. The "ceaseless maddening sound of the tide" describes not just the movement of the sea but the constant flow of her own desires, which become maddening for not being accepted or reciprocated. We can understand the "things" of "things died" as an erotic spark that has burned out. The profound loneliness of an un-fulfilled "I" "in the room where we two lie," the brokenness and distorted sense of self that come from walking through life feeling dead inside, are movingly depicted by the final three lines, which formally and emotionally rupture the poem. It is as if the poet, in her inability to break from conventional form in a repressive, unforgiving society, breaks the form of the poem, so that the poem itself can speak the truth, the disappointed love that dare not speak its name.

CÉSAR VALLEJO

———

"Black Stone Lying on a White Stone"

(1930)

The Peruvian poet César Vallejo lived in Paris from 1923 to 1938. His dire poverty, his brooding exile and bitter sense of displacement, his growing rage over social inequities and the naked suffering of others, all seemed to overwhelm him. And yet during the last fifteen years of his life, he wrote 110 poems that are his most lasting achievement. *Poemas humanos,* which his widow, Georgette Vallejo, published posthumously in 1939, is one of the most humane, sorrowful, and agonized works of modernism.

Here is Vallejo's most iconic poem, "Piedra negra sobre una piedra blanca," in which he foresees his own death. The poem is undated, but on January 2, 1930, Vallejo sent it along with two other poems in a letter to a Peruvian friend.

Black Stone Lying on a White Stone

I will die in Paris, on a rainy day,
on some day I can already remember.
I will die in Paris — and I don't step aside —
perhaps on a Thursday, as today is Thursday, in autumn.

It will be a Thursday, because today, Thursday, setting down
these lines, I have put my upper arm bones on
wrong, and never so much as today have I found myself
with all the road ahead of me, alone.

César Vallejo is dead. Everyone beat him,
although he never does anything to them;
they beat him hard with a stick and hard also

with a rope. These are the witnesses:
the Thursdays, and the bones of my arms,
the solitude, and the rain, and the roads . . .

(Translated by Robert Bly and John Knopefle)

Vallejo apparently got the idea for "Piedra negra sobre una piedra blanca"
on a wet day in Paris in the late twenties. He was wearing a black overcoat and
sat down on a white stone bench in a state of utter dejection. The Cuban critic
Eugenio Florit suggests that Vallejo's sonnet "recalls the ancient practice of me-
morializing a fortunate event with a white stone, an unfortunate one with a
black." Vallejo may have thought of himself as a black stone atop a white grave-
stone.

Some of Vallejo's biographers believe that Vallejo's "memory" of his own
death was inspired by a waking dream, which had the feeling of a premonition;
it came to him on a visit to Peru in 1920. Inadvertently mixed up in a political
feud for which he was eventually imprisoned, anxiously hiding from the police
at a friend's house in Trujillo, Vallejo dreamed that he was witnessing his own
death in Paris, surrounded by people he did not know or recognize. Some of
the details of Vallejo's daydream turned out to be eerily prescient, close to the
circumstances of his actual death eighteen years later, on April 15, 1938. It was
not a Thursday, though, but rather Good Friday.

Vallejo's self-elegy has a disruptive, estranging effect in almost every trans-
lation. Yet it is nearly impossible to replicate its exact rhythms and its gram-
mar in English. The poem is a sonnet written in loose hendecasyllables, the
eleven-syllable lines that have been one of the staples of Spanish poetry since
the Renaissance. What is especially striking is how Vallejo disorders the typical

argumentative logic of the fourteen-line form by constantly careening back-
ward and forward in time. He uses four different Spanish verb tenses, which
shift jarringly from one to the other without warning.

The sonnet begins in the future tense: "Me moriré en Paris con aguacero,"
which Bly and Knopefle translate as "I will die in Paris, on a rainy day." A more
literal translation would read: "I will die in Paris in a downpour." The stormy
weather creates a feeling of foreboding, and the line reads as a prediction of the
speaker's own death. However, in the second line we learn that he already has
a memory of this day ("una día del cual tengo ya el recuerdo"), as if his death
had happened before he predicted it. The third line explains that he will die
in Paris, a fate he won't try to avoid ("— and I don't step aside —"), and then
suggests that it might happen on a Thursday, just like today, the day he's writ-
ing the poem, in the fall. The first five lines lurch between the future and pres-
ent tenses, sometimes within the same line ("I *will die* in Paris — and I *don't
step* aside —"). These fluctuations flatten time, giving the sense that the future
exists in the present; also, they indicate that the speaker in the present is un-
flinchingly facing his future death.

He repeats that his death will be on a Thursday. Why? In answer, Vallejo
employs a word from the language of argumentation — "because" — but with
a surreal twist: "because today, Thursday, setting down / these lines, I have
put my upper arm bones on / wrong." In other words, in writing the very lines
we are reading, the speaker has attached his arm bones incorrectly, as if arms
could be put on and taken off like a shirt. It's interesting to examine Vallejo's
word choices, which are both inventive and strange, both to get a sense of the
original Spanish and to understand that translation is more an art than a sci-
ence. For example, the phrase Vallejo used for "setting down" is "que proso," a
coinage that makes a present-tense verb, *proso*, out of the noun *prosa*, meaning
"prose"; therefore, a literal translation would be something like "as I prose."
He also pairs a Latinate anatomical word — *húmeros*, "the upper arm bones,"
with a colloquial phrase — "me he puesto a la mala," "I put it on the hard way,"
to suggest some sort of difficult medical arm-reattachment procedure. This
image points not only to the extreme effort of this arm reattachment and the
resulting feeling of bodily estrangement, but also to the effort of writing the
lines, which makes this reattachment necessary. Vallejo also introduces an-
other verb tense, the present perfect — "I have put," "have I found" — which
indicates an action that occurred in the past or begins in the past and contin-

ues into the present. Whereas the first five lines bring the future into the present, the following three lines bring the past into the present. The speaker also predicts that he will die on a Thursday, like "today," because "never so much as today have I found myself / with all the road ahead of me, alone." The octave closes with the speaker coming to understand the existential isolation of his solitude.

Vallejo has written one of the most startling voltas in the long history of the sonnet. It's worth noting an obvious visual cue signaling this turn in the Spanish version: whereas every line in the octave ends with an *o* sound, the ninth line ends with the word *pegaban*, "they were beating," which abruptly breaks this pattern. The ninth line also turns from the first person to the third person — the speaker speaking *as* himself becomes the speaker speaking *about* himself — to declare that "César Vallejo is dead." Because Vallejo again uses the present-perfect *ha muerto*, this clause is sometimes rendered as "César Vallejo has died." It's as if the poet has penned his own death announcement. In the Spanish text a comma instead of a period follows this statement — "César Vallejo ha muerto, le pegaban" — which causally links the beating to his death.

The following line employs another radical shift in tense. In a note to her translation of the poem, Rebecca Seiferle points out that the hendecasyllabic count also breaks down here in the tenth line, where "the interruption of time is most noticeable and dramatic, when the past tense of 'César Vallejo has died' and 'le pegaban' ('they kept hitting him' but also 'they used it to hit him') is followed by 'él les haga nada' ('he does nothing to them')." The shifting and flattening of time are simultaneously enacted in the poem's grammar and its rhythm. Interrupting the past tense with the present tense reminds us that the poet composing his own death notice is still alive, protesting the injustice of the brutalities he's suffered by writing them down. Therefore, the proclamation "Cesar Vallejo is dead" points to the death of identity, the loss of self he feels as he contemplates his journey alone.

The last stanza concludes the sonnet by naming the witnesses to the violence he has endured. In keeping with the surreal tone of the poem, the witnesses are not people but five key elements of the poem: "the Thursdays, and the bones of my arms, / the solitude, and the rain, and the roads." (Bly and Knopefle inexplicably add the word "and" to the last line, which in the original reads, "la soledad, la lluvia, los caminos . . .") The final line of the sestet trails off in an ellipsis after "roads," as if literalizing the feeling of ongoing loneliness expressed in the final line of the octave: "with all the road ahead of me, alone."

Therefore, it's no accident that this line begins with "the solitude" and ends with "the roads." Given that the entire list of witnesses stands as a summary of the poem itself, it is as if Vallejo, like Keats in "This living hand," means for this poem to speak for him as his witness long after his death, which he has so forcefully predicted, comes to pass.

ALFONSINA STORNI

"I'm Going to Sleep"

(1938)

"Voy a dormir" is the last poem the Argentine poet Alfonsina Storni wrote. She was suffering from terminal cancer and had cut herself off from even her closest friends and family members. It was October 25, 1938; she was only forty-six. Before she died, she posted three letters: one to her son Alejandro, one to a friend whom she asked to care for her family, and a third to the Argentine newspaper *La Nación,* with this farewell poem.

I'm Going to Sleep

Teeth of flowers, bonnet of dew,
hands of grass, you, lovely nursemaid,
turn down the earthen sheets for me
and the quilt of weeded moss.

I'm going to sleep, my nurse, tuck me in,
put a lamp on my headboard;

a constellation; whichever you like;
both are fine; lower the light a little.

Leave me alone: you hear buds bursting open . . .
An unearthly foot rocks you from above
and a bird sketches you a few beats

so you'll forget . . . Thanks. Oh, a favor:
if he calls again on the phone
tell him not to insist, that I've gone . . .

(Translated by Lauren K. Watel)

After writing in classical forms such as the Petrarchan sonnet earlier in her career, Alfonsina Storni, like many modernist writers of the time, began to experiment and disrupt these forms, which had come to be considered somewhat stale. This poem follows the pattern of all the poems in her final book, *Mask and Clover* (*Mascarilla y trébol*). She termed the form an *antisoneto,* or anti-sonnet — in other words, a sonnet that works within, and yet against, the traditional form. The Peruvian avant-garde poet José Carlos Mariátegui published a short piece called "El anti-soneto" in a journal in Lima in 1928. Writing about his contemporary Martín Adán, he pronounced "the definitive, evident, irrevocable decease of the sonnet" and called the anti-sonnet "the sonnet that is no longer a sonnet, but its negation, its opposite, its critique, its renunciation."

Storni's last poem maintains the eight- and six-line structure of a Petrarchan sonnet, which she divides into two quatrains and two tercets. Like César Vallejo's surreal sonnet "Black Stone Lying on a White Stone," this poem is written in fourteen hendecasyllabic lines. Storni's use of expressive punctuation forces a series of stops and starts as the poem unfolds, continually interrupting the flow of the basic eleven-syllable line, just as Vallejo's constant shifts in tense disrupt time within and between lines. Though adhering to a conventional stanzaic form and meter, Storni chose not to use rhyme in her sonnet; she thereby creates a feeling of spontaneity and freedom within the prescribed form.

"I'm Going to Sleep" is a poem of leave-taking. The title announces the speaker's intention to "go to sleep," by which she means the final sleep, death.

The connection between sleep and death goes back to antiquity. In Greek mythology Hypnos, the god of sleep, and Thanatos, the god of death, were said to be children of Nyx, the goddess of night. The Spanish word *cementerio* ("cemetery") derives from Greek (*koimeterion*) and Latin (*koemeteriun*) words for "sleeping place," from *koiman,* "to put to sleep," and from *keimai,* "I lie down." As in many Romantic poems, Storni's speaker conflates sleep and death; however, here she literalizes the connection to a remarkable degree by depicting an oddly cozy bedroom scene, where a tender nursemaid will put her to bed for her final sleep.

The poem begins with three images that isolate aspects of an implied person — "teeth," "bonnet," and "hands" — and modifies each with an image from nature — "flowers," "dew," and "grass." This trio of strange juxtapositions instantly links the as-yet-unnamed person to the pastoral. In the middle of the second line we learn that these objects stand in for, and characterize, an addressee, the "you" of the poem, whom the speaker envisions as a beloved nursemaid. She instructs this woman to prepare a bed for her; it has, however, "earthen sheets" and a "quilt of weeded moss," which suggest a bed in the ground, or a grave. Because her nursemaid is turning down her bed, the "I" assumes the role of a child, the nurse her caretaker.

After saying that she's "going to sleep," the speaker, like a child afraid of the dark, asks the nursemaid to tuck her in and leave a lamp on the headboard. In the next line she mentions another lighting option — "a constellation; whichever you like." Here the poem casually conflates the human and the cosmic, as if the pastoral nursemaid also has supernatural powers and can wield an entire constellation as easily as a lamp, as she prefers; "both are fine." Notice this quatrain's unusual use of semicolons, which create a longer pause than commas do, and isolate each phrase, for emphasis. The octave ends with an additional request: for the nursemaid to "lower the light a little," as if the speaker wants the room darker so she can fall asleep.

The sestet signals a shift in the tone and the action of the poem. The speaker says, "Leave me alone," as though she's ready to fall asleep by herself. A colon follows the word "alone," indicating another longer pause, and then the imperative ("tuck me in," "lower the light") switches to the declarative ("you hear buds bursting open . . ."). The "buds bursting open" evoke shoots emerging from the earthy bed and allude to the flowering of new life, perhaps the afterlife.

The ellipsis at the end of this line again signifies a break in time, a "bursting open" of the poem into what appears to be a switch in point of view. In the next two and a half lines the nurse seems to be addressing the speaker in her bed. As if to comfort a child, the nurse says, "An unearthly foot rocks you from above / and a bird sketches you a few beats // so you'll forget . . ." Just as the nurse can put a constellation on the headboard, she can also rock the "earthen" bed with an "unearthly foot." Storni combines a verb, *traza,* associated with visual art and meaning "trace or draw," with a musical term, *compases,* meaning "beats or measures," to evoke the arcs and the rhythm of a bird's wings in flight, which will lull the sleeper into forgetfulness.

After another ellipsis in the first line of the final stanza, the point of view seems to switch back to the speaker, who thanks the nursemaid for her soothing words. One last thing occurs to her: "Ah, un encargo" ("Oh, a favor:"). She tells the nursemaid that "if he calls again on the phone / tell him not to insist, that I've gone . . ." There's an informal feeling in this last request, as if the speaker has just gone out for a while. It's impossible to know the identity of this "he" who suddenly appears at the end of the poem — he could be a specific man or anyone who might call, even life itself — but whoever he is, she wants him to stop insisting, because she has left for good. The sestet ends with another ellipsis as the poem trails off and opens out in the same way that César Vallejo's self-elegy does.

Alfonsina Storni knew when she wrote this poem that she was going to sleep for the last time. Shortly after writing and sending it, she walked into the Atlantic Ocean at Mar de Plata. This strangely peaceful anti-sonnet, which views death as an earthly sleep ushered in by a loving nursemaid, both worldly and otherworldly, turned out to be a tenderly felt and carefully composed suicide note.

JULIA DE BURGOS

—

"To Julia de Burgos"

(1938)

J ulia de Burgos was a feminist, a civil rights activist, a Puerto Rican *indepen-dentista,* and a committed internationalist in the first half of the twentieth century. She was also a poet of the Americas influenced by Walt Whitman's inclusive free-verse catalogs, Pablo Neruda's passionate early love songs, which she memorized, and Alfonsina Storni's unabashed erotic poems. She refer-enced the title of Miguel de Unamuno's famous philosophical tract *Del sen-timiento trágico de la vida* to describe Storni's "profundity of life and tragic sense of life," which also describes de Burgos's passionate sense of herself as a writer.

De Burgos splits herself off into two parts in her highly self-conscious and self-accusing poem "To Julia de Burgos" ("A Julia de Burgos"), which she pub-lished in Puerto Rico in 1938. She was twenty-four years old.

To Julia de Burgos

Already people are muttering that I am your enemy
because they say that in verse I give the world your I.

They lie, Julia de Burgos. They lie, Julia de Burgos.
What rises in my poems isn't your voice; it's my voice,
because you are the trappings and I am the essence;
and the deepest chasm lies between the two.

You are a cold doll of the social lie,
and I, the virile spark of human truth.

You, honey of courtesan hypocrisies, not I;
who undress my heart in all my poems.

You are like your world, selfish; not I;
who risk everything to be what I am.

You are merely the sickly matronly lady;
not I; I am life, strength, woman.

You are your husband's, your master's; not I;
I'm nobody's, or everybody's, because to all, to all,
I give myself in my pure feeling and my thinking.

You ripple your hair and paint yourself; not I;
the wind ripples me; the sun paints me.

You are a domestic lady, resigned, submissive,
tied to the prejudices of men; not I;
I am Rocinante running rampant
following horizons of God's justice.

You're not in charge of yourself; everyone's in charge
of you; your husband, your parents, your relatives,
the priest, the couturier, the theater, the club,

the car, the jewels, the banquet, the champagne,
heaven and hell, and the what-will-they-say social.

As for me, no, only my heart is in charge in me,
only my thought; the one in charge in me is I.

You, flower of aristocracy; and I, flower of the village.
You have everything in you and you owe it to everyone,
while I, my nothing I owe to no one.

You, stuck to the static ancestral dividend,
and I, a one in the sum of the social denominator,
we are the duel to the death that fatally approaches.

When the multitudes run riotous
leaving behind ashes of burnt-out injustices,
and when the multitudes run with the torch
of the seven virtues, against the seven sins,
against you, and against all the unjust and the inhumane,
I will be among them with the torch in my hand.

(Translated by Lauren K. Watel)

The title of this poem, "To Julia de Burgos," immediately signals that the poet is writing to herself, as in a letter, a memo, or an editorial. The poem begins by jumping into the scenario that requires this self-address: "Already people are muttering that I am your enemy / because they say that in verse I give the world your I." This sets out the basic terms of the poem's argument, that the writer is seen as her own enemy by giving away her "I" in her poetry. De Burgos intentionally ends this initial couplet with the words *tu yo,* which mean both "your I" and "you I." The rest of the poem will go on to dramatize the conflict between the "you" and the "I."

The next line — "They lie, Julia de Burgos. They lie, Julia de Burgos." — is composed of two short declarative sentences. Addressing herself by name twice, as if chastising herself for believing that lie, she protests that the people muttering about her are wrong. She goes on to explain that "What rises in my poems isn't your voice; it's my voice." In this line she clarifies that the "I" is the speaker in her poems, her poet-self, and the "you" is another self. The next line summarizes the difference between these two selves: the "you" is represented by "the trappings," the "I" by "the essence." By the fifth line of the poem we understand that on the most basic level she considers the "you" superficial, the "I" profound. To underscore the opposition between them, de Burgos ends the quatrain asserting that "the deepest chasm lies between the two."

The poem then goes on to elaborate on the opposition between the "I" and the "you." After the second stanza each subsequent unrhyming stanza consists of one sentence that adds to the terms of this contrast. The third stanza poses "you" as "a cold doll of the social lie" and "I" as "the virile spark of human truth," making it explicit that the "you" stands for the compromised societal self, while the "I" represents the poetic self who is committed to truth. Given the terms of this comparison, a "cold doll" and a "virile spark," one begins to see "To Julia de Burgos" as a radically gendered poem. Each subsequent stanza depicts the conflict between the "you" of the social persona, seen as variously trapped and disempowered by feminine passivity and conventional feminine roles, and the "I" of the writer persona, seen as aligned with Romantic ideals beyond the stereotypically feminine, such as virility, purity of thought, strong womanhood, the natural world, and struggles for justice.

As the high rhetorical language and stark oppositions of each stanza begin to accumulate, the sense of a fierce struggle between two irreconcilable selves becomes more and more apparent. The "I" consistently criticizes and rejects her social identity as a performance of womanhood, "honey of courtesan hypocrisies," while she valorizes her writer identity, the truer, freer self that is expressed in her poems. The poem categorizes the "you" as deceitful, selfish, weak, vain, and the "I" as honest, self-affirming, strong, attuned to nature. The "I" seems disgusted by her submissive domesticity and compares her artistic self to Don Quixote's legendary horse, Rocinante, who has unseated his rider and is now "running rampant" on the hunt for justice. There is an inside joke here, since when de Burgos was growing up, Rocinante was the name of her father's horse; her own horse, Nacional, goes unmentioned. The poem returns repeatedly to the issue of control, of ownership of the female self. Whereas the "you" belongs to a husband, a master, the "I" belongs to nobody. One might even say that the speaker conceives of the "you" as her body, her physical self, which must operate in the social world and submit to control by external forces, which she enumerates in a list:

> You're not in charge of yourself; everyone's in charge
> of you; your husband, your parents, your relatives,
> the priest, the couturier, the theater, the club,
> the car, the jewels, the banquet, the champagne,
> heaven and hell, and the what-will-they-say social.

In contrast, the speaker prizes her inner spirit, the "I" of her own feeling and mind, the lyric "I" of the poem, which can operate in the world of the imagination without restrictions and must submit to no one: "As for me, no, only my heart is in charge in me, / only my thought; the one in charge in me is I."

As the poem draws to a close, de Burgos's appraisal of bourgeois manners, trappings, and values expands to a broader commentary on class and wealth inequality. She aligns the "you" of the self with the aristocracy, the "I" with the village. In the penultimate stanza she continues this economic critique, envisioning herself as a society of one, split between "You, stuck to the static ancestral dividend, / and I, a one in the sum of the social denominator." She is all too aware that a revolution, a "duel to the death," is coming between these opposing forces. As if to signal formally the culmination of her argument, in the original Spanish de Burgos triple-rhymes this tercet. The final six-line stanza, which in Spanish consists of three rhyming couplets, ends on a vision of this revolution, in which the "multitudes run riotous / leaving behind ashes of burnt-out injustices." "You" makes her last appearance in the penultimate line, an object of the multitudes' wrath, associated with "all the unjust and the inhumane." The "I" in the last line, conversely, stands in their midst, like the Statue of Liberty, with a torch in her hand.

What is most powerful, even revolutionary, about de Burgos's poem is its unflinching probing of the self, which is imagined as a battleground; the conflict splits the writer in two while offering a systematic social critique. This ingenious poetic move influenced many Spanish-language poems, including Jorge Luis Borges's "Borges and I" ("Borges y yo," 1957) and Jaime de Biedma's "Against Jaime Gil de Biedma" ("Contra Jaime Gil de Biedma," 1968). Vanessa Pérez Rosario points out that similar confrontations between warring aspects of the self will appear in Gabriela Mistral's "The Other" ("La otra," 1954), Anne Sexton's "Her Kind" (1960), and Sylvia Plath's "Three Women: A Poem for Three Voices" (1962). Julia de Burgos, a fierce innovator, provided a model for incisive feminist self-critique that forcefully equates the personal with the political.

ANNA AKHMATOVA

—

"In Memory of M. B."

(1940)

This elegy by Anna Akhmatova honors the memory of Mikhail Bulgakov, a Russian doctor turned writer who composed plays, fiction, nonfiction, and various forms of journalism. He is most famous for his comic masterpiece *The Master and Margarita,* a fantastical modernist novel about, among other things, the devil's visit to the Soviet Union. Akhmatova wrote "In Memory of M. B." just after Bulgakov's death in March 1940, during the nightmares of the Stalinist terror. The poem is part of the elegiac cycle "Wreath to the Dead" (1938–61):

> *In Memory of M. B.*
>
> Here is my gift, not roses on your grave,
> not sticks of burning incense.
> You lived aloof, maintaining to the end
> your magnificent disdain.
> You drank wine, and told the wittiest jokes,
> and suffocated inside stifling walls.

Alone you let the terrible stranger in,
and stayed with her alone.
Now you're gone, and nobody says a word
about your troubled and exalted life.
Only my voice, like a flute, will mourn
at your dumb funeral feast.
Oh, who would have believed that half-crazed I,
I, sick with grief for the buried past,
I, smoldering on a slow fire,
having lost everything and forgotten all,
would be fated to commemorate a man
so full of strength and will and bright inventions,
who only yesterday, it seems, chatted with me,
hiding the tremor of his mortal pain.

(Translated by Stanley Kunitz with Max Hayward)

In the title of this poem Akhmatova uses the initials, rather than the full name, of the deceased. This is the first clue that the poet is writing under precarious political conditions that require extreme secrecy and discretion. Bulgakov had personally been blacklisted by Stalin. Most of his work was banned during his lifetime, very few of his plays were permitted to be performed, and he was prevented from leaving the country when he desperately desired to emigrate. Given his outcast status when he died, it was probably too dangerous to refer to him by his full name. Akhmatova instead addresses Mikhail Bulgakov directly, in the present tense, reinforcing a sense of a private communication between two intimates.

The poem's first lines, "Here is my gift, not roses on your grave, / not sticks of burning incense," also allude to the public erasure of figures thought to be political dissidents. For fear of reprisals the speaker doesn't dare observe traditional rituals of public mourning; instead, she must write a poem in private as her funereal offering. Just a title and two lines have already hinted at ways in which a tyrannical government silences its opponents. Silence and speech, private and public expression, will become one of the main themes of the poem.

As Joanna Trzeciak points out, this poem in Russian consists of a single stanza in what Russian scholars call "undivided quatrains." This means that each four-line unit acts as if it were a stand-alone quatrain. Akhmatova established an elaborate formal system, impossible to replicate in translation, involving a regular *abab* rhyme scheme with alternating masculine and feminine rhymes, as well as a pattern of metrical symmetry, switching between iambic pentameter and iambic hexameter.

Osip Mandelstam once observed that the roots of Akhmatova's art lie in the nineteenth-century novel, in Tolstoy, Turgenev, and Dostoevsky, and that her poetic form "was developed with a glance at psychological prose." In the first stanza the poet brings a prose writer's eye to her characterization of Bulgakov. She paints a portrait of a writer who, as much as he wanted to see his work published and performed, refused to become a mouthpiece for the government; rather, he bravely, stubbornly maintained his "magnificent disdain." Though he kept up a cosmopolitan persona, drinking wine and telling "the wittiest jokes," privately he "suffocated inside stifling walls." Here Akhmatova literalizes as "stifling walls" the oppressive political forces that prevented him from traveling outside the country to live in artistic and political freedom.

Akhmatova also effectively characterizes the isolation Bulgakov must have felt for much of his life, given both his blacklisting by Stalin and his ongoing poor health. He suffered from serious injuries sustained on the front as a Red Cross doctor in World War I, from a near-fatal bout with typhus, and from an inherited kidney disorder. Emphasizing his dignity, his aloofness, and his private, solitary suffering, the speaker ends the stanza with the end of Bulgakov's life: "Alone you let the terrible stranger in, / and stayed with her alone." Reversing the usual idea of death as an active force, hunting people down and taking them away, she describes Bulgakov as an active participant in his own end, as he *lets in* death, "the terrible stranger," and *stays with* her, as if he's faced death stoically, with great poise.

The second stanza begins with a powerful depiction of a double silence: "Now you're gone, and nobody says a word / about your troubled and exalted life." Here the speaker refers to both the silence of the deceased and the silence of his would-be mourners, who can't publicly grieve a person who's been deemed a "non-person." Then there is the silence of the "dumb funeral feast," which the speaker must counter with her "voice, like a flute." Trzeciak points out that the diction and language Akhmatova uses to begin the second stanza are strongly reminiscent of early nineteenth-century elegies from the Russian Golden Age. Even though the poet will mourn Bulgakov, the flute's piercing notes can sound only in the poem, in silence rather than performed in public, like the "gift" from the first stanza. The flute is also a reference to the elegiac tradition in poetry: ancient Greek elegies were chanted aloud and traditionally accompanied by a flute, the instrument of grief.

The speaker's sorrow expands from mourning the friend she has lost to mourning the life she has lost. Writing about Eugenio Montale, Joseph Brodsky observed that "death as a theme always produces a self-portrait." That becomes apparent here. Like Bulgakov, Akhmatova suffered from a ban on her work. Her ex-husband was prosecuted and shot; her son was arrested and imprisoned; many of her friends were killed, including Mandelstam, her greatest ally, who had been deported and died in a Siberian labor camp. She lived in poverty, trying to get her son released. No wonder Akhmatova's speaker describes herself as "half-crazed" and "smoldering on a slow fire," which parallels Bulgakov's "suffocating inside stifling walls." Given that she is "sick with grief for the buried past" — another devastating sort of silence exercised by tyrannical governments is erasure of the past — and "having lost everything and forgotten all," she is astonished that it has fallen to her to remember "a man / so full of strength and will and bright inventions." The poem closes with an indelible snapshot of the deceased writer, "who only yesterday, it seems, chatted with me, / hiding the tremor of his mortal pain." Even as he is speaking to his friend, Bulgakov is hiding his suffering, which summarizes in microcosm life during the Stalinist era.

Bulgakov diligently worked on *The Master and Margarita* until the month before his death, but the book wasn't published until 1967, in Paris. Similarly, although Akhmatova penned her elegy in 1940 from her house in Leningrad, it wasn't published until 1966. And yet, as Bulgakov puts it in one of the most memorable lines from his brilliant satire, "manuscripts don't burn." "In Memory of M. B." is a poem of memorialization and self-preservation. Here Akhmatova quietly but defiantly speaks on behalf both of Bulgakov and herself. She speaks against the many silences imposed by an autocratic regime, but especially against death, the ultimate silence.

MIKLÓS RADNÓTI

"The Fifth Eclogue"

(1943)

Miklós Radnóti's poems have a doleful intimacy and intensity. This Hungarian poet of the first half of the twentieth century clung with a desperate serenity to the classical values of the Western poetic tradition at a time when those values had been undermined by the horrors of two world wars. Like his Russian contemporary Osip Mandelstam, Radnóti wrote with a deeply felt subjectivity about thoroughly modern concerns, and his poems were filled with a growing sense of uncertainty and dread. However, both poets tried to impose a sense of personal control over the era's horrific and uncontrollable social calamities by their insistence on the aesthetic and moral ideals of antiquity, such as the clarity of poetic form, the virtues of reason, and the philosophical rectitude of Stoicism.

The eclogue is a short dialogue or soliloquy with a formal poetic structure. The term originated with Virgil's *Eclogues* (originally titled *Bucolics*), which dates from the mid-30s BCE, though an underlying theme of many eclogues — an urban poet turning to the countryside for sustenance — was first established by Theocritus in the *Idylls* (third century BCE). In 1938, Radnóti translated Virgil's ninth eclogue, an experience that instigated his own dark pastorals. Radnóti's eight eclogues comprise a discontinuous series that he wrote in the late 1930s and early 40s. The sixth eclogue is missing, though many scholars now identify the poem "Fragment" ("Töredék") as the sixth.

Radnóti's eclogues are written in hexameters, the classical six-foot metrical line that is well-suited to Hungarian if somewhat long for English, in which the five-foot pentameter line serves as a baseline. Radnóti calls on the shepherd muse to assist him in trying to preserve the values of civilization against the barbarities of war. "Pastoral Muse, O help me!" he exclaims in "The Third Eclogue," "this age must murder its poets." These poems sing to overcome terror, invoking the splendors of memory, the landscape of childhood, and the necessity of love when "reason falls apart."

Here is the bluntest and most startling poem in the sequence:

The Fifth Eclogue

FRAGMENT
To the memory of György Bálint

Dear friend, you don't know how cold this poem made me quake,
how afraid I was of words. Even today I tried to escape them.
I wrote half-lines.

            I tried to write about other things,
but it was no use. This terrible, hidden night calls me:
"Talk about him."

            Fear wakes me, but the voice
is silent, like the dead out there in the Ukrainian fields.
You're missing.

            And even autumn doesn't bring news.

                    In the forest
the promise of another furious winter whistles today. In the sky,
clouds heavy with snow fly past and halt.
Who knows if you're alive?

            Even I don't know today. I don't shout
angrily if they wave their hands painfully and cover their faces
and don't know anything.

            But are you alive, wounded?

Do you walk among dead leaves, circled by the thick smell of forest mud,
or are you a smell too?

> Snow drifts over the fields.

He's missing—the news hits.

> And inside, my heart pounds, freezes.

Between two of my ribs, a bad, ripping pain starts up,
quivers, and in my memories, words you spoke a long time ago
come back sharply and I feel your body's as real
as the dead's—

> And I still can't write about you today!

November 21, 1943

(Translated by Steven Polgar, Stephen Berg, and S. J. Marks)

In the spring of 1943, Radnóti was serving a ten-month stint of forced labor. When he heard that a close friend, the essayist and critic György Bálint, had been dispatched as a labor serviceman to Ukraine, he got the idea for "The Fifth Eclogue" ("Ötödik ecloga"). After returning home in November, with the grim news of his friend's plight on his mind, Radnóti wrote and dated the poem, which he dedicated to the memory of Bálint. Radnóti's fifth eclogue seems composed in a state of confusion, uncertain as to whether his friend is dead or alive. But the dedication suggests a darker truth, which he unconsciously knows but cannot accept: his friend has already died. Later, he learned that Bálint had in fact perished in a field hospital in Ukraine.

Radnóti formally modernizes the classical eclogue by marking it as a fragment, which suggests something broken off or detached from the whole, something imperfect or incomplete. The Romantic poets treated the fragment as a radiant moment freed from temporality, but the modernists reinvented it as an acutely self-conscious mode of writing that breaks the flow of time, leaving gaps and tears. It is a form of disruption. Radnóti designates his pastoral a "fragment" because his knowledge of its subject's fate is incomplete. He dreads the closed circle, the completeness, of an elegy.

Radnóti dedicates the poem to the memory of his friend and then addresses Bálint in the present tense, as if conversing with him, a move reminiscent of Akhmatova's in "In Memory of M. B." In Hungarian the poem begins with some hard percussives, a persistent knocking of *d* and *r* sounds: "Drága barátom, hogy didergtem e vers hidegétol." They mimic the poet's quaking—from the cold and from his fear of words. With its clipped sentences and dropped lines, the poem visually reflects the difficulty of writing a poem one fears writing, which is why it keeps breaking off and interrupting itself — "I wrote half-lines. / I tried to write about other things, / but it was no use."

As in many of the poems in this anthology, including Thomas Hardy's "The Voice" and Edward Thomas's "The Owl," a nonhuman natural element, the night, cries out to the poet, saying, "Talk about him." The line then drops to "Fear wakes me," as if the speaker has been in a sort of dream state. Now that he's awake, the voice of the "terrible, hidden night . . . is silent, like the dead out there in the Ukrainian fields." This reference to the dead brings his friend's plight back to mind in the following line: "You're missing." After this, the line drops again, as if the shock of this statement sends the poet's pen jolting downward. Notice that the poem repeats this pattern to the end; the line drops whenever Radnóti forces himself to write something he finds hard to accept.

In addition to his fragmenting of the classical eclogue form, Radnóti also updates it by giving nature a radically different role. His agonized version might be considered a sort of anti-eclogue. Whereas nature in the eclogue usually served as a place of escape, a peaceful idyll harkening back to a more innocent, Eden-like past, a simple refuge from the bustle and confusion of the city, in this eclogue the natural world offers no escape from the horrors of the so-called civilized world. The speaker characterizes the night as "terrible, hidden," "the Ukrainian fields" as full of corpses, the winter as "furious." Autumn brings no news of his friend, and clouds "halt" like soldiers and "wave their hands painfully and cover their faces / and don't know anything." Throughout the poem elements of the natural world offer none of the usual consolations and only reinforce the sense of dread.

Questioning his friend directly as to his circumstances, the speaker asks if he is "alive, wounded? / Do you walk among dead leaves, circled by the thick smell of forest mud . . ." Then, at a devastating line break, he wonders, "or are you a smell too?" After this awful question the line again drops, to "Snow drifts over the fields." In another context drifting snow could be a peaceful image. However, as the speaker contemplates the decomposition of his friend's body, this snow seems to cover over and annihilate everything. In the next line, the earlier sentence "You're missing" turns into "He's missing — the news hits." It's as if, after the dropped line combining the smell of decomposition with the obliterating snow, he must tell himself the news again and let it sink in, as if for the first time. After his heart "pounds, freezes," recalling the first line's "cold" and "quake," he feels "a bad, ripping pain" between his ribs. The memory of his friend's voice, the very words he spoke, come back to him. Where the speaker states, "I feel your body's as real / as the dead's —" the line breaks hard after the dash, like a lash of pain. Now he can no longer avoid knowing what he has suspected all along. But it's too much to bear, and in the final dropped line the speaker must fragment this elegy, which he can't seem to complete: "And I still can't write about you today!"

Radnóti finished his seventh and eighth eclogues after he had been drafted for hard labor and assigned to work in a copper mine in Bor, Yugoslavia. He was taken from the mine and driven westward across Hungary in a forced march, and there, near the town of Abda sometime between November 6 and November 10, 1944, along with a group of twenty-one other prisoners, he was killed and tossed into a mass grave by members of the Hungarian armed forces. He was thirty-five years old. After the war, Radnóti's wife had his body exhumed, and his last poems were found in his field jacket, written in pencil in a small Serbian exercise book that is now known as "The Bor Notebook." These poems have literally risen from the grave to give Radnóti's final testimony.

CZESŁAW MIŁOSZ

———

"Café"

(1944)

What occurred in Poland was an encounter of a European poet with the hell of the twentieth century, not hell's first circle, but a much deeper one," Czesław Miłosz declared in his 1983 collection of lectures, *The Witness of Poetry*. "This situation is something of a laboratory, in other words: it allows us to examine what happens to modern poetry in certain historical conditions." What Miłosz meant by "historical conditions" was the complete disintegration of European culture — "the sudden crumbling of all current notions and criteria" — between 1939 and 1945. Polish poets felt the need to respond in a radical way to the disgrace of Europe — how it was sinking into inhumanity, how it was complicit in genocide — by trying to remake poetry from the ground up. It was starting over again after what seemed like the end of the world.

The poet in Poland experienced history on his pulse, Miłosz argued, and by writing his own experiences he was also writing the experiences of others, speaking the unspeakable. "What can poetry be in the twentieth century?" he wondered. "It seems to me there is a search for the line beyond which only a zone of silence exists, and that on the borderline we encounter Polish poetry. In it a peculiar fusion of the individual and the historical took place, which means the events burdening a whole community are perceived by a poet as touching him in a most personal manner. Then poetry is no longer alienated." Part of Miłosz's lifelong project was to write as if poetry "is no longer a foreigner in society." He had made a poetic model out of shared trauma.

Many of Miłosz's friends and fellow poets died during the Nazi occupation, especially during the Warsaw Uprising, an extensive though ultimately unsuccessful attempt waged by the Polish underground resistance to liberate Warsaw from the Germans in the summer of 1944. All his early war and postwar poems are haunted by survivor's guilt. Here is his poem "Café":

Café

Of those at the table in the café
where on winter noons a garden of frost glittered on windowpanes
I alone survived.
I could go in there if I wanted to
and drumming my fingers in a chilly void
convoke shadows.

With disbelief I touch the cold marble,
with disbelief I touch my own hand.
It — is, and I — am in ever novel becoming,
while they are locked forever and ever
in their last word, their last glance,
and as remote as Emperor Valentinian
or the chiefs of the Massagetes, about whom I know nothing,
though hardly one year has passed, or two or three.

I may still cut trees in the woods of the far north,
I may speak from a platform or shoot a film
using techniques they never heard of.
I may learn the taste of fruits from ocean islands
and be photographed in attire from the second half of the century.

But they are forever like busts in frock coats and jabots in some monstrous
    encyclopedia.

Sometimes when the evening aurora paints the roofs in a poor street
and I contemplate the sky, I see in the white clouds
a table wobbling. The waiter whirls with his tray
and they look at me with a burst of laughter
for I still don't know what it is to die at the hand of man,
they know — they know it well.
Warsaw, 1944

"Café," which Miłosz translated himself, is the fourth poem in "Voices of
Poor People," a six-part sequence of moral outrage and loss included in *Res-
cue* (*Ocalenie*, 1945), one of the first books printed in postwar Poland. The
poem is written in a clear-cut, fairly plain-style free verse. Like other Polish
poets of his generation and the half-generation that followed, which included
Tadeusz Różewicz, Zbigniew Herbert, and Wisława Szymborska, Miłosz dis-
trusted so-called pure poetry — that is, poetry that turns away from the world,
that seeks, as the French Symbolist poet Stéphane Mallarmé put it, "to purify
the language of the tribe." As Witold Gombrowicz formulates it in his witty
and influential polemic "Against Poets," "The minute the poets lost sight of a
concrete human being and became transfixed with abstract Poetry, nothing
could keep them from rolling down the incline into the chasm of the absurd."
Miłosz put human beings at the center of his work and committed himself to a
forthright and seemingly guileless language that could communicate directly.
"Try to understand this simple speech as I would be ashamed of another. / I
swear, there is in me no wizardry of words," he tells a dead friend in his poem
"Dedication."

Miłosz chose a rather unassuming title, "Café," which serves both as the
poem's initial setting and as an indelible vision at the end of the poem. Cafés,
especially those deemed "artistic" cafés, were important local gathering places
for Polish poets, writers, artists, and intellectuals of all sorts in the interwar
period. The first three-line sentence explains the significance of this unnamed
café: "Of those at the table in the café / where on winter noons a garden of
frost glittered on windowpanes / I alone survived." Notice the suspenseful ef-
fect Miłosz achieves by first populating the café with "those at the table," then
providing a luminous visual detail, the noon frost on the windowpanes. Only

in the third line does Miłosz's speaker reveal the fact that "I alone survived." This simple, poignant declaration echoes the announcement in Job 1:15 made by a messenger who has witnessed a massacre: "And I alone have escaped to tell you." In referencing this passage, Miłosz posits himself as a messenger, the sole survivor of a massacre, who must relate the story to others. The stanza ends with another three-line sentence, this one in the conditional tense: "I *could* go in there if I wanted to." It suggests the ability to enter a place his friends can no longer enter. However, he knows that if he went inside, his fingers would touch only "a chilly void" and he would summon only "shadows."

In the second stanza the speaker is suddenly inside the café, perhaps in his imagination, where "with disbelief" he touches "the cold marble" of the table and, implicitly, the tomb. He then touches his own hand, as if estranged from his own body, from his own physical warmth. Notice how the following line stutters and interrupts itself when the speaker tries to express the astonishment of his continuing existence, separating the personal pronoun from the "to be" verbs with dashes and a comma — "It — is, and I — am." He sees his hand's presence and his own presence in the world as in a constant state of flux, "in ever novel becoming," which he differentiates from his friends' absence from the world, which he sees as static, since "they are locked forever and ever / in their last word, their last glance," frozen in their youthful identities. They have become as distantly historical as the fourth-century Roman emperor Valentinian or the little-known, ancient nomadic tribe of the Massagetes, though only a short time has passed.

In the third stanza the speaker lists some of the things he might do in the future, such as cutting lumber, giving a speech, making a movie, or learning the taste of exotic fruits. He repeatedly uses the modal verb "may," which indicates not only what he *might* do, if he feels like it, but also what he *can* do, what being alive *allows* him to do. The last activity on the list, being "photographed in attire from the second half of the century," contrasts with the image of his dead friends as "busts in frock coats and jabots in some monstrous encyclopedia." While his photograph would show him dressed in up-to-date fashions, his friends' encyclopedia entry depicts them as statues cut off at the shoulders and absurdly dressed in out-of-date frock coats and jabots, those decorative cloth pieces worn at the throat by men in the seventeenth and eighteenth centuries.

After this chilling image of anachronistic busts in the encyclopedia of the dead, the last stanza begins with the vibrant image of a colorful evening sunset that "paints the roofs in a poor street." When the speaker looks at the sky, he sees "in the white clouds / a table wobbling." Just as he does in the first stanza with "I alone survived," Miłosz waits to reveal what the speaker sees in the clouds by enjambing lines 2 and 3 to startling effect, bringing the café back into the poem. There's a wonderful aural and associative subtlety in the linking of "white clouds" and "a table wobbling." Notice the repetition of *w, t,* and *l* sounds in both phrases, as well as the visual image of the table's unmentioned white tablecloth; the *white* clouds must have reminded him of it. Czesław Miłosz elaborates on this vision, repeating some of the same sounds in "The *wai*ter *whir*l*s w*ith his *t*ray." The next line, where his friends regard him "with a burst of laughter," seems to add lively detail to this whimsical scene. However, the enjambment after "laughter" dramatically changes the tone, as the laughter and the café scene vanish into the final two lines of the poem: "for I still don't know what it is to die at the hand of man, / they know — they know it well."

Whereas "Café" begins at a café where the speaker's friends are present only as potentially summoned shadows, the poem ends at another café, where the speaker is an outsider. He cannot join his friends at the table because of his ignorance of a certain type of death, "at the hand of man," and their intimate knowledge of it; this forms a barrier between them that cannot be crossed. Though his friends have gained a bitter wisdom that the speaker lacks, they paid for it with their lives.

KADYA MOLODOWSKY

"Merciful God"

(1945)

The Yiddish poet Kadya Molodowsky was born in 1894 in Bereza Kartuska, a shtetl in White Russia. She participated fully in Jewish literary life, first in Warsaw, Poland, where she lived from 1921 to 1935, teaching Yiddish and Hebrew and publishing four collections of poems. After a move to New York City she supported herself by writing for the Yiddish press. She was a rebellious modernist who showed great sympathy for "all impoverished women who scour burnt pots" ("Poor Women") and a feminist who defied traditional roles and considered herself an exiled outsider.

Because she was living in the United States, Molodowsky was not caught directly in the maelstrom of the Holocaust, as were the Jewish poets Paul Celan, Nelly Sachs, or Avrom Sutzkever, for example. However, because of her close identification with the Jews and the Jewish culture of eastern Europe, she felt a deep personal anguish about the events unfolding in the fall of 1944. "The bitter news about *khurbm poyln* [the destruction of Poland] began to arrive," she wrote in her autobiography. "In agitation, I began to tear at the fingers of my hands. One finger became so badly infected that it required surgery."

The unthinkable hatred that was fueling the mass destruction of people and cities altered the very lens through which Jews viewed the world. Molodowsky describes this sweeping shift in perspective in her introduction to a book of Yiddish Holocaust poetry: "All our concepts changed: concepts of earth and heaven, and of the human being; we even perceived nature differently. The foundations of the world changed their forms." The poet responded to the Holocaust and its devastating aftermath with a singular book of poems, *Only King David Remained* (*Der meylek Dvid akleyn iz geblibn*), which Molodowsky called "a tombstone for a life that had vanished." As she explained in her collection of *khurbm-lider* (poems lamenting the destruction), "I saw in succession before my eyes a Jewish world that had been destroyed, Jewish cities, destruction and pain. I gave this book the name *Only King David Remained,* in order to say that the Jewish people was no more, all that remained was King David alone with his sorrow-crown on his head."

The book sets a defiant and sardonic tone by beginning with the poem "Merciful God" ("El khanun").

Merciful God

Merciful God,
Choose another people,
Elect another.
We are tired of death and dying,
We have no more prayers.
Choose another people,
Elect another.
We have no more blood
To be a sacrifice.
Our house has become a desert.
The earth is insufficient for our graves,
No more laments for us,
No more dirges
In the old, holy books.

Merciful God,
Sanctify another country,
Another mountain.
We have strewn all the fields and every stone

With ash, with holy ash.
With the aged,
With the youthful,
And with babies, we have paid
For every letter of your Ten Commandments.

Merciful God,
Raise your fiery brow,
And see the peoples of the world —
Give them the prophecies and the Days of Awe.
Your word is babbled in every language —
Teach them the deeds,
The ways of temptation.

Merciful God,
Give us simple garments
Of shepherds with their sheep,
Blacksmiths at their hammers,
Laundry-washers, skin-flayers,
And even the more base.
And do us one more favor:
Merciful God,
Deprive us of the Divine Presence of genius.

(Translated by Kathryn Hellerstein)

The poem's title comes from the term *El khanun* ("Merciful God" or "God of Mercy"), which most notably appears in Exodus 34:6–7. After God has made a covenant with Moses, the people violate it by worshiping a golden calf, a betrayal known in rabbinic literature as "that deed." In his rage for this act of rebellion God destroys the original tablets bearing the Ten Commandments. However, when Moses intervenes on the people's behalf, God allows him to carve a second set of tablets; God then descends to him in a cloud and addresses him, describing Himself as merciful:

And the LORD passed by before him, and proclaimed, The LORD, The LORD God, merciful and gracious, longsuffering, and abundant in goodness and truth,

Keeping mercy for thousands, forgiving iniquity and transgression
and sin . . .

This passage became known as the "Shlosh-esrei Middot" ("Thirteen Attributes of God"), which are recited or chanted on many Jewish holidays, as well as while the Torah is being taken from the ark for that day's procession and reading, to enable Jews of any era to renew their covenant with God.

Each stanza in Molodowsky's poem begins with the apostrophe "Merciful God." An apostrophe is a mode of direct address; the poet turns to address a God or gods, the muse, a dead or absent person, a natural object, a thing, an imaginary quality or concept. Starting the poem with "Merciful God" sets up the expectation that, as in a typical prayer, the speaker will be asking God for something uplifting, like compassion, patience, peace, or strength. However, in the second and third lines, Molodowsky upends this expectation by asking God to "Choose another people, / Elect another." She makes this startling request on behalf of Jews because "We are tired of death and dying." The rest of the poem is an argument against, and a rejection of, the covenant of Exodus, which has brought unthinkable misery to the Jewish people. To be chosen, to be sanctified or made holy, is to be cursed, and she beseeches God to choose someone else.

The entire poem overflows with the language of diminishment, annihilation, and exhaustion. It is also filled with references to the Tanakh, or Hebrew Bible. After the horrors of World War II, the Jews have been utterly depleted, in body and in spirit. "We have no more prayers"; "We have no more blood / To be a sacrifice." In an implicit reference to the House of Israel, which in Exodus represents God's covenant with the chosen people, she declares, "Our house has become a desert." So many people have died, "The earth is insufficient for our graves." The speaker wants nothing more from God, "No more laments," "No more dirges." Sacred elements of Jewish tradition that God granted the Jews following their covenant — "the old, holy books," "the prophecies and the Days of Awe," "the deeds / The ways of temptation" — she wants God to give to "another country, / Another mountain," "the peoples of the world."

Alluding to the crematoria of the Holocaust, the speaker declares, "We have strewn all the fields and every stone / With ash, with holy ash." The purposeful addition here of "*holy* ash" emphasizes the poet's conclusion that God's sanctification of the Jewish people has brought them to ruin. She points out the unacceptable price of having accepted this covenant, whose very language ironically includes the command not to kill: "With the aged, / With the youthful, / And with babies, we have paid / For every letter of your Ten Commandments."

In the concluding stanza, Molodowsky's speaker rejects the tradition in Jewish culture of a special calling to scholarly pursuits and the life of the mind; instead, she asks God to let the so-called Chosen People become un-chosen, ordinary people who work with their hands as "shepherds with their sheep, / Blacksmiths at their hammers, / Laundry-washers, skin-flayers." The poem ends, like Alfonsina Storni's "I'm Going to Sleep," with the speaker making a last request: "And do us one more favor: / Merciful God, / Deprive us of the Divine Presence of genius." Rather than ask God to bless her people, she requests deprivation, her final renunciation of that special, chosen status, which was seen as the "genius" of the Jewish people.

Molodowsky's poem, which she deliberately dated 1945, is a prayer to end all prayers, since her last request asks God to withdraw, thus negating any need for additional prayer. Oddly, even somewhat wittily, in all her bitter weariness she never seems to doubt the existence of God, an irony that places her in a long counter-tradition of Jewish lamentations that curse God while continuing to evoke Him. Her poem thus becomes what the scholar David Roskies labels "a sacred parody." As the translator and critic Kathryn Hellerstein puts it, "Molodowsky thus responds to the destruction of European Jewry with her own act of annihilation." If God's power is to offer a holy covenant to the Jewish people, Molodowsky uses her power in "Merciful God" to break that covenant, not by worshiping a false idol, but by refusing the covenant itself.

PRIMO LEVI

——

"Shemà"

(1946)

The Italian Jewish writer Primo Levi wrote this poem on January 10, 1946, when the Nuremberg Trials were gathering momentum. He first called it "Psalm" and used it, untitled, as the epigraph to his first book, *If This Is a Man* (*Se questo e un uomo,* 1947), a memoir chronicling the eleven months he spent in Auschwitz. He took the memoir's title from the fifth line in the poem, "Consider if this is a man." When Levi republished the poem in August 1964, he changed its title to "Shemà." The poem could also serve as an epigraph to his entire poetic oeuvre, which is filled with a rage and desperation often tempered in the rest of his work:

> *Shemà*
>
> You who live safe
> In your heated houses
> You who come home at night to find
> Hot food and friendly faces:

Consider if this is a man,
Who toils in the mud
Who knows no peace
Who fights for half a loaf
Who dies at a yes or a no.
Consider if this is a woman,
With no hair and no name
With no more strength to remember
With empty eyes and a womb as cold
As a frog in winter.

Ponder that this happened:
I consign these words to you.
Carve them into your hearts
At home or on the street,
Going to bed or rising:
Tell them to your children.
Or may your house fall down,
May illness make you helpless,
And your children turn their eyes from you.

(Translated by Jonathan Galassi)

Levi was primarily a prose writer. A chemist by profession as well as by temperament, he likened writing poems to an irrational illness, "the fruit of emotionality," which sometimes came over him. Yet intermittently he felt the need to write poems and often compared himself to Coleridge's ancient mariner because of his compulsion to tell his story to everyone he met. "I had a torrent of urgent things I had to tell the civilized world," he said. "I felt the tattooed number on my arm burning like a sore." Though the German philosopher Theodor Adorno notoriously declared that "to write poetry after Auschwitz is barbaric," Primo Levi profoundly disagreed. "Soon after the war," he said, "I thought that poetry was more appropriate than prose to express what I had inside of me. By saying poetry I am not thinking of lyrics. In those years I would have amended Adorno's statement: After Auschwitz, we cannot write poems except about Auschwitz."

When Levi changed the title of his poem from "Psalm," a sacred song or hymn, to "Shemà," he also changed its emphasis. The later title refers to a specific text known as the Shemà, which is the most common Jewish prayer. Levi learned this prayer as a twelve-year-old boy studying for his bar mitzvah in Turin. It begins, "Hear, O Israel, the Lord Our God, the Lord is One." Beyond this well-known first line the Shemà is a central prayer in Jewish services, consisting of three paragraphs drawn from three different passages in the Torah.

Because the word *Shemà* means "listen" or "hear," the title of the poem also constitutes its first command. The poem starts with the word "You" and goes on to address this "you" as its intended listener. Who is this "you" who is supposed to listen? The traditional Shemà is addressed to the Jewish people, starting with Moses's own words in the Torah: "Shemà Yisrael" ("Listen, Israel"). Levi's Shemà identifies, in its first four-line stanza, a much broader intended audience: anyone who is safe, living in "heated houses," where they can "come home at night to find / Hot food and friendly faces." The stanza ends with a colon, indicating that the poem has finished specifying who should listen and that the message to them now follows.

The longer second stanza is indented for emphasis and divided into two equal five-line parts. Both begin with the word "Consider," the second command of the poem. The first half asks us to contemplate "if this is a man." Notice the repetition of the word "Who" at the beginning of the next four lines. Levi purposely employs anaphora (the repetition of the same word at the beginning of a series of lines), which is one of the poetic strategies seen in the lists and catalogs of the Hebrew Bible. Rather than use punctuation to end-stop the lines, Levi enjambs them, so that the list runs together, as if to express the speaker's outrage: "Who toils in the mud / Who knows no peace / Who fights for half a loaf / Who dies at a yes or a no." The list creates a portrait of sorts — the verbs progress from "toil" to "know" to "fight" to "die" — which forces us to consider if "this" creature, who "toils in the mud" without rest like a driven animal, who has been reduced to starvation, and whose life hinges on the whims of others, is still a human being.

The second half of the stanza asks us to contemplate "if this is a woman." Rather than repeat "Who" at the start of each line, Levi paradoxically uses "With," followed by another enjambed list, this one composed of things the woman does *not* have: "no hair and no name," "no more strength," "empty eyes and a womb as cold / As a frog in winter." Once more the list forces us to contemplate whether "this" creature, who is all lack, all emptiness, without memory, vision, or hope for the future, is still a human being. And hauntingly, the "womb as cold / As a frog in winter" contrasts with the "heated houses" and "Hot food" of the people being addressed in the first stanza.

The last stanza returns to the left margin and begins with the word "Ponder," the poem's third command. Levi's speaker wants readers to think about the fact that a man and a woman endured circumstances so harrowing as to dehumanize them completely. The next five lines draw directly from Deuteronomy 6:6–7; these verses also make their way into the traditional Shemà:

And these words, which I command thee this day, shall be in thine heart:
And thou shalt teach them diligently unto thy children, and shalt talk
of them when thou sittest in thine house, and when thou walkest by the way,
and when thou liest down, and when thou risest up.

With the fourth command of the poem the speaker insists that we should "Carve" his words into our hearts. He intentionally uses a verb that invokes cutting into something with a sharp object to inscribe it, a potentially violent and painful marking. Levi famously told the interviewer Ferdinando Camon that the Holocaust sewed a yellow Star of David not only on his sleeve but also on his heart. Therefore, he wants everyone to bear on their very hearts the knowledge of the atrocities done to innocent people in this malignant era and to carry this knowledge wherever they go, during all times of day.

In the final command of the poem, "*Tell* them to your children," the speaker instructs readers that it is not enough to carve his words into their hearts so that they will remember the horrors of the past; additionally, they must make sure to pass on the story to future generations, to keep the memory alive. He ends the poem in a near-biblical fury with a three-line curse, which he wishes on anyone who dares to forget: "Or may your house fall down, / May illness make you helpless, / And your children turn their eyes from you." Levi's speaker, in this fierce warning, reminds us that if we take for granted our "heated houses" and "friendly faces," if we forget the suffering endured by the man and the woman, this anti-Adam and anti-Eve in the hellish anti-garden of the Holocaust, we will lose our houses, our health, and our future, as our children will no longer recognize us.

The traditional Shemà in many modern contexts has been understood as a declaration of unity or oneness, whether divine or human; conversely, Levi's lyric manifesto meditates on the nothingness of human beings who have been reduced to something less than human. He thus changes the very direction and nature of the original prayer. In doing so, though, and by calling the poem "Shemà," he also reminds us that that the Shemà is the prayer that is recited not only at bedtime in observant Jewish households, but also at the threshold of death, a place from which he has recently returned. This poem stands as a prayer for all those who crossed that threshold in the horrific years of the Holocaust, so that they will be remembered.

NÂZIM HIKMET

—

"On Living"

(1948)

Nâzım Hikmet is one of the great Turkish poets of social consciousness, a figure comparable, say, to the Spanish poets Federico García Lorca and Miguel Hernández. Like them, he was a Whitmanesque poet of the empathic imagination who felt his way into the lives of other people, and who put his wild creative energies at the service of a humane vision. Hikmet was politically minded and devoted to the international left, had a Romantic inclination to utopianism, but was temperamentally allergic to authoritarian constraints on the literary imagination. He was an iconoclastic Marxist who valued people over ideology; ultimately, his political and artistic stance put him at odds with Turkish authorities.

In January 1938, Hikmet was arrested on a trumped-up charge of inciting the Turkish armed forces to revolt because military cadets were reading his poems. He was sentenced to twenty-eight years in prison. In his *Memoirs*, Pablo Neruda recounts Hikmet's story of how he was treated after his arrest:

Accused of attempting to incite the Turkish navy into rebellion,
Nâzım was condemned to the punishments of hell. The trial was held

on a warship. He told me he was forced to walk on the ship's bridge until he was too weak to stay on his feet, then they stuck him into a section of the latrines where the excrement rose half a meter above the floor. My brother poet felt his strength failing him. The stench made him reel. Then the thought struck him: my tormentors are keeping an eye on me, they want to see me drop, they want to watch me suffer. His strength came back with pride. He began to sing, low at first, then louder, and finally at the top of his lungs. He sang all the songs, all the love poems he could remember, his own poems, the ballads of the peasants, the people's battle hymns. He sang everything he knew. And so he vanquished the filth and his torturers.

It's no accident that Hikmet finds, through singing, the strength to frustrate his captors' desire to destroy him. Just as an act of creative, melodic self-expression helped the poet overcome this miserable situation, a similar act, writing poetry, helped him endure years of imprisonment. His translator Mutlu Konuk points out that in prison Hikmet began to write more directly, more seriously, less topically. Over a thirteen-year period of incarceration he composed some of his greatest short lyrics as well as his long, collage-like epic poem, *Human Landscapes from My Country*. Here is his free-verse manual for living:

On Living

I
Living is no laughing matter:
　　　you must live with great seriousness
　　　　like a squirrel, for example —
　I mean, without looking for something beyond and above living,
　　　　I mean living must be your whole life.
Living is no laughing matter:
　　　you must take it seriously,
　　　so much so and to such a degree
　that, for example, your hands tied behind your back,
　　　　　your back to the wall,
　or else in a laboratory

in your white coat and safety glasses,
    you can die for people —
even for people you've never seen,
even though you know living
    is the most real, the most beautiful thing.
I mean, you must take living so seriously
    that even at seventy, for example, you'll plant olive trees —
    and not for your children, either,
    but because although you fear death you don't believe it,
    because living, I mean, weighs heavier.

II
Let's say we're seriously ill, need surgery —
which is to say we might not get up
        from the white table.
Even though it's impossible not to feel sad
        about going a little too soon,
we'll still laugh at the jokes being told,
we'll look out the window to see if it's raining,
or still wait anxiously
        for the latest newscast . . .
Let's say we're at the front —
    for something worth fighting for, say.
There, in the first offensive, on that very day,
    we might fall on our face, dead.
We'll know this with a curious anger,
    but we'll still worry ourselves to death
    about the outcome of the war, which could last years.
Let's say we're in prison
and close to fifty,
and we have eighteen more years, say,
        before the iron doors will open.
We'll still live with the outside,
with its people and animals, struggle and wind —
        I mean with the outside beyond the walls.
I mean, however and wherever we are,
    we must live as if we will never die.

III

This earth will grow cold,
a star among stars,
                and one of the smallest,
a gilded mote on blue velvet —
            I mean *this,* our great earth.
This earth will grow cold one day,
not like a block of ice
or a dead cloud even
but like an empty walnut it will roll along
                in pitch-black space . . .
You must grieve for this right now
— you have to feel this sorrow now —
for the world must be loved this much
                        if you're going to say "I lived" . . .

February 1948

(Translated by Randy Blasing and Mutlu Konuk)

Hikmet called poetry "the bloodiest of the arts," by which he meant that poetry strikes at the most painful and vulnerable aspects of our lives, pierces the protective emotional layers we hide behind, and draws blood. In titling his poem "On Living" Hikmet cuts straight to the most basic question about our existence: how should we live? The poem consists of a three-part argument that attempts to answer this question and, in doing so, to persuade the reader, and the poet himself, of the rightness of his thinking, his experience. For this reason, he speaks in a tone of openhearted didacticism, as he intends for the poem to instruct.

Part I tackles the question of how to live in the first two lines: "Living is no laughing matter: / you must live with great seriousness." The speaker addresses a "you" in a somewhat relaxed manner, as if chatting with a close friend; however, despite this seemingly casual way of speaking, he continually hammers home the point that "you" must live "seriously." Repeating the phrase "for example," Hikmet outlines four scenarios of serious living. The first, amusingly, is to live "like a squirrel." He explains this odd simile: "I mean, without looking for something beyond and above living, / I mean living must be your whole life." Here in microcosm is his overarching argument, which seems deceptively simple yet strangely difficult to achieve, that one must live with intense commitment, with one's full attention on living.

The second scenario positions the reader with "hands tied behind your back, / your back to the wall," like a prisoner about to be executed; the third locates the reader as a scientist "in a laboratory, in your white coat and safety glasses." Hikmet's speaker then posits a standard by which to determine whether a person, whatever their situation, indeed lives seriously: engaging in life "to such a degree / that . . . you can die for people— / even for people you've never seen." Serious living thus involves solidarity with others and a willingness to die, while recognizing that life is "the most beautiful thing." The fourth scenario envisions the reader, grown older, ready to "plant olive trees" in order to keep engaging with life, culminating in the idea that "although you fear death you don't believe it, / because living, I mean, weighs heavier." Part I ends on the premise that, despite humans' awareness of their mortality, faith in the act of living must outweigh fear of death.

It's interesting to note how the poem mimics the poet engaged in the act of thinking. The repeated use of the qualifier "I mean" suggests that he's refining his argument as he's writing the poem. Varied line lengths, dropped lines, and jagged spacing across the page likewise give the impression of thinking in action. Note the expressive spacing he uses to describe the person to be executed:

> that, for example, your hands tied behind your back,
> your back to the wall,

Like the Russian futurist Vladimir Mayakovsky, one of his models, Hikmet exploits the visual resources of typographical design throughout the poem to re-create the movement of his argument and to isolate phrases for emphasis.

Part II begins with the line "Let's say we're seriously ill, need surgery—"; immediately we can see that Hikmet has changed tactics. The "I" and the "you" of Part I have become a communal "we," and the use of "for example" to introduce a particular scenario becomes "Let's say we're." After elaborating on a scenario related to illness—"which is to say we might not get up / from the white table"—the speaker concludes that nonetheless "we'll still laugh at the jokes being told." In other words, even as we face imminent death, we still align ourselves with life. He repeats this "Let's say we're . . . we'll still" mode of argument in the second scenario: "Let's say we're at the front . . . / we'll still worry ourselves to death / about the outcome of the war." The final scenario of this part takes on a special significance and authority, a deeper depth charge, since it is clearly his own:

> Let's say we're in prison
> and close to fifty,
> and we have eighteen more years, say,
>   before the iron doors will open.
> We'll still live with the outside . . .

Part II concludes by restating the poem's thesis on how to live: "I mean, however and wherever we are, / we must live as if we will never die."

In Part III, Hikmet again changes perspective, dropping the personal pronouns and personal scenarios for a more impersonal, totalizing view of death: "This earth will grow cold." Both scenarios in this final section imagine earth utterly devoid of life, and the poem becomes an elegy for the planet. In luminous images the speaker describes this future lifeless earth as "a gilded mote on blue velvet" and "like an empty walnut" rolling along in darkness. After acknowledging and envisioning this bleak future, he calls upon us to grieve now for the end of all life on earth. The last lines of the poem bring back the "you" and the "I" to clinch his argument about the way we should live: "for the world must be loved this much / if you're going to say 'I lived' . . ." The poet who suffered years of imprisonment and torment by his captors nonetheless understood, and urgently wanted others to understand, that the way to live, the way for life to overshadow death, is to love.

WELDON KEES

"Aspects of Robinson"

(1948)

W eldon Kees invented a self-revealing character named Robinson, a fig-
ure known by only his last name, making him nearly anonymous, and
thus Kees inscribed the existential dilemmas of American life at midcentury.
There are four Robinson poems in all, which date from 1944–49: "Robinson,"
"Robinson at Home," "Aspects of Robinson," and "Relating to Robinson." In
all of them, Robinson is a figure in absentia, a middle- or upper-middle-class
Everyman, a person missing from his own life.

Kees used himself as a template for his portrait of Robinson, a self-portrait
without a self. His first readers immediately noticed a connection to Robin-
son Crusoe. Robinson is living in Manhattan, but he's essentially alone on a
small island. Scholars have subsequently pointed out that there is an American
character named Robinson in Louis-Ferdinand Céline's *Journey to the End of
the Night* and in Franz Kafka's *Amerika;* all these Robinsons drift in and out
of an alienating city. Céline's and Kafka's modernist Crusoe-like updates are,
however, more unprincipled and degenerate than Kees's bourgeois figure, who
more closely resembles T. S. Eliot's Prufrock.

Here is "Aspects of Robinson":

Aspects of Robinson

Robinson at cards at the Algonquin; a thin
Blue light comes down once more outside the blinds.
Gray men in overcoats are ghosts blown past the door.
The taxis streak the avenues with yellow, orange, and red.
This is Grand Central, Mr. Robinson.

Robinson on a roof above the Heights; the boats
Mourn like the lost. Water is slate, far down.
Through sounds of ice cubes dropped in glass, an osteopath,
Dressed for the links, describes an old Intourist tour.
—Here's where old Gibbons jumped from, Robinson.

Robinson walking in the Park, admiring the elephant.
Robinson buying the *Tribune,* Robinson buying the *Times.* Robinson
Saying, "Hello. Yes, this is Robinson. Sunday
At five? I'd love to. Pretty well. And you?"
Robinson alone at Longchamps, staring at the wall.

Robinson afraid, drunk, sobbing Robinson
In bed with a Mrs. Morse. Robinson at home;
Decisions: Toynbee or luminol? Where the sun
Shines, Robinson in flowered trunks, eyes toward
The breakers. Where the night ends, Robinson in East Side bars.

Robinson in Glen plaid jacket, Scotch-grain shoes.
Black four-in-hand and oxford button-down,
The jeweled and silent watch that winds itself, the brief-
Case, covert topcoat, clothes for spring, all covering
His sad and usual heart, dry as a winter leaf.

"Aspects of Robinson" gives us a figure of social banality, existential terror.
Robinson is a postwar man of the world, who lives in the middle ranks. James
Reidel, Kees's assiduous biographer, suggests that Robinson's "accouterments,
pastimes, preferences, drugs, drinks, women, books, and death wish are cata-

logued and could almost be the precious, fragile, ironic layers that protect the anima within."

The poem offers us glimpses, facets, angles, perspectives — the many faces of Robinson. Kees was a cinephile and there's a cinematic quality to the successive images of Robinson, whom we see in various urban tableaux. The poem itself unfolds in five five-line stanzas. There seems to be something a little beyond reason in the way that Kees pushes past the symmetrical quatrain. The rhythm is mostly a loose iambic pentameter. This poem concerns a figure in social situations. Kees came from Beatrice, Nebraska, and though he met many people during his years in New York, he was never entirely comfortable in the city. He took Eliot's dim view of a spiritually bankrupt society.

The novelist Charles Baxter has observed that "Aspects of Robinson" "is a dark cousin of a Frank O'Hara 'I-do-this-I-do-that poem': what's so pleasurable in O'Hara, the flaneur walking down the street and enjoying the sunny spectacle of life, is, in Weldon Kees, drained of all pleasure, like the perceptions of a veteran from World War II, who has been traumatized in some way and can't enjoy anything, despite the signs and symbols of prosperity and material middle-class life." As a poem, "Aspects of Robinson" is full of lists, this-and-that, one thing after another, but it's difficult to make the connection between experiences.

Stanza 1, scene 1: Robinson is playing cards at the Algonquin, the famous literary hub and hotel. It's a posh locale. But there's no natural light, the people outside are "ghosts" blown past the door, and the taxis streak the avenues with garish colors. The city has an air of unreality, the feeling of an urban hell. It's only a few blocks away but Robinson seems to need a taxi to get to Grand Central Station.

Stanza 2, scene 2: Robinson has taken a trip out to Brooklyn Heights. He is standing on the roof, looking down at the river. Like figures out of Dante, the boats below "Mourn like the lost." There's a kind of discordance to the scene. On the one hand, we seem to be in the middle of a cocktail party. A foolish osteopath dressed for golf is talking about an old tourist trip to Russia, which would have been more remarkable in 1948 than it is now. On the other hand, Robinson is standing on the spot where someone committed suicide: "Here's where old Gibbons jumped from, Robinson." Robinson is addressed at the end of the sentence rather than at the beginning. Indeed, his name opens and closes the first two stanzas with a kind of insistence, as if to prove he exists.

The next three stanzas present us with a catalog of Robinson's daily life. The tempo speeds up and the poem takes on a notational, almost ethnographic quality. It's described in present participles, as if filmed from above: Robinson walking in Central Park, admiring a large caged animal; Robinson buying the dailies; Robinson on the phone politely accepting an invitation. Robinson sitting by himself at Longchamps, a New York restaurant whose walls were covered with versions of Degas's paintings of the Longchamp racetrack. When a friend complained to Kees that Robinson wouldn't be sitting alone in a fashionable restaurant staring at the wall, Kees replied that he could see the point, "even though I have empirical proof that this happens frequently enough: often you get seated at a crummy table where there is nothing else to stare at except a wall — and sometimes when very tired and too much involved with people and things, a wall is just the ticket."

Robinson is getting around, keeping up appearances, but in the fourth stanza, we get the dark underlying truth: "Robinson afraid, drunk, sobbing Robinson / In bed with a Mrs. Morse." Kees uses the adulterous Mrs. Morse here as a prop, a move he got from Eliot: "Has anyone ever mentioned that Eliot uses people frequently as objects?" he wondered. The people have names, but they are practically anonymous. Robinson starts the morning in floral swimming trunks, looking out at the waves, but he ends it in bars on the East Side. At home in bed, he tries to decide whether to read the fashionable historian Toynbee, who is primarily known for his twelve-volume *Study of History,* or simply take a luminol and drop off. Kees loved crime novels and certainly knew that luminol is often used to detect blood at crime scenes. Note how he has also been building up and pressing down on the sound of the letter *l:* "elephant," "Hello," "love," "well," "alone," "Longchamps," "luminol." The sound helps thread together the various glimpses of Robinson, who can barely hold himself together.

The last stanza unfolds in one long sentence fragment, which provides, as the poet Dana Gioia puts it, "an anatomy, simultaneously individual and impersonal, of contemporary alienation."

> Robinson in Glen plaid jacket, Scotch-grain shoes.
> Black four-in-hand and oxford button-down,
> The jeweled and silent watch that winds itself, the brief-
> Case, covert topcoat, clothes for spring, all covering
> His sad and usual heart, dry as a winter leaf.

The various brands — the "Glen plaid jacket," "Scotch-grain shoes," "oxford button-down," and so on — have a satirical bite. The expensive watch silently winds itself, the season turns to spring, and everything is renewed, except Robinson. Hence the telling line break on the word "brief- / Case." The poem closes with its only end-rhyme: "brief" and "leaf."

The existential despair that flows beneath this poem is stated outright in the last line. Everything Robinson does and wears covers up "His sad and usual heart, dry as a winter leaf." The word "usual" is cuttingly well placed here. It suggests that Robinson is not at all unique. He's not the only one roaming the streets and the subways, drinking in bars, traveling back and forth to a white-collar job. There are a million Robinsons out there. Weldon Kees was nearly one of them.

GWENDOLYN BROOKS

———

"The rites for Cousin Vit"

(1949)

"The rites for Cousin Vit" is the sixth piece in a sequence of fifteen poems called "The Womanhood" in Gwendolyn Brooks's second book, *Annie Allen* (1949), which traces the life of a young woman growing up and coming into her womanhood in a Black working-class neighborhood in Chicago during and after World War II. Annie is the unnamed, nearly absent speaker, who serves as a stand-in for Brooks herself:

> ### The rites for Cousin Vit
>
> Carried her unprotesting out the door.
> Kicked back the casket-stand. But it can't hold her,
> That stuff and satin aiming to enfold her,
> The lid's contrition nor the bolts before.
> Oh oh. Too much. Too much. Even now, surmise,
> She rises in the sunshine. There she goes,
> Back to the bars she knew and the repose
> In love-rooms and the things in people's eyes.

Too vital and too squeaking. Must emerge.
Even now she does the snake-hips with a hiss,
Slops the bad wine across her shantung, talks
Of pregnancy, guitars and bridgework, walks
In parks or alleys, comes haply on the verge
Of happiness, haply hysterics is. Is.

Brooks delivered her "rites" in the form of an elegiac Petrarchan sonnet, which divides into an octave (with the rhyme scheme *abbacddc*) and sestet (*efggef*). The durable sonnet form has been transformed over the centuries. Now the scene has shifted from Italy to Chicago and the heavenly Laura has been replaced by the earthy Cousin Vit. Indeed, the sonnet form has been stretched to accommodate its fiery subject. The poem has a vernacular streak, an elliptical syntax, and a vital energy delivered in a skillfully balanced and brisk iambic pentameter.

Brooks told the interviewer Studs Terkel that Vit was based on a friend of hers "who had the irrepressibility that seems unconfinable even in death." Brooks took her name from the Latin word *vita*, meaning "life." Vit seems larger than life, too vigorous to die. Brooks elevates her to a "cousin" and thus claims the disreputable Vit as a necessary part of her extended family. Cousin Vit is getting her last rites, but she is also getting her human rights.

The poem begins with two sentence fragments, in which a first-person subject, an "I" or "We," is implied but not stated. The two first lines begin emphatically with stressed past-tense verbs, the second one followed by a stressed adverb: "Cárried," "Kícked báck." The focus is on Vit being carried out the door in a casket. The door is a threshold, the coffin a container: "But it can't hold her." The second line is enjambed, as if lineation can't hold her either; the tense immediately changes from past to present. Vit had a rebellious spirit that couldn't survive in a world of "stuff and satin aiming to enfold her." The words "hold her" cling tightly to "enfold her." Vit may have been haphazard, but she wouldn't likely be hemmed in by mere mortality.

We notice how the unnamed narrator mutters to herself and nods her head: "Oh oh. Too much. Too much. Even now, surmise . . ." The critic John Gery suggests that this playful line "subverts any profound sense of grief or loss at Vit's departure" and "undermines our ability to take her life too seriously." But playfulness doesn't automatically mean mockery. On the contrary, the narrator doesn't seem to be mocking Vit's life so much as recognizing and celebrating it. Yes, Vit may have been an outlaw, Brooks seems to suggest, shaking her head, but she was *our* outlaw.

What the narrator "surmises" is that Vit "rises in the sunshine." The next phrase has a cinematic quality: "There she goes." Vit is off to the places she frequented. Notice how the fragment stands apart at the end of the ninth line: "Must emerge." There's no apparent religious context to the poem, but the down-to-earth and sensuous Vit is implicitly, metaphorically, even sinfully being compared to the risen Christ. This refers us back to the title and gives a surplus of meaning to the word "rites," a solemn ceremony for a not very solemn person.

The risen Vit returns to her old sketchy haunts, the bars and "love-rooms." The way that the narrator describes Vit's dancing is especially noteworthy (Brooks fills the line with a single clause and makes much of the *s* and *sh* sounds: "Even now *she* doe*s* the *s*nake-hip*s* with a hi*ss*") because it connects Vit both to Eve and to the serpent. She is part of "the womanhood." Vit drinks wine (notice how the *s* and *sh* sounds slur in "*S*lop*s* the bad wine acro*ss* her *sh*antung"), which makes for a kind of secular communion, and shamelessly gossips about subjects large and small ("talks / Of pregnancy, guitars and bridgework"). She is tied to the neighborhood, the community, and, instead of going quietly to the cemetery, she "walks" — notice the emphatic enjambment — "In parks or alleys."

In a giddy, over-the-top way Brooks presses the *h* sound in the last two lines: "comes *h*aply on the verge / Of *h*appiness, *h*aply *h*ysterics is." The word "haply," which means "perhaps," seems cheerful in such proximity to "happiness." But that happiness is not quite attained. There is an excessive wildness in the word "hysterics," which points to the way that Vit lived, "on the verge," and presumably how she died.

The last word, "Is," half-rhymes with "hiss," the most disjunctive rhyme in the poem. A sentence unto itself, it abruptly cuts off the poem. "Is." A verb alone. Being itself. Two contradictory positions are being simultaneously embraced here. On one hand, the poem is evidently an elegy, a last rite. On the other hand, it also suggests that Vit still exists — she is too unruly to be contained. As a poem, "The rites for Cousin Vit" simply refuses to accept that someone so alive could consent to the indignity of being buried, and so it becomes an elegy that denies death.

STEVIE SMITH

———

"Not Waving but Drowning"

(1953, 1957)

All poets are misfits and oddballs, but there is something especially discomfiting and even improbable about the English poet Stevie Smith. "Who and what is Stevie Smith?" Ogden Nash asked in a Dorothy Parker–esque moment: "Is she woman? Is she myth?" Wearing a childlike pinafore and white lace stockings, telling a puzzled reporter, "I'm probably a couple of sherries below par most of the time," chanting or singing her poems in a high, off-pitch voice at poetry gatherings in the 1960s ("She chanted her poems artfully off-key, in a beautifully flawed plainsong that suggested two kinds of auditory experience," Seamus Heaney once said: "an embarrassed party-piece by a child halfway between giggles and tears, and a deliberate *faux-naif* rendition by a virtuoso"), she seems so unlikely and, in retrospect, necessary: a welcome tonic, a heartbreaking brightness we were seeking all along. We still relish this figure, who arrived like a Blakean thunderclap with all the freshness, frivolity, and forthrightness of childhood, with all the sad and caustic insight of long experience. Thinking about her elemental poems, which are so cheeky and rash, so stingingly honest, impertinent, and deathward-leaning, so filled with mordant wit and comic desperation ("learn too that being comical," she explains in a poem about Jesus, "does not ameliorate the desperation"), I keep wanting to adapt something Randall Jarrell once wrote about Walt Whitman. Someone might have put on her tombstone STEVIE SMITH: SHE HAD HER NERVE.

Stevie Smith understood that a lot of people carry around a sense of sad deficiency. They pretend to fit in, though in truth they don't feel at home in the world at all. They keep up a semblance of normalcy, but sometimes, as she said, "they get tired and the brave pretense breaks down and then they are lost." Here is her lethal masterpiece, "Not Waving but Drowning," which she wrote during a low ebb in April 1953. She published it a year later and then revised it as the title poem of her fifth book, *Not Waving but Drowning* (1957):

Not Waving but Drowning

Nobody heard him, the dead man,
But still he lay moaning:
I was much further out than you thought
And not waving but drowning.

Poor chap, he always loved larking
And now he's dead
It must have been too cold for him his heart gave way,
They said.

Oh, no no no, it was too cold always
(Still the dead one lay moaning)
I was much too far out all my life
And not waving but drowning.

Smith got the idea for this twelve-line poem from a newspaper report about a man drowning. You can feel the grave submarine laughter and the plunging depths behind its fatal misunderstanding. We are meant to be disconcerted by its comic awfulness, by the spooky fact that the man in the poem is already dead but still moaning, still suffering. Will May, the editor of *All the Poems of Stevie Smith,* points out that in a typed draft Smith accompanied the poem with the illustration of a man being hauled from the water, but later replaced it with the purposely disjunctive drawing of a bedraggled girl. She is shown from the waist up, her wet hair hanging over her face. This is a sly, androgynous way of crossing genders, suggesting that the drowned man is also a drowned woman.

In *A History of Twentieth-Century British Women Poets,* Jane Dowson and Alice Entwistle argue that Smith's subterranean subject is "undisclosed emotional undertow," a persistent theme of poems by women. The fact that there are no quotation marks setting off what seems to be the dead man's speech in lines 3 and 4 suggests that the speaker of the poem is ventriloquizing the dead man's words. This tells us not just about the speaker but also about the ventriloquist. The emotion is thus partly revealed and partly concealed under the surface.

This deceptive little poem unfolds over three quatrains that rhyme *abcb.* Rhyming every other line, as in a ballad, gives a feeling of intermittency. In the first stanza, for example, the rhyme scheme disconnects two words, "man" and "thought," and links two others through a disconcerting near or slant rhyme, "moaning" and "drowning."

Notice how the linguistic register of the poem changes in the second stanza. Here the speaker takes on an ordinary social voice, what a couple of British people might say, standing in a crowd on the shore. Thus, the poem moves between speech and commentary. Here are the usual clichés about a person whom they knew a little. He was a "poor chap" who loved "larking," which is to say that he was something of a prankster, a fellow who concealed his melancholy under a mischievous surface, perhaps like Smith herself. The third line — "It must have been too cold for him his heart gave way" — is by far the longest in the poem and seems a bit drawn out, as if running together an entire conversation. Note too the iron shock of the foreshortened twelfth line, which is the shortest one in the poem: "They said." The exact rhyme with the word "dead" is inescapable.

Smith loved Robert Browning, especially his poem "Childe Roland to the Dark Tower Came," which was ingrained in her memory since childhood. See, for example, her poem "Childe Rolandine." Smith's biographer Frances Spalding points out that the dying man in "Not Waving but Drowning" can hear the people on the beach talking about him just as "Childe Roland" overhears a discussion about his burial. In both poems, this adds a ghostly element to the man's isolation.

The statement "They said" is immediately countered in the last stanza by an exclamation: "Oh, no no no." The speaker insists that the drowning man's heart didn't give away because the water was too cold for him this one time;

no, "it was too cold always." The man was always out there drowning. The next phrase is parenthetical, "(Still the dead one lay moaning)," and reminds us of his continual suffering. The word "always" emphatically does not rhyme with "life," but the slant rhyme of "moaning" and "drowning" does recur, once more clinching the connection. So too the poem returns to the startled and aggrieved voice of the drowned one himself, who goes on suffering an isolation that kills. We also recognize that the third line of the poem — "I was much further out than you thought" — is now transformed into the allegorical penultimate line — "I was much too far out all my life."

No one ever forgets the final declaration in this poem. It seems there is an element of confession here, as if Stevie Smith was somehow speaking both about someone else and about herself. She kept her nerve and created a fitting epitaph: "I was much too far out all my life / And not waving but drowning."

TADEUSZ RÓŻEWICZ

"In the Midst of Life"

(1955)

Tadeusz Różewicz was a poet of dark refusals, hard negations. He was a naked or impure poet ("I crystallize impure poetry," he wrote), an anti-poet relentlessly, even ruthlessly determined to tell the truth, however painful. He scorned the idea of the poet as prophet and provoked from the margins — a stubborn outsider. He dwelled in uncertainties and doubts, in the insecure, gray areas of life, and stripped poetry down to its essentials: words alone on a page. He was bracingly clear and shunned the floridities, the grand consolations, of the traditional lyric. His characteristic free-verse style was a non-style, a zero-sum game. "I have no time for aesthetic values," he declared. Rather, he treated modern poetry as "a battle for breath" and wrote with an anxious, prolific, offhanded urgency. He was a wary, bemused seer of nothingness. He is the Samuel Beckett of modern Polish poetry.

Różewicz belonged to a brilliant generation of Polish poets — the half generation after Czesław Miłosz — initiated in the apocalyptic fires of history. He was a crucial part of the firmament — the "Generation of Columbuses" — that included Krzysztof Baczyński (1921–1944), Tadeusz Gajcy (1922–1944), and

Zdzislaw Stroiński (1921–1944), all of whom died in the Warsaw Uprising, as well as Zbigniew Herbert and Wisława Szymborska, who survived to become major poets. He grew up during one of the few periods of independence in Polish history and came of age during the horrific years of World War II. Poland lost six million people during the war, nearly one-fifth of its population, and all young writers felt the crushing burden of speaking for those who did not survive the German occupation. Różewicz's own brother was murdered by the Gestapo in 1944, and he himself served in a guerilla unit of the Home Army. He felt that he had been led to slaughter and yet survived. For him, poetry — or at least one kind of poetry — was murdered during the war. The Holocaust loomed over everything.

The war was such a traumatic event for the new generation of Polish poets that it called all moral and aesthetic values into question. Those who survived could never believe in the future again. Nor could they revert to traditional forms of poetry. They rejected the aesthetics of elaborate, ornamental, or sonorous language. No more intricate meters and rhymes, no more fancy metaphors. It was as if poetry had to be reinvented from the ground up. Różewicz fostered this distrust of rhetoric. He was among the first to catch the mood, in a stripped-down poetry of drastic simplicity. "I felt that something had forever ended for me and for mankind, something that neither religion nor science nor art had succeeded in protecting."

Here is a poem from 1955 that reads like a new kind of primer. It was published in the book *An Open Poem* (1956) and struck Polish poetry like a thunderclap:

> ## In the Midst of Life
>
> After the end of the world
> after death
> I found myself in the midst of life
> creating myself
> building life
> people animals landscapes
>
> this is a table I said
> this is a table
> on the table is bread a knife

a knife is to cut bread
people live on bread

man must be loved
I studied night and day
what must be loved
I answered man

this is a window I said
this is a window
beyond the window is a garden
in the garden I see an apple tree
the apple tree is in bloom
the blossoms fall
the fruits form
ripen

my father picks an apple
that man picking the apple
is my father

I sat in the doorway of my house
that old woman who
is leading a goat by a rope
is more necessary
and more precious
than the seven wonders of the world
anyone who thinks and feels
that she is not necessary
is a mass-murderer

this is a man
this is a tree this is bread

people eat to live
I repeated to myself
human life is important

human life is of great import
the value of life
outweighs the value of all things
created by man
man is a great treasure
I kept repeating stubbornly

this is water I said
I stroked the waves with my hand
and talked to the river
water I said
nice water
this is me

a man was talking to the water
talking to the moon
the flowers the rain
talking to the earth
the birds
the sky

the sky was silent
the earth was silent
if he heard a voice
flowing
from earth water and sky
it was the voice of another man

(Translated by Magnus J. Krynski and Robert A. Maguire)

A feeling of unreality haunts this poem. The world had come to an end, everything had seemingly died, including the speaker, and yet he somehow finds himself immersed in the flow again, trying to figure things out, creating himself, building life. Różewicz jams together on one line "people animals landscapes," as if they all are of the same order of reality. The speaker is filled with a sense of amazement too. After all the cruelty, hatred, and destruction, simple things seem somehow to have endured, against all odds. Hence: "this is a table I said / this is a table." He seems to be reassuring himself of the usefulness and meaning of the most ordinary things: "on the table is bread a knife / a knife is to cut bread / people live on bread." The objective world alone seems to be real. Or is it?

The speaker has come through a great trauma and must learn everything again. He distrusts all abstractions, all overarching concepts. He is reciting the ABCs of the Communist glorification of the common man: "man must be loved / I studied night and day." It is as if he is trying to convince himself of something impossible to believe: "what must be loved / I answered man." He looks up from his study: "this is a window I said / this is a window." It is as if by saying something he can reassure himself that it exists. He is stunned that the natural world still seems to be out there: "beyond the window is a garden." He can see an apple tree, as in the original garden. He also reassures himself that individuals have survived: "my father picks an apple / that man picking the apple / is my father." Notice the grammatical shift from "my father" to "that man." Here the emphasis changes from the fact that his father is picking an apple to the fact that the man picking the apple is, in fact, his father. It all has an air of utter estrangement.

For a moment, the poem takes on an anecdotal quality: "I sat in the door-way of my house." Like the window, the doorway is a threshold point that connects the inside to the outside, the man to the world. The most radical claim in the poem is that an old woman walking past his house with a goat "is more necessary / and more precious" than even the seven wonders of the world: "anyone who thinks and feels / that she is not necessary / is a mass-murderer." Różewicz is clearly aware of the extreme nature of his insistent declaration. But the underlying premise doesn't seem that outlandish — that every person truly matters, that each person must be valued, no matter how simple or ordinary, that the world has seen what happens when we dehumanize people and sacrifice them in the name of an idea. Nothing should be more valuable than a human life. What the war has taught him is that anyone who devalues ordinary individuals as somehow "unnecessary" is complicit in the machinery of mass murder.

All the while, the speaker keeps trying to reassure himself that "human life is important" because he has seen how unimportant it really is, how easy it was to destroy, how many people had been obliterated. It had become harder and harder to believe the general truism that "man is a great treasure," which he keeps stubbornly repeating, trying to convince himself. In the next stanza there is also a comic moment when the speaker strokes and pets the water, like an unruly or dangerous animal: "nice water," he says reassuringly, "this is me." But, of course, the water is indifferent and does not recognize him. The river is oblivious.

At the end of "In the Midst of Life," the speaker goes on talking to the elements, to the universe itself. It all seems completely natural. He doesn't seem unhinged. But neither is he like the legendary Orpheus, who could animate the world with his music. The water, the moon, the flowers, the rain, the earth, the birds, the sky — none of them speak back to him. The natural world never answers. On the contrary, the only real possibility for communication is with another person, "the voice of another man."

"In the Midst of Life" is a poem of great residual bitterness and alienation. It has a desperate clarity. And what Różewicz finally seems to have come to is a carefully qualified ethical stance toward other human beings.

DAHLIA RAVIKOVITCH

———

"On the road at night there stands the man"

(1959)

Dahlia Ravikovitch was one of the leading poets of the so-called Genera-
tion of the State, a group of Hebrew writers who came of age following
the establishment of the State of Israel in 1948. She inherited her love of po-
etry from her father, an engineer who emigrated from Russia via China in the
early 1930s. She was six years old when he was killed in a car accident, mowed
over by a drunken Greek soldier serving in the British army. Soon afterward,
her mother took her to live on a kibbutz without telling her that her father had
died. She only learned about it two years later from another kid on the play-
ground. The trauma of his death would be one of the defining experiences of
her life — and her poetry.

Here is an untitled poem from her first book, *The Love of an Orange* (1959),
which was published when she was twenty-three years old:

> On the road at night there stands the man
> Who once upon a time was my father.
> And I must go down to the place where he stands
> Because I was his firstborn daughter.

Night after night he stands alone in his place
And I must go down and stand in that place.
And I wanted to ask him: Till when must I go.
And I knew as I asked: I must always go.

In the place where he stands, there is a trace of danger
Like the day he walked that road and a car ran him over.
And that's how I knew him and marked him to remember:
This very man used to be my father.

Not one word of love does he speak to me
Though once upon a time he was my father.
And even though I was his firstborn daughter
Not one word of love can he speak to me.

(Translated by Chana Bloch and Chana Kronfeld)

Ravikovitch's poem has a solid symmetrical structure of four quatrains. It has a cohesive surface and a clear logic. Look again at the beginning:

On the road at night there stands the man
Who once upon a time was my father.
And I *must* go down to the place where he stands
Because I was his firstborn daughter.

Like her contemporary Yehuda Amichai, Ravikovitch was influenced by the English Metaphysical poets, mostly through the advocacy of T. S. Eliot, and learned the language of poetic argument from such writers as John Donne and George Herbert. Here, as in a Metaphysical poem, the language of causality operates throughout. The speaker begins by stating that she *must* go down to the road precisely *because* of her identity as an eldest daughter. The language of argumentation gives a feeling of rationality to this poem, but there is also something irrational in its very premise. After all, the lyric is driven by the speaker's compulsive need to return to the scene of the accident, the spot where her father was killed. It is powered by an obsession, which is repeated night after night, to "go down to the place where he stands."

There is a fantastical quality to all of this. The poem begins at an odd remove: "On the road at night there stands the man." The inversion puts the road first and the man second. And we don't learn that the man was her father until the end of the second line. Indeed, the father himself becomes an imaginary figure. This seems evident in the fairy tale language that opens and closes the poem: "On the road at night there stands the man / Who *once upon a time* was my father." This recurs as: "Not one word of love does he speak to me / Though *once upon a time* he was my father." Perhaps the man was once a genuine or real father long ago, but now he has been transformed into a ghost keeping watch on the road where he was murdered. And this becomes a sentence for his daughter too, who must always return to the fateful place of the accident. Notice the lack of a question mark in what is seemingly a question: "And I wanted to ask him: Till when must I go. / And I knew as I asked: I must always go."

The speaker of Ravikovitch's poem has a repetition compulsion. She cannot help herself and seems fixated on returning and marking her father's place so that she can remember him. The site has replaced her memory. Ravikovitch's translators note that in Hebrew the phrase "marked him to remember" evokes a passage from the Passover Haggadah, where Rabbi Judah created a mnemonic device in order to remember the ten plagues. Whenever she returns, the speaker in the poem feels a vague foreboding, a trace or fear of danger, a ghostly intimation that recalls the day that her father was simply out walking along and was suddenly killed by a car. She was never there to see it. Now she is witness to his erasure.

The firstborn daughter returns every night and yet, despite her loyalty, her father cannot respond or acknowledge her. The change in tense from the past to the present in the last two lines is revealing: "And even though I *was* his firstborn daughter / Not one word of love *can* he *speak* to me." Her father's silence is painful and seems withholding, though it will never be broken. It's especially pointed to say that he cannot reassure her with a single word of love —and here she uses the auxiliary verb *can* —because, in fact, he is unable to speak at all. His silence is shattering, unnatural, permanent, and as a result her love will forever go unreciprocated. All of this has a quasi-logical and hallucinatory quality that befits the language of trauma.

In a perceptive psychoanalytically oriented book on Ravikovitch and the poetics of trauma, the scholar Ilana Szobel suggests that a more revealing translation of that last line would be "I always knew, I was forever beholden" —a statement that embodies Ravikovitch's personal experiences and poetic commitments, a declaration "that may be read as a poetic articulation of the nature of her trauma." Ravikovitch was a searing feminist, a stirring love poet, and a political activist, but she was also always a poet of unresolved mourning, forever beholden.

Her unnamed early poem, the portal to her work, is devastatingly sad because it enacts mourning without resolution, grief without end.

—

"Poem of the Gifts"

(1960)

Jorge Luis Borges is mostly known for his mind-bending metaphysical parables that cross the boundaries between the short story and the essay. But Borges always identified himself first as a reader, then as a poet. He found the borders between genres permeable and lived in an imaginary world created by books. "If I were asked to name the chief event in my life, I should say my father's library," he said in 1970. "In fact, sometimes I think I have never strayed outside that library."

Borges suffered from hereditary weak eyesight and eventually became the sixth generation of his family to go blind. This was an especially unfortunate fate for the reader and writer who in 1955 became the director of Argentina's National Library. He served for eighteen years, possibly the happiest years of his life, though the external world gradually faded to a gray fog. It was as if he was coming home again to his father's library, though now with greater resources and riches. But then his blindness deprived him of the freedom of reading. He said, "Little by little I grew to understand the strange irony of events. I had always imagined Paradise under the aspect of a library ... And there was I, in some way the center of 900,000 volumes in various languages.

I discovered that I could hardly make out the title pages or the spines. I then wrote 'Poem of the Gifts.'"

Here is "Poema de los dones," which was initially dedicated to Borges's friend and collaborator, the prose writer María Esther Vázquez:

Poem of the Gifts

No one should read self-pity or reproach
into this statement of the majesty
of God, who with such splendid irony
granted me books and blindness at one touch.

Care of this city of books he handed over
to sightless eyes, which now can do no more
than read in libraries of dream the poor
and senseless paragraphs that dawns deliver

to wishful scrutiny. In vain the day
squanders on these same eyes its infinite tomes,
as distant as the inaccessible volumes
that perished once in Alexandria.

From hunger and from thirst (in the Greek story),
a king lies dying among gardens and fountains.
Aimlessly, endlessly, I trace the confines,
high and profound, of this blind library.

Cultures of East and West, the entire atlas,
encyclopedias, centuries, dynasties,
symbols, the cosmos, and cosmogonies
are offered from the walls, all to no purpose.

In shadow, with a tentative stick, I try
the hollow twilight, slow and imprecise —
I, who had always thought of Paradise
in form and image as a library.

Something, which certainly is not defined
by the word *fate,* arranges all these things;
another man was given, on other evenings
now gone, these many books. He too was blind.

Wandering through the gradual galleries,
I often feel with vague and holy dread
I am that other dead one, who attempted
the same uncertain steps on similar days.

Which of the two is setting down this poem —
a single sightless self, a plural I?
What can it matter, then, the name that names me,
given our curse is common and the same?

Groussac or Borges, now I look upon
this dear world losing shape, fading away
into a pale uncertain ashy-gray
that feels like sleep, or else oblivion.

(Translated by Alastair Reid)

Borges wrote poetry throughout the 1920s, mostly under the aegis of a vanguard Imagist sect called the Ultraists, but then it mysteriously deserted him as he went on to create a new kind of narrative prose in such books as *Universal History of Infamy* (*Historia universal de la infamia,* 1935), *The Garden of Forking Paths* (*El jardin de senderos que se bifurcan,* 1941), and *Ficciones* (1944). The fabulist returned to poetry in 1950s with a more direct and straightforward style, a beguiling and deceptive simplicity, and dictated his poems to classical meters.

Borges's book *The Maker* (*El hacedor,* 1960) is divided into two parts. The first half consists entirely of prose parables. The second half commences with "Poem of the Gifts" and continues with a group of lineated poems. There is no discord between the pieces in prose and the lyrics in verse. And yet in the prologue to his book *In Praise of Darkness* (*Elogio de la sombra,* 1969), Borges also makes a point about emotion in the lyric: "Beyond its rhythm, the typographical layout of free verse is there to inform the reader that what awaits him is not facts or reasoning, but poetic emotion."

There might be some justification then in thinking that the pressure of feeling determined the lineated form of "Poem of the Gifts." That feeling is intense, but it is also quiet and restrained. Borges also confesses, "After many years I realize (not without a bit of sadness) that in all my efforts in free verse I just went from one classical meter to another." "Poem of the Gifts" looks like free verse, but it mostly unfolds in Spanish as a series of twelve-syllable lines, or alexandrines. Borges was indebted to John Milton's Petrarchan sonnet on his blindness. He might have recalled that Robert Bridges called his own alexandrines "neo-Miltonics." The regular quatrains also give the poem a feeling of orderliness and symmetry.

Borges said that he wanted the first lines of the poem to sound "calm, like a prayer." It's the sort of prayer one might recite to oneself while moving through a labyrinth of books in a quiet building. The speaker treats the central irony of the poem without self-pity or rage but with a kind of wistfulness. The gift he has been given is complicated. Borges uses the plural to refer to "libraries of *dreams*" ("*los sueños*"), but Reid translates it as singular, "libraries of *dream*." After all, the books outside of his office are now just as distant to him as the books that perished in the fire at Alexandria. Borges always linked blindness to books, to reading and learning. He evokes the Greek story of King Tantalus, who was punished by Zeus to eternal thirst and hunger in Hades despite being placed in a pool of water and almost within reach of a fruit tree. Tantalus's name became the origin of the verb *tantalize*.

The speaker projects his own condition onto the place — "this blind library." It's as if the bookshelves, the walls themselves, hold the key to the mysteries of the universe ("symbols, the cosmos, and cosmogonies"), but he cannot use this key to open the tantalizingly close door — it's "all to no purpose." The fiction writer Leonard Michaels called Borges "a master of controlled estrangement," an apt term for the image of the blind custodian tentatively making his way through the library:

> In shadow, with a tentative stick, I try
> the hollow twilight, slow and imprecise —
> I, who had always thought of Paradise
> in form and image as a library.

Moving forward, the speaker invokes his double, a man no longer alive, whom he identifies as himself. "I am that other dead one, who attempted / the same uncertain steps on similar days," he confesses, and then wonders: "Which of the two is setting down this poem — / a single sightless self, a plural I?" This seems like a metaphysical ploy, as in many of Borges's short stories, but here it also turns out to have a literal meaning. At the end of the poem, Borges evokes Paul Groussac (1845–1929), a French intellectual and naturalized Argentine whom he greatly admired. Groussac was the second blind director of the National Library, after José Marmol, who directed the library from 1858 to 1871. Groussac lived on the first floor of the Biblioteca Nacional de Argentina, where he served for forty-four years, and eventually also went blind. Borges's double is also his predecessor, and the poet seems to speak for either or both as he faces an ash-gray world. Finally, like Alfonsina Storni in her last poem, "I'm Going to Sleep," Borges invokes the ancient connection between sleep and death. He suggests that this precious world is "losing shape, fading away" into a grayness that feels like sleep, which is temporary, or else oblivion, which is permanent.

GWEN HARWOOD

———

"In the Park"

(1961)

The Australian poet Gwen Harwood deserves to be better known in the United States. She published her early poem "In the Park" in the magazine *The Bulletin* in 1961 under the pseudonym Walter Lehmann. She liked "masques, masquerades, wigs and beards," and this was the first of the thirteen pseudonyms that she would employ over the course of her career. Two years later, she claimed the poem under her own name in her first book, *Poems* (1963).

It was especially difficult for a woman poet, particularly one who was writing about domestic life, to make her way in Australia in the 1950s. As the Australian writer Susan Sheridan puts it, "In 1959, in Tasmania, an unknown poet called Gwen Harwood started a guerilla war on incompetent literary editors by sending out her poems under male pseudonyms." Harwood's suspicions about sexism were verified and suddenly her poems were readily accepted. Her outrage grew. In 1961, she submitted two sonnets on the lovers Abelard and Eloisa to *The Bulletin* under her first male nom de guerre. After they were published, it was revealed that the two poems read acrostically, "So Long Bulletin, Fuck All Editors."

Here is "In the Park":

In the Park

She sits in the park. Her clothes are out of date.
Two children whine and bicker, tug her skirt.
A third draws aimless patterns in the dirt.
Someone she loved once passes by — too late

to feign indifference to that casual nod.
"How nice," *et cetera.* "Time holds great surprises."
From his neat head unquestionably rises
a small balloon . . . "but for the grace of God . . ."

They stand a while in flickering light, rehearsing
the children's names and birthdays. "It's so sweet
to hear their chatter, watch them grow and thrive,"
she says to his departing smile. Then, nursing
the youngest child, sits staring at her feet.
To the wind she says, "They have eaten me alive."

"In the Park," or as Elizabeth Lawson aptly dubbed it, "In the Dreaded Park," is a carefully crafted and explosive Petrarchan sonnet. The rhythm is a steady iambic pentameter, the rhyme scheme is exact: *abba cddc efg efg.* An unnamed woman sits in the park with her three children and encounters a man whom "she loved once." The poem has the drama of a short story — it is presented from a third-person center of consciousness — and the concision of a lyric poem. Despite the original male signature, it takes a female point of view. Harwood gleefully told an interviewer that someone once said to her, "Only a man could have written that poem with the necessary self-detachment."

The poet Eavan Boland recalls that she "began to write in an Ireland where the word 'woman' and the word 'poet' seemed to be in some sort of magnetic opposition to each other." The situation was the same in Australia. Harwood was afraid of being typecast as a housewife and excluded from the rank of poets; she also had a husband and four children, and she wanted or needed the cover of a male pseudonym. She mined domestic life for subject matter, but she was also troubled when critics identified her with the protagonist of her suburban poems.

Harwood's interviews are filled with disclaimers. She said, "I am horrified at the tendency of people to identify the I with the author . . . I keep saying that the I of the poems is not the I making jams jellies pickles and chutneys." She insisted on what W. B. Yeats called "a phantasmagoria," the gap between the poet who creates and "the bundle of accidents and incoherence that sits down to breakfast," though in Harwood's case she probably also made that breakfast for her family. She distanced herself from the domestic rounds and said, "The I of my poems is an entirely operatic I." When one interviewer told her that she saw "an impulse of self-expression" in "In the Park," Harwood retorted, "But it says she sits in the park. Her clothes are out of date. Mine are never out of date." She explained that the poem originated when she "saw that woman and felt [her] way into what she was thinking."

Yet there was obviously some part of Harwood that recognized the domestic claustrophobia described in "In the Park." She understood the experience and created a powerfully gendered scene. Notice how the poem starts with short stabbing declarative sentences and three carefully end-stopped lines.

> She sits in the park. Her clothes are out of date.
> Two children whine and bicker, tug her skirt.
> A third draws aimless patterns in the dirt.

There is a long pause at the end of the first quatrain: "Someone she loved once passes by — too late . . ." The rhymes are strategically deployed: the words "skirt" and "dirt" are clenched together while "date" is held off and then paired with the word "late." The drama of the poem is triggered by an unexpected meeting.

There is a telegraphic use of dialogue in the second quatrain. An entire polite conversation can be inferred from it: "'How nice,' et cetera. 'Time holds great surprises.'" The sheer rote boredom of that "et cetera" lands with a heavy weight, like the multisyllabic word "unquestionably." The rhyming links "surprises" to "rises" and ironically pairs "nod" with "God." There's a surreal or postmodernist moment at the end of the stanza, where the narrator describes "a small balloon" rising over the man's head, like a dialogue bubble from a comic strip, to project or exteriorize his thought: "but for the grace of God . . ." The idea trails off, but the woman is certain of his secret relief, which shames her.

The Petrarchan sonnet turns in the last six lines. It is as if a camera now looks down on two people standing in the flickering light, making polite conversation, that awkward chatter between former lovers who were once extremely close but no longer know each other. The woman gives the conventional assurances about the sweetness of motherhood. But then the man leaves, and the woman is left to her own devices, nursing her child, staring down at her feet. "To the wind she says, 'They have eaten me alive.'"

This last line is a small bomb detonating in a carefully constructed domestic scene. For the female character, the idea of being eaten alive seems especially bitter after her conversational assurances about how sweet it is to see the children "grow and thrive." The final rhyme, "thrive" and "alive," is brutally pointed. The woman may speak to the wind, as in a visionary poem — think of how often in Romantic poetry, speaking to the wind is a sign of poetic inspiration, a creative and destructive inspiriting force ("Not I, not I, but the wind that blows through me!" D. H. Lawrence declares in "Song of a Man Who Has Come Through") — though here it is not at all a sign of prophetic power. Rather, the image speaks to the woman's loneliness and isolation. She looks down, as if in defeat, and addresses the wind because there is no one she can really talk to, no one she can tell the truth to.

This poem has an air of postnatal depression, the feeling of being devoured by life, a sense of inescapable confinement. It's not a matter of whether the woman loves her children or not. It's a question of how life seems to be closing in around her. Gwen Harwood had the wherewithal to capture that anguished experience in a furious formal poem, a fiercely controlled and vehement sonnet.

ROBERT HAYDEN

———

"The Whipping"

(1962)

I once saw a documentary about Robert Hayden that showed him moving through his old neighborhood on Detroit's east side, talking about his past and pointing out the familiar landmarks of his childhood. The trouble was that few of those landmarks remained. A warehouse had replaced the house where he was born, and across the street, a parking lot and power plant stood in place of the house where he was raised. As Hayden paused there — gentle, nearsighted, bundled up against the January cold — it was easy to understand why displacement was one of his main poetic subjects.

The old, poor neighborhood where he had grown up, the main Black section of the city, which was called "Black Bottom" because it rested on fertile farmland, no longer existed. Hayden explained that an entire neighborhood "which had been fairly cohesive had been destroyed." The cultural center of that neighborhood was called "Paradise Valley." Many of Hayden's most personal poems are a rescue operation for that troubled paradise. The poet Michael Harper recalled that at one time Hayden wanted to collect all his poems about Paradise Valley as a special gift for friends. The collection would have included "Elegies for Paradise Valley," "Free Fanta-sia: Tiger Flowers," "Homage to the Empress of the Blues," "The Rabbi," "Summertime and the Living...," "The Whipping," and "Those Winter Sun-days."

Hayden could be nostalgic about his neighborhood, but he also knew that he came from a dysfunctional home. He was born Asa Sheffey, but his par-ents soon separated and left him with their neighbors, William and Sue Ellen Hayden, who raised him as their son and renamed him Robert Earl Hayden. He learned years later that they never formally adopted him. He was bound to his childhood as the foster son of poor, working-class people and remained committed to what he liked to call "folk" people: poor, uneducated, dignified, all those who quietly fulfilled what he called "love's austere and lonely offices" ("Those Winter Sundays"). But he also refused to sentimentalize his past — as a child growing up his primary desire was to escape the world that surrounded him — and he determined to remember it accurately.

Here is his poem "The Whipping" from *A Ballad of Remembrance* (1962):

The Whipping

The old woman across the way
    is whipping the boy again
and shouting to the neighborhood
    her goodness and his wrongs.

Wildly he crashes through elephant ears,
    pleads in dusty zinnias,
while she in spite of crippling fat
    pursues and corners him.

She strikes and strikes the shrilly circling
    boy till the stick breaks
in her hand. His tears are rainy weather
    to woundlike memories:

My head gripped in bony vise
    of knees, the writhing struggle

> to wrench free, the blows, the fear
>   worse than blows that hateful
>
> Words could bring, the face that I
>   no longer knew or loved. . . .
> Well, it is over now, it is over,
>   and the boy sobs in his room,
>
> And the woman leans muttering against
>   a tree, exhausted, purged —
> avenged in part for lifelong hidings
>   she has had to bear.

Hayden told an interviewer that this poem was motivated by his need to recall the past and rid himself of the pain of so much of it. "I was often abused and often hurt physically," he confessed. His foster parents simply "didn't know how to handle children." Yet, here as elsewhere in Hayden's work, there is a certain detachment, a formal distancing and reticence. This is true of even his most personal poems. Experience has been transposed into art. Here, this is evident in the six elastic, carefully crafted quatrains, which indent the second and fourth lines; in the way the poet balances the enjambments and isolates phrases for emphasis; in the way he rhythmically drives the poem forward. He capitalizes the first letter of each stanza, a quiet formality, and divides the poem neatly in half.

"The Whipping" begins in the present, turns to the past, and then returns to the present with a new awareness and knowledge. It's the formula that Wordsworth created in "Tintern Abbey." The poem thus takes the form of a crisis lyric — it enacts a mental transport. The central memory is triggered as the speaker watches an old woman — "The old woman" — across the way who is whipping a boy — "the boy" — yet again. Neither the woman nor the boy is identified by name. If the scene didn't make such a visceral impression, they'd almost seem like allegorical figures. This whipping is something that obviously happens periodically. The old woman doesn't hide the fact, either. The fourth line knowingly isolates and balances the phrase "her goodness and his wrongs." The boy dramatically crashes through the plants, struggling to escape, pleading in the flowers where he is trying to hide, while the woman, despite her "crippling" weight, "pursues and corners him."

The scene is violent. Notice the hissing *s* and *sh* sounds that enact it: "*She strikes* and *strikes* the *sh*rilly *c*ircling / boy till the *s*tick break*s* . . ." The violence breaks the boy into tears and breaks the speaker too. Suddenly he is catapulted back into his own past, into the experience of being bludgeoned and screamed at by a loved one disfigured by rage. This is a dark, troubled instance of what Proust deemed "involuntary memory."

"The Whipping" is an action-packed poem, but one notices the slightly stiff and removed diction of "His tears are rainy weather / to woundlike memories." It's as if the speaker is distancing himself from what he is about to remember and face. The meaning then cleverly turns on a colon placed precisely midway through the poem. That colon splits open the poem and marks a calculated turn from the third to the first person. Memory explodes. The next six lines enact a transformation. Look at how strategically the lines unfold:

> My head gripped in bony vise
> of knees, the writhing struggle
> to wrench free, the blows, the fear
> worse than blows that hateful
>
> Words could bring, the face that I
> no longer knew or loved. . . .

These lines depict the speaker's futile struggle to break free. Notice the repetition of the letter *w*, which weaves together the words "writhing," "wrench," "worse," and "Words." There's also a wrenching line and stanza break, which creates a sort of double emphasis, between "hateful" and "Words." The ellipsis marks the end of a sentence; a beating has trailed off. It also signals a memory that is too much to bear. When the speaker returns to the present tense ("Well, it is over now, it is over"), he is talking both about the boy in his room and about himself as a child.

Hayden complicates the moral resonance at the end of the poem by suggesting that the woman (the neighbor in the present and, by implication, the adult in his own past) has been avenging a lifetime of secret hurts. There is a pun on the word "hidings." "I got a few hidings like that," Hayden remembered, referring to the way he was beaten. But here the word also refers to what this poor, heavyset, pain-ridden woman had been forced to conceal for her entire life. The woman's secret hurts don't justify or excuse her abusive behavior, but they do help to explain it. She has been "purged" and "avenged," though only "in part." Hayden understands the way that violence has been passed down from generation to generation. It was a brutal cycle that needed to be broken.

Robert Hayden could come to such a large understanding only through the writing of the poem itself. "The Whipping" is an acutely observant poem, a reckoning, and testimonial. As Gwendolyn Brooks said, "Life is right there, in the finished piece."

ROBERT LOWELL

———

"Night Sweat"

(1963)

N ight Sweat" appeared as the penultimate poem in *For the Union Dead* (1964), which Robert Lowell wrote during a period when he was especially worn out from his bipolar disorder, which caused regular bouts of depression and mania. It was still a few years before he started taking lithium, which offered him a lifeline. He said about the book:

> Depression's no gift from the Muse. At worst, I do nothing. But often I've written, and wrote one whole book — *For the Union Dead* — about witheredness. It wasn't acute depression, and I felt quite able to work for hours, write and rewrite. Most of the best poems, the most personal, are gathered crumbs. I had better moods, but the book is lemony, soured, and dry, the drouth I had touched with my own hands. That, too, may be poetry — on sufferance.

Lowell was able to make something lasting out of his depression in "Night Sweat," a crisis poem with a lyrical flair and a certain rhetorical grandiloquence that is rare for a poem dampened by such a dark spirit.

Night Sweat

Work-table, litter, books and standing lamp,
plain things, my stalled equipment, the old broom —
but I am lying in a tidied room,
for ten nights now I've felt the creeping damp
float over my pajamas' wilted white . . .
Sweet salt embalms me and my head is wet,
everything streams and tells me this is right;
life's fever is soaking in night sweat —
one life, one writing! But the downward glide
and bias of existing wrings us dry —
always inside me is the child who died,
always inside me is his wish to die —
one universe, one body . . . in this urn
the animal night sweats of the spirit burn.

Behind me! You! Again I feel the light
lighten my leaded eyelids, while the gray
skulled horses whinny for the soot of night.
I dabble in the dapple of the day.
A heap of wet clothes, seamy, shivering,
I see my flesh and bedding washed with light,
my child exploding into dynamite,
my wife . . . your lightness alters everything,
and tears the black web from the spider's sack,
as your heart hops and flutters like a hare.
Poor turtle, tortoise, if I cannot clear
the surface of these troubled waters here,
absolve me, help me, Dear Heart, as you bear
this world's dead weight and cycle on your back.

The poet Elizabeth Bishop especially loved this poem. In a letter to Lowell in 1963, she called it "very beautiful, musical, spontaneous," and said that it was "a wonderful, perfectly natural poem — very *sympathetic.*" The words "spontaneous" and "perfectly natural" jump out because the poem does have a feeling of spontaneity and naturalness, though that feeling is hard-won, since the poem is crafted as a double sonnet. The first stanza is a Shakespearean sonnet, which consists of three four-line units and a summarizing couplet. The rhyme scheme is tight: *abbacdcdefefgg.* Indeed, Lowell lifted this section and reprinted it as a part of a sequence of five poems called "April's End" in his book of improvisational sonnets, *Notebook 1967–1968.* The second half of the poem is a Petrarchan sonnet, which consists of two parts, an octave and a sestet. The rhyme scheme is different: *ababcaacdeffed.* The change in format from one kind of a sonnet to another also signals a change in feeling.

"Night Sweat" begins with a sense of spiritual torpor. The speaker reveals his artistic incapacity through images of sexual impotence: "plain things, my stalled equipment, the old broom . . ." The night sweat itself becomes a sign of spiritual anguish: "Sweet salt embalms me and my head is wet." Steven Axelrod and others have argued that the trope of night sweat is indebted to the so-called terrible sonnets of Gerard Manley Hopkins, especially "I wake and feel the fell of dark, not day." There's a Hopkinsian echo in the consonance of "*w*ilted *w*hite" followed by "*S*weet *s*alt." For Lowell, as for Hopkins, there's a kind of confusion between sexual energy and writing. The speaker explicitly links "one life, one writing" to "one universe, one body." He feels himself being wrung dry and emptied out by life.

When Lowell reprinted "Night Sweat" in his *Selected Poems* (1976), he decided to jam it together as one section in twenty-eight continuous lines. He had always felt that the second section was weaker than the first and thought the difference dissolved when it was printed as one unit. But I am following Lowell's friend and editor Frank Bidart in keeping the division. As Bidart explains in his preface to Lowell's *Collected Poems,* the reader needs to feel the break between these two balanced units of equal length. Each is formally different. The first stanza closes: "one universe, one body . . . in this urn / the animal night sweats of the spirit burn." As Bidart explains: "The heavy sense of closure embodied by this final rhymed couplet reflects a closed system. In an earlier line, 'always inside me is the child who died.' The spirit cannot escape the body which, one with the universe, is an urn in which the sweating spirit is encased and burns."

The second section turns with a sudden exclamation: "Behind me! You!" Another person, a sudden lightness, enters the room. It made greater formal sense for Lowell to mark this volta with a stanza break. The reader experiences the dramatic change. The night turns into day and the spirit lightens as "Night Sweat" turns from a sense of cold defeat to one of warm domestic con nection — a crying baby, a rescuing wife. It is now directed to Elizabeth Hard-wick, Lowell's loyal, long-suffering wife and friend. The liquid sounds enact the change ("Again I feel the light / lighten my leaded eyelids"). There is even a desultory Hopkinsian moment, or parody, as "Glory be to God for dappled things" turns into "I dabble in the dapple of the day." The word "light" recurs and morphs into "your lightness alters everything." This self-portrait of the artist becomes a semi-humorous quasi-love poem, a longed-for connection.

The husband notices that his wife's "heart hops and flutters like a hare." All those *h* sounds hop along. He addresses his love directly as "Poor turtle, tortoise," which shows a rueful self-awareness of what he has put her through. In this race, she is both the tortoise and the hare. He knows the dead weight of the world the turtle bears on her back. He also knows that on his own he cannot "clear / the surface of these troubled waters," and calls on his love to absolve and help him, addressing her directly as "Dear Heart." In a sympathetic and authoritative study of Lowell's manic depression, Kay Jamison calls the ending "a tribute and supplication — from husband to wife, and drowning man to lifeline."

There is a modified or partial "spiritual recovery" in the second half of the poem. Bidart characterizes the qualified release in the final eight lines in this way: "The poet's optimism ('your lightness alters everything') is partly rein-forced but partly denied by the cyclical final rhymes (*abccba*). Transformation is not decisively closed off by a rhymed final couplet, but the agent of transfor-mation still must bear 'this world's dead weight,' the cycle that will return, that cannot be shaken off."

"Night Sweat" is the work of a committed artist — one life with only one writing — seeking to bear "the downward glide / and bias of existing." It is also a poem of partial liberation, a recognition of interdependence. At the end it turns to the beloved in a wry tribute to the rescuing power of love.

ANNE SEXTON

—

"Wanting to Die"

(1964)

Anne Wilder, a friend and psychotherapist, wrote this to Anne Sexton early in 1964: "I love living and the things and objects that are available here on Earth. Like blades of grass, for example." She asked Sexton about her inexplicable attraction to suicide. It didn't take long before she got a reply in the form of a poem:

> *Wanting to Die*
>
> Since you ask, most days I cannot remember.
> I walk in my clothing, unmarked by that voyage.
> Then the almost unnamable lust returns.
>
> Even then I have nothing against life.
> I know well the grass blades you mention,
> the furniture you have placed under the sun.

But suicides have a special language.
Like carpenters they want to know *which tools.*
They never ask *why build.*

Twice I have so simply declared myself,
have possessed the enemy, eaten the enemy,
have taken on his craft, his magic.

In this way, heavy and thoughtful,
warmer than oil or water,
I have rested, drooling at the mouth-hole.

I did not think of my body at needle point.
Even the cornea and the leftover urine were gone.
Suicides have already betrayed the body.

Still-born, they don't always die,
but dazzled, they can't forget a drug so sweet
that even children would look on and smile.

To thrust all that life under your tongue! —
that, all by itself, becomes a passion.
Death's a sad bone; bruised, you'd say,

and yet she waits for me, year after year,
to so delicately undo an old wound,
to empty my breath from its bad prison.

Balanced there, suicides sometimes meet,
raging at the fruit, a pumped-up moon,
leaving the bread they mistook for a kiss,

leaving the page of the book carelessly open,
something unsaid, the phone off the hook
and the love, whatever it was, an infection.
(February 3, 1964)

In the poem Wilder has been transformed into a nameless interlocutor, possibly a therapist, the one who kicks off this lyric by inquiring about Sexton's compulsion to kill herself, which the interlocutor cannot understand. According to Sexton's biographer Diane Middlebrook, when Wilder asked this question, Sexton was not particularly thinking about destroying herself; rather, she was considering how to write about it — again. She had already published her first two books, *To Bedlam and Part Way Back* (1960) and *All My Pretty Ones* (1962) and had confessed to two attempts at suicide.

At the time that she wrote "Wanting to Die" Sexton was especially interested in Arthur Miller's new play, *After the Fall,* which centered on the self-destructiveness of a character obviously based on Miller's celebrity ex-wife, Marilyn Monroe. Sexton's former classmate and friendly competitor Sylvia Plath had committed suicide by asphyxiating herself about a year earlier, and you can feel Plath's presence hovering somewhere in the background too. As evidence: Sexton included "Wanting to Die," along with her poem "Sylvia's Death," an elegy she wrote just six days after Plath's suicide, in a brief memoir that she composed about Plath called "The Bar Fly Ought to Sing" (1970). She states outright that the poem "was written directly for both of us and for that place where we met: 'Balanced there, suicides sometimes meet.'" She also recalls how they used to reminisce in loving detail about their first suicide attempts. Like Plath's, Sexton's fascination with death was specific, lurid, and fervent. And yet she also referred to suicide, almost offhandedly, as "the opposite of the poem." If that is true, then, as the critic Philip McGowan suggests, "suicide becomes anti-poetry." It is an impulse against language.

In the poem, however, Sexton rejects her own formulation when she declares that "suicides have a special language." That language takes her to the edge of nullity, nothingness itself. Wilder's initial probing question about suicide triggered what Sexton called a "morbid free association," which she appended to a letter in mid-January 1964: "We live at such contrasts . . . you and me . . . me lapping the edges . . . me testing death . . . me raging at the corpse, the bread that I took for a kiss, the love, an infection." In "Wanting to Die," Sexton has organized these raw associations into eleven clearly organized tercets, a lucid thirty-three-line exposition.

The speaker in Sexton's poem is obsessed with dying perfectly. She confesses to her desire to die, yet the poem itself is vividly alive. In the first stanza, she describes her state of mind as cloudy and confused. She sees her desire for death in metaphorical terms as a voyage, a journey without return. The speaker feels an "unnamable lust" coming over her, something almost carnal she cannot control. And yet her argument is weirdly poised and logical. The speaker herself is not overcome by this uncontrollable feeling. Notice how at the beginning of the poem each line is a sentence, a station in the argument. The subject matter is boiling hot — one feels the percolating undertow, the raging lust for death — but the reasoning is cool-headed. Reread the opening with a focus on the language of argumentation:

> *Since you ask,* most days I cannot remember.
> I walk in my clothing, unmarked by that voyage.
> *Then* the almost unnamable lust returns.
>
> *Even then* I have nothing against life.
> *I know well* the grass blades you mention,
> the furniture you have placed under the sun.
>
> *But* suicides have a special language.
> Like carpenters they want to know *which tools.*
> They never ask *why build.*

This language, which we associate with essayistic thinking, continues throughout; hence phrases such as "In this way" and "I did not think" and "and yet." The somewhat detached argumentative side of the poem may be one of its spookier aspects. In an almost matter-of-fact way, Sexton's speaker compares suicides to carpenters, tradesmen, people who make and repair things. She takes for granted that she is one of them.

Middlebrook suggests that Sexton's thoughts about suicide were pretty well entrenched by 1964, and so were her practices. She knew *"which tools"* — she planned to combine alcohol with an overdose of pills. She considered this "the woman's way out," as she told her psychiatrist Dr. Orne, who had encouraged her to write poetry after she had tried to commit suicide in 1956.

The speaker in "Wanting to Die" is completely clear, unsentimental, and certain about her statements. She doesn't hesitate. She knows exactly what she is talking about, even though she keeps describing her own behavior as irrational, as when she characterizes her battle with suicide as possessing the enemy, eating the enemy, which works its "magic" on her. This tension between rationality and irrationality is one of the defining features of this painfully sad poem.

Sexton's speaker keeps coming up with creative ways for characterizing suicide and her own will to die. She wants to control the moment of death itself, to take herself to the threshold. She is fascinated by the boundary. She sexualizes her own terminology throughout, using the words "lust," "passion," "kiss." She speaks of suicides as stillborn and dazzled; she refers to death as something like candy, "a drug so sweet / that even children would look on and smile." She equates death with "a sad bone." She refers to an "old wound" in her body and portrays the body itself as a "bad prison." The subject is death, but there is something curiously enthusiastic about the way the poem keeps generating metaphors for it. The two final stanzas hit a higher register, a feverish lyrical pitch. Like the moon, a typical image of high romance, the language is slightly pumped up:

> Balanced there, suicides sometimes meet,
> raging at the fruit, a pumped-up moon,
> leaving the bread they mistook for a kiss,
>
> leaving the page of the book carelessly open,
> something unsaid, the phone off the hook
> and the love, whatever it was, an infection.

Despite its lyric height, the poem ends in a kind of speechlessness, the final silence of suicide, which permanently cuts things off. Hence the book left "carelessly open" and the phone left hanging off the hook. This is eerily reminiscent of the end of Alfonsina Storni's suicide lyric, "I'm Going to Sleep." The suicide inevitably leaves something unresolved, something never to be finished. In the end, even love seems only a final betrayal, something the speaker cannot comprehend ("whatever it was"), not a nourishment but a physical invasion of the body, "an infection." Anne Sexton's fascination with death followed her to the end.

ROSE AUSLÄNDER

"My Nightingale"

(1965)

Rose Ausländer was born in 1901 as Rosalie Scherzer in Czernowitz, a city in the northern region of Bukovina, when it was part of the Austro-Hungarian Empire. She came from a traditional German-speaking Jewish family and had a seemingly idyllic childhood in the city known as "Little Vienna" and "Jerusalem on the Prut." The same world shaped both her and Paul Celan, whom she met during the war; they faced the same torturous history. At the end of World War I, Czernowitz was united with the Kingdom of Romania, but during World War II the Nazis took it over. Later it was returned to Romania, forming part of the Soviet Union. It is now a city in Ukraine.

A promising student, Scherzer gave up her studies after her father died, in 1920. She immigrated to the United States when she was nineteen years old, married her fellow student Ignaz Ausländer when she was twenty-two, and separated from him three years later. But she was extremely close to her mother, who was an invalid, and kept returning to take care of her. Ausländer's first book, *The Rainbow* (*Der Regenbogen*), was printed in Czernowitz in 1939. Two years later, German troops occupied the city. Along with her brother, Max, she and her mother were trapped in the ghetto, often hiding out in cellars, but they somehow survived. Later she testified that "while we waited for death, there were those of us who dwelt in dream-words — our traumatic home amidst our homelessness. To write was to live."

Ausländer was living in New York when her mother died in Romania in 1947. Overwhelmed by grief, she suffered a physical and psychological breakdown that lasted more than a year. She wrote many poems in response to the great loss of her life, including "The Mother" ("Die Mutter"), which declares, "I am her shadow and she my light." My favorite is "My Nightingale" ("Meine Nachtigall"), which appeared in her second book, *Blind Summer* (*Blinder Sommer*), published in Vienna in 1965.

My Nightingale

My mother was a doe in another time.
Her honey-brown eyes
and her loveliness
survive from that moment.

Here she was —
half an angel and half humankind —
the center was *mother*.
When I asked her once what she would have wanted to be
she made this answer to me: a nightingale.

Now she is a nightingale.
Every night, night after night, I hear her
in the garden of my sleepless dream.
She is singing the Zion of her ancestors.
She is singing the hills and beech-woods
of Bukowina.
My nightingale
sings lullabies to me
night after night
in the garden of my sleepless dream.

(Translated by Eavan Boland)

Like Dahlia Ravikovitch's poem to her father, "On the road at night there stands the man," there's a fairy tale or mythological element to Ausländer's acutely felt, highly personal poem for her mother. It's like a lost story from Ovid's *Metamorphoses*. To emphasize the fairy tale dimension, one translation even begins: "Once upon a time my mother was a doe." Ausländer suggests that the qualities of a doe, which seem to have come to her mother from some other world, could still be seen in her. There's a sense of foreboding or ominousness hovering in the fourth line, in the feeling that her mother's fragile allure from a previous life could somehow still "survive from that moment."

The sense of the mother being somewhat otherworldly is emphasized in the assertion "Here she was / half an angel and half humankind." Ausländer felt a special kinship with the German poet Else Lasker-Schüler and translated her poem "Meine Mutter" into English (as "My Mother"); it begins with the question "Was she the great angel / who walked at my side?" The death of the mother was overwhelming for both poets, who felt the loss as total. After all, the center of the child's world, the center of the universe itself, was *mother*. Ausländer italicizes the word for emphasis.

As a poem, "My Nightingale" begins to turn when the speaker wistfully asks her mother what creature she would have liked to be, and she answers dreamily: *a nightingale*. Birds have often figured in poetry as messengers from the beyond. The nightingale — a small, secretive, solitary songbird that goes on singing late into the night — has had a special metaphorical and symbolic power for artists. It fills an apparently irresistible need to attribute human feelings to the bird's pure and persistent song. Poets, who are often nocturnal creatures, have identified with "spring's messenger, the sweet-voiced nightingale," as Sappho calls it. The history of these representations begins with one of the oldest legends in the world, the violent tale of Philomela, whose tongue was cut out and who was changed into a nightingale, which laments in darkness but nonetheless tells its story in song. As a European poet, Ausländer was certainly conscious of this long tradition, including the way the Romantic poets utilized the bird as a symbol of imaginative freedom. Remember John Keats's dramatic exclamation: "Thou wast not born for death, immortal Bird!"

"My Nightingale" subtly triggers and alters the tradition. The poem structurally turns in the third and final stanza: "Now she is a nightingale." The mother may have been a doe in a past life, "another time," but now she has been transfigured into something loftier, a bird, a figure of transcendence. The present tense is compelling because the reader understands immediately that the mother has been utterly transformed. She was always only partly of this world anyway. The poem now becomes a living testament, an elegy taking place in the present tense. Every night the mother's song haunts the speaker's "sleepless dream," which is not an actual dream but a reverie under the magical spell of night, an associative or waking dream. As a nightingale, the mother sings of the world she loved as a woman: the Zion or Promised Land of her Jewish ancestors, the beautiful hills and trees of her native Bukovina. The maternal song is a nightly ritual, a lullaby, though a lullaby that keeps her daughter awake "in the garden of my sleepless dream."

Here the daughter becomes the listener and the mother the unseen songster, whose heartrending music testifies to what she loved. The message has been heard. And the poem itself captures the woebegone plaintiveness of the mother's nightingale song.

RANDALL JARRELL

———

"Next Day"

(1965)

Randall Jarrell threw himself fully into the role of a woman in a triad of poems strung across his work: "The Face," "The Woman at the Washington Zoo," and "Next Day." Each of these women stands both as herself and as a sort of Everywoman or, as Jarrell understood it, Every-person, a figure who is both ordinary and exceptional. This common fate is something that happens to everyone, Jarrell suggests: at first you mature and gain knowledge, but then, inevitably, something goes wrong. Jarrell's androgynous poems unnervingly pursue the moment when something invisibly turns and goes awry, when the naked self radically breaks down its last defenses.

"Next Day" is the lead poem in the last collection that Jarrell prepared for publication, *The Lost World* (1965), his finest book.

> *Next Day*
>
> Moving from Cheer to Joy, from Joy to All,
> I take a box
> And add it to my wild rice, my Cornish game hens.

The slacked or shorted, basketed, identical
Food-gathering flocks
Are selves I overlook. Wisdom, said William James,

Is learning what to overlook. And I am wise
If that is wisdom.
Yet, somehow, as I buy All from these shelves
And the boy takes it to my station wagon,
What I've become
Troubles me even if I shut my eyes.

When I was young and miserable and pretty
And poor, I'd wish
What all girls wish: to have a husband,
A house and children. Now that I'm old, my wish
Is womanish:
That the boy putting groceries in my car

See me. It bewilders me he doesn't see me.
For so many years
I was good enough to eat: the world looked at me
And its mouth watered. How often they have undressed me,
The eyes of strangers!
And, holding their flesh within my flesh, their vile

Imaginings within my imagining,
I too have taken
The chance of life. Now the boy pats my dog
And we start home. Now I am good.
The last mistaken,
Ecstatic, accidental bliss, the blind

Happiness that, bursting, leaves upon the palm
Some soap and water —
It was so long ago, back in some Gay
Twenties, Nineties, I don't know . . . Today I miss
My lovely daughter

Away at school, my sons away at school,

My husband away at work — I wish for them.
The dog, the maid,
And I go through the sure unvarying days
At home in them. As I look at my life,
I am afraid
Only that it will change, as I am changing:

I am afraid, this morning, of my face.
It looks at me
From the rear-view mirror, with the eyes I hate,
The smile I hate. Its plain, lined look
Of gray discovery
Repeats to me: "You're old." That's all. I'm old.

And yet I'm afraid, as I was at the funeral
I went to yesterday.
My friend's cold made-up face, granite among its flowers,
Her undressed, operated-on, dressed body
Were my face and body.
As I think of her I hear her telling me

How young I seem; I *am* exceptional;
I think of all I have.
But really no one is exceptional,
No one has anything, I'm anybody,
I stand beside my grave
Confused with my life, that is commonplace and solitary.

"Next Day" unfolds through ten shapely, symmetrical six-line stanzas with cuttingly abbreviated second and fifth lines, which rhyme throughout. These are practically the only rhymes until the end of the poem, and each one has its own poignancy. As the poem progresses, the reader starts to anticipate the connections. Most of them link subjects as well as sounds, almost telling a story in themselves as "wisdom" rhymes with "become," "wish" is tied to "womanish," and "years" to "strangers." The word "taken" morphs into "mistaken," "water" links to "daughter," "maid" to "afraid," and "me" to "discovery." The final two rhymes bring finality: "yesterday" connects to "body" and "have" falls into "grave."

"Next Day" is a dramatic monologue. We hear in it the plaintive intelligence of a suburban housewife who wants to be seen and heard. Jarrell may have been making a male assumption here — that a woman can't bear the way she has become invisible to others. The poem begins on a light note; it has a humorous detachment, a comic self-consciousness. The speaker puns on the obsessively cheerful names of household detergents (Cheer, Joy, All). She makes a sly connection between the purchased and the purchasers, the "Cornish game *hens*" and the "slacked or shorted, basketed, identical / Food-gathering *flocks*." The poem pivots on the word "overlook" and ruefully quotes William James's pragmatic idea that "Wisdom" — notice the emphatic line and stanza break — "Is learning what to overlook." Thus, the aging speaker, who seems to have read James's *Principles of Psychology* (volume 2, chapter 22), wryly accepts that "I am wise / If that is wisdom." These witticisms are so characteristic of Jarrell himself that it seems he has tellingly projected and inscribed his own voice onto the voice of a woman at the supermarket, who has his own wit and knowledge. The mask slips.

So much of this poem is about what can't be overlooked. The speaker notices that the boy carrying groceries to her car doesn't see her. She has now become sexually invisible. The wild feelings she once had, the accidental ecstasies she stumbled upon in her youth, seem to leave nothing behind. Her own erotic past has suddenly become remote ("It was so long ago, back in some Gay / Twenties, Nineties, I don't know"). This throws her into a dizzying sense of abandonment and loss, and so she especially misses her daughter, who is away at school, her sons, who are also away at school, and her husband, who is away at work. She is a person of privilege — she has a maid, after all, and a dog for company — but that doesn't rescue her from the brutalities of aging. The speaker wants desperately to be seen; though she is gendered as an ordinary woman, the wistfulness seems to be Jarrell's own:

> As I look at my life,
> I am afraid
> Only that it will change, as I am changing:
>
> I am afraid, this morning, of my face.

The poem hits a higher pitch in the final two stanzas. It takes on an anecdotal quality as the speaker suddenly remembers going to her friend's funeral the day before. Immediately the title, "Next Day," comes into focus. The ruthless insight and the depth of ordinary courage it takes for the speaker to recognize herself in her dead friend, *as* her dead friend, to confront her own bewildering and commonplace fate, almost seem heroic. The poetic technique operates in such a seamless and unassuming way that it's easy to overlook: look at how the rhetorical argument relentlessly pushes the voice to its heart-rending conclusion, as in a Shakespeare sonnet ("And yet"; "But really"), and note the timely, ferocious progression of triple adjectives in the fourth line ("Her *undressed, operated-on, dressed* body"). It's worth pausing to unpack the indignity implied in these three successive adjectives. First, the friend was *undressed,* or stripped down (we recall how earlier in the poem the speaker has remarked, "How often they have *undressed* me, / The eyes of strangers!"). But instead of being the object of a fantasy, she has now been *operated-on,* that is, subjected to a failed surgery or surgeries. Finally, she is *dressed* again, though now as a corpse. It's hard to ignore the implication that food is also *dressed* — that is, cleaned and prepared. This secondary meaning seems to apply since the speaker in the supermarket has stated outright that for so many years she "was good enough to eat." Jaunty surface meets sinister undertow as the speaker equates her friend's dead body to herself. So too the rhymes in the last stanza of "Next Day" act as a ghostly haunting of sounds; it's not just the irrefutable connection of "have" and "grave," but also the identical rhyme on the word "exceptional" and the off-rhyme on the words "anybody" and "solitary" that drive home the inexorable truth: "no one is exceptional, / No one has anything, I'm anybody."

It was characteristic of Jarrell to put his technique in the service of what he took to be an ordinary woman's voice. Jarrell's poem is not authentic or convincing because he learned about and understood female experience per se, but because he credited himself with what he called "a semi-feminine mind," and he mined his indeterminate sexual identity to project himself into another skin, another body, another self. He used all the imagination and technique available to him to propel himself across a divide, which is to say that he both recognized and displaced himself in the guise of an unnamed woman coming home from the supermarket.

J. V. CUNNINGHAM

—

"Montana Fifty Years Ago"

(1967)

J. V. Cunningham was a poet and scholar of scrupulous exactitude. He had a rigorous intelligence, a full command of the classical tradition, and a dry, demanding sense of poetic form. He was committed to what he called "the bare plain style," poetry freed from ornamentation, and prized clarity as well as brevity. "The mature style is what we could call the plain style if we met it in the Renaissance," his mentor Yvor Winters wrote in "The Plain Style Reborn" (1967). Cunningham's poems are quietly moving too. Like Ben Jonson and Edwin Arlington Robinson, two of his primary models, or Edgar Bowers and Thom Gunn, two of his contemporaries, he often generalized the situations in his poems, though the feeling is personal and somehow breaks through. As Gunn said about Fulke Greville, "the generality is a summation of experience and not an evasion of it."

Here is "Montana Fifty Years Ago," a poem of heartache that concludes *Poems and Epigrams (1960–1970)*. It is written in blank verse so skillfully varied that it sounds like natural speech. There is a deft syncopation between the sentences and the lines.

Montana Fifty Years Ago

Gaunt kept house with her child for the old man,
Met at the train, dust-driven as the sink
She came to, the child white as the alkali.
To the West distant mountains, the Big Lake
To the Northeast. Dead trees and almost dead
In the front yard, the front door locked and nailed,
A handpump in the sink. Outside, a land
Of gophers, cottontails, and rattlesnakes,
In good years of alfalfa, oats, and wheat.
Root cellar, blacksmith shop, milk house, and barn,
Granary, corral. An old *World Almanac*
To thumb at night, the child coughing, the lamp smoked,
The chores done. So he came to her one night,
To the front room, now bedroom, and moved in.
Nothing was said, nothing was ever said.
And then the child died and she disappeared.
This was Montana fifty years ago.

Cunningham's bare-bones style was well-suited to his evocation of Montana in the past. He told an interviewer that the poem refers to the dry-land ranch where he spent each summer, growing up in Montana. "The poem 'Montana Fifty Years Ago' is an attempt to summarize not so much my own experience, but to put into form the kind of situation out at the ranch."

"Montana Fifty Years Ago" is a companion to his poem "Montana Pastoral," which also derives from those summers on the ranch, which, he took care to note, was thirty-six miles from Billings, over the rimrock in the Wheat Basin Country. Both poems are rugged western pastorals — rural, spare, unsentimental. The speaker is at a remove from the people he is writing about. Cunningham wrote "Montana Fifty Years Ago" in 1967, which sets the scene in 1917, part of a remote western world, far from the raging war. He was six years old at the time of the poem's events. He was fifty-six and teaching Renaissance literature at Brandeis University when he wrote it.

The poem comes full circle. It begins by naming a state (Montana) and a time (Fifty Years Ago), which was far off but still possible to remember, and concludes by summarizing it ("This was Montana fifty years ago"). It dramatizes a situation that stands for the whole. The very name of the woman in the poem, Gaunt, marks her as a type. We understand immediately that she embodies the characteristics of gauntness. One thinks of her as extremely lean and angular, probably haggard, like Dorothea Lange's photograph of a migrant mother. According to *The American Heritage Dictionary,* the secondary meaning of the word *gaunt* is "bleak or desolate," and that applies here too. Gauntness implies privation, being too thin, the opposite of maternal fecundity. It evokes an era.

The opening line sets the scene with a chiseled and concise sentence: "Gaunt kept house with her child for the old man." The relationship is transactional. The woman and her unnamed child are compared to their destination. She is "dust-driven as the sink / She came to," the innocent child "white as the alkali." This strange chemical comparison suggests that the child is like white alkali, a mixture of salts that forms a white crust on the soil. Since the mother is like the sink, it may be worth mentioning that an alkali can also be defined as a base that dissolves in water. The old man who owns the place is never named. We never learn the name or even the gender of the child, who is thus something of a generic figure. The poem seems to be saying: these are the sorts of people who lived there then, this was the place.

Cunningham characterizes a rugged world. What the land was like, what grew there, what stood on the property. Much of the poem turns out to be a series of short catalogs. He renders in sentence fragments a world of tasks, hard work, open country. By the end of the day, there is nothing to do but thumb a dated *World Almanac.* The chores are done, the child sick. The poem employs a highly condensed plot: a nearly anonymous woman with a child arrived to do the cooking and cleaning for an old man who simply moved into her room, which therefore became their bedroom. What was their relationship? Was it anything more than a convenience, two people huddled for comfort in a lonely place?

We have no idea how these people felt about their situation because everything was unspoken between them. The poem concludes with three one-line sentences, each neatly balanced and end-stopped, each a declaration unto itself.

1. Nothing was said, nothing was ever said.
2. And then the child died and she disappeared.
3. This was Montana fifty years ago.

Why is this reticence so heartbreaking? Because no one ever spoke of what was happening to them; because a child died and the mother disappeared, without saying a word, and was never heard from again; because an old man was deserted and once more left to endure an unspeakable loneliness. It's not just the suffering of these three unnamed people we are talking about, who fall outside of recorded history; it's all of Montana in 1917, a bleak and beautiful western world, now forever gone but captured in a short poem.

— —

"For the Anniversary of My Death"

(1967)

W. S. Merwin's work reached one of its peaks in his bleak, apocalyptic book *The Lice* (1967). The ruthless authenticity, the stark, stripped-down style and prophetic feeling, the utter seriousness and desperate sense of a coming extinction, what one critic calls its "cool radiance," enlarged the sense of what poetry can do in the world, which seemed as if it were coming to end. The book has the feeling of last things. "If I were not human I would not be ashamed of anything," Merwin confesses ("Avoiding News by the River"); "I who have always believed too much in words" ("Fly").

The Lice was also the first full-length book in which Merwin dropped punctuation entirely. Like the French poets Guillaume Apollinaire and Jean Follain, whom he translated, he would never pick it up again in poetry. He had come to believe that poetry, more so than prose, has a strong relationship to the spoken word. Using punctuation felt like the nailing the words to the page. Rather, he sought the movement and lightness of the spoken word. So too he had found a way to make silence an integral part of his music.

There was also a new metaphysical dimension to some of his poems, such as "For the Anniversary of My Death":

For the Anniversary of My Death

Every year without knowing it I have passed the day
When the last fires will wave to me
And the silence will set out
Tireless traveler
Like the beam of a lightless star

Then I will no longer
Find myself in life as in a strange garment
Surprised at the earth
And the love of one woman
And the shamelessness of men
As today writing after three days of rain
Hearing the wren sing and the falling cease
And bowing not knowing to what

"For the Anniversary of My Death," which is carefully divided into two
parts, like a theorem in algebra, has a clear and clever premise, a universal rec-
ognition. Every year we pass our death-day, just as we do our birthday, but
without knowing it. We can never mark this fateful day in advance. An anni-
versary is usually something we celebrate, but this one goes unnoticed. In fact,
it will be unknown to us until the very end. Realizing this, we must now ap-
proach every day with a sense of unease and awe.

Merwin's poem of self-mourning begins with this recognition ("Every year
without knowing it I have passed the day") and immediately moves into the
realm of farewell on a cosmic scale. The images are elemental, the abstractions
immense: the "last fires" that wave, the silence that sets out like the beam of
a remote star. A "lightless star," an apparent oxymoron, is a dead star. Silence
is characterized as a "Tireless traveler." We usually associate tirelessness with
human beings who work energetically, continuously. But here silence is the
one who is indefatigable. The end of everything is undeniable. The universe is
filled with an eternal chill.

An intricate web of sound operates throughout the first stanza. There is
also a stateliness to the rhythm. Listen to the alliterations: "*will wave*," "*silence
will set*," "*Tireless traveler*." The vowel sounds, especially the long *a*'s and *i*'s,
carefully echo each other in these five end-stopped lines. Merwin is known for

his piercingly plain style, but the thickness of sounds here seems more reminiscent of Tennyson or Dylan Thomas.

"For the Anniversary of My Death" is structured in such a way that it reads like a thirteen-line sonnet, what the poet John Hollander deemed "thirteeners." The first five-line stanza characterizes what happens every year. The imagery, though, places us outside of time, in the realm of eternity. There is an enormous leap, a decisive break, between the two parts of the poem, like a space for meditation. The second eight-line stanza shifts the poem on the word "Then." This word is consequential. The poem now focuses on the period after the speaker will have died. Contemplating his own death, he finds himself cherishing the earth as he knows it, enumerating what will be lost. He characterizes life as something he found himself wearing like "a strange garment," which can — which must — be taken off. Recall that César Vallejo described how his upper arm bones could be put on and taken off like a shirt or a jacket — *a strange garment* — in "Black Stone Lying on a White Stone." The physical or bodily recognition of death estranges experience; hence, "Then I will no longer / Find myself in life as in a strange garment / Surprised . . ." The act of being surprised takes over the speaker — and the poem.

Merwin specifically contrasts the "love of one woman" to the larger "shamelessness of men." He notes the singing of the wren, the ongoing falling of the rain. Indeed, the song of the wren begins at the precise moment that the rain ceases. Like John Keats in his last desperate fragment, "This living hand," Merwin now brings the writing of poetry itself into the poem with sudden immediacy: "As today writing after three days of rain." It is as if the ceasing of the rain finally enabled him to contemplate the hard truth of his own mortality. It focuses attention on the moment, and he becomes fully present to himself: "As today writing after three days of rain / Hearing the wren sing and the falling cease / And bowing not knowing to what." In the end, everything will be lost. This reality heightens the ways in which the earth continues to astonish us.

"For the Anniversary of My Death" is an elemental poem. There is a sense of inscrutability in the way it ends. The closure is open-ended since Merwin finds himself unexpectedly bowing, out of respect, as if in prayer, to some greater unnamed force, some large and unknown mystery.

MURIEL RUKEYSER

"Poem"

(1968)

"We are a people tending toward democracy at the level of hope," Muriel Rukeyser wrote in her treatise *The Life of Poetry* (1949). But then she added this: "on another level, the economy of the nation, the empire of business within the republic, both include in their basic premise the concept of perpetual warfare." Rukeyser understood the way that warfare has been interwoven into our history, and she opposed it with a notion of democratic possibility. She said, "To be against war is not enough, it is hardly a beginning... We are against war and the sources of war."

Rukeyser spent much of her life opposing war and trying to imagine peace. She was concerned with root causes and democratic imperatives. Here is a poem that she wrote at the height of the Vietnam War:

Poem

I lived in the first century of world wars.
Most mornings I would be more or less insane,

The newspapers would arrive with their careless stories,
The news would pour out of various devices
Interrupted by attempts to sell products to the unseen.
I would call my friends on other devices;
They would be more or less mad for similar reasons.
Slowly I would get to pen and paper,
Make my poems for others unseen and unborn.
In the day I would be reminded of those men and women
Brave, setting up signals across vast distances,
Considering a nameless way of living, of almost unimagined values.
As the lights darkened, as the lights of night brightened,
We would try to imagine them, try to find each other.
To construct peace, to make love, to reconcile
Waking with sleeping, ourselves with each other,
Ourselves with ourselves. We would try by any means
To reach the limits of ourselves, to reach beyond ourselves,
To let go the means, to wake.

I lived in the first century of these wars.

"Poem" is the work of a citizen-poet. It is written in free verse and pitched at the level of speech, not song. The poem is compressed into twenty lines, nineteen of them in a single stanza, one that breaks off on its own, freestanding. The title, "Poem," is outwardly bland and generic but inwardly ambitious because it suggests that something can be made from words and crafted into a living entity. There is still hope in the making of art. The first sentence — a line unto itself — is part pronouncement, part lament: "I lived in the first century of world wars." Rukeyser thus begins with the declaration that she is living inside a large and appalling history, a new era of global conflicts. It is an unprecedented time of killing, a nuclear world, the first century.

The second line immediately brings the poem down a notch by turning to something more daily: "Most mornings I would be more or less insane." The writer and activist Michael True points out that the word "insane," which lands with a jolt at the end of the line, is surprising in a way that the Russian poet Joseph Brodsky found characteristic of American poetry: "it violates the preconceived music of the meter with its linguistic content."

Rukeyser's poem is also surprising in the way that it is written using the modal verb "would," the past-tense form of "will," and thus talks about the past somewhat hypothetically, more or less as it happened nearly every day:

> The newspapers would arrive with their careless stories,
> The news would pour out of various devices
> Interrupted by attempts to sell products to the unseen.

Rukeyser refers here to the negligent lies of officials and the almost offhanded complicity of newspapers, which once took the government at its word. She employs the word "devices" to suggest both pieces of electronic equipment and underlying schemes, ruses, and maneuvers. The Vietnam War was the first conflict delivered and sold to people through their television sets, experienced in living rooms and bars. She notes the omnipresence of the news underwritten by advertising, the secret business driving it. This is capitalism at work — devices selling products to people who have been turned into consumers. Rukeyser was writing in the mid-to-late sixties. She was eerily prescient in perceiving the power of *devices,* such as TV sets, as a means of selling things to strangers. But the word "unseen," which lands at the end of the fifth line, will also come back to suggest poetic exchange. It will be reclaimed by the poet.

Rukeyser's poem changes when it turns to the act of writing poetry itself: "Slowly I would get to pen and paper, / Make my poems for others unseen and unborn." This is the structural turn in the poem — the recognition that the poet is a daily maker (the artist doesn't stand apart) and the poem a made thing, a message sent out to strangers, those alive now, yet somehow "unseen," and others yet "unborn." The doubling of the prefix *un-,* which means "not," takes on a positive energy here. The poem is a capsule sent out into the unknown, a gift freely given and taken.

"Poem" progresses through a hypothetical day, beginning in the morning and ending at night. Over its course an unlikely hopefulness sets in as the speaker remembers "those men and women / Brave, setting up signals across vast distances, / Considering a nameless way of living, of almost unimagined values." The poet emphasizes the adjective "Brave" by lifting it out of its normal position ("those brave men and women"), placing it after the nouns "men" and "women," and using it to hold and then kick off a new line. The implication is that it takes courage to imagine a new and still-unarticulated way of life, to create values that have not yet been imagined.

As daylight darkens and night brightens, the poem moves from memory to imagination. It transforms the act of imagining into a communal exercise. Like Guillaume Apollinaire in "The Pretty Redhead" and Nâzım Hikmet in his manifesto "On Living," Rukeyser shifts from the "I" ("I would be reminded") to a "We" ("We would try to imagine them, try to find each other"). This social turn to the common work — what Adrienne Rich would call "the dream of a common language" — is an effort to build a better world. Rukeyser sets up what she elsewhere calls "exemplary lives" as models, figures like Pablo Neruda and Käthe Kollwitz, who connected art to social justice, who used it to link their personal lives to political subjects.

Rukeyser has tried to imagine them, she says,

> To construct peace, to make love, to reconcile
> Waking with sleeping, ourselves with each other,
> Ourselves with ourselves.

First of all, peace is not something that automatically comes to us, but something to be constructed, like a work of art. It is something made, like love. Rukeyser is unusual as a political poet because she is careful to locate the enemy within as well as outside herself. It's true, she argues, that we need to become reconciled with one another, but we also need to reconcile our conscious and unconscious minds, "Waking with sleeping," "Ourselves with ourselves." She offers a fraught psychological recognition: we are all divided within; we need to unite with others and also make peace with ourselves. Rukeyser would return to this theme in later poems, such as "Waking This Morning," where she characterizes herself as "a violent woman" who is trying to be "non-violent" one day at a time. She recognizes this as especially challenging because the days are often filled with violence.

There is great hopefulness in the ideal that "We would try by any means / To reach the limits of ourselves, to reach beyond ourselves, / To let go the means, to wake." This awakening means not just being well-informed and up to date, but also coming into a state of greater awareness, of fuller consciousness. She seems to anticipate the current notion of being *woke* — that is, fully alert to discrimination or injustice of any sort. For her, this meant going beyond the self. The final line stands alone, reverberating back through the poem, echoing and changing the beginning:

I lived in the first century of these wars.

Michael True finds a great reconciliation in this last line, a perennial optimism, which associates the violence within with the violence without, "peacemaking in the individual and peacemaking in the social order." This has an appealing utopianism. But perhaps the last line also suggests that warfare is ongoing, that people will have to live through a second and third century of never-ending conflict. So far Rukeyser's prediction has proved prescient — we are now living in that second century. But the dream too is inscribed into her poem: "We are a people tending toward democracy at the level of hope."

ETHERIDGE KNIGHT

"The Idea of Ancestry"

(1968)

I've never been able to shake what Etheridge Knight said on the back cover of his first book, a thirty-two-page chapbook, *Poems from Prison* (Broadside Press, 1968): "I died in Korea from a shrapnel wound, and narcotics resurrected me. I died in 1960 from a prison sentence and poetry brought me back to life." One might say that, in a roundabout way, his early life led him to enlist in the army and serve in the Korean War, which led him to narcotics, which forced him to the criminal side of the street, which landed him in prison, which finally led him to poetry. As the poet Terrance Hayes puts it, "Knight's biography is a story of restless Americanness, African Americanness, and poetry. It has some Faulknerian family saga in it, some midcentury migration story, lots of masculine tragedy, lots of soul-of-the-artist lore."

Knight started writing poetry in prison in order to transform his rage, which was killing him. His sentence was brutally unfair, and he was so furious that he could scarcely remember his first months in jail. He was transferred from one prison to another. Writing poetry literally became a way to save himself. Knight was already an expert at "toasts," a Black vernacular form that prefigured rap and has its roots in the oral traditions of enslaved Africans. The poems are long improvised narratives about rough, rowdy, and fearless heroes, who all have what the folklorist Roger Abrahams deems the "amorality" of the trickster. Knight carried his trickster mentality and gift for the vernacular into his written verse, which he often recited from memory. His poems are decidedly literary, but he never lost his sense of street language. And his true underlying subject was always freedom.

Here is his iconic early poem "The Idea of Ancestry":

The Idea of Ancestry

1

Taped to the wall of my cell are 47 pictures: 47 black
faces: my father, mother, grandmothers (1 dead), grand-
fathers (both dead), brothers, sisters, uncles, aunts,
cousins (1st & 2nd), nieces, and nephews. They stare
across the space at me sprawling on my bunk. I know
their dark eyes, they know mine. I know their style,
they know mine. I am all of them, they are all of me;
they are farmers, I am a thief, I am me, they are thee.

I have at one time or another been in love with my mother,
1 grandmother, 2 sisters, 2 aunts (1 went to the asylum),
and 5 cousins. I am now in love with a 7-yr-old niece
(she sends me letters written in large block print, and
her picture is the only one that smiles at me).

I have the same name as 1 grandfather, 3 cousins, 3 nephews,
and 1 uncle. The uncle disappeared when he was 15, just took
off and caught a freight (they say). He's discussed each year
when the family has a reunion, he causes uneasiness in
the clan, he is an empty space. My father's mother, who is 93
and who keeps the Family Bible with everybody's birth dates
(and death dates) in it, always mentions him. There is no
place in her Bible for "whereabouts unknown."

2
Each fall the graves of my grandfathers call me, the brown
hills and red gullies of mississippi send out their electric
messages, galvanizing my genes. Last yr / like a salmon quitting
the cold ocean-leaping and bucking up his birthstream / I
hitchhiked my way from LA with 16 caps in my packet and a
monkey on my back. And I almost kicked it with the kinfolks.
I walked barefooted in my grandmother's backyard / I smelled the old
land and the woods / I sipped cornwhiskey from fruit jars with the men /
I flirted with the women / I had a ball till the caps ran out
and my habit came down. That night I looked at my grandmother
and split / my guts were screaming for junk / but I was almost
contented / I had almost caught up with me.
(The next day in Memphis I cracked a croaker's crib for a fix.)

This yr there is a gray stone wall damming my stream, and when
the falling leaves stir my genes, I pace my cell or flop on my bunk
and stare at 47 black faces across the space. I am all of them,
they are all of me, I am me, they are thee, and I have no children
to float in the space between.

Knight said that he started making up the poem "The Idea of Ancestry"
one time when he had been in solitary confinement for thirty or forty days.
Called by a number rather than a name for five years, he had begun to forget
who he was. Thus, he tried to reconnect to his roots, his extended family, by
imagining forty-seven photographs taped to the wall of his cell. His sister Eu-
nice Knight-Bowens, who did so much to keep his legacy alive, also confirmed
that the poem wasn't actually composed in a prison cell at the Indiana State
Penitentiary in Terre Haute, where her brother was serving what would turn
out to be an eight-year sentence for armed robbery, but rather in solitary con-
finement, where he couldn't possibly have access to a trove of family photo-
graphs. But in his mind he was crossing a divide. By imagining that he could
see the faces of relatives on the walls of the "hole," he was seeking and establish-
ing the connections that would wind him back to the world.

Knight's poem consists of forty-two lines divided into two distinct parts.

The first section, in long Whitmanesque lines, borders on prose and creates a feeling of spaciousness within confinement. We never lose sight of his physical imprisonment, but we also respond to the freedom of his imagination. This section begins with a catalog of his extended family, living and dead. The enjambment in the first line emphasizes that these are " 47 black / faces." Knight doesn't have the opportunity for a face-to-face encounter, which the French philosopher Emmanuel Lévinas views as the basis for human sociality, but he does seem "ordered and ordained" by his relationship to the faces in his family photographs. His African American heritage consoles him as he scrolls through the list. Notice the emphatic enjambment ("They *stare* / across the space at me sprawling on my bunk") as he traverses the gulf, a kind of void, between his bunk and the wall. The rhythm builds off repetition, and the stanza intensifies:

> I know
> their dark eyes, they know mine. I know their style,
> they know mine. I am all of them, they are all of me;
> they are farmers, I am a thief, I am me, they are thee.

This refrain is a realization of identity and difference. Knight's speaker asserts that he knows each and every one of the family members and they "know" him too; he is not just one but "all of them." This is a statement of solidarity. At the same time, he has taken a path that separates him from them, a painful recognition expressed in four short sentences jammed together in the culminating line of the stanza: "they are farmers, I am a thief, I am me, they are thee." The word "thee" — an archaic or dialect word for "you" — has a kind of biblical formality here, a definite feeling of otherness.

The feeling changes with the next stanza, which begins: "I have at one time or another been in love with my mother ..." We normally reserve the idea of being in love for erotic attachments, but the speaker uses these words to catalog his affection for all the women in his family: his grandmother, who is mentioned five times in the poem, his two sisters and two aunts (including the one sent to an asylum, whose story is left untold), and five cousins. The list ends with his seven-year-old niece, who writes to him in a child's hand. She is the only one he can imagine smiling at him, perhaps because of her innocence.

The next stanza turns to the men in the poet's short ancestry. We learn that Etheridge Knight had the same name as one grandfather, three cousins, three nephews, and an uncle. The poem then becomes chattier, telling about an uncle who just took off and (supposedly) hopped a freight train. This is where we learn about the annual family reunion and the unknown uncle as an "empty space" there, a recognition that rebounds back to the speaker. He remembers how his ninety-three-year-old grandmother never forgets her lost young one. "There is no / place in her Bible for 'whereabouts unknown.'" The line hovers at the word "no" before dropping down to "place," and then the implacable coldness and impersonality of the phrase "whereabouts unknown" registers. The stanza ends with a feeling of being lost, with an underlying terror that the speaker too will someday become an empty space.

Notice how the punctuation radically changes in the second half of the poem. Memory speeds up, and Knight starts abbreviating words and jamming them together. He also starts using the slash as a punctuation mark. This presses activities together even as it separates him from others. Knight explained his signature style in an interview with Patricia L. Hill in 1978: "My lines, my form, everything is simply meant to approximate the spoken words. When I leave out periods, or use slash marks, or jam words together, or pull them apart, or leave a space, it's simply meant to try to help the reader say . . . [the poem] the way I say it." He is trying out a new mode of punctuation to notate the way the poem sounds to him.

The second section dramatically picks up the pace of the poem. It begins with a sense of ritual, a return to the place where he was born: "Each fall the graves of my grandfathers call me, the brown / hills and red gullies of mississippi send out their electric / messages, galvanizing my genes." The speaker's dead grandfathers, now rooted in the ground of his native Mississippi, seem to be calling out and activating some biological code within him. This ritual feeling then turns to a particular reminiscence ("Last yr") of hitchhiking home under the spell of addiction, which he almost "kicked" under the spell of his kin. He implicitly contrasts his life in the city with the world of his rural family ("I walked barefooted in my grandmother's backyard / I smelled the old / land and the woods"). The soothing warmth saves him for a little while, but then addiction takes over again. He was "almost contented" because he had "almost" caught up with and found himself again. But that doubling of the word *almost* is painful:

That night I looked at my grandmother
and split / my guts were screaming for junk / but I was almost

contented / I had almost caught up with me.
(The next day in Memphis I cracked a croaker's crib for a fix.)

The last five-line stanza returns to the present tense. The poem circles back to the beginning, interlacing the warm natural imagery of rural life with the brutal reality of imprisonment: "This yr there is a gray stone wall damming my stream, and when / the falling leaves stir my genes, I pace my cell or flop on my bunk / and stare at 47 black faces across the space." The speaker's two worlds are colliding, summoning the musical refrain of the poem. He reiterates with new understanding his sense of identity and difference ("I am all of them, / they are all of me, I am me, they are thee"), but now adds a harsh recognition: "and I have no children / to float in the space between." His own childlessness haunts him because he has nothing and no one to fill the empty space between his ancestry and himself. This enlarges the sense of solitary confinement that launched the poem in the first place.

"The Idea of Ancestry" is a crucial poem of the African American family, but it is also relevant to anyone who can trace their lineage back only two or three generations. It is a poem of connection and disconnection, of imprisonment, memory, and freedom.

JOHN BERRYMAN

"Henry's Understanding"

(1969)

Henry is the ironic hero of John Berryman's signature sequence collected in *The Dream Songs* (1969). In the first installment, *77 Dream Songs* (1964), Berryman took pains to separate himself from Henry and treat him as a persona, a character different from himself. He always closely resembled his main character, who often served as what Richard Poirier called a "performing self," but the separation started to relax and break down in the second part, *His Toy, His Dream, His Rest* (1968). Henry becomes a very thin persona. In Berryman's last two books, *Love & Fame* (1971) and *Delusions, Etc. of John Berryman* (1972), the mask slips entirely, and there doesn't seem any perceptible distance between the character Henry and the poet who created him.

At night I return to Berryman's last, needy, grief-stricken poems. Lyrics such as "He Resigns," "Henry by Night," and "Henry's Understanding" have a terrifying clarity and simplicity, a dark vulnerability and honesty, a wounded splendor.

Henry's Understanding

He was reading late, at Richard's, down in Maine,
aged 32? Richard & Helen long in bed,
my good wife long in bed.
All I had to do was strip & get into my bed,
putting the marker in the book, & sleep,
& wake to a hot breakfast.

Off the coast was an island, P'tit Manaan,
the bluff from Richard's lawn was almost sheer.
A chill at four o'clock.
It only takes a few minutes to make a man.
A concentration upon now & here.
Suddenly, unlike Bach,

& horribly, unlike Bach, it occurred to me
that *one* night, instead of warm pajamas,
I'd take off all my clothes
& cross the damp cold lawn & down the bluff
into the terrible water & walk forever
under it out toward the island.

The title, "Henry's Understanding," establishes a third-person perspective; there is a clear demarcation between the creator and the main character. This sense of character carries through the first line, "He was reading late, at Richard's, down in Maine." Like Berryman, Henry is reading at his friend Richard Blackmur's house in Maine. The second line turns into a question, which mimics someone trying to remember exactly when something happened: "Was he 32?" This question also changes the poem. By the third line the pretense of a third person or objective perspective falls away and the poem takes place entirely in the first person. This becomes an unabashedly personal or subjective lyric.

The Dream Songs have a nervous energy and rely on a slangy, idiosyncratic lingo. The ampersands help create a quirky informality and offhandedness. Berryman's signature style carries over to "Henry's Understanding," though here the colloquial language has a more plainspoken eloquence. Stylization seems to break down under the weight of feeling.

So too "Henry's Understanding" utilizes the characteristic form that Berryman invented for the Dream Songs. The poem consists of eighteen lines: three six-line verse paragraphs. It works like an extended three-part sonnet. Berryman often rhymed stanza by stanza, but here only the middle stanza of the poem rhymes (*abcabc*). The rhythm has a ghost of pentameter beat, which is dramatically foreshortened in the third and sixth lines. Isolate the third line in each stanza, for example, and you get the full effect of the end-stopped lines:

> my good wife long in bed.

> A chill at four o'clock.

> I'd take off all my clothes

The terrifying premonition of this poem is that the speaker will one day commit suicide by walking into the sea. Foreknowledge doesn't seem to help save him. He re-creates with electric clarity the feeling of being in a guest bedroom at a friend's house in Maine. It is 4 a.m., and all he needs to do is put his book down and go to sleep. In the first stanza, he repeats the word "bed" at the end of three lines in a row — as if trying to convince himself that if he goes to sleep, everything will be better in the morning. But 4 a.m. is the pit of all hours, the dark night of the soul.

Berryman uses rhyme to emphasize the end-words in the middle stanza. The place, "P'tit Manaan," links to an essential figure, "a man"; the word "sheer," which suggests that the bluff from the lawn was both steep and diaphanous, connects to "here," meaning "this very place, this world, the present"; and the time, "four o'clock," turns into the name of the exemplary composer Johann Sebastian "Bach." The poet presses down on the decisive moment:

> It only takes a few minutes to make a man.
> A concentration upon now & here.

He reverses the word order in the idiom "here and now" and thus changes its emphasis. The word "now" becomes paramount, and the phrase lands on the word "here." It's as if a certain moment in time determines a person's fate.

The poem turns on the word "Suddenly" at the end of the second stanza. The speaker contrasts himself to Bach, the great composer of spiritual joy. It's not just that he is "unlike Bach" (the line and stanza break create extra emphasis) but that he is "horribly, unlike Bach," who found salvation in music. The word "horribly" hovers. "Suddenly" and also "horribly," it occurs to the speaker what he is going to do.

Many of the poems in the collection *Delusions, Etc. of John Berryman* sound a religious note. They are idiosyncratic prayers filled with spiritual anguish and longing. But the conversion does not hold. As expressed in "Henry's Understanding," as in "He Resigns," Berryman's speaker will not be able to defend himself against his own alcoholic depression. And so there is a dark inevitability to the last stanza of "Henry's Understanding," a hopeless realization that he would someday take off all his clothes and walk naked across "the damp cold lawn & down the bluff / into the terrible water & walk forever / under it out toward the island." Notice how the line breaks mimic the action, the plunge from "down the bluff" and the landing on the word "into," the long hovering pause over the phrase "walk forever" and the recognition that he is going "under it out toward . . ." He is drowning himself by walking into the water but, as the poet A. Alvarez noted in a review, the tone is somehow open-ended. Maybe he will eventually arrive somewhere after all, some lost place that he had longed for since childhood.

John Berryman was irreversibly damaged by life and obsessed by suicide. He passed on January 7, 1972, some three years after he wrote "Henry's Understanding." But perhaps it would be consoling to think that in some sense he entered the terrible water and then walked forever under it out toward the island.

L. E. SISSMAN

—

"A Deathplace"

(1969)

In 1965, L. E. Sissman, an advertising executive, discovered that he had Hodgkin's disease, an incurable illness that he recognized as "routinely fatal." He was thirty-seven years old and thereafter worked with a palpable sense of time's urgency. Chemotherapy gave him intermissions of health for eleven more years. But he had been "introduced" to dying, and from then on wrote ardently, incessantly, as if his life depended on it. His days were numbered ("numbers" is an old name for poems), and he numbered them in return. That's how he emerged as a poet. Or as he put it, "Instead of a curtain falling, a curtain rose. And stayed up, revealing a stage decked in defining light."

Sissman's first book was titled *Dying: An Introduction* (1968). It was as if his entire life had been a preparation for this honorable, somewhat formal meeting, which would spur him to become the poet he was meant to become, even as it drained the world of its substance. There is a breezy effortlessness to the epigrammatic couplets and flexible blank-verse lines weighted with earthly observations. *Dying: An Introduction* has a verbal gaiety, a joyous exuberance, a sense of fleeting grace undaunted but deepened by fatal illness. It also has the gravity of late knowledge, of memories saved from oblivion and held up to the light.

    Sissman carried the same spirit into his next book, *Scattered Returns* (1969), which opens with "A Deathplace."

A Deathplace

Very few people know where they will die,
But I do: in a brick-faced hospital,
Divided, not unlike Caesarean Gaul,
Into three parts: the Dean Memorial
Wing, in the classic cast of 1910,
Green-grated in unglazed, Aeolian
Embrasures; the Maud Wiggin Building, which
Commemorates a dog-jawed Boston bitch
Who fought the brass down to their whipcord knees
In World War I, and won enlisted men
Some decent hospitals, and, being rich,
Donated her own granite monument;
The Mandeville Pavilion, pink-brick tent
With marble piping, flying snapping flags
Above the entry where our bloody rags
Are rolled to be sponged and sewn again.
Today is fair; tomorrow, scouring rain
(If only my own tears) will see me in
Those jaundiced and distempered corridors
Off which the five-foot-wide doors slowly close.
White as my skimpy chiton, I will cringe
Before the pinpoint of the least syringe;
Before the buttered catheter goes in;
Before the I.V.'s lisp and drip begins
Inside my skin; before the rubber hand
Upon the lancet takes aim and descends
To lay me open, and upon its thumb
Retracts the trouble, a malignant plum;
And, finally, I'll quail before the hour
When the authorities shut off the power

In that vast hospital, and in my bed
I'll feel my blood go thin, go white, the red,
The rose all leached away, and I'll go dead.
Then will the business of life resume:
The muffled trolley wheeled into my room,
The off-white blanket blanking off my face,
The stealing, secret, private, *largo* race
Down halls and elevators to the place
I'll be consigned to for transshipment, cased
In artificial air and light: the ward
That's underground; the terminal; the morgue.
Then one fine day when all the smart flags flap,
A booted man in black with a peaked cap
Will call for me and troll me down the hall
And slot me into the black car. That's all.

The jaunty rhythm and rhyme in this poem seem kindred to the work of Joseph Brodsky or Frederick Seidel, a comic postmodern timing that suddenly swerves and plunges into something more disturbing. There's something civic or sociable about the form. Sissman begins with a simple premise — "Very few people know where they will die, / But I do" — and then starts to roll out the iambic pentameter lines with easy fluency. He warms up by describing the three wings of the hospital, which he knows so well and gleefully compares to "Caesarean Gaul." Julius Caesar's *Gallic Wars* famously begins with the sentence "Gaul is a whole divided into three parts." The ironic description of the three wings of the hospital almost operates as a weaponized defense against the true realization that the speaker comes to in this poem. For example, we can almost feel the nasty, satirical pleasure he gets out of describing the formidable Maud Wiggin as "a dog-jawed Boston bitch / Who fought the brass down to their whipcord knees / In World War I . . ." The way he fools around with consonance (from "*Green-gr*ated" to "un*gl*azed" and "*B*uilding" to "*Bos*-ton *b*itch" to "*br*ass") increases the sense of playfulness.

The first line of this poem doesn't rhyme — as if to isolate the observation ("Very few people know where they will die") — but after that the poem flies along on heroic couplets, which sometimes extend to three lines. The rhyming iambic pentameter, or five-stress, couplet was introduced into English by Chaucer in "The Prologue to the Legend of Good Women" and used for most of *The Canterbury Tales.* It has sometimes been nicknamed riding rhyme, probably because the pilgrims reeled off such rhymes while riding to Canterbury. John Dryden and Alexander Pope discovered that the closed form of the couplet was well suited to aphoristic wit. Sissman rides along and enjambs lines describing the hospital in one long stanza of forty-five lines.

Everything starts to change when the speaker describes the entry "where our bloody rags / Are rolled to be sponged and sewn again." One-third of the way through, then, the poem turns:

> Today is fair; tomorrow, scouring rain
> (If only my own tears) will see me in
> Those jaundiced and distempered corridors
> Off which the five-foot-wide doors slowly close.

It comes as a surprise, perhaps to the speaker as much as to the reader, when the scouring rain makes him think wistfully of his own tears. He projects a kind of animal sickness onto the yellow corridors themselves, which seem both "jaundiced and distempered." The doors close. Thereafter the nonchalance gives way and the tone darkens considerably.

Now the speaker chronicles something more personal, emotionally closer to home — the predictable sequence of events related to his own death. We feel it as he begins to cringe while delineating the surgery, including "the pinpoint of the least syringe," "the buttered catheter," the lisping and dripping I.V., and then the "malignant plum," his death sentence. The poem pauses for the word "finally," and the speaker begins to quail "before the hour / When the authorities shut off the power / In that vast hospital . . ." Sissman captures the eerie feeling of a hospital at night. The power shut-off signifies the speaker's approaching death. He details how blood thins from red to white, the color leaches out of everything, and the end comes abruptly. He doesn't say "and I die," but instead "and I'll go dead," as if the power generator has shut off in him too.

Soon the lights go up again, and throughout the hospital the business of life resumes. The speaker imagines what comes next with uncanny precision, though even then he can't resist playing with the word "blank," which is buried in two other words: "The off-white *blank*et *blank*ing off my face." So too he captures the feeling of a "*largo* race," which is to say a "race / Down halls and elevators" with a tempo that is slow and dignified, like the music for a funeral procession. Step by step, he pictures how he will be transferred to the morgue and then slotted into a black car by an undertaker. The poem closes with a matter-of-fact, resigned shrug, a simple two-word declaration: "That's all."

L. E. Sissman carried on his anguished playfulness for two more books, *Pursuit of Honor* (1971) and *Hello, Darkness* (1978), a characteristically jaunty title for his posthumously published collected poems. His last poems show us a decent man, a good citizen, and an "innocent bystander" looking with relentless honesty and clairvoyance at the hard details and harsh realities of his own passing.

—■—

"They Feed They Lion"

(1969)

T hey Feed They Lion" is a magisterial celebration of rage. The poem is so rhetorically charged, so rhythmically driven, that it is, in a stylistic sense, a verbal machine unlike any other in Philip Levine's work. But in another thematic sense, it is the culmination of Levine's early work, which begins in silence and failure (the desperate hush of "Silent in America"; the failure of poets who don't write in "My Poets"). Levine's first books — from *On the Edge* (1963) to *They Feed They Lion* (1972) — obsessively return to the subject of the voicelessness of the oppressed. As his work developed, he increasingly insisted on defiantly transforming blankness into language, refusing to be quieted. The theme of the necessity of violently breaking silence peaks in a poem that celebrates the racial rebellion and social insurrection of the Detroit riots of 1967. The oppressed speak through wildly destructive action.

They Feed They Lion

Out of burlap sacks, out of bearing butter,
Out of black bean and wet slate bread,

Out of the acids of rage, the candor of tar,
Out of creosote, gasoline, drive shafts, wooden dollies,
They Lion grow.
                     Out of the gray hills
Of industrial barns, out of rain, out of bus ride,
West Virginia to Kiss My Ass, out of buried aunties,
Mothers hardening like pounded stumps, out of stumps,
Out of the bones' need to sharpen and the muscles' to stretch,
They Lion grow.
                  Earth is eating trees, fence posts,
Gutted cars, earth is calling in her little ones,
"Come home, come home!" From pig balls,
From the ferocity of pig driven to holiness,
From the furred ear and the full jowl come
The repose of the hung belly, from the purpose
They Lion grow.
                  From the sweet glues of the trotters
Come the sweet kinks of the fist, from the full flower
Of the hams the thorax of caves,
From "Bow Down" come "Rise Up,"
Come they Lion from the reeds of shovels,
The grained arm that pulls the hands,
They Lion grow.
                  From my five arms and all my hands,
From all my white sins forgiven, they feed,
From my car passing under the stars,
They Lion, from my children inherit,
From the oak turned to a wall, they Lion,
From they sack and they belly opened
And all that was hidden burning on the oil-stained earth
They feed they Lion and he comes.

Levine noted that he wrote "They Feed They Lion" when he returned to
Detroit just after the riots to see what had happened to his hometown. He was
scared by what he found, especially because the riots took place in the neigh-
borhood where he had grown up. He was now both an insider and an outsider.
The poem refers to driving around the city, which is its actual backdrop — a

white man passing through Black neighborhoods ("From all my white sins forgiven, they feed, / From my car passing under the stars"). He registers it all with shock, a roiling mix of emotions.

Here is his story of how he came up with the title, a startling linguistic formula:

> I was working alongside a guy in Detroit — a black guy named Eugene — when I was probably about twenty-four. He was a somewhat older guy, and we were sorting universal joints, which are part of the driveshaft of a car. The guy who owned the place had bought used ones, and we were supposed to sort the ones that could be rebuilt and made into usable replacement parts from the ones that were too badly damaged. So we spread them out on the concrete floor, and we were looking at them carefully, because we were the guys who'd then do the job of rebuilding them. We had two sacks that we were putting them in — burlap sacks — and at one point Eugene held up a sack, and on it were the words "Detroit Municipal Zoo." And he laughed and said, "They feed they lion they meal in they sacks."

This memory also jumpstarts the action. The poet takes the joke — using the detritus of junked autos as food for the wild animals of Detroit — and transforms it into the metaphor that drives the poem. As you reread the first stanza, note too the anaphoric repetition of the phrase "Out of," the deliberate rhythmic balance — a caesura neatly divides each of the first five lines — and growing musical drive. The repetition of the letter *b* in the first two lines threads together the words, and so does the *d* in the next two lines.

> Out of *b*urlap sacks, || out of *b*earing *b*utter,
> Out of *b*lack *b*ean || and wet slate *b*read,
> Out of the aci*d*s of rage, || the can*d*or of tar,
> Out of creosote, gasoline, || *d*rive shafts, woo*d*en *d*ollies,
> They Lion grow.

Everything is incendiary and combustible here. Levine uses "acids," a word related to chemistry, to characterize the intense emotional state "of rage"; he takes the quality of "candor," or frankness, and applies it to "tar," a sticky black liquid made from thick oil. "Creosote," an extremely flammable byproduct of wood combustion, also consists mainly of tar, a highly flammable viscous liquid, and so it's obvious what will happen if you place it next to gasoline.

The word "Lion" leaps out of the fifth line. In this poem, Levine uses this word, which is always capitalized, as both noun (as in "the Lion") and verb (as in "to Lion"). "They" becomes both subject (as in "They Feed") and possessive pronoun (as in "They Lion," meaning "Their Lion"). This sinuous syntactical energy and ambiguity give the poem a sweeping musical and rhetorical authority, a sense of a city about to burn, a psychological understanding of what motivates people to move from "Bow Down" to "Rise Up."

Levine marshals the Black vernacular to summon up the Great Migration, the movement of millions of African Americans from the rural South to the industrializing North. Detroit, among other cities, was completely transformed from about 1900 to 1940, when the population of Wayne County, Michigan, grew from around 350,000 to more than two million. By 1967, African Americans represented more than 40 percent of Detroit's overall population. In Levine's dramatic condensed version, the journey north mixes with the growth of a rough beast, a mythical Lion, slouching not toward Bethlehem, as in W. B. Yeats's "The Second Coming," but toward a gritty Midwestern city, which would suffer its own apocalypse. The poem rides the vernacular, and yet the long lines — and the rhetorical repetition of the phrase "Out of" — move the language beyond everyday speech into the realm of prophecy:

> Out of the gray hills
> Of industrial barns, out of rain, out of bus ride,
> West Virginia to Kiss My Ass, out of buried aunties,
> Mothers hardening like pounded stumps, out of stumps,
> Out of the bones' need to sharpen and the muscles' to stretch,
> They Lion grow.

Levine compresses the long bus ride by citing two locations, "from West Virginia to Kiss My Ass," as if "Kiss My Ass," that familiar colloquialism, was actually the name of a city or state. In other words, he uses an insult to identify a place, a state of mind, and the pissed-off attitude that could be found in the urban Midwest. He recognizes that what is growing emerges from the people who have come before, out of "buried aunties"; out of the hard work of women, "Mothers hardening like pounded stumps"; and out of the failed land, "out of stumps." It's as if an animal is coming together out of the land and the people: "Out of the bones' need to sharpen and the muscles' to stretch."

In the next section, Levine recognizes the importance of the pig to Black culture, especially Black Southern culture, and he uses this most despised of animals to create movement toward a furious sacrifice, a near-sacred reckoning. The riots began when the police raided an after-hours bar, or "blind pig." Formally, the lengthening stanzas enact the feeling that something violent is ominously building: a Lion (that most majestic of African creatures) is growing. The poet Paul Zweig once noted that this Lion "is a mockery of St. Mark's biblical lion," a winged, roaring, triumphant symbol of Christian salvation, because when this lion comes "man and earth will be devoured by one hunger." The words "Out of" are now replaced by phrases beginning with the word "From." Something is growing that cannot be stopped.

> Earth is eating trees, fence posts,
> Gutted cars, earth is calling in her little ones,
> "Come home, come home!" From pig balls,
> From the ferocity of pig driven to holiness,
> From the furred ear and the full jowl come
> The repose of the hung belly, from the purpose
> They Lion grow.
> From the sweet glues of the trotters
> Come the sweet kinks of the fist, from the full flower
> Of the hams the thorax of caves,
> From "Bow Down" come "Rise Up,"
> Come they Lion from the reeds of shovels,
> The grained arm that pulls the hands,
> They Lion grow.

Levine fuses a host of influences into a daring new whole in "They Feed They Lion." The splendid twists and turns of colloquial Black speech marry the incantatory rhythms of the biblical prophets, and the influence of earlier poets can also be felt, as in the anaphora of Christopher Smart's "Jubilate Agno":

For a man speaks HIMSELF from the crown of his head to the sole of his feet.

    For a LION roars HIMSELF complete from head to tail.

    Likewise Walt Whitman's "Out of the Cradle Endlessly Rocking" creates the stylistic model for moving from

> *Out of* the cradle endlessly rocking,
> *Out of* the mocking-bird's throat, the musical shuttle,
> *Out of* the Ninth-month midnight . . .

to

> *From* the memories of the bird that chanted to me,
> *From* your memories, sad brother, from the fitful risings and fallings
>   I heard,
> *From* under that yellow half-moon late-risen and swollen as if with
>   tears . . .

So too in his memoir-essay "The Poet in New York in Detroit," Levine acknowledges his debt to Federico García Lorca, especially the sequence *Poet in New York,* and stated that he could never have written the opening lines of "They Feed They Lion" if he hadn't discovered the furious confrontation of images in "The King of Harlem." Levine also learned something from the wildly inventive mixed-diction language of John Berryman and Dylan Thomas. For example, the phrase "From my five arms and all my hands" comes right out of Thomas's playbook. Here Levine exaggerates the image of arms and hands to give the feeling of something monstrous continuing to grow.

    Levine cryptically employs a host of religious echoes and allusions as this thirty-three-line poem builds to its final apocalyptic conclusion:

>   From my five arms and all my hands,
> From all my white sins forgiven, they feed,
> From my car passing under the stars,
> They Lion, from my children inherit,
> From the oak turned to a wall, they Lion,

From they sack and they belly opened
And all that was hidden burning on the oil-stained earth
They feed they Lion and he comes.

The sacrifice has been laid out. The rebellion has come, the meek have inherited the earth, or whatever is left of it in the industrial Midwest. This is Detroit, the Motor City, where Nature has come to its dead end — the oak turned to a wall — and the oil-stained earth is burning. All hell has been loosed and an overdue reckoning has come to America.

——

"The Small Square"

(1972)

The Portuguese poet Sophia de Mello Breyner Andresen said that poetry requires "unflagging intransigence." She believed that a poem "speaks not of ideal life but of actual life: the angle of a window; the reverberation of streets, cities, rooms; shadows along a wall; the appearance of faces; the silence, distance and shine of stars; the breathing of night; the perfume of the linden-flower and oregano." Andresen's sensuous and textured depiction of "actual life," her feeling for the physicality of the world, is what she brings to "The Small Square," which is also powered by something eerie and unseen: the mysterious presence of death, the ruthless passage of time.

The Small Square

My life had taken the shape of the small square
That autumn when your death was meticulously getting ready
I clung to the square because you loved
The humble and nostalgic humanity of its small shops
Where clerks fold and unfold ribbons and cloth

I tried to become you for you were going to die
And all life there would cease being mine
I tried to smile the way you smiled
At the newsagent at the tobacconist
And at the woman without legs selling violets
I asked the woman without legs to pray for you
I lit candles before all the altars
Of the churches located on one side of this square
For as soon as I opened my eyes I saw I read
The vocation of eternity written on your face
I summoned the streets the places the people
That had been witnesses of your face
In hopes they would call you in hopes they would unravel
The fabric that death was weaving in you

The speaker of "The Small Square" ("A pequena praça") remembers a time when her life itself had narrowed to the shape or form of a little square, "the small square," the only one that had come to matter. The poem is an autumnal reminiscence and takes place in the past tense. It will prove to be an elegy. Just as Anna Akhmatova addresses Mikhail Bulgakov in her elegy "In Memory of M. B.," so too does Andresen speak directly to her beloved: "That autumn when your death was meticulously getting ready." That season — and fall is the season of dying things — Death operated as a very scrupulous, active, and tireless agent, who overlooked nothing.

"The Small Square" mourns an actual (and not an ideal) life, a real person. It does not internally identify the "you" who is being addressed. But the speaker's intimate knowledge of the person's daily schedule and domestic routine, life lived at the most granular level, as well as her comfortableness in the town plaza, suggests that she is probably talking about her mother, perhaps even taking her mother's place.

Andresen was born and raised in Porto, Portugal, and the geography of the square itself suggests that she is describing Praça dos Leões in central Porto, where two churches share a single corner. This is the rambling square where her mother lived much of her life. This appears to be an autobiographical poem about the poet's mother, which is how the various translators of the poem understand it. Nonetheless, it is noteworthy that the speaker is so intimate and familiar with the person she is talking to, so involved in the recollection of trying to intervene in this person's rapidly approaching death, that she doesn't think to identify her (or him) for the reader. Our recognition that a mother is being evoked is the sort of leap explained by ethnomethodology. The sociologist Harvey Sacks, for example, gives the remarkable example of a two-year-old who says, "The baby cried. The mommy picked it up." Almost everyone automatically assumes that the mommy is the mother of that baby, though this is not linguistically clear. A form of social intelligibility is operating, a way to make sense of the world.

There is a bit of magical thinking going on here — it's as if by returning to her mother's provincial square, the speaker can somehow forestall her mother's death: "I clung to the square because you loved / The humble and nostalgic humanity of its small shops." Through an act of projection, we get a sense of the humble, nostalgic humanity of the mother from her feeling for the shops themselves. The speaker tries to reinhabit the little place that her mother most loved — and thus stand in her stead. This is powerfully evoked in the line that joins the "you" and the "I," mother and daughter — "*I* tried to become *you* for *you* were going to die" — which is so haunting, it takes a moment to realize that this thought runs over into the next line, connected by the conjunction "And": "And all life there would cease being mine." The daughter will have no claim on the life of the square once her mother dies. It doesn't belong to her.

The lines of this poem are stately and mostly end-stopped — each begins with a capital letter and makes its own emphatic gesture — though the entire poem pushes forward without any punctuation, as if to emphasize the relentlessness of time. Nothing stops until the end. The heightened feeling — an accelerating gloom, a kind of mourning in advance — gives a special sheen to the description of the little square. The speaker goes through the motions of trying to become her mother as she makes her mother's daily rounds and reenacts her encounters with the locals: "I tried to smile the way you smiled / At the newsagent at the tobacconist / And at the woman without legs selling violets." But the poem turns when she encounters the woman without legs, an emblematic figure. One moment the speaker is smiling at her, the next she is asking her to pray for her mother.

It is implied that the mother is religious — she once lit candles at the churches crowded on one side, or, more specifically, on one corner of the square. There is a logic, an argument being developed here. The speaker recalls how she herself lit candles before every altar because "as soon as I opened my eyes I saw I read / The vocation of eternity written on your face." The beautiful phrase "vocation of eternity" suggests a kind of call or summons to a world beyond time. She could see as well as read the dedication that was now being inscribed on her mother's face.

The speaker can no longer pretend to be her mother:

> I summoned the streets the places the people
> That had been witnesses of your face
> In hopes they would call you in hopes they would unravel
> The fabric that death was weaving in you

We normally think of witnesses as people, but here the streets and places are also invoked to try to prevent the inevitable. It's as if the people and places the dying mother has cared about can somehow keep her attached to the earth. But the enemy is now weaving a fabric that can never be unraveled. It is not so much that the mother is putting on a shroud but, much more painful, that the shroud is being woven into her very body.

As it progresses, "The Small Square" reveals itself, reluctantly, as an elegy. The poem recalls how hard the poet tried to prevent her mother's death. But by the time she had come to write this poem — and by the time we are reading it — it was already too late.

"Under One Small Star"

(1972)

Wisława Szymborska was a canny ironist and rapturous skeptic, a philosophically oriented writer who raised universal questions nonchalantly, with an offhanded charm. She looked at the world with the eye of a disabused lover, and her poems — wise, funny, personal — carry the sting of long experience. Like her Polish contemporaries Zbigniew Herbert and Tadeusz Różewicz, she mounted a sly defense of individual subjectivity against collectivist thinking, and her poems, like theirs, are subversive in the way they force us to reconsider received opinions. The rejection of dogma constituted the basis of her personal ethics.

Here is the concluding poem of her seventh book, *Could Have* (1972):

Under One Small Star

My apologies to chance for calling it necessity.
My apologies to necessity if I'm mistaken, after all.
Please, don't be angry, happiness, that I take you as my due.
May my dead be patient with the way my memories fade.

My apologies to time for all the world I overlook each second.
My apologies to past loves for thinking that the latest is the first.
Forgive me, distant wars, for bringing flowers home.
Forgive me, open wounds, for pricking my finger.
I apologize for my record of minuets to those who cry from the depths.
I apologize to those who wait in railway stations for being asleep today
    at five a.m.
Pardon me, hounded hope, for laughing from time to time.
Pardon me, deserts, that I don't rush to you bearing a spoonful of water.
And you, falcon, unchanging year after year, always in the same cage,
your gaze always fixed on the same point in space,
forgive me, even if it turns out you were stuffed.
My apologies to the felled tree for the table's four legs.
My apologies to great questions for small answers.
Truth, please don't pay me much attention.
Dignity, please be magnanimous.
Bear with me, O mystery of existence, as I pluck the occasional thread from
    your train.
Soul, don't take offense that I've only got you now and then.
My apologies to everything that I can't be everywhere at once.
My apologies to everyone that I can't be each woman and each man.
I know I won't be justified as long as I live,
since I myself stand in my own way.
Don't bear me ill will, speech, that I borrow weighty words,
then labor heavily so that they may seem light.

(Translated by Clare Cavanagh and Stanisław Barańczak)

I too am sorry — if I don't do justice to a poem of such rueful self-aware-
ness. I don't want to sound too certain about a poem about uncertainty. In her
Nobel Prize lecture, Szymborska confessed that she especially valued the little
statement "I don't know." She said, "Poets, if they're genuine, must also keep
repeating 'I don't know.'" This sentence was her mantra. Interrogation was her
method. She liked to take inventory and explore all the ramifications of an
idea to see what it would yield.

"Under One Small Star" is just such a catalog. The poem sets its course
and establishes its tone right from the beginning. In this syntactically repeti-
tive work, almost every line forms a complete sentence. The sentences line up

and accumulate meaning as the poem progresses. It is also a litany, a form that operates through a series of parallel structures. "Litany" has its etymological roots in French and Latin words related to prayer or supplication. What's unusual about Szymborska's litany of apologies is who is addressed in it.

We think of apologizing to people, not to concepts, and so it's odd and funny to witness an apology to the philosophical idea of indeterminism or probability — "chance" — for "calling it necessity." The speaker is sorry that what was random or accidental appeared to be inevitable. But then in the second line she immediately retracts that assertion: "My apologies to necessity if I'm mistaken, after all." So, which is it? She doesn't pretend to know. These questions matter: Did the universe come into being by accident or design? Are the things that happen random or somehow determined? But neither scientists nor philosophers can agree on the right answer, if there is one.

Szymborska's speaker then proceeds to apologize to different categorical entities such as happiness, her dead, and time. There is something impossible about apologizing to abstractions that do not have the human capacity to forgive. Happiness can't get angry, the dead are presumably never impatient, and time doesn't notice what is being overlooked as it is passing. But the speaker knows what she takes for granted, how much she is forgetting about the people who have passed away, and just how much of the world she is constantly missing. Her guilt is remorseless.

The speaker of this poem is filled with a wry sense of inadequacy as she begs forgiveness from everything she can think of — from inanimate objects as well as from emotions and concepts, from places as well as from groups of people, anthropomorphizing everything. She repeatedly apologizes for her limitations — a fading memory, a desire for small pleasures, a "record of minuets." There is genuine suffering in the world, and she finds herself continually overlooking it, hence this line about refugees: "I apologize to those who wait in railroad stations for being asleep today at five a.m." The center of the poem is her apology to the falcon; it judges her with an unswerving gaze that cannot change — because the bird turns out to be dead.

For all the humor in this poem, there's a slightly bitter taste to the idea that humans need to apologize to everything, and that nothing can be held in place for long. The speaker finds herself narrowing the world to make it manageable, thereby trivializing it, and feels unequal to the world's constant sufferings and travails. She keeps giving small answers to large questions. Most of her limitations simply reflect the nature of being alive. What is true for her turns out to be true for everyone. We cannot fathom the full mystery of existence. We cannot live fully soulful lives. All viewpoints are incomplete, all efforts inadequate: "My apologies to everything that I can't be everywhere at once. / My apologies to everyone that I can't be each woman and each man." Each of us stands in our own way. Empathy matters but it has limits. It is ultimately impossible to transcend our individuality. There is no one to forgive us for our separateness.

Szymborska takes these limitations personally and uses them to define her attitude toward poetry. The conclusion to this mini-epic of apologies stands as an *ars poetica:* "Don't bear me ill will, speech, that I borrow weighty words, / then labor heavily so that they may seem light."

Richard Hugo

——

"Degrees of Gray in Philipsburg"
(1973)

Richard Hugo said that "Degrees of Gray in Philipsburg" was the poem he had been trying to write for twenty years. He wrote it in four hours after one visit to a Montana mining town. It's partially an ethnographic description of the town, but, more accurately, it's a projection of his own feelings onto it. Hugo was a poet of place and Philipsburg served as one of what he termed "triggering towns," places that activated his imagination, his feelings and thoughts. "The poem is always in your hometown," he explained, "but you have a better chance of finding it in another." He also recognized that not just any whistle-stop would do: "Though you've never seen it before, it must be a town you've lived in all your life." Philipsburg seemed to fit the bill. Hugo took emotional possession of it, and his poem is a clear-eyed portrait of a Western mining town in the late stages of collapse. But it's even more a portrait of Richard Hugo coming to terms with himself; his style as well as his perspective was colored by a strong sense of masculinity. He was also a Western poet of remorseless self-scrutiny.

"Degrees of Gray in Philipsburg" is the last poem in Hugo's finest collection, *The Lady in Kicking Horse Reservoir* (1973). Notice how the phonic blend of *gr* sounds in the title binds the words together: "De*gr*ees of *Gr*ay." It is as if the poet is gauging the amount or level of the color gray in Philipsburg. Gray is a neutral color, literally a color "without color," the hue of the cloud-covered or ashen sky that hovers over this Montana town. It has overtones of gloom.

Degrees of Gray in Philipsburg

You might come here Sunday on a whim.
Say your life broke down. The last good kiss
you had was years ago. You walk these streets
laid out by the insane, past hotels
that didn't last, bars that did, the tortured try
of local drivers to accelerate their lives.
Only churches are kept up. The jail
turned 70 this year. The only prisoner
is always in, not knowing what he's done.

The principal supporting business now
is rage. Hatred of the various grays
the mountain sends, hatred of the mill,
The Silver Bill repeal, the best liked girls
who leave each year for Butte. One good
restaurant and bars can't wipe the boredom out.
The 1907 boom, eight going silver mines,
a dance floor built on springs —
all memory resolves itself in gaze,
in panoramic green you know the cattle eat
or two stacks high above the town,
two dead kilns, the huge mill in collapse
for fifty years that won't fall finally down.

Isn't this your life? That ancient kiss
still burning out your eyes? Isn't this defeat
so accurate, the church bell simply seems
a pure announcement: ring and no one comes?
Don't empty houses ring? Are magnesium
and scorn sufficient to support a town,

not just Philipsburg, but towns
of towering blondes, good jazz and booze
the world will never let you have
until the town you came from dies inside?

Say no to yourself. The old man, twenty
when the jail was built, still laughs
although his lips collapse. Someday soon,
he says, I'll go to sleep and not wake up.
You tell him no. You're talking to yourself.
The car that brought you here still runs.
The money you buy lunch with,
no matter where it's mined, is silver
and the girl who serves your food
is slender and her red hair lights the wall.

"Degrees of Gray" consists of forty-two lines divided into four irregular stanzas, which operate like paragraphs. It begins emphatically, provisionally: "You might come here Sunday on a whim." The sentence and the line coincide. The tone is informal, conversational — the rhythm has a strong iambic base — and the speaker is talking directly to "you," though we still don't know who that "you" is. He could be addressing any visitor, any reader who might whimsically decide to drive over to Philipsburg, Montana, for the day. The language is offhand and plainspoken. He could also be speaking to himself.

The next sentence changes things dramatically: "Say your life broke down." That's a hypothetical of an entirely different magnitude because it is so acutely sad. The sentence is a supposition — a vision: "Let's say, for example . . ." Like a car, your life has now broken down.

The third sentence, which is carefully enjambed for effect, turns the poem into an indirect confession: "The last good kiss / you had was years ago." That initial phrase, which James Crumley borrowed for his hard-boiled detective novel *The Last Good Kiss,* sets the almost noirish tone. The supposition is a confession: the speaker's life has already broken down.

The rest of the stanza — and much of the rest of the poem — gives us the portrait of a town on its last legs. The streets were laid out by "the insane," which suggests they don't have any rhyme or reason, and the hotels couldn't make it because there weren't enough visitors.

The businesses are failing or failed. The only institutions still going are the churches and bars and, it turns out, the churches are all empty. So too the jail is out of date, and the lone prisoner has been there so long that he doesn't remember what he might have done.

You might come here on a whim, but when you get here you discover that the town you are visiting is all too grimly real. It externalizes what you are feeling. Hugo had a keen sense for the vernacular, a gift for portraying Montana towns in collapse. As a free-verse poet, he was especially good at balancing the sentence and the line. When you reread the second stanza, notice the extra pause at the end of each line, as if you are hesitating on the edge of a cliff and then go tumbling over. Every enjambment provides a new punch, a new meaning, to the sentence.

The first sentence sets the tone. The line break coils a surprise. The reader expects to hear the name of an actual business but instead gets an out-of-control feeling:

> The principal supporting business now
> is rage. Hatred of the various grays
> the mountain sends, hatred of the mill,
> The Silver Bill repeal, the best liked girls
> who leave each year for Butte. One good
> restaurant and bars can't wipe the boredom out.
> The 1907 boom, eight going silver mines,
> a dance floor built on springs —
> all memory resolves itself in gaze,
> in panoramic green you know the cattle eat
> or two stacks high above the town,
> two dead kilns, the huge mill in collapse
> for fifty years that won't fall finally down.

This stanza encapsulates a short history of the boom-and-bust cycle of a typical Montana town. The second line clarifies the meaning of the title: "Hatred of the various grays / the mountain sends . . ." The grays are gradations of fog, but they also take on an emotional hue. Hugo captures something of the fury of people left behind. There is a reference to the Sherman Silver Purchase, which was repealed in 1893 and drastically lowered the price of silver. "The Silver Bill Repeal" and "the best liked girls" are placed on the same line, which suggests that it's because of the repeal that those girls leave for the big city. The single decent restaurant and — the speaker bites down on the letter *b* — "*b*ars can't wipe the *b*oredom out." Freud taught us that boredom is the flip side of rage. There's a reference to the boom in 1907 and then the bust that inevitably followed. Notice how the repeated alliterative use of the letter *f* in the last line — "*for fifty* years that won't *fall finally* down" — threads four words together. It repeatedly makes your upper front teeth lightly touch your bottom inside lip and then pushes the air through your mouth.

So, what's left of this gutted town with only a few men left in it? The line "all memory resolves itself in gaze" is a good contemporary description of what used to be called topographical poetry, which Samuel Johnson defined as "*local poetry,* of which the fundamental subject is some particular landscape . . . with the addition . . . of historical retrospection, or incidental meditation." John Denham inaugurated the genre with his poem "Cooper's Hill" (1642), but he couldn't have envisioned a late-twentieth-century topographical poem of grazing cattle and two dead kilns, an enormous mill that has been collapsing for half a century but never entirely falls. That's more in the line of William Blake.

The third stanza consists entirely of questions. Talking to himself, and also to us — "Isn't this your life?" — the speaker is wondering about the exactitude of his projection. His own loneliness and defeat seem accurately embodied in the day of rest in an empty town, Sunday in Philipsburg. But then he enlarges the question:

> Are magnesium
> and scorn sufficient to support a town,
> not just Philipsburg, but towns
> of towering blondes, good jazz and booze
> the world will never let you have
> until the town you came from dies inside?

He has identified so completely with Philipsburg that he wonders if it's representative of what life itself has become — for him, for Montana, for civilization itself.

The final stanza gives a determined answer to the questions he has just posed: "Say no to yourself." The poem pivots and takes on a sort of Yeatsian gaiety and resolve. It moves into the present tense. The speaker is now explicitly talking to himself but also to the old man who can still laugh, to the good folks of Montana, to all of us. The poet Joanna Klink argues that here "Hugo offers us a city-map straight into, through and — in a very fleeting, tenuous way — out of despair."

> The old man, twenty
> when the jail was built, still laughs
> although his lips collapse. Someday soon,
> he says, I'll go to sleep and not wake up.
> You tell him no. You're talking to yourself.
> The car that brought you here still runs.
> The money you buy lunch with,
> no matter where it's mined, is silver
> and the girl who serves your food
> is slender and her red hair lights the wall.

The speaker in Hugo's poem digs in and finds consolation, light. He responds to the second line of the poem ("Say your life broke down") with a recognition that the car still runs — and so does your life. The money may be mined elsewhere, but it can still buy things here. There is a faint tinge of the erotic in his vision of the slender waitress whose hair provides a luminous light on the wall. The world can still be lit from within.

It turns out that Richard Hugo, for all his despair, was also a poet of gritty optimism.

—

"On This Side of the River"

(1975)

Stephen Berg had an idiosyncratic voice — forthright, nervous, intimate, self-questioning. One might call him a confessional poet except he kept emptying out and interrogating the self that is the basis of that mode, which he felt was too narrowly interpreted. He wrote in the wake of Whitman's "Song of Myself," Eliot's *Four Quartets,* Lowell's *Life Studies.* He demanded utter authenticity in art — individuality of feeling, depth of sincerity. He was a fragmented postconfessional, a spiritual seeker, a poetic magpie, an antic skeptic, an agnostic Jew who kept looking for justice, for wisdom, and for God, who inevitably disappointed him.

Berg treated poetry as a soul-making activity, and one of the striking things about his poems, which are so intimate, is that they are also so oddly literary. He was a devoted reader. He read as a poet reads — avidly, intuitively, unreasonably. He experienced poetry on his pulse, and other people's work stimulated much of his best work. He consistently turned other writers' poems and stories to his own ends. They are interwoven into the fabric of his work. One might say that these figures delivered him to himself. He had a gift for fusion.

In 1969, Berg and Robert Mezey borrowed a phrase from the Spanish poet Juan Ramón Jiménez — *poesia desnuda* — for the title of their anthology *Naked Poetry,* which they followed seven years later with *The New Naked Poetry.* These anthologies of free-verse poetry in open forms followed their conviction that "the strongest and most alive poetry in America has broken the grip of traditional meters and had set out, once again, into 'the wilderness of unopened life.'" That last phrase, which they borrowed from D. H. Lawrence's essay on Walt Whitman ("Ahead of all poets, pioneering into the wilderness of unopened life, Whitman"), certainly marked Berg's own path. He had a firm commitment to organic form and moved to eschew ornamentation, to let his poems "take shape from the shapes of their emotions." At least that's what he claimed. He also let them take shape from the shapes of other people's work, which he translated and revised constantly. He craved contact, a Dante who kept seeking Virgilian guides. He was obsessive and went on his nerve.

Berg's book *Grief* (1975) is a collection of poems with narrative values, lyrical perceptions, and psychological motives. His colloquial idiom and special mode — sometimes comic, sometimes tragic — is painstakingly clear. He employed it to ask large unanswerable questions. Here is a primary example, which begins with a haiku by the Japanese poet Kobayashi Issa (1763–1828):

On This Side of the River

To Millie

Simply trust:
don't the petals also flutter down
just like that?
— Issa

I undress and lie down next to you in bed
and throw one of my legs across yours, I wait
until you are completely lost
then slide my head on the pillow with yours.
Your hair gets caught in my teeth.
I stretch a little to rub my head against yours, so
gently neither of us can feel it,
my breath goes and returns with yours.
There is a moon. Clouds streak its face.

At this late hour by the river the cherry trees stand alone,
black tongueless sentinels
that report nothing.
Wind shakes the flowers that hang over the water,
on the other side families sit down to eat.
I know it.
Not one petal has been torn loose,
and I lie here with my hands on you, not moving,
seeing us today under the trees
sitting with our legs crossed facing each other, talking,
and try to remember what we said.
Get up. I want you to explain
what no couple has ever understood —
the silence, our two skins, the fact that one dies first.
One angry face the color of the
blossoms flashes up and leaves.
The moon pours in. I begin telling you about
my life like the cabdriver in the story
who plows all night through Moscow desperate
for someone to listen to him and winds up at dawn
standing under a streetlamp, snow chilling his mouth,
telling his horse how terrible life is because his
five-year-old son died yesterday, and not one passenger would listen,
pulling the nag's ear down to his mouth, whispering deep
into it his unbearable story.

Berg first published this poem without the haiku and added the three lines from Issa when he reprinted it in his *New and Selected Poems* (1992). He had decided that he needed to start his own poem with the simple advice of another. It isn't easy to "simply trust," to put oneself in the hands of whatever fate comes. But, Issa asks, isn't that how petals fall? Isn't that how nature itself works?

The speaker in Berg's poem, who is trying to take this lesson to heart, is some version of himself, a presumed person but not quite a full-fledged separate entity. Berg liked to blur the distance between the writer and speaker, to create the feeling of human warmth, the fiction of an actual presence. It's the sort of move that Robert Lowell made in his poem "Night Sweat."

Listen to the relaxed opening:

> I undress and lie down next to you in bed
> and throw one of my legs across yours, I wait
> until you are completely lost
> then slide my head on the pillow with yours.

We are present to the casual intimacy here, the telling detail ("Your hair gets caught in my teeth"), the close contact ("I stretch a little to rub my head against yours, so / gently neither of us can feel it, / my breath goes and returns with yours"). The address is so direct that it feels almost artless. It begins with a reference back to Issa's haiku, to a moment of stopped time before the petal falls:

> Not one petal has been torn loose,
> and I lie here with my hands on you, not moving,
> seeing us today under the trees
> sitting with our legs crossed facing each other, talking
> and try to remember what we said.
> Get up. I want you to explain
> what no couple has ever understood —
> the silence, our two skins, the fact that one dies first.

The turn to his wife, Millie — "Get up. I want you to explain . . ." — is especially revealing because the speaker needs his spouse to talk to him, to tell him what he cannot come to terms with, which is that a husband and wife, two people who seem inextricably linked, are still ultimately separate despite their intimacy. They are mortal. But, of course, his wife is asleep, she is not talking at all — this is what *he* is secretly telling *her*. It is at this precise moment that the poet introduces Chekhov's story "Grief." The move is characteristic of Berg's method. All the poems in the first section of *Grief,* for example, are self-described as coming after Chekhov stories.

> The moon pours in. I begin telling you about
> my life like the cabdriver in the story
> who plows all night through Moscow desperate
> for someone to listen to him and winds up at dawn

standing under a streetlamp, snow chilling his mouth
telling his horse how terrible life is because his
five-year-old son died yesterday, and not one passenger would listen,
pulling the nag's ear down to his mouth, whispering deep
into it his unbearable story.

The speaker recognizes his dependency here. The light pours in, he notes, a natural illumination. It also has a symbolic resonance, a sense of illumination. He knows that he can't describe precisely what he means, his past, his secret life, his own grief. Instead he needs the Chekhov story, which gives its title to Berg's volume, as a stand-in to talk about his own experience. He becomes like that desperate cabdriver, who is trying to tell an unacceptable story, to describe and alleviate his suffering. No one will listen to him but a poor unsuspecting animal.

Berg is seeking to capture an extreme feeling about life itself as it is lived and described, not over there, say, on the other side of the river, the transcendental side, the afterlife, but over here, on this side of the great divide, the earthly side. He has a palpable feeling of urgency. We feel ourselves listening to a man speaking to his sleeping wife. He is confessing some dreadful secret to her, to the ether — the subject is suffering — and to us, his future readers, his unseen listeners, who will someday overhear "his unbearable story."

PHILIP LARKIN

———

"Aubade"

(1977)

Philip Larkin essentially wrote from personal experience. His verbal antennae seemed precisely attuned to unhappiness. "Happiness writes white," he often quipped, quoting the French novelist Henry de Montherlant, who stated that "happiness writes in white ink on a white page." Larkin understood poetry as "emotional in nature and theatrical in operation." His carefully honed style combined a self-deprecating, razorlike wit with an unshakable sense of worldly disappointment, of desires unfulfilled and dreams thwarted.

Larkin famously remarked to an interviewer, "Deprivation is for me what daffodils were for Wordsworth," which is both funny and acute, since the misery of diminished and unfulfilled experience is his enduring subject. The tone of sour majesty, of sardonic resignation infused with wordless romantic yearning, is something we might call Larkinesque. It is difficult to think of him as young—this man who seemed to have been born middle-aged, regretting a past that never took place and terrified of oncoming death.

Here is Larkin's last truly great poem, which appeared in the Christmas issue of the *Times Literary Supplement* in 1977. One would be hard-pressed to find another poem that so purposefully upends and refutes the positive Christmas vision.

Aubade

I work all day, and get half-drunk at night.
Waking at four to soundless dark, I stare.
In time the curtain-edges will grow light.
Till then I see what's really always there:
Unresting death, a whole day nearer now,
Making all thought impossible but how
And where and when I shall myself die.
Arid interrogation: yet the dread
Of dying, and being dead,
Flashes afresh to hold and horrify.

The mind blanks at the glare. Not in remorse
— The good not done, the love not given, time
Torn off unused — not wretchedly because
An only life can take so long to climb
Clear of its wrong beginnings, and may never;
But at the total emptiness forever,
The sure extinction that we travel to
And shall be lost in always. Not to be here,
Not to be anywhere,
And soon; nothing more terrible, nothing more true.

This is a special way of being afraid
No trick dispels. Religion used to try,
That vast, moth-eaten musical brocade
Created to pretend we never die,
And specious stuff that says *No rational being
Can fear a thing it will not feel,* not seeing
That this is what we fear — no sight, no sound,
No touch or taste or smell, nothing to think with,
Nothing to love or link with,
The anaesthetic from which none comes round.

And so it stays just on the edge of vision,
A small unfocused blur, a standing chill
That slows each impulse down to indecision.
Most things may never happen: this one will,
And realisation of it rages out
In furnace-fear when we are caught without
People or drink. Courage is no good:
It means not scaring others. Being brave
Lets no one off the grave.
Death is no different whined at than withstood.

Slowly light strengthens, and the room takes shape.
It stands plain as a wardrobe, what we know,
Have always known, know that we can't escape,
Yet can't accept. One side will have to go.
Meanwhile telephones crouch, getting ready to ring
In locked-up offices, and all the uncaring
Intricate rented world begins to rouse.
The sky is white as clay, with no sun.
Work has to be done.
Postmen like doctors go from house to house.

Larkin's "Aubade" is a terrifying spiritual confrontation with oblivion.

Remember that the aubade is traditionally a dawn song expressing the regret of lovers parting at daybreak. It has no fixed metrical form. It also typically recalls the joy of two lovers joined in original darkness. But there is no beloved at all in Larkin's crossover poem at dawn, his anti-aubade, which has a precedent in bleak modern aubades with the same title by William Empson and Louis MacNeice. He establishes the sense of isolation right from the beginning. Instead of heralding the light at 4 a.m., "Aubade" is a dawn song that starts in darkness and sees only "Unresting death, a whole day nearer now, / Making all thought impossible but how / And where and when I shall myself die."

Larkin wrote the first three stanzas of his poem in 1974, worked on it intermittently over the next three years, and finally completed it after his mother's death in the fall of 1977. Christopher Fletcher relates it to John Betjeman's poem "Before the Anaesthetic, or a Real Fright" and suggests that Larkin answers his friend's question — "Is it extinction when I die?" — with a declaration about "The sure extinction that we travel to / And shall be lost in always." Larkin's letters are peppered with comments about his terror of the finality of death. He referred to "Aubade" as his "in-a-funk-about-death poem." "Aubade," he said, "the death thing, or rather 'fear-of-death thing.'" He wrote to a friend, "I don't know that I ever expected much of life, but it terrifies me to think it's nearly over." He said that he dreaded "endless extinction."

There are times when the bleakness of Larkin's message seems undercut by the technical poise and understated virtuosity of the poem, which consists of five exceptionally well-crafted ten-line stanzas. The rhyme scheme is *ababccdeed*. The poem unfolds in a fluent iambic pentameter, except for the penultimate foreshortened line, or half-line, which sets up the conclusive aperçu of each stanza. The language seems down to earth, close to speech, and yet somehow reaches greater heights of eloquence.

Larkin uses rhyme so tactically that it works as a strategic weapon. For example, he yokes "night" to "light," "stare" to "there," and "die" to "horrify"; he presses together "dread" and "dead," "never" and "forever," "here" and "anywhere." There is grim merriment in the way he rhymes "afraid" and "brocade" and reduces the whole of religion to "That vast, moth-eaten musical brocade / Created to pretend we never die." The phrase "nothing to think with" leads with dark inevitability to the lilting line "Nothing to love or link with." He takes the uplifting Yeatsian spiritual word "vision" and undercuts it with "indecision," which echoes and inverts T. S. Eliot's "Love Song of J. Alfred Prufrock": "And time yet for a hundred indecisions, / And for a hundred visions and revisions." He undermines "brave" with "grave" and tunes "shape" to "escape." He also expertly presses the consonants, like the *d* sounds in "yet the *d*read / Of *d*ying, and being *d*ead," which is followed in the next line with the aspirated *h* sounds of "*h*old and *h*orrify." He uses alliteration to connect and cross lines, as in "*t*ime / *T*orn" and *c*limb / *C*lear." It is strange how the precision of certain rhymes and repetitions can still give us frissons of verbal pleasure even when the subject matter is so bleak.

Larkin was well known for his love of the blues. In a book called *Larkin's Blues,* B. J. Leggett suggests that the first line of "Aubade" is a blues line: "I work all day, and get half-drunk at night." It's a line in the continuous present tense. He argues that "working and drinking are the common properties of the blues, drinking most often as a way of coping with despair." So too the second line alludes to "one of the most common of all blues openings — 'woke up this morning' — but rephrasing it in nonblues language."

Larkin's poem begins in the first-person singular but drops the "I" in the second stanza and never picks it up again. The poem thereafter universalizes, speaking in the first-person plural for all of us. It may have been a necessary psychological strategy. For example, it might be more natural to say, "*My mind* blanks at the glare," though the second stanza begins, "*The mind* blanks at the glare." It may be that the glower of his own death was so great that he needed to displace it. He italicizes the sentence "*No rational being / Can fear a thing it will not feel*" so that it will sound like a quotation, but it's not a sentiment he can possibly embrace because it is precisely what "we fear — no sight, no sound, / No touch or taste or smell . . ." Larkin's speaker can't look at his own death directly — "The anaesthetic from which none comes round. // And so it stays just on the edge of vision." Throughout the poem this vision keeps blurring and coming back into focus. The poet cannot fend off the central premise of his poem, even as he keeps finding clever aphoristic ways of phrasing the dilemma, as when he hyphenates "furnace-fear," alliterates "*Being brave*," and presses the *d*'s, *n*'s, and *w*'s in the line "*Death is no different whined at than withstood.*"

The last stanza marks the final transition point of the aubade: "Slowly light strengthens, and the room takes shape." The room comes into focus, "plain as a wardrobe," and brings with it the fateful helpless knowledge of what we all know but can't escape or accept: death is one day closer now. Meanwhile, morning comes on and "telephones crouch, getting ready to ring / In locked-up offices." Archie Burnett, Larkin's remarkably assiduous editor, has tracked down virtually all his sources, such as his deliberate borrowing here from Barbara Pym's *A Glass of Blessings,* one of his favorite novels, for the unusual image of "the telephone crouching on the floor alone, ringing unheeded." There is a stoic recognition that time never stops. The sky may be sunless, but "Work has to be done" and mail must be delivered: "Postmen like doctors go from house to house."

Larkin's gloomy prognosis has sparked extreme reactions from other poets. The universalizing change from the first-person singular into the first-person plural, the quiet transformation of "I" into "we," may be one of the reasons. The poem's powerful force field is so negative that it demands that the reader reckon with it. Seamus Heaney considered it "the definitive post-Christian English poem, one that abolishes the soul's traditional pretension to immortality and denies the Deity's immemorial attribute of infinite personal concern." Czesław Miłosz, a formidable critic, was troubled by the nihilism of "Aubade." He called it "a high poetic achievement" but also protested:

> And yet the poem leaves me not only dissatisfied but indignant, and I wonder why myself. Perhaps we forget too easily the centuries-old mutual hostility between reason, science and science-inspired philosophy on the one hand and poetry on the other? Perhaps the author of the poem went over to the side of the adversary and his ratiocination strikes me as a betrayal? For, after all, death in the poem is endowed with the supreme authority of Law and universal necessity, while man is reduced to nothing, to a bundle of perceptions, or even less, to an interchangeable statistical unit. But poetry by its very essence has always been on the side of life.

Miłosz couldn't bear the thought of life without redemption.

C. K. Williams responded to Miłosz's argument with the counterclaim that there is a "redemptive gravity" in Larkin's work. Heaney too argued that a poem with such generative energy does not side with the adversary. Yet he concurred that, "for all its heartbreaking truths and beauties, 'Aubade' reneges on what Yeats called the 'spiritual intellect's great work.'"

It's possible to find oneself vacillating about "Aubade." Death has vindictive force in the poem, and yet the last line seems oddly encouraging. Larkin made a revealing comment about it in 1984: "Some doctor read that last line 'Postmen like doctors go from house to house' and said, 'It's years you know since doctors did house to house visiting.' But I said 'No. It isn't postmen, comma, like doctors, comma, but just postmen like doctors.' I meant the arrival of the postman in the morning is consoling, healing."

It turns out that as long as we're alive, another morning arrives even after the darkest night of the soul. The dailiness of life starts all over again. Larkin's negativity weights the evidence, but the generating form of the poem reaches out to an unseen listener, a human other, and suggests that the poem, perhaps despite itself, stands on the side of life.

WILLIAM MEREDITH

"Parents"

(1978)

Many of William Meredith's most significant poems revolve around one mysterious insight into common human experience. He probed the dark complexities of human conduct with a quiet humor and determination. He was writing a modest form of wisdom poetry. Here's the poem "Parents" from his finest book, his last single collection, *The Cheer* (1980). Meredith added the dedication when he reprinted the poem in *Partial Accounts: New and Selected Poems* (1987).

Parents

(for Vanessa Meredith and Samuel Wolf Gezari)

What it must be like to be an angel
or a squirrel, we can imagine sooner.

The last time we go to bed good,
they are there, lying about darkness.

They dandle us once too often,
these friends who become our enemies.

Suddenly one day, their juniors
are as old as we yearn to be.

They get wrinkles where it is better
smooth, odd coughs, and smells.

It is grotesque how they go on
loving us, we go on loving them.

The effrontery, barely imaginable,
of having caused us. And of how.

Their lives: surely
we can do better than that.

This goes on for a long time. Everything
they do is wrong, and the worst thing,

they all do it, is to die,
taking with them the last explanation,

how we came out of the wet sea
or wherever they got us from,

taking the last link
of that chain with them.

Father, mother, we cry, wrinkling,
to our uncomprehending children and grandchildren.

"Parents" explores the complex doubleness of our relationship to those strange familiars, "these friends who become our enemies." The couplet form seems especially appropriate for a poem about the duality and duplicity of parents. The couplet, two successive lines of poetry, is the most elementary of units, just like the parental unit. Here each of the unrhymed couplets has the heft and authority of an epigram. The poem follows an arc from our first un-comprehending sense of the existence of our parents to our final bleak recognition after their deaths. It's not a confessional poem — we don't learn anything specific about Meredith's own parents — but a poem generalized from personal experience. In this way it's like J. V. Cunningham's remembrance in "Montana Fifty Years Ago."

In his *Paris Review* interview, Meredith said that the idea for "Parents" came to him after he'd gone to a Thanksgiving dinner where the host couple had three surviving parents, who were in attendance. These three seemed to him charming, interesting people, about his own age, while to their children they seemed, as parents normally do, embarrassing, tacky, stupid, and tedious, albeit lovable. He saw his friends' suffering and he remembered such suffering himself. That was the trigger.

There are just thirteen two-line stanzas in "Parents," yet it packs in a life-time of observations. The first eight couplets are closed, which means that the sense and syntax come to conclusion at the end of the second line, and each one has a feeling of self-containment and enclosure. To start: our parents never seem entirely human to us and we have no idea what they might really be like: "What it must be like to be an angel / or a squirrel, we can imagine sooner." In the beginning, each of the parents' actions seems like a kind of betrayal to the child. The first line postulates something, say, "The last time we go to bed good," which the second line radically modifies: "they are there, lying about darkness." All the pressure hinges on the word "lying": as we grow older, we find our parents' attempts to reassure us simply misleading.

In almost every couplet, the second line contains a kind of punch line. Think of the pause between the first observation, "It is grotesque how they go on / loving us," and the second one, "we go on loving them." The word "gro-tesque" is unexpected in this context and carries a comic hideousness. The first line is rueful and exasperated: "It is grotesque how they go on." The line break hovers and hesitates. The drop down to "loving us" has the deadpan timing of a good joke. Worse yet is the wry knowledge: "we go on loving them." So too a precise sense of timing governs the colon and the line break in "Their lives: surely / we can do better than that." It's almost as if the word "surely" had been underlined. The word contains an attitude, all those years of rolling our eyes and condescending to our parents.

There is a turn in the ninth stanza of this poem. Two-thirds of the way through the poem we come to the first open-ended two-line stanza. A couplet is considered open when the sense carries forward past the second line into the next line or lines. "Everything / they do is wrong, and the worst thing, // they all do it, is to die . . ." "*Everything* they do is wrong" seems like something that a teenager might say. But then the tone shifts. The phrase "they all do it" is an interruption, an explanation. It creates a sense of time slipping by, of parents passing on, of children left behind with no final explanations.

There is a keen psychological understanding in the last couplet, in the recognition that each of us continues to carry on a one-sided lifelong conversation with our parents long after they have died. This conversation is literally incomprehensible to the next generations. Even as we ourselves age, we go on crying out to the people who created and formed us. We are forever linked to them. No matter how much we continue to call on and question them, though, we never get back an answer.

HAYDEN CARRUTH

———

"Essay"

(1978)

Hayden Carruth's poem "Essay" first appeared in his book *Brothers, I Loved You All* (1978). He titled it this way because of the essayistic or discursive movement of the text, which follows his thought process and makes an argument. It sounds like a piece of prose and moves like a poem. It may not be entirely coincidental that in the mid-seventies the poet Robert Pinsky made the case for just this kind of poem in his book *The Situation of Poetry*. The discursive poem, he argued, is an explanatory poem that moves across a wide swatch of territory: "It is speech, organized by its meaning, avoiding the distances and complications of irony on one side and the ecstatic fusion of the speaker, meaning, and subject on the other. The idea is to have all the virtues of prose, in addition to those qualities and degrees of precision which can be called poetic." Carruth was already employing the essayistic mode that Pinsky was calling for. He too was making a statement and accessing a terrain. He would also use the method in other poems, such as "Essay on Love" and "Essay on Death."

Essay

So many poems about the deaths of animals.
Wilbur's toad, Kinnell's porcupine, Eberhart's squirrel,
and that poem by someone — Hecht? Merrill? —
about cremating a woodchuck. But mostly
I remember the outrageous number of them,
as if *every* poet, I too, had written at least
one animal elegy; with the result that today
when I came to a good enough poem by Edwin Brock
about finding a dead fox at the edge of the sea
I could not respond; as if permanent shock
had deadened me. And then after a moment
I began to give way to sorrow (watching myself
sorrowlessly the while), not merely because
part of my being had been violated and annulled,
but because all these many poems over the years
have been necessary — suitable and correct. This
has been the time of the finishing off of the animals.
They are going away — their fur and their wild eyes,
their voices. Deer leap and leap in front
of the screaming snowmobiles until they leap
out of existence. Hawks circle once or twice
above their shattered nests and then they climb
to the stars. I have lived with them fifty years,
we have lived with them fifty million years,
and now they are going, almost gone. I don't know
if the animals are capable of reproach.
But clearly they do not bother to say good-bye.

You can hear the ghost of blank verse in Carruth's even-keeled free-verse lines. The poem operates in the middle range — above speech and below song. It begins informally — "So many poems about the deaths of animals" — as if we've been dropped into the midst of a conversation that the speaker is carrying on partly with himself, partly with his poetry peers. He goes on to prove his point by referring to Richard Wilbur's "The Death of a Toad," Galway Kinnell's "The Porcupine," and Richard Eberhardt's "On a Squirrel, Crossing the

Road, in New England." This is a poem of thinking in action. The speaker doesn't bother to cover up the fact that he can't remember who wrote a poem about cremating a woodchuck. I myself don't recall any poems like this by Anthony Hecht or James Merrill, but there is a good poem by Maxine Kumin about trying to kill woodchucks. But perhaps that's not the point. None of these pieces particularly matter — he could have listed many more. It's the sheer number of poems about dead animals that seems to have deadened the genre. The speaker doesn't exempt himself from this critique, either. He feels that the experience of writing about dead animals has been used up. And it is coming across a decent-enough lyric by a decent-enough poet, the British writer Edwin Brock, that sends him over the top.

The poem structurally turns in the middle of the eleventh line, as the speaker observes his own feeling, as if from a distance: "And then after a moment / I began to give way to sorrow (watching myself / sorrowlessly the while) ...". The warm or sorrowful feeling of the poet and the cool or unashamed reasonableness of the essayist are battling it out. The poem employs the language of argumentation ("*not merely because* / part of my being had been ... annulled, / *but because* all these many poems over the years / *have been necessary* — suitable and correct") to make a conclusive point: "This has been the time of the finishing off of the animals."

The language noticeably changes after the speaker makes this short, sad, direct statement: "They are going away." The drier essayistic mode yields to a kind of lyricism when he talks about the bodies and voices of wild animals. He repeats the word "leap" three times to enact the way that the deer leaping away from "screaming snowmobiles" somehow end up leaping out of existence itself. Likewise the hawks regretfully circle their "shattered nests" just once or twice before climbing "to the stars." People have always felt connected to animals. We've observed the ways we are both like and unlike them. Notice how the speaker links his own time span to our long human history. "I have lived with them fifty years," he recalls. "We have lived with them fifty million years." The heart lurches over the line break and the conjunction in the next line: "and now they are going, almost gone." We feel the desperate progression from "going" to "almost gone."

The animals may not reproach us, but the end of this poem is a reproach. "Essay" sharpens into an unexpected elegy for the animals, who leave without saying goodbye. There is no ritual farewell. Carruth's new kind of animal poem, which he had resisted writing, has now become a pointedly political poem. He had overcome his own objection to animal poems and reversed his original argument, thereby refreshing the genre. In doing so, he created an acute essay-poem about the extinction of different species, an accusation against human beings, and a humane lyric about the death of animals.

JAMES SCHUYLER

"Arches"

(1978)

James Schuyler is often celebrated as a poet who celebrated the everyday and ordinary, what he called "the pure pleasure of / Simply looking." He took a walk or peered through his window, and the poem became the daily record of what he saw. He had a keen eye and reveled in particularity. But Schuyler was afflicted by periodic bouts of mental illness, and he was often looking at life from the outside, as through a looking glass. The reason that daily life takes on such a luminous glow in a great deal of his work is because he was effectively cut off from it much of the time. He cherished the familiar because it was never quite familiar enough, never something that he could take for granted. He reminds me of the eighteenth-century English poet Christopher Smart, in the way his work spotlights and exaggerates familiar things. Both fastened themselves to daily life as a meaningful way to hold on to the world.

It's not necessary to pathologize Schuyler's enthusiasms or the way that he took pleasure in describing ordinary things. But looking at some of his work from this angle does help account for its psychological pressure, its odd intensities. The language is plain but seems psychologically lit from within. He looked hard at things, but he wasn't an Objectivist poet, like Louis Zukofsky or George Oppen. There is an inner nervousness driving his work.

Schuyler's mental health was fragile, and he was institutionalized several times in the 1970s. In 1975 he wrote "The Payne Whitney Poems" while he was interned at the Payne Whitney Psychiatric Clinic in New York City. He published the entire eleven-poem cycle in the *New York Review of Books* in 1978. The diary-like series subsequently appeared in *The Morning of the Poem* (1980). Here, as the poet David Herd suggests, "Schuyler presents in miniature many aspects of his work: the importance of observation, a fascination with the vicissitudes of weather, a fondness for the collage-like list (as in 'Sleep'), and, throughout the cycle, a sense that in writing one might better make oneself at home in one's world."

"The Payne Whitney Poems" are nervous, low-key, focused on the daily, and sometimes funny. The speaker keeps "wigging in" and "wigging out"; the wires in his head are always crossing.

Here's the poem "Arches":

> *Arches*
>
> of buildings, this building,
> frame a stream of windows
> framed in white brick. This
> building is fireproof; or else
> it isn't: the furnishings first
> to go: no, the patients. Patients
> on Sundays walk in a small garden.
> Today some go out on a group
> pass. To stroll the streets and shop.
> So what else is new? The sky
> slowly/swiftly went blue to gray.
> A gray in which some smoke stands.

The title runs into the first line and the poem sets off on its own hesitant string of thoughts. As so often happens in Schuyler's poems, the speaker is looking out the window and recording what he sees, as if the window serves as protection against what the philosopher Gaston Bachelard calls "exterior dizziness." He is engaged but slightly removed from it all. The lines are cut short, the rhythm jittery. There isn't much to hold on to. What's striking is how immediately Schuyler's speaker begins adapting ("Arches // of buildings, this building") and correcting ("This / building is fireproof; or else / it isn't") what he observes. The buildings narrow to a single building. The poem itself is visually "framed." The speaker is looking through the enclosure of his own window and through the arches that "frame a stream of windows / framed in white brick."

Everything is provisional; every statement leads to a revision. This building is fireproof or, whoops, it isn't. There's dry, grim humor in the recognition that in a fire the patients will go before the furnishings. The uncapitalized word "patients" is repeated, this time capitalized. This simple language indicates that the speaker has come through a great catastrophe and needs to remember how to use language again. It is very shaky and tentative.

There is a tiny drama here. The speaker is looking at the windows of the other buildings, at the patients walking in the garden on Sunday. He isn't one of them. They're free, or somewhat free, to stroll about; he is not. He takes a moment to ask himself, "So what else is new?" It is almost as if he is trying to think of something interesting to tell a visitor. He seems slightly desperate to come up with something fresh in a place where life has come to a standstill, where nothing new seems to happen. That's why he turns to the weather:

> The sky
> slowly/swiftly went blue to gray.
> A gray in which some smoke stands.

Schuyler manages to capture the texture of a small moment in time, how the day darkens and dusk sets in, simultaneously slowly and swiftly. No other poet would have jammed those words together as "slowly/swiftly." A person is sitting or standing by the window as the day closes shop. As soon as he describes the sky going from blue to gray, he immediately corrects this observation, noting a "gray in which some smoke stands." The three alliterative *s* sounds — "*s*ome *s*moke *s*tands" — enact the way that the day comes to a lingering and yet sudden close. Something can still be seen, something preserved. Something is left standing. But it is mist and vapor.

The poet Michael Hofmann hears an undertone of nervous amusement in this poem, despite everything. He writes: "However halting, impaired, almost uncommunicative the poem, I still have the perverse sense that the station to which it is tuned, however low, is merriment. The sentences may be mumbled and reluctant and short and full of wrong turnings, but there is still a low ebb of wit in them — in the macabre speculation, in the observation of others like or unlike himself, in the unexpectedly fluent linkage of smoke and fire. It is, in other words, and perhaps again unexpectedly, literary." This is well said about a poem that is somehow hesitant and yet sure of itself. It seems quietly aware of its own construction, of being made in front of us. The speaker of this poem is ill, but the poet who crafted it was healthily — *slowly/swiftly* — making a new kind of poem.

NAOMI SHIHAB NYE

"Kindness"

(1978, 1994)

As a poet, Naomi Shihab Nye brings a fresh perspective to the world. Her poems are neighborly and hard-won, playful and instructive, canny and wise. She pays close attention to things that might otherwise be overlooked — sometimes by gazing at them directly, sometimes by catching them out of the corner of her eye. Nye, a Palestinian American poet, travels widely and often relies on Middle Eastern and Latin American sources. Her poems seem to have a sort of homespun clarity, though many bring back lessons learned on the road. She reminds me of William Stafford, one of her formative models, in the sly, unexpected way that she sidles up to a subject. Here is her poem "Kindness":

> *Kindness*
>
> Before you know what kindness really is
> you must lose things,
> feel the future dissolve in a moment
> like salt in a weakened broth.

What you held in your hand,
what you counted and carefully saved,
all this must go so you know
how desolate the landscape can be
between the regions of kindness.
How you ride and ride
thinking the bus will never stop,
the passengers eating maize and chicken
will stare out the window forever.
Before you learn the tender gravity of kindness
you must travel where the Indian in a white poncho
lies dead by the side of the road.
You must see how this could be you,
how he too was someone
who journeyed through the night with plans
and the simple breath that kept him alive.

Before you know kindness as the deepest thing inside,
you must know sorrow as the other deepest thing.
You must wake up with sorrow.
You must speak to it till your voice
catches the thread of all sorrows
and you see the size of the cloth.
Then it is only kindness that makes sense anymore,
only kindness that ties your shoes
and sends you out into the day to gaze at bread,
only kindness that raises its head
from the crowd of the world to say
It is I you have been looking for,
and then goes with you everywhere
like a shadow or a friend.

In lyric poetry, the topic of kindness has been consistently undermined by sentimentality—there are hundreds of inauthentic poems telling us to be nice to each other—and there aren't many poets who have treated it seriously as something earned from experience. One of the few modern poems that stands behind Nye is Sylvia Plath's "Kindness," which Plath wrote in the last week of her life. But Plath treats the subject with dark irony and mordant wit ("Kindness glides about my house. / Dame Kindness, she is so nice!") and destroys the saccharine sentiment that sometimes surrounds it. Nye takes a different approach. She treats actual kindness as something that does not just glide along on the surface. Rather, it is shadowed by suffering. Like Guillaume Apollinaire, she wants "to explore kindness the enormous country where everything is silent."

The recognition that jumpstarts this poem is that the speaker did not know the true or real meaning of kindness until something disastrous happened to her. "Before you know what kindness really is / you must lose things." In the first published version of this poem, she took an even more extreme position and said, "you must lose everything," but later Nye decided that statement was too melodramatic. What's crucial is how she complicates the idea of kindness. The "you" in this poem operates as a kind of double addressee. At first the speaker seems to be addressing each of us, an intimate but somehow generalized "you," as if she is treating the reader as a confidant. The poem never entirely loses that feeling, but as it progresses it becomes clearer and clearer that the speaker is first of all talking to herself. That's because the poem becomes anecdotal. The speaker is recounting the story of something that explicitly happened to her. The reader is then put in the position of a listener.

"Kindness" appeared in Nye's first book of poems, *Different Ways to Pray* (1980), where she dated it to "Colombia, 1978." She has sometimes called herself the "secretary" for this poem and described the story behind it. One week after they were married, she and her husband set off to travel the length of South America by bus. At the end of the first week of their journey, their bus was held up, they were robbed of everything, and someone was murdered. They were naturally very shaken up. Afterward, a stranger noticed their distress and came up to them in the plaza where the bus had let them off. He was unexpectedly kind and apologized for what had happened to them. It was a simple gesture that helped them get their bearings. After the stranger had gone, Nye's husband hitchhiked off to a larger city to see if he could redeem their traveler's checks. That's when she sat in a plaza in Popayán and transcribed this poem. She said that a female voice seemed to be speaking to her out of air.

Just as Wordsworth's sonnet "Surprised by joy" is as much about sorrow as it is about joy, so Nye's poem is as much about sorrow as it is about kindness. The poem is an argument delivered with the confidence of hard experience:

"Before you know . . . / you must . . ." The poise of each line, the way the first sentence breaks down, as if naturally, into four syntactical units, reinforces the sense of assurance.

> Before you know what kindness really is
> you must lose things,
> feel the future dissolve in a moment
> like salt in a weakened broth.

Nye follows this pattern of breaking the lines into distinct end-stopped units through the poem, which hones down on the losses as it progresses. Notice the consonance ("*feel the future*") that enforces the very large claim that one's entire future simply dissolves like salt in a weak soup.

The anaphoric repetition in the way the speaker describes money, "*What you held* in your hand, / *what you counted* and carefully saved," and the consonance that binds together the words "held" and "hand," "counted" and "carefully," emphasizes that the loss of money stands for an even greater loss, and that this loss must happen, she suggests, so that you can experience the desolate landscape between "the regions of kindness." So far, the landscape still seems generalized, though it immediately narrows to something more specific, more actual: a bus ride that seems to go on and on in a South American country. In just four lines, Nye creates the feeling of being on an interminable trip.

But then the speaker abruptly comes up against an awful and very specific death, which stands at the heart of the poem.

> Before you learn the tender gravity of kindness
> you must travel where the Indian in a white poncho
> lies dead by the side of the road.
> You must see how this could be you,
> how he too was someone
> who journeyed through the night with plans
> and the simple breath that kept him alive.

The sense of sorrow in the poem is changed immeasurably by the death of the "Indian in a white poncho." The speaker doesn't even know his name. He's the one who has lost everything. She recognizes that he was just like her, like all of us, someone with plans, a person with a life ahead of him. Nye yokes a force to a quality in order to describe "the tender gravity of kindness." We don't normally think of gravity, a natural phenomenon, as something that is tender, something dear or considerate. And we don't typically apply that force field to a quality like kindness, which suggests a way of behaving toward one another. But kindness has a strong gravitational pull in this poem, an inevitability. It is something that must be earned by gazing at the death of another person and realizing that it could be you lying in that ditch by the side of the road.

As a poem, "Kindness" is structured around three repetitions: "Before you know," "Before you learn," and "Before you know." Notice the parallelism in the two lines that kick off the second stanza: "Before you know kindness as the deepest thing inside, / you must know sorrow as the other deepest thing." The speaker in this poem is certain of what she has just learned. That's what gives her the insistence to keep repeating "You must." One sorrow *must* come to stand for all the other sorrows; experience must be experienced and enlarged. Nye's poem is a way of returning to first things. That's why kindness becomes so elemental, something very simple and basic, like tying your shoes and sending you out to look for bread. The speaker doesn't have any money and so she can't really buy bread. Sorrow has singled you out, Nye argues, and now so must kindness, which "raises its head / from the crowd of the world." In other words, kindness has been lost in the crowd, in the multiplicity of everything we do, but now it recognizes you. A single group of people, the crowd, has been enlarged into "the crowd of the world." The image has become allegorical.

At the end of the poem, kindness is personified and talks both to the speaker and to us at the same time. Notice how the poet presses together the entities "I" and "you":

> It is I you have been looking for,
> and then goes with you everywhere
> like a shadow or a friend.

Nye closes the poem with a delicate simile. After kindness speaks, it never leaves you alone again. It always travels with you "like a shadow" — a dark figure, an inseparable companion or follower — "or a friend," a trusted confidant, someone bound to you by mutual affection. Kindness is one or the other, not both. In other words, it goes with you all the time whether you want it to or not. Perhaps, then, it is better to befriend it.

Henry James said that "three things in human life are important: the first is to be kind, the second is to be kind, and the third is to be kind." Naomi Shihab Nye suggests that such kindness must be earned by sorrow. There aren't many poets whose lifework I would describe as kindhearted. But kindness has shadowed Nye's work for the past forty years. She has gone on to other sorrows and other tragedies, but her empathic imagination, her shadow or friend, has always accompanied her.

—•—

"The Woman on the Bridge over the Chicago River"

(1979)

Allen Grossman was a unique figure in postmodern American poetry. He practiced the high Romantic mode with remarkable confidence. Stylistically, he was an heir to W. B. Yeats, Wallace Stevens, and Hart Crane, his three major precursors, though in a sense he de-historicized Romanticism. He treated the impulse toward transcendence as a permanent feature of the lyric. Grossman believed that "Poems create poets," rather than the other way around, and here is one of the poems that "created" him. It is the title poem of his second collection.

The Woman on the Bridge over the Chicago River

Stars are tears falling with light inside.
In the moon, they say, is a sea of tears.
It is well known that the wind weeps.
The lapse of all streams is a form of weeping,
And the heaving swell of the sea.

                       Cormorants
Weep from the cliffs;
The gnat weeps crossing the air of a room;
And a moth weeps in the eye of the lamp.
Each leaf is a soul in tears.

                                    Roses weep
In the dawn light. Each tear of the rose
Is like a lens. Around the roses the garden
Weeps in a thousand particular voices.
Under earth the bones weep, and the old tears
And new mingle without difference.
A million years does not take off the freshness
Of the calling.

                  Eternity and Time
Grieve incessantly in one another's arms.
Being weeps, and Nothing weeps, in the same
Night-tent, averted,
Yet mingling sad breaths. And from all ideas
Hot tears irrepressible.

                        In a corner
Of the same tent a small boy in a coat
Sobs and sobs,
                        while under the Atlantic
Depth and Darkness grieve among the fountains,
And the fountains weep out the grieving sea.

O listen, the steam engines shunt and switch
Asleep in their grieving. A sad family
In the next house over shifts mournfully
About staining the dim blind. The boy looks up
As the grieving sound of his own begetting
Keeps on,

And his willow mother mars her mirror
Of the lake with tears.

                                                 It is cold and snowing
And the snow is falling into the river.
On the bridge, lit by the white shadow of
The Wrigley Building,
A small woman wrapped in an old blue coat
Staggers to the rail weeping.

                              As I remember,
The same boy passes, announcing the fame
Of tears, calling out the terms
In a clear way, translating to the long
Dim human avenue.

"The Woman on the Bridge over the Chicago River" presents a world made from tears. It's as if God, who is noticeably absent from the poem, had created a universe that does nothing else but weep, a universe of lamentation. We are now inhabiting some surreal or inverted version of Genesis. And yet, as Tom Lutz points out in *Crying: A Natural and Cultural History of Tears,* weeping is an exclusively human activity. We are the only species that cries for emotional reasons. Indeed, crying is a human universal. Grossman's poem therefore projects onto the cosmos a distinctively human feeling. It is an act of catharsis.

It's worth pointing out that there isn't much crying going on in modernist poetry, which cultivated aesthetic rigor and control, ironic distance. T. S. Eliot and Ezra Pound, for example, were highly defended against too much feeling in poetry, which they considered sentimental and effeminate. Masculinist styles also emphasized stoicism. There is not much stoicism in Grossman's wet lyric, however, which enacts a late Romantic alternative to a dry modernist aesthetic. It proposes a different idea about masculinity and feeling. It has a maternal source.

The title declares that this poem is going to be about a woman standing on a bridge overlooking the Chicago River. She is placed in a suspended or liminal position. But the supposed subject doesn't come back into the poem until the penultimate stanza: "A small woman wrapped in an old blue coat / Staggers to the rail weeping." It's not until the poem heads toward its conclusion that we understand how the whole universe of sadness has finally come back down to her.

Everything is keening. There is a startling beauty in the opening image of this poem: "Stars are tears falling with light inside." Falling stars may be tears — a sadness dropping from above — but they also have a brightness within. Notice the odd, rhetorical interpolations in the next two sentences: "In the moon, *they say,* is a sea of tears. / *It is well known* that the world weeps." The speaker is bringing in a community of other people to concur that the stars, the moon, the wind, and the sea are all crying. The tears falling from the sky above the bridge join with the tears flowing below it. The speaker suggests that this is something all of us intuitively understand.

The second stanza unites cormorants weeping from cliffs, a gnat weeping as it crosses through the air of a room, and a moth weeping in the eye of a lamp. The weeping carries on inside houses too. It is everywhere. Think of the psalm-like or spiritual declaration "Each leaf is a soul in tears." It's as if there is a soul in all living things, as the Neoplatonists believed, and each soul grieves to be united with the whole. The third stanza suggests that this weeping continues to be fresh and yet it is as old as time, as death itself. The mourning never gets old: "A million years does not take off the freshness / Of the calling."

Every sentence in this poem is a declaration. In the fourth stanza, philosophical abstractions and ideas also begin to weep. Wisława Szymborska may have apologized to these abstractions in her poem "Under One Small Star," but Allen Grossman observes them crying. William Blake stated, "Eternity is in love with the productions of time." In Grossman's revision, Time is also weeping in Eternity's arms. Being grieves, presumably because it must die, but Nothing also grieves, presumably because it does not exist. It's as if the concepts, which take on life, could sadly intermingle breaths. We don't usually think of ideas as having feelings, but here a mournfulness undergirds them: "And from all ideas / Hot tears irrepressible." Thinking itself becomes a form of weeping.

Most autobiographical and epiphanic poems begin with the literal and move into the visionary. They situate us in a place and time and then shift into some other timeless realm. That's the Wordsworthian strategy in such poems as Anthony Hecht's "A Hill," Elizabeth Bishop's "In the Waiting Room," and James Wright's "A Blessing." But Grossman reverses the mode. He begins in the high visionary mode and turns to the autobiographical content, or the seemingly autobiographical content, only in the second half of the poem.

There is a tent where Being and Nothing turn away from each other yet intermingle, and it is in this same tent that we find a small boy wearing a coat and sobbing uncontrollably. We do not know who the boy is, but we do learn that he is crying while the large allegorical figures of Depth and Darkness are grieving "among the fountains, / And the fountains weep out the grieving sea." His crying is underpinned by all the grief under the Atlantic Ocean. This poem shuttles repeatedly between intimacy and expansiveness, between the miniature and the gigantic.

"O listen," the speaker cries out, and part of what we listen to is a thicket of *s* sounds: "the *s*team engines *s*hunt and *s*witch / A*s*leep in their grieving." It's as if he himself is surprised to find himself in a city of trains. We observe a sorrowful family, presented in the third person, who are weeping so badly that their tears stain the blinds. We witness a boy who hears the sad sound of his own "begetting," a word with an almost biblical feeling. The boy grieves, and goes on grieving, over his own birth, that primal separation, and so does his "willow mother." The poet doesn't say "willowy mother," which would suggest her shape, but "willow mother," which makes her nearly a mythological creature, part tree, part person. The repetition of the letter *m* slowly sounds out what is happening, how the "*m*other *m*ars her *m*irror / Of the lake with tears."

Grossman continues to move from the universal to the local, from the general to the particular, in the next-to-last stanza, where we are once more reminded that the poem is situated in downtown Chicago. The stanza sets the scene in the present tense, in winter: "It is cold and snowing / And the snow is falling into the river." The mysterious woman — we have been waiting for her to show up all along — now appears on the bridge, which is lit by the large white shadow of the Wrigley Building. The last stanza turns from the present to the past and marks this scene as a personal memory:

> As I remember,
> The same boy passes, announcing the fame
> Of tears, calling out the terms
> In a clear way, translating to the long
> Dim human avenue.

At the end of the poem, the woman on the bridge becomes in some sense the speaker's mother. The speaker himself becomes the boy. This is an archetypal situation. One of the stranger things that Grossman told the poet Mark

Halliday, in their stimulating conversations published as *The Sighted Singer,* is that he considers it a commonplace that persons write poems for their mothers. He said, "My poetry is, in the most literal sense, the speech of my mother, or rather, the completion of the speech of my mother." He embraces an idea, which would seem extreme even for Freud, that a son's poetic work fulfills his mother's spoken and unspoken desires. "The sense in which my poetry is organized to justify hope goes deep back into a personal history of intimacy, of a mother who was restlessly and in some sense destructively dissatisfied with the world around her. The prolongation and, as it were, consummation of her will toward a golden world is as voracious an account as I can give of my motive to art." In "The Woman on the Bridge over the Chicago River," the poet vows to complete the weeping speech of his mother, his first beloved.

One implication of Grossman's thinking is that poetry originates with our mothers, who first gave us speech, the texture of sounds, our mother tongue. They gave us the words that became our world and, in the process, sentenced us to ourselves. The maternal origin thus points to the "source of the world, the deep source of art, the point of intersection between nothing and something; both for myself as an individual, as the mother is, and myself as the member of a cosmos which did itself have a beginning." The mother is thus both an individual person and a larger principle of inception and parentage.

Grossman also noted that the speaker in "The Woman on the Bridge over the Chicago River" vows to write a book against our vanishing. He rebels against our mortal forgetfulness. The phrase "the fame / Of tears" evokes the traditional dream of eternal Fame, a longstanding literary ideal that goes back to ancient Greece, to Homer and to Theogenes, who promised his beloved that she would be "known / To people of all time, your name imperishable." In a sense, the speaker of this poem remembers the boy who is "calling out the terms" and vows to translate it into human speech. What he remembers is a monumental sadness, the sadness of mother and son, a grief with a depth beyond reason, and he vows to forever memorialize it in a visionary poem.

We read poems for all sorts of reasons — to be challenged, disturbed, consoled, recognized. We look to poetry for articulations, for knowledge. It is inevitable that we also ask *What is poetry for?* Allen Grossman answers this question with firm resolve: "Poetry is a principle of power invoked by all of us against our vanishing."

ANTHONY HECHT

—

"The Book of Yolek"

(1981)

In 1945, Anthony Hecht was a twenty-two-year old private in the US Army's Ninety-Seventh Infantry Division when he participated in the liberation of the Flossenbürg concentration camp. By the time his unit arrived to help free the camp, more than thirty thousand people had died there, and the SS personnel had fled. Prisoners were dying from typhus at the rate of five hundred a day. As Hecht explained in a book-length interview with Philip Hoy:

> Since I had the rudiments of French and German, I was appointed to interview such French prisoners as were well enough to speak, in the hope of securing evidence against those who ran the camp. Later, when some of these were captured, I presented them with the charges leveled against them, translating their denials or defenses back into French for the sake of their accusers, in an attempt to get to the bottom of what was done and who was responsible.

Hecht found the whole experience "inexpressibly horrible" and was forever changed by what he witnessed in a remote area of northeastern Bavaria.

Later, he tried to come to terms with the totality of what was done and who was responsible in a group of formally crafted, emotionally intense Holocaust poems, which includes "Rites and Ceremonies," "'More Light! More Light!,'" "It Out-Herods Herod, Pray You Avoid It," "Persistences," and "The Book of Yolek."

"The Book of Yolek" is a sestina with a sacred or religious feeling. It reads like one of the lost or apocryphal books of the Bible. A small boy has perished and refuses to be forgotten. The German epigraph is Martin Luther's translation of a verse in the Gospel of John (19:7), which translates as "We have a law, / And by that law he must die." In the Gospel, the demand is attributed to the Jews who sought the death of Jesus. But Hecht ironically lifts the statement from its original context and uses it as an epigraph, where it now constitutes the German justification for killing children, including one named Yolek.

The Book of Yolek

Wir haben ein Gesetz,
Und nach dem Gesetz soll er sterben.

The dowsed coals fume and hiss after your meal
Of grilled brook trout, and you saunter off for a walk
Down the fern trail, it doesn't matter where to,
Just so you're weeks and worlds away from home,
And among midsummer hills have set up camp
In the deep bronze glories of declining day.

You remember, peacefully, an earlier day
In childhood, remember a quite specific meal:
A corn roast and bonfire in summer camp.
That summer you got lost on a Nature Walk;
More than you dared admit, you thought of home;
No one else knows where the mind wanders to.

The fifth of August, 1942.
It was morning and very hot. It was the day
They came at dawn with rifles to The Home
For Jewish Children, cutting short the meal

Of bread and soup, lining them up to walk
In close formation off to a special camp.

How often you have thought about that camp,
As though in some strange way you were driven to,
And about the children, and how they were made to walk,
Yolek who had bad lungs, who wasn't a day
Over five years old, commanded to leave his meal
And shamble between armed guards to his long home.

We're approaching August again. It will drive home
The regulation torments of that camp
Yolek was sent to, his small, unfinished meal,
The electric fences, the numeral tattoo,
The quite extraordinary heat of the day
They were all forced to take that terrible walk.

Whether on a silent, solitary walk
Or among crowds, far off or safe at home,
You will remember, helplessly, that day,
And the smell of smoke, and the loudspeakers of the camp.
Wherever you are, Yolek will be there, too.
His unuttered name will interrupt your meal.

Prepare to receive him in your home some day.
Though they killed him in the camp they sent him to,
He will walk in as you're sitting down to a meal.

Hecht marshals the form of the sestina to enact a kind of walk. An intricate verse form created and mastered by the Provençal poets, the sestina is a thirty-nine-line poem consisting of six six-line stanzas and one three-line envoi (or "send-off"). The six end-words of the first stanza are repeated, in a prescribed order, as end-words in each of the subsequent stanzas. The concluding tercet includes all six of the end-words. One feature of the form is its tendency to generate a narrative even as it circles back on itself as the end-words recur. It has a sense of expansiveness but also a sense of compulsive returning.

It is evident from "The Book of Yolek" that Hecht had been thinking seriously about the sestina as a form. He was trying to figure out how it operates, to achieve maximum impact. This formal preoccupation is confirmed in one of his letters: "And it occurred to me that because of the persistent reiteration of those terminal words, over and over in stanza after stanza, the sestina seemed to lend itself especially well to a topic felt obsessively, unremittingly."

"The Book of Yolek" has a few explicit sources. One was a memorable photograph from the Warsaw ghetto, which Hecht describes: "It's of a small boy, perhaps five or six, wearing a shabby peaked hat and short pants, his hands raised and a bewildered, forlorn look on his face as he gazes off at something to the side of the camera, while behind him uniformed, helmeted soldiers keep their rifles trained on him, as one of them looks directly at the camera without the least expression of embarrassment."

Hecht also said that the poem derived from Hanna Mortkowicz-Olczakowa's fictionalized account of the last walk of the Jewish educator Janusz Korczak, who witnessed the deportation of the Jews from the Warsaw ghetto (he called it *"The district of the damned!"*) and tried to stop the liquidation of children's homes and orphanages. Among the children were "little Hanka with lung trouble, Yolek who was ill . . ." The sixty-four-year-old Korczak, whose health had been ruined, refused to part with more than two hundred children and adolescents from the Children's Home, who were in his charge, and he insisted on going with them to their deaths in the Treblinka extermination camp. New evidence suggests that Mortkowicz-Olczakowa's account, which begins, "The day was Wednesday, 5th August, 1942, in the morning," is highly romanticized. The truth was far darker. But Hecht's ruthless formal and moral scrupulousness avoids the trap of sentimentalizing Korczak's last walk and promising Yolek and his classmates "eternal glory."

"The Book of Yolek" is written in a skillfully varied, seemingly effortless blank verse. The poem begins deceptively, at a leisurely pace. It is addressed to a "you," using the second person, which creates a sense of intimacy, of someone talking to himself. It's a way for the poet to speak to himself as well as to someone else. We feel invited in. This effect is heightened by the present tense. The first stanza is one sentence that ambles across six lines. The speaker is camping out. The coals are still hot after a fresh meal — is there an intimation of what's to come in the way they "fume and hiss"? — as he saunters off for a walk amid the midsummer hills at twilight. It's all quite lovely. This feeling is clinched in

the alliterative repetition of the letter *d* in the last line: "In the *d*eep bronze
glories of *d*eclining *d*ay." The reader who knows German will have picked up a
darkness lurking in the epigraph, but otherwise we have no idea what the true
subject of this poem is going to be.

The second stanza, which is divided neatly into two sentences, moves to
the implied speaker's childhood memory of being at summer camp: "You re-
member, peacefully . . ." He finds himself recalling the time he got lost on a
hike and suddenly felt an unexpected fear and homesickness, more than he al-
lowed himself to admit. The poem then turns on the line "No one else knows
where the mind wanders to."

Where the mind of the speaker abruptly wanders to, in fact, is a very par-
ticular day. Notice that Hecht doesn't render it as "August 5, 1942," but instead
writes it out, "The fifth of August, 1942," as in a formal document. The first
line is a fragment, the second obsessively repeats the fateful timing: "*It was*
morning . . ."; "*It was* the day . . ." Two things continue to happen throughout
the rest of the poem. The story of five-year-old Yolek, and the other children
forced to march to their fate, is narrated; we get a dramatic sense of their "ter-
rible walk." At the same time, there is always a person in the present tense re-
calling what happened. He is bedeviled and unable to forget. Hence the lines,
which open the next three stanzas:

How often you have thought about that camp . . .

and

We're approaching August again. It will drive home . . .

and

Whether on a silent, solitary walk
Or among crowds, far off or safe at home,
You will remember, helplessly, that day . . .

Hecht's poem has a quiet, hypnotic insistence. Sometimes this is deliv-
ered through anaphora ("Yolek who had bad lungs, who wasn't a day / Over
five years old"), sometimes through consonance ("silent, solitary"), sometimes
through changes in verb tense ("you *were driven* to"; "It *will drive* home"). But

the fundamental formal achievement is the extremely adept use of the six end-words: "meal," "walk," "to," "home," "camp," and "day." Each of these words begins innocently enough but then takes on a much darker meaning over the course of the poem. Hecht finds multiple uses for "home," "day," "meal," and "walk," a word that serves as both a noun and a verb.

Take the word "camp." It begins innocuously enough in the phrases "set up camp" and "summer camp." But at the end of the third stanza and the beginning of the fourth, the word takes on an entirely different connotation: "In close formation off to a special camp. // How often you have thought about that camp." This is the first time that we understand the word to mean "death camp." Hecht is fulfilling the prescribed form and putting "camp" at the center of the poem. And we are experiencing the way a word migrates from innocence to horror.

Something equally transformative happens to the word "to," which begins the poem as an inconsequential preposition but later becomes a consequential date, "1942," and, even more haunting, part of the noun "tattoo." It takes on a kind of inevitability as an adverb ("Wherever you are, Yolek will be there, too") and a dark fatefulness in the penultimate line ("Though they killed him in the camp they sent him to").

The six end-words are ordained to come together in the final three lines. The envoi becomes an injunction. The speaker is still talking to himself, but now, very pointedly, he also seems to be addressing each of us. Reminiscent of Primo Levi's poem "Shemà," the envoi makes clear the Jewish injunction to remember the dead:

> Prepare to receive him in your home some day.
> Though they killed him in the camp they sent him to,
> He will walk in as you're sitting down to a meal.

Yolek has been transformed into a kind of Elijah figure. On Passover, Jews all over world pour the prophet Elijah a cup of wine and open the door for him, inviting him to enter as a guest who will signal the advent of the Messiah. Thus far, Elijah has tarried and never come back. And neither has Yolek. At the end of Anthony Hecht's testimonial poem, each of us is left at home, opening the door and sitting down to a meal, forever waiting for a murdered boy to return.

—◆—

"Mr Cogito and the Imagination"

(1983)

Zbigniew Herbert was an avant-garde classicist — a stubbornly idiosyncratic poet of isolation, disinheritance, and grief, a poet of "historical irony" (the phrase is Czesław Miłosz's), continually confronting his own experience and juxtaposing it with that of the past, seeking grounds for what he called "universal compassion." He deliberately cultivated a cool, economical, and anti-rhetorical style, dispensing with punctuation in his poems and eschewing grandiose effects.

Herbert was attracted to philosophy — he had a long correspondence with the Polish philosopher Henryk Elzenberg — and in the early 1970s he adopted the persona Pan Cogito, or Mr Cogito, his playful stand-in, whose name originated in Descartes's famous Latin proposition *Cogito, ergo sum* ("I think, therefore I am"). Some of the Mr Cogito poems are written in the first person, others in the third person, but all of them give Herbert the wry perspective and distance of a figure who speaks both as himself and as someone else, a sort of Polish Everyman, who knows European philosophy. He has had Herbert's life experiences. Mr Cogito is not a full-fledged dramatic persona, as in a poem

by Robert Browning. He is a filter, or as the critic Hugh Kenner said about El-
iot's figure J. Alfred Prufrock, "a name plus a voice."

Here is "Mr Cogito and the Imagination," which appears in *Report from a
Besieged City* (1983):

Mr Cogito and the Imagination

I
Mr Cogito has never trusted
the tricks of the imagination

the piano at the top of the Alps
played concerts false to his ear

he had no regard for labyrinths
the Sphinx filled him with disgust

he lived in a cellarless house
without mirrors or dialectics

jungles of tangled images
were never his homeland

he rarely got carried away
on the wings of a metaphor
he then plunged like Icarus
into the arms of the Great Mother

he adored tautologies
explanations
idem per idem

a bird is a bird
slavery slavery
a knife a knife
death is death

he loved
a flat horizon
a straight line
earth's gravity

2
Mr Cogito
will be counted
among the species *minores*

he will receive indifferently
the verdict of men of letters

he employed the imagination
for wholly different purposes

he wanted to make of it
an instrument of compassion

he longed to understand fully

— Pascal's night
— the nature of a diamond
— the prophets' melancholy
— the wrath of Achilles
— the fury of mass murderers
— the dreams of Mary Stuart
— the fear of Neanderthals
— the last Aztecs' despair
— Nietzsche's long dying
— the Lascaux painter's joy
— the rise and fall of an oak
— the rise and fall of Rome

in order to revive the dead
and maintain the covenant

Mr Cogito's imagination
moves like a pendulum

it runs with great precision
from suffering to suffering

there is no place in it
for poetry's artificial fires

he wants to be true
to uncertain clarity

(Translated by Alissa Valles)

Mr Cogito is a poet-philosopher and this is his aesthetic manifesto. It has a light touch and a serious purpose. The poem is divided into two parts. The first part lists some of the things that Mr Cogito distrusts, what he especially dislikes, what repels him. The second section points out some of the primary things that, by contrast, compel him. He recognizes that he is going against the grain of much twentieth-century thought, but he is determined to make his case for what he believes to be the true role and purpose of the imagination.

The poem begins with Mr Cogito's innate skepticism, asserting that "Mr Cogito has never trusted / the tricks of the imagination," and immediately takes a swipe at the French poet Arthur Rimbaud, who coined the phrase "the piano in the Alps" ("After the Flood") as an image for the Romantic sublime, music at its transcendental peak. The premise of Rimbaud's image is that the artist is playing the music of the spheres, invoking some otherworldly power. Mr Cogito doesn't elaborate or explain, but to him these concerts sound false.

Mr Cogito distrusts labyrinths, which have intricate corridors and secret passageways in which most people get completely lost, and he is disgusted by the Sphinx, a mythical creature with a human head and the body of a lion, presumably because, according to Greek legend, it devoured all travelers who could not decipher its riddle. Intellectually speaking, Mr Cogito doesn't like mountaintops or basements; by implication he doesn't trust the promise of secret knowledge, occult or labyrinthine thinking. He explicitly doesn't like mirrors or "dialectics," which suggests Hegelian or Marxist thinking. The implication is that one gets tied in knots trying to figure them out. The reader starts to detect an oppositional political undercurrent running through the poem.

Mr Cogito declares himself against Surrealism or Surrealist thinking — "jungles of tangled images / were never his homeland" — and metaphors that carry one away to another realm. He then purposefully mixes up metaphors and mythologies by stating that when he did get carried away "he then plunged like Icarus / into the arms of the Great Mother." This is to say that he becomes like the son of Daedalus, who flies too close to the sun and pays for it with his life. The Great Mother is a reference to the psychologist Erich Neumann's invocation of the Mother Goddess as an archetypal figure, and there is a subtle dig here at extravagant Jungian, or archetypal, interpretations of Greek myths.

What is Herbert so bothered about? Like many poems that we have been considering, "Mr Cogito and the Imagination" takes a key structural turn. It pivots in the seventh stanza with this statement: "he adored tautologies / explanations / *idem per idem*." The legal term *idem per idem* means "the same for the same." This is almost comically reductive, but it's clear that Mr Cogito wants to keep things simple, even obvious. Herbert was supremely a poet of thought — self-questioning, philosophically self-conscious, a tragic post-Cartesian who recognized that fantasy can have a high price, that calling things by false names has ethical and political implications. He had lived through the political consequences of official Soviet lies — he wrote this poem during a period of martial law in Poland — and recognizes how crucial it is to question political double-speak, the so-called dialectics used to excuse totalitarian thinking. That's why it's so crucial to recognize that

> a bird is a bird
> slavery slavery
> a knife a knife
> death is death.

The poem rapidly changes categories — from a bird to slavery, from a knife to death — in order to unmask the concrete truth of things. There is something to be said, then, not just for intoxication but also for disenchantment in poetry. It is healthy to look out and see "a flat horizon / a straight line," and to feel "earth's gravity." Herbert counters the impulse toward transcendence and brings us down to earth.

The second section of the poem begins by dryly observing that Mr Cogito knew that his position would force him to be counted "among the species *minores*" — that is, part of a lesser species. He accepts his literary fate and receives "indifferently / the verdict of men of letters." Herbert was indifferent to aesthetic fashion and exemplary in his determination to treat the imagination as "an instrument of compassion." He believed that it is essential for poetry to have humane ends in an inhumane world.

Here is the list of those things that Mr Cogito wanted to consider to the very end. It is a compelling catalog of subject rhymes:

> — Pascal's night
> — the nature of a diamond
> — the prophets' melancholy
> — the wrath of Achilles
> — the fury of mass murderers
> — the dreams of Mary Stuart
> — the fear of Neanderthals
> — the last Aztecs' despair
> — Nietzsche's long dying
> — the Lascaux painter's joy
> — the rise and fall of an oak
> — the rise and fall of Rome

The list begins with "Pascal's night," the philosophical wager that human beings bet their lives on: whether or not God exists. It's a metaphysical question. Think of what is called Pascal's "night of fire," that late night in November 1654 when the French scientist and skeptic had a dramatic encounter with God, which he then wrote down and sewed into the lining of his coat, his Memorial. This theological reference is followed by a puzzle about "the nature of a diamond," the formation and miracle of an earthly gem. The poem has moved from the heavens to the earth. The prophets are melancholy because they know what is coming, what human beings are going to do to one another.

Herbert's catalog moves from metaphysical questions to historical ones. Mr Cogito wants to know about the nature of religious faith and the miracle of nature, but he also wants to learn about the victims of history, both individual and collective. Compelled by the rage and madness of some ("the wrath of Achilles"), which leads to the fear and despair of others ("the dreams of Mary Stuart"), the catalog certainly points to the horrors of history ("the fury of mass murderers"). Mr Cogito wants to understand the primal despair of those on the point of extinction ("the fear of Neanderthals"). What must it have been like to be one of the last Aztecs? They were facing not only individual death but also the obliteration of an entire people, their whole history, their complete civilization. A large collective or communal suffering is then followed by the sustained death throes of one of Europe's great philosophers; the suffering of a horse in the street tipped Nietzsche into madness. But Mr Cogito doesn't just meditate on suffering; he also focuses on the mysteries of creation and the joys of artistic creativity. He refers to the ecstasy of the first painters, who captured the movement of animals on the walls of a French cave. He concludes by paralleling the cycle of nature ("the rise and fall of an oak") with the cycle of a civilization ("the rise and fall of Rome").

Herbert provides an essential corrective to what he calls "the artificial fires" of poetry and provides a greater imaginative imperative — a desire to bring the dead back to life and "maintain the covenant." He keeps human suffering in view. Precision matters; accuracy is essential. He remains faithful not just to what we know but also to what we don't or cannot know, to what he names "uncertain clarity." He was a model of integrity, a hero of consciousness, unwavering in his humanity.

C. K. WILLIAMS

"From My Window"

(1983)

C. K. Williams had a large social imagination. He was a poet of disquietude, of psychological extremes, and probed the sorrows of a diligent, self-reflexive consciousness. In his first two books, *Lies* (1969) and *I Am the Bitter Name* (1971), he showed less interest in exploring linkages and connections than in what he called "varieties of disjunctive consciousness." His early work, influenced by the Surrealism of the French dramatist Antonin Artaud and the Peruvian poet César Vallejo, subverted logical connections and struggled to enact the movement of the mind as it swoops, hovers, and moves in at least three different directions. Unsparingly honest and violently self-divided ("I am going to rip myself down the middle into two pieces," he declared in "Halves"), his poems were also motivated by a ferocious political consciousness, almost breaking apart from frustration and rage over the lies of the social and political worlds. He especially despised the war in Vietnam.

The decisive moment in Williams's work came when he began to put things into his poems rather than take them out, to become a poet of inclusive consciousness. He enlarged and extended his lineation even further than Walt Whitman's long free-verse lines, which harken back to the King James Bible, the model for prose in English. The test for Williams was to see how far he could push and shape that line before it faltered and turned into prose poetry. By using the line as the longest possible rhythmic unit, he forced himself to break the abbreviated rhetorical code, the conventional shorthand, that seems to characterize so much of the poetry of any given period. As if heeding Robert Frost's directive to dramatize ("Everything written is as good as it is dramatic," Frost said), Williams also became an insistent storyteller, burrowing his social message into the substance and political unconscious of his poems.

Williams started to use his long, rangy, capacious line in *With Ignorance* (1977) and then perfected it in *Tar* (1983). He had become a storyteller, which is to say that he borrowed some devices from narrative fiction to build anecdotes into stories and make keen social observations. He also used the line as a container for consciousness, for observing people in social situations, usually doing something outrageous, sometimes unwillingly, and often breaking a public norm. There's an element of voyeurism in his poems. He was watchful and often caught himself in the act of seeing something that he shouldn't be seeing. He observed others doing the same thing. He was willing to confront hard truths — about himself as well as others — and his poems can be discomfiting to read. He said, "Poetry confronts in the most clear-eyed way just those emotions which consciousness wishes to slide by."

That clear-eyed view especially relates to the poem "From My Window," the opening gambit in *Tar:*

From My Window

Spring: the first morning when that one true block of sweet, laminar,
            complex scent arrives
from somewhere west and I keep coming to lean on the sill, glorying
            in the end of the wretched winter.
The scabby-barked sycamores ringing the empty lot across the way
            are budded — I hadn't noticed —
and the thick spikes of the unlikely urban crocuses have already broken
            the gritty soil.
Up the street, some surveyors with tripods are waving each other left
            and right the way they do.
A girl in a gym suit jogged by a while ago, some kids passed, playing
            hooky, I imagine,

and now the paraplegic Vietnam vet who lives in a half-converted
        warehouse down the block
and the friend who stays with him and seems to help him out come
        weaving towards me,
their battered wheelchair lurching uncertainly from one edge of the
        sidewalk to the other.
I know where they're going — to the "Legion": once, when I was
        putting something out, they stopped,
both drunk that time, too, both reeking — it wasn't ten o'clock — and
        we chatted for a bit.
I don't know how they stay alive — on benefits most likely. I wonder
        if they're lovers?
They don't look it. Right now, in fact, they look a wreck, careening
        haphazardly along,
contriving, as they reach beneath me, to dip a wheel from the curb so
        that the chair skewers, teeters,
tips, and they both tumble, the one slowly, almost gracefully sliding
        in stages from his seat,
his expression hardly marking it, the other staggering over him,
        spinning heavily down,
to lie on the asphalt, his mouth working, his feet shoving weakly and
        fruitlessly against the curb.
In the storefront office on the corner, Reed and Son, Real Estate, have
        come to see the show.
Gazing through the golden letters of their name, they're not, at least,
        thank god, laughing.
Now the buddy, grabbing at a hydrant, gets himself erect and stands
        there for a moment, panting.
Now he has to lift the other one, who lies utterly still, a forearm
        shielding his eyes from the sun.
He hauls him partly upright, then hefts him almost all the way into
        the chair but a dangling foot
catches a support-plate, jerking everything around so that he has to
        put him down,
set the chair to rights, and hoist him again and as he does he jerks the
        grimy jeans right off him.
No drawers, shrunken, blotchy thighs: under the thick, white coils

of belly blubber,

the poor, blunt pud, tiny, terrified, retracted, is almost invisible in the
       sparse genital hair,

then his friend pulls his pants up, he slumps wholly back as though he
       were, at last, to be let be,

and the friend leans against the cyclone fence, suddenly staring up at
       me as though he'd known,

all along, that I was watching and I can't help wondering if he knows
       that in the winter, too,

I watched, the night he went out to the lot and walked, paced rather,
       almost ran, for how many hours.

It was snowing, the city in that holy silence, the last we have, when
       the storm takes hold,

and he was making patterns that I thought at first were circles, then
       realized made a figure eight,

what must have been to him a perfect symmetry, but which, from
       where I was, shivered, bent,

and lay on its side: a warped, unclear infinity, slowly, as the snow
       came faster, going out.

Over and over again, his head lowered to the task, he slogged the path
       he'd blazed,

but the race was lost, his prints were filling faster than he made them
       now and I looked away,

up across the skeletal trees to the tall center city buildings, some,
       though it was midnight,

with all their offices still gleaming, their scarlet warning beacons
       signaling erratically

against the thickening flakes, their smoldering auras softening portions
       of the dim, milky sky.

In the morning, nothing: every trace of him effaced, all the field pure
       white,

its surface glittering, the dawn, glancing from its glaze, oblique,
       relentless, unadorned.

The narrator begins by setting a city scene: it's the end of winter, the first
real morning of spring, and he keeps coming back to the window to drink it

all in. Williams uses three adjectives — "sweet," "laminar" (a word borrowed from physics, as in a laminar flow, to suggest a constant nonturbulent stream), and "complex" — to describe the scent coming from somewhere to the west. The narrator seems newly awake and observes that the sycamores have now budded ("I hadn't noticed"). The natural scene alerts him to what is unfolding below — the surveyors, the girl in a gym suit, some kids passing by, probably skipping school, and now the paraplegic Vietnam vet and his friend weaving unsteadily from one side of the sidewalk to the other. He knows where they are going — to the "Legion" — and how they get drunk in the morning. He doesn't speculate, but the vet in a wheelchair is probably suffering from some form of posttraumatic stress disorder. The speaker is curious about the two of them ("I wonder if they're lovers?" he idly speculates) and how they manage to survive, probably "on benefits."

The main action of the poem is the untoward accident that takes place in the street below, the vet in a wheelchair tumbling to the ground, his friend staggering over him. The narrator of the poem observes what is happening to them through a window, which, as in Cavafy's poem "The God Abandons Antony," serves as a sharp transition point between inside and outside. But here the narrator has a sort of double consciousness. He is not only witnessing what is going on in the street below but also notices two other people, Reed and his son, who are likewise observing, from their storefront window, what has become a "show." Oddly, they see everything through the lettering of their names, a curious, privileged position. Everyone is separated by glass; no one can hear what anyone else is saying. Williams's narrator is looking down, and the others are looking out at the spectacle. What happens next is painful: the vet's friend inadvertently pulls off the crippled man's pants and everyone sees the "blotchy thighs" and the "poor, blunt pud." The narrator can't look away but can't bear the exposure either, and yet he can't deny it is happening because Reed and Son are also seeing precisely what he is seeing. And then the man in the street, the vet's friend, looks up and sees the narrator observing it all from the window above. He watches him watching. Those indoors and outdoors are locked in a shameful moment that feels endless. The narrator can't avoid the fact that he has become a guilty spectator to another person's suffering.

And then the poem moves to the memory of the night that the speaker saw the vet's friend — he isn't given a name — going out and making a figure eight in the snow. That night the narrator became an unintended witness to the small drama of a person trying to make a mark in a snowfall that was quickly erasing it. The poem has thus moved from a new morning to the memory of night.

The narrator finds something sacred in the scene and remembers "the city in that holy silence, the last we have." He can't help noticing the difference in perspectives. Whereas the man in the snow probably thinks he is making a figure with perfect symmetry, the observer above sees that it is flawed, "shivered, bent" — "a warped, unclear infinity." That's the view at ground level. But the narrator has a more elevated view. Notice how he looks up over "the skeletal trees" to the lights gleaming in some Center City buildings, even at midnight, which, as we have seen from other poems, almost always signals an epiphany. The lights are a naturalistic detail, but the light itself is not natural. Standing at the window at midnight, he is also standing on the threshold between one day and the next, the inner and outer worlds, earth and heaven. In many visionary poems, such as W. B. Yeats's "All Souls' Night" ("Midnight has come") and Walt Whitman's "A Clear Midnight," the midnight hour is symbolically clear and almost transparent, not cloudy or obscure, and signals a kind of commerce between this world and the next. But Williams's narrator has a much more mixed view. He views the gleaming lights as "scarlet warning beacons signaling erratically," as if their "smoldering auras" are somehow a warning of the ruthless natural force coming down at us from "the dim, milky sky." For a moment the two figures in this poem, one down below in the snow, one standing above at the window, are alone in the universe.

It's a fleeting revelation. The narrator recalls that on the following morning, all traces of the man in the snow have been effaced; the cold, clear, glittering field is unmarked, "pure white." Once more Williams employs three surprising adjectives — "oblique" (not straightforward), "relentless" (unabated), and "unadorned" (plain and simple) to describe the dawn. He also presses the consonants *gl* in the last line ("*gl*ittering," "*gl*ancing," "*gl*aze") to suggest the almost incandescent, angular, shining light of the new day. The narrator of C. K. Williams's vigilant poem finds himself staring into a beauteous oblivion.

—

"Night Song"

(1983)

Throughout her fierce and unsparing fourth book, *The Triumph of Achilles* (1985), Louise Glück treats the sexual desire to lose the self to another as an erotic version of the longing for oblivion and death, a joyous illusion, but an illusion nonetheless. She poses that longing against artistic consciousness, the desire to leave behind "exact records." Lovers have a deep-seeded need to try to merge and become one, but it comes at a high cost — the loss of consciousness, of self. Here is "Night Song," which appeared in *The New Yorker* in 1983 and was subsequently published as the fifth section of her nine-part sequence, "Marathon," in *The Triumph of Achilles*.

Night Song

Look up into the light of the lantern.
Don't you see? The calm of darkness
is the horror of Heaven.

We've been apart too long, too painfully separated.
How can you bear to dream,
to give up watching? I think you must be dreaming,
your face is full of mild expectancy.

I need to wake you, to remind you that there isn't a future.
That's why we're free. And now some weakness in me
has been cured forever, so I'm not compelled
to close my eyes, to go back, to rectify —

The beach is still; the sea, cleansed of its superfluous life,
opaque, rocklike. In mounds, in vegetal clusters,
seabirds sleep on the jetty. Terns, assassins —

You're tired; I can see that.
We're both tired, we have acted a great drama.
Even our hands are cold, that were like kindling.
Our clothes are scattered on the sand; strangely enough,
they never turned to ashes.

I have to tell you what I've learned, that I know now
what happens to the dreamers.
They don't feel it when they change. One day
they wake, they dress, they are old.

Tonight I'm not afraid
to feel the revolutions. How can you want sleep
when passion gives you that peace?
You're like me tonight, one of the lucky ones.
You'll get what you want. You'll get your oblivion.

It's as if we are overhearing an extremely personal, albeit one-sided conversation, a monologue so ardent that it wants to rise above speech, to become a song. It hits a heightened pitch, like a nocturne, and presents a night scene, an all-night vigil. This is a sort of counterpart poem to Stephen Berg's "On This Side of the River," where a gruelingly self-conscious male speaker addresses his sleeping female lover. In "Night Song," a hypervigilant female speaker dramatically addresses her sleeping male lover. But whereas Berg's poem has a distinctly urban milieu, the two figures in Glück's poem seem to have gone to a cabin by the sea, far from the lights of the city.

It's late at night. The speaker's tone is urgent, her voice low, reckless, intent: "Look up into the light of the lantern," she tells him. The liquid *l*'s link the three words — "Look," "light," "lantern" — and help emphasize the command to see. The lantern is a realistic detail, but it is also a metaphor for the solitary light of consciousness. This is reminiscent of a moment in an elegy by the Czech poet, Jiří Orten, where he states outright: "Now, when everything's running short, / I can't stand being here by myself. The lamplight's too strong."

The second line kicks off with a question: "Don't you see?" Here the emphasis can fall on any one of the three words: "*Don't* you see?"; "Don't *you* see?"; "Don't you *see*?" The speaker is more alert than her sleeping lover. She seems impatient with him for dropping off to sleep and leaving her awake and alone with her insights.

The speaker's next thought is unexpected. She is sounding a warning to her lover — she can't understand why he doesn't also recognize that "The calm of darkness / is the horror of Heaven." The line break emphasizes the calmness of darkness, and the *h* sound presses together the unlikely pairing of "horror" and "Heaven." The word "Heaven" is capitalized, as it is here, only when referring to the dwelling place of the Lord. The promise of an afterlife is usually thought of as reassuring, but for Glück's speaker it is appalling because it means mortal death, the end of time.

The lovers are exhausted, spent, cold. The specifics of their situation are sketchy, but we infer from the previous parts of the sequence that they have come together after a long and possibly final absence, remembered their severed past, acted their parts in a "great drama," made love as if stamping or branding each other's bodies. Now while one sleeps and dreams — expectant, oblivious — the other keeps herself awake by talking to him with a passionate, perhaps even terrified intensity, telling him what she has learned, bringing him her news, her argument. In the first sentence, the word "apart" opens up into the word "separated," and the speaker presses down on the adverb "too":

> We've been apart too long, too painfully separated.
> How can you bear to dream,

> to give up watching? I think you must be dreaming,
> your face is full of mild expectancy.
>
> I need to wake you, to remind you that there isn't a future.
> That's why we're free. And now some weakness in me
> has been cured forever, so I'm not compelled
> to close my eyes, to go back, to rectify—

Glück poses the difference between sleeping and waking as an opposition between clarity and dreaming, consciousness and forgetfulness, living in the present moment against expecting a future. The speaker's vigilant intensity, her doomed foreknowledge, is contrasted to her lover's mildness, his escape from consciousness, his faith in a future that she believes doesn't exist. We're free precisely because we don't have any expectations of time. We must watch ourselves in the moment, she seems to be telling him; we must live inside it. The speaker has cured herself of what she calls a weakness, a need to go back over the past, to correct things. She is frustrated with her lover for sleeping, which seems like an escape. Consciousness is the only weapon against an oblivion that separately will be claiming each of us.

In an essay about "Night Song," called "The Dreamer and the Watcher," Glück suggests that for her the sleeping lover is a figure of Eros, the ravishing god of love, whereas the watcher is a version of Psyche, the mortal woman who, at whatever cost, insists on knowledge. Glück's observer doesn't long for the lightness of the body; rather, she valorizes the presence of the watcher, an acute artistic consciousness. The theme of the watcher and the sleeper is part of a larger argument about the integrity of the human self. She poses the existential longing for solitude against the lover's longing for dissolution.

The lovers exist in a liminal space. They are left with only an old-fashioned lantern burning in the night. Outside, the world has been stripped down to essentials: the beach still, the sea cleansed of anything superfluous. Seabirds, which seem to have regressed to vegetal life, sleep on a narrow structure at the edge of the coastline. The speaker calls the terns "assassins." Why? Perhaps because they are harbingers of oblivion. The word seems to bring her up short and she breaks off this train of thought: "You're tired; I can see that. / We're both tired, we have acted a great drama."

These lines put me in mind of Galway Kinnell's "Wait" (1980), a poem that stands against suicide and states outright:

Wait.
Don't go too early.
You're tired. But everyone's tired.
But no one is tired enough.

Glück's lovers are naked; they have acted their parts in a passion play. A little while ago the heat between them was so great that their hands were like kindling wood. The flames might have burned their clothes and reduced them to ashes. Now everything has gone cold. The speaker too was one of the dreamers, but now she desperately needs to tell her lover what she has discovered, the wisdom she has come to. The lover is close by but also somehow out of reach:

> I have to tell you what I've learned, that I know now
> what happens to the dreamers.
> They don't feel it when they change. One day
> they wake, they dress, they are old.
>
> Tonight I'm not afraid
> to feel the revolutions. How can you want sleep
> when passion gives you that peace?
> You're like me tonight, one of the lucky ones.
> You'll get what you want. You'll get your oblivion.

Glück's speaker has come back with the news that lovers are always lost in a dream, that dreamers don't feel the textured passage of time. They are unaware of what is happening to them. One day they wake up, get dressed again, and discover they are old. It has all passed in a dream. But she believes in consciousness rather than peace. The line break at the end of the first line of the last stanza emphasizes her attitude toward time passing: "I'm not afraid / to feel the revolutions."

By the end of this dramatic monologue, the speaker's possibly unconscious impatience and near-anger with her lover for sleeping so peacefully ("How can you want sleep / when passion gives you that peace?") peaks and coalesces in a muted accusation and judgment delivered as two declarative sentences pressed into one line: "*You'll* get what *you* want. *You'll* get *your* oblivion." She doesn't say, "*We'll* get what *we* what. *We'll* get *our* oblivion."

In conclusion, Glück's speaker realizes, and argues with a kind of vengeance, that both the watcher and the dreamer are alike: they are both "lucky" because they will get release, freedom from the burdens of selfhood. They will be fulfilled. In the end, the human stand-ins for Eros and Psyche will both find oblivion, the end of life itself, negation and nonbeing. Consciousness is what we have until then.

SHARON OLDS

———

"The Race"

(1983)

Sharon Olds wrote "The Race" in the days or weeks after her father died in the early autumn of 1983. He was seventy years old. It was intended to be a freestanding individual poem, though it eventually founds its place at the heart of her thematically linked collection *The Father* (1992).

The Race

When I got to the airport I rushed up to the desk,
bought a ticket, ten minutes later
they told me the flight was cancelled, the doctors
had said my father would not live through the night
and the flight was cancelled. A young man
with a dark brown moustache told me
another airline had a non-stop
leaving in seven minutes. See that
elevator over there, well go
down to the first floor, make a right, you'll

see a yellow bus, get off at the
Pan Am terminal, I
ran, I who have no sense of direction
raced exactly where he'd told me, a fish
slipping upstream deftly against
the flow of the river. I jumped off that bus with those
bags I had thrown everything into
in five minutes and ran, the bags
wagged me from side to side as if
to prove I was under the claims of the material,
I ran up to a man with a white flower in his breast,
I who always go to the end of the line, I said
Help me. He looked at my ticket, he said
Make a left and then a right, go up to the moving stairs and then
run. I lumbered up the moving stairs,
at the top I saw the corridor,
and then I took a deep breath, I said
Goodbye to my body, goodbye to comfort,
I used my legs and heart as if I would
gladly use them up for this,
to touch him again in this life. I ran, and the
bags banged against me, wheeled and coursed
in skewed orbits, I have seen pictures of
women running, their belongings tied
in scarves grasped in their fists, I blessed my
long legs he gave me, my strong
heart I abandoned to its own purpose,
I ran to Gate 17 and they were
just lifting the thick white
lozenge of the door to fit into
the socket of the plane. Like the one who is not
too rich, I turned sideways and
slipped through the needle's eye, and then
I walked down the aisle toward my father. The jet
was full, and people's hair was shining, they were
smiling, the interior of the plane was filled with a
mist of gold endorphin light,

I wept as people weep when they enter heaven,
in massive relief. We lifted up
gently from one tip of the continent
and did not stop until we set down lightly on the
other edge. I walked into his room
and watched his chest rise slowly
and sink again, all night
I watched him breathe.

"The Race" has a desperate emotional urgency. The action is so immediate that it takes a moment to register that it takes place in the past tense. It's a flash of memory that unfolds across one long stanza of fifty-six lines. The plot is deftly established in the first five lines. The father won't make it through the night, the doctors have said, and the daughter needs to get to him before he dies. Flying is the only option, but "the flight was cancelled," a point reiterated for emphasis. The rest of the poem builds momentum and carefully recreates a woman's wild rush through the airport. We know what's at stake in "the race."

Olds has an intuitive feeling for velocity in a poem. Here her run-on sentences and tense enjambments work perfectly to dramatize the experience. We feel the gap between the urgency of the situation and the utter anonymity of the airport, a neutral public space. The poem moves rapidly, but the speaker takes time to observe everything carefully; for example, she notes that a "young man" has "a dark brown moustache." She fluently embeds his exact speech into her sentence:

> See that
> elevator over there, well go
> down to the first floor, make a right, you'll
> see a yellow bus, get off at the
> Pan Am terminal, I
> ran . . .

That yellow bus inevitably evokes a school bus. One of the striking things here is the dramatic calm that overcomes the speaker — "I who have no sense of direction / raced exactly where he'd told me" — and how she compares herself to "a fish / slipping upstream deftly against / the flow of the river." A. R.

Ammons said that a poem is a walk, but this one is much faster than that — it's a race to the finish.

Linger for a moment over the simile of the suitcases wagging the woman from side to side "as if / to prove I was under the claims of the material." The suggestion is not just that the bags are controlling her, like a dog, but that "the material," the trip, the outer physical world, is placing its claim on her. So too the white flower in the man's breast seems like a hopeful sign. All this is embedded in a run-on sentence that ends with a plea whose poignancy outstrips its occasion, a simple airport request: "*Help me.*"

The poem then pauses for another set of directions. Notice the long, slow line that ends curtly after the first word of the next line: "Make a left and then a right, go up to the moving stairs and then / run." Soon the pace picks up again:

> I said
> Goodbye to my body, goodbye to comfort,
> I used my legs and heart as if I would
> gladly use them up for this,
> to touch him again in this life.

The poem moves fluently between the mundane details of the airport run and statements of the largest emotional import. Now the woman in the poem compares herself to photographs she has seen of other women running, as if in wartime; now she links herself to her father and claims her separation from him too: "I blessed my / long legs he gave me, my strong / heart I abandoned to its own purpose."

Olds takes the time to invert one of Jesus's sayings — "It is easier for a camel to go through the eye of a needle, than for someone who is rich to enter the kingdom of God" (Mark 10:25) — as she describes the fortunate physical entry into the plane itself: "Like the one who is not / too rich, I turned sideways and / slipped through the needle's eye." Note the next displacement. The speaker doesn't say that she heads toward her seat, but rather "I walked down the aisle toward my father." This has the magical feeling of a wedding. Or, as Olds has put it, "A very small girl in 1945 might have at some point assumed, without knowing she was assuming, that when she grew up she too might take her turn at marrying her father."

What follows is an amazing description of the interior of a plane in a "gold endorphin light" — which brings a fairy tale element to the feeling created by hormones. The endorphins released during a long, hard sprint are projected onto the light itself, completing the analogy: "I wept as people weep when they enter heaven, / in massive relief." There is a pun on the word "relief," which first of all suggests a great release from anxiety. The word also has a geographical meaning and refers to the highest and lowest elevation points in an area. That's a view one might get when one "enters heaven."

The poem lifts, like the plane itself, and concludes with one sentence that tumbles forward:

> We lifted up
> gently from one tip of the continent
> and did not stop until we set down lightly on the
> other edge. I walked into his room
> and watched his chest rise slowly
> and sink again, all night
> I watched him breathe.

The words "gently" and "lightly" suggest the way that a daughter might touch her dying father. There is a feeling of utter calm as the speaker sits back and flies across the country, which she characterizes in just three and a half lines. She elides the flight; she doesn't bother with the arrival at the other airport, the drive across the city. Instead, she cuts ahead and enters the room where her father is still alive. The race has been worth it. She has made it in time.

"The Race" is a determined, single-minded poem. Olds doesn't show any of the ambivalence toward the father that is evident in many of her other poems. She succeeds in reaching him. She also succeeds in capturing the feeling of a woman in the middle of life, running and flying to catch her father before he dies, racing to watch him breathe for the last time.

—

"In Memory of the Unknown Poet, Robert Boardman Vaughn"

(1984)

Donald Justice was a scrupulous tactician of melancholy and loss who approached his subjects with "a love that masquerades as pure technique" ("Nostalgia of the Lakefronts"). His dark, exacting villanelle for a lost friend, "In Memory of the Unknown Poet, Robert Boardman Vaughn," appeared in his fifth collection, *The Sunset Maker* (1987).

In Memory of the Unknown Poet, Robert Boardman Vaughn

But the essential advantage for a poet is not to have a beautiful world with which to deal: it is to be able to see beneath both beauty and ugliness; to see the boredom, and the horror, and the glory.

T. S. Eliot

It was his story. It would always be his story.
It followed him; it overtook him finally —
The boredom, and the horror, and the glory.

Probably at the end he was not yet sorry,
Even as the boots were brutalizing him in the alley.
It was his story. It would always be his story,

Blown on a blue horn, full of sound and fury,
And signifying, O signifying magnificently
The boredom, and the horror, and the glory.

I picture the snow as falling without hurry
To cover the cobbles and the toppled ashcans completely.
It was his story. It would always be his story.

Lately he had wandered between St. Mark's Place and the Bowery,
Already half a spirit, mumbling and muttering sadly.
O the boredom, and the horror, and the glory.

All done now. But I remember the fiery
Hypnotic eye and the raised voice blazing with poetry.
It was his story. It would always be his story —
The boredom, and the horror, and the glory.

Here Justice makes excellent use of the villanelle form, which has its roots in Italian folk song. It entered English poetry in the nineteenth century as a type of light verse, but took on a more majestic life in the twentieth century. You can see that it consists of nineteen lines divided into six stanzas — five tercets and one quatrain. The first and third lines become the refrain lines of alternate stanzas and the final two lines of the poem. These lines rhyme throughout, as do the middle lines of each stanza. Thus the entire poem builds upon two repeated lines and turns on two rhymes. That's why it's a form of compulsive returns. Justice recognized that the villanelle's insistent repetitions are well suited to a poetry of loss. Here he transforms it into an elegy.

Robert Boardman Vaughn was an old friend of Justice's from his Miami days. Laurence Donovan, who knew Vaughn from their time in high school, described him as a "gaunt, wild-eyed apparitional figure," a dreamer and adventurer who "haunted the fishing piers of St. Croix and St. Thomas and the bars of Coconut Grove and New York City with the frenzied and compelling talk that was enlivened by the alcohol that finally destroyed him." Vaughn had a tragic fate; he was beaten to death in the streets of Manhattan.

Vaughn was a poet manqué. In a book-length interview with Philip Hoy, Justice noted that his view of Vaughn's poetry would always be colored by his memory of him as a friend. "He led too ragged and dangerous a life to settle down and concentrate on writing poems. In a way, the life he chose to live became his most fully realized art." Justice also recalls him in the poem "Portrait with One Eye":

> You have identified yourself
> To the police as quote
> Lyric poet. What else? —
> With fractured jaw. Orpheus,
>
> Imperishable liar!
> Your life's a poem still,
> Broken iambs and all.
> Jazz, jails — the complete works.

Justice's villanelle has a compressed plot — a narrative can be inferred from it. In this sense, it is a story-poem. The opening line — "It was his story. It would always be his story" — suggests that what happened to Vaughn was somehow fated, ordained. It followed and overtook him. This line keeps returning as we discover the sordid details of Vaughn's deterioration and death. But this story is counterpointed by the sustaining grandeur and larger perspective, what lies underneath the beauty and the ugliness, "the boredom, and the horror, and the glory."

Justice lifted a phrase from a passage in T. S. Eliot's essay "The Use of Poetry" (1933) and uses it as a recurring line. He picks up the second part of Eliot's thought here:

> It is an advantage to mankind in general to live in a beautiful world;
> that no one can doubt. But for the poet is it so important? We mean
> all sorts of things, I know, by Beauty. But the essential advantage for a
> poet is not to have a beautiful world with which to deal; it is to be able
> to see beneath both beauty and ugliness; to see the boredom, and the
> horror, and the glory.

Justice heard the rhythmic lyricism in Eliot's aesthetic declaration. It was a brilliant creative stroke to take the last part of Eliot's sentence and apply it to the life of Robert Boardman Vaughn.

Everything in Justice's poem is interwoven; everything seems to rhyme. There is an echo chamber reverberating through all nineteen lines. The first and third lines rhyme off the letters *ry* ("story" / "glory" / "sorry" / "fury" / "hurry" / "Bowery" / "fiery" / "poetry"). The middle lines rhyme off the letters *ly* ("finally" / "alley" / "magnificently" / "completely" / "sadly"). There is not a single harsh one-syllable, or masculine, rhyme in the entire poem.

Justice's skill in employing the villanelle form seems to be effortless. Pause a moment over a few of the local effects. For example, in the third stanza, he references a famous speech in *Macbeth* (act 5, scene 5, lines 19–28) by slipping in Vaughn's love of jazz ("It would always be his story // Blown on a blue horn") and attaching it to Shakespeare's declaration that life is "a tale / Told by an idiot, full of sound and fury, / Signifying nothing." But instead of completing the line with the phrase "Signifying nothing," Justice defies expectation and exclaims that Vaughn's story was indeed signifying something: "O signifying magnificently / The boredom, and the horror, and the glory." Justice thus wrings a fresh meaning out of Shakespeare's well-worn declaration.

There is something clear-eyed and unblinking about the way that Justice imagines how his friend was kicked to death in an alley: "I picture the snow as falling without hurry / To cover the cobbles and the toppled ashcans completely." The first line is, as the poet Robert Mezey puts it, "calm, steady, almost nerveless." Mezey finds something dry and nearly cruel in the phrase "without hurry." There is also an intricate pattern of sounds in the next line, a weave of repeated *c*'s and a few well-timed and plosive *pl*'s. These are threaded together by the quiet *o*'s and *a*'s ("To *c*over the *c*obbles *a*nd the t*oppl*ed *a*sh*ca*ns *c*om*pl*etely"). This stanza is followed by a description of his friend's sad last days. The last phrase bites down on the letters *mu:* "Lately he had wandered between St. Mark's Place and the Bowery, / Already half a spirit, *mu*mbling and *mu*ttering sadly." This is followed by the only modification in Eliot's phrase, the tiny but telling open-mouthed exclamation, *O:* "O the boredom, and the horror, and the glory."

A sad resignation begins the final stanza: "All done now." Vaughn's troubled life is over. But this recognition is somehow countered by the sublimity of memory, the recollection of a friend vividly alive: "But I remember the fiery

/ Hypnotic eye and the raised voice blazing with poetry." This is a moment rescued out of time. Donald Justice elliptically tells the tale of Robert Boardman Vaughn's sorry death in this high lyric, but he also gives great distinction and even majesty to his friend's story. He counters his loss with an unforgettable poetic music.

GERALD STERN

—◆—

"The Dancing"

(1984)

Gerald Stern is an American original — a Romantic poet with a sense of humor, an Orphic voice living inside of history, a sometimes comic, sometimes tragic visionary crying out against imprisonment and shame, singing of loneliness and rejuvenation, dreaming of social justice and community. He is like some ecstatic Maimonides writing his own idiosyncratic guide for the perplexed, converting his losses, transforming death and sadness into beautiful singing.

Here is a one-sentence poem that appears in his fifth book, *Paradise Poems* (1984):

> The Dancing
>
> In all these rotten shops, in all this broken furniture
> and wrinkled ties and baseball trophies and coffee pots
> I have never seen a post-war Philco
> with the automatic eye
> nor heard Ravel's "Bolero" the way I did

in 1945 in that tiny living room
on Beechwood Boulevard, nor danced as I did
then, my knives all flashing, my hair all streaming,
my mother red with laughter, my father cupping
his left hand under his armpit, doing the dance
of old Ukraine, the sound of his skin half drum,
half fart, the world at last a meadow,
the three of us whirling and singing, the three of us
screaming and falling, as if we were dying,
as if we could never stop — in 1945 —
in Pittsburgh, beautiful filthy Pittsburgh, home
of the evil Mellons, 5,000 miles away
from the other dancing — in Poland and Germany —
oh God of mercy, oh wild God.

"The Dancing" picks up velocity as it goes. It begins in the present tense — the speaker is rummaging through thrift shops, looking at discarded items, discovering what he can never find again. He is nostalgically searching for something ineffable that can never be recovered, his past. Many of Stern's poems begin in places that have been worn out, such as out-of-date stores, empty restaurants, abandoned city lots, the waste places of nature. They begin in the ruins. There is, by implication, a long life that precedes his poems, which often start in a state of exuberant exhaustion.

"The Dancing" turns on the memory of hearing Maurice Ravel's one-movement orchestra piece "Boléro" in 1945. The idea of regeneration through music is one of Stern's central motifs. "It's only music that saves me," he asserts in "Romania, Romania." So too dancing with joy, but with an undercurrent of sorrow, is one of the recurring features of his work. One of his later collections, for example, is called *Save the Last Dance* (2008). A book of his quirky drawings is titled *Dancing with Tears in My Eyes* (2014).

In the poem "The Dancing," the dance rhythms of Ravel's piece suddenly catapult the speaker back into his adolescence. He was twenty years old in 1945 and, like some euphoric Proust, he recalls a paradise of three, a young man and his Old World parents, losing themselves and dancing wildly in their tiny living room on Beechwood Boulevard in Pittsburgh. The specific place matters. In their frenzied joy, the world is transformed into a "meadow," a place of harmony.

But then the poem takes an unexpected turn. The year 1945 has vast historical significance. The lyric vibrates and turns into a Holocaust poem. The speaker remembers the city of his childhood, which he describes with an oxymoron: "beautiful filthy Pittsburgh." He can't resist taking a potshot at the barons of his hometown, "the evil Mellons." But he also summons up what he terms that "other dancing." Dancing now becomes something metaphorical, not just an experience in America, but also a liberation in Europe. By swerving this way Stern becomes a political as well as a personal poet, turning his attention back to the historical world, remembering that one family's heaven exists alongside another's hell. What seemed to be a strictly personal remembrance takes on greater historical resonance. For while one branch of the family was dancing in Pittsburgh, another branch was experiencing the liberation of Poland and Germany.

The poem concludes with a sudden invocation of God, which gives it the feeling of prayer: "oh God of mercy, oh wild God." This line presses together a strangely split or two-pronged God. The first phrase invokes the traditional merciful God. Recall that Kadya Molodowsky borrowed this same phrase, *El khanun* ("Merciful God" or "God of Mercy"), which most notably appears in Exodus 34:6–7, for the title of her bitterly ironic Holocaust poem "Merciful God." Stern invokes this benevolent presence as a figure who enables a family's ecstasy, who lets a small apartment be transformed into a momentary paradise. But the second phrase invokes some other darker and deeper force, a "wild God." In his poem "Hurt Hawks," Robinson Jeffers states, "The wild God of the world is sometimes merciful to those / That ask mercy." But whereas Jeffers progresses from wildness to mercy in thinking about God, who is not a transcendent figure but one "of the world," Stern does precisely the opposite. In the last line he binds together a merciful God with a more uncontrollable one, an incomprehensible transcendent force and figure who will never be contained or understood.

This world is our only paradise, Gerald Stern teaches us in "The Dancing." It is a world of ironies and ecstasies, a world with a long memory, a world of joy tempered by sorrow and suffering.

JOY HARJO

———

"For Anna Mae Pictou Aquash,
Whose Spirit Is Present Here and in the
Dappled Stars (for we remember the story
and must tell it again so we may all live)"

(1985)

J oy Harjo is an American poet with a generous gift for storytelling. As a citi-
zen of the Mvskoke tribal nation, she believes that every story she tells links
her to her ancestors and connects her to us. She tends to think of each poem as
a ceremonial object, which has the potential to create change. Here is an elegy
with a magical title that appeared in her book *In Mad Love and War* (1990).
Harjo subsequently released a dramatic recitation of it with her band, Poetic
Justice (1998). It was her first song.

> *For Anna Mae Pictou Aquash, Whose Spirit Is Present Here and
> in the Dappled Stars (for we remember the story and must tell it
> again so we may all live)*

Beneath a sky blurred with mist and wind
    I am amazed as I watch the violet
heads of crocuses erupt from the stiff earth
    after dying for a season,
as I have watched my own dark head

appear each morning after entering
the next world
      to come back to this one,
          amazed.
It is the way in the natural world to understand the place
           the ghost dancers named
after the heartbreaking destruction.
          Anna Mae,
             everything and nothing changes.
You are the shimmering young woman
          who found her voice,
when you were warned to be silent, or have your body cut away
from you like an elegant weed.
You are the one whose spirit is present in the dappled stars.
(They prance and lope like colored horses who stay with us
      through the streets of these steely cities. And I have seen them
      nuzzling the frozen bodies of tattered drunks
      on the corner.)
This morning when the last star is dimming
           and the buses grind toward
the middle of the city, I know it is ten years since they buried you
the second time in Lakota, a language that could
          free you.

I heard about it in Oklahoma, or New Mexico,
how the wind howled and pulled everything down
in a righteous anger.
      (It was the women who told me) and we understood
          wordlessly
the ripe meaning of your murder.
      As I understand ten years later after the slow changing
          of the seasons
that we have just begun to touch
      the dazzling whirlwind of our anger,
we have just begun to perceive the amazed world the ghost dancers
      entered
          crazily, beautifully.

Joy Harjo and Anna Mae Pictou Aquash were close to the same age. Aquash, the most visible woman of the American Indian Movement (AIM), was a much-loved community member. She was the sort of First Rights Activist — knowledgeable, funny, hardworking, and courageous — that Harjo and many of her friends looked up to. The two probably met briefly at a Native rights meeting in New Mexico or Arizona. They were both working toward a more compassionate and just world for Native peoples.

Aquash was brutally killed in December 1975. The murder was hard to process. Harjo wrote "For Anna Mae . . ." for an event honoring her memory ten years later, in Boulder, Colorado. The long and elaborate title gives the poem the feeling of a ceremonial text. It can be broken down into two parts. The first operates as a dedication with an indigenous sense that the spirit lives on beyond the body and dwells in the universe itself: "For Anna Mae Pictou Aquash, Whose Spirit Is Present Here and in the Dappled Stars." The second half of the title, set off in parentheses, is an insistent reminder: "(for we remember the story and must tell it again so we may all live)." Like Holocaust poems by Primo Levi and Anthony Hecht, such as "Shemà" and "The Book of Yolek," this poem ritually obligates us to remember and retell the tale, not just for the sake of the dead, but for our own. Harjo's poem then becomes just such a necessary retelling.

Harjo's note to the poem is helpful, though reading even this bare narration of the facts is enough to arouse feelings of unresolved fury:

> In February 1976, an unidentified body of a young woman was found on the Pine Ridge Reservation in South Dakota. The official autopsy attributed death to exposure and alcohol. The FBI agent present at the autopsy ordered her hands severed and sent to Washington for fingerprinting. John Trudell, one of the leaders of the American Indian Movement, rightly called this mutilation an act of war. Her unnamed body was buried. When Anna Mae Pictou Aquash, a young Micmac woman who was an active American Indian Movement member, was discovered missing by her friends and relatives, a second autopsy was demanded. It was then discovered that she had been killed by a bullet fired at close range to the back of her head. She had not died of exposure and there was no alcohol in her blood. Her killer or killers have yet to be identified.

As she notes in the poem, Harjo was writing this poem of remembrance a full decade after the execution. At the time it was thought that Aquash had been killed by the FBI. Based on recent investigations, however, it appears that she likely was murdered by her AIM brothers after being falsely accused of being an FBI informant.

Harjo's memorial poem uses much of the page as, to use William Carlos Williams's phrase, a "field of action." Charles Olson called this approach "composition by field." Formally, Harjo ventures out into the open, and the lineation gives her poem a feeling of spaciousness. It is as if by breathing these long lines she could give breath again to the person she is memorializing. The long, extended lines are roughly similar in number of syllables and beats. By lowering and indenting lines, she also isolates and thus emphasizes certain phrases and thoughts.

Harjo has said that while composing the opening of the poem she kept thinking of how a young woman's body was found at the first thaw in a ditch in South Dakota, at a time when crocuses and other green life were breaking through the freeze. That is the doorway through which the memory of Aquash entered. Thus, the poem begins with a sense of wonderment at the resurrection of the natural world: "I am amazed as I watch the violet / heads of crocuses erupt from the stiff earth / after dying for a season." Williams captures a similar sense of violent rebirth in his iconic poem "Spring and All," where he observes how things "grip down and begin to awaken." Harjo's speaker links this natural awakening to the way she gets up after a night of dreaming: "as I have watched my own dark head / appear each morning after entering / the next world / to come back to this one, / amazed." The word "amazed" is emphatically given its own line. This feeling of astonishment will recur at the end of the poem.

The next sentences further connect the natural to the human world through a reference to the ghost dancers: "It is the way in the natural world to understand the place / the ghost dancers named / after the heartbreaking destruction." Harjo compacts a history here and connects it to the natural cycle. The Ghost Dance was a ceremony created by Plains Indians in the nineteenth century to rehabilitate their culture in response to the Indian Wars. It supposedly ended at the massacre at Wounded Knee in 1890, though, as prophesied, it was revitalized in the 1970s. It stands as a reclamation of values, of tribal spirituality and unification. As it is for Gerald Stern, dancing is an important motif in much of Harjo's work — she elsewhere has noted that "Dancing in the

Bible was a celebration of life" — and here she connects it to "naming," the traditional work of the poet. It signals her grief-stricken determination that the world will be renewed "after the heartbreaking destruction." She must bear a heavy grief for the destruction of a people and a culture.

At this point the poem addresses Anna Mae Pictou Aquash directly — "Anna Mae, / everything and nothing changes" — and praises her great determination and courage:

> You are the shimmering young woman
> who found her voice,
> when you were warned to be silent, or have your body cut away
> from you like an elegant weed.

Harjo tells an alternative story about Aquash and refuses to let her be defined by her murder and mutilation. She praises her beauty and righteousness, her militant determination. Aquash refused to be silenced. The present tense is crucial here because it suggests that there is something in Aquash that will never be killed: "You *are* the one whose spirit is present in the dappled stars."

Harjo introduces an indigenous image of nature and contrasts it to the modern urban world. Something spiritual still infuses our degraded planet. Hence the parenthetical comment that compares the dappled stars to colored horses, as if they take bodily form:

> (They prance and lope like colored horses who stay with us
> through the streets of these steely cities. And I have seen them
> nuzzling the frozen bodies of tattered drunks
> on the corner.)

Like horses, the stars "nuzzle" the drunks awake. The poem then returns to a dawn light:

> This morning when the last star is dimming
> and the buses grind toward
> the middle of the city, I know it is ten years since they buried you
> the second time in Lakota, a language that could
> free you.

"For Anna Mae Pictou Aquash . . ." declares itself as an anniversary ritual or ceremony to mark and memorialize her second, or true, burial. This implies that this second event was the moment when Aquash found her Native resting place, her natural home, in the language that liberated her to embrace her heritage and become herself.

The poem structurally turns precisely at the point of its one stanza break, its single pause. Notice how the speaker projects onto nature the rage she feels: "I heard about it in Oklahoma, or New Mexico, / how the wind howled and pulled everything down / in a righteous anger." This is the other side of fury, the righteous anger pushing change forward. John Ruskin coined the term "pathetic fallacy" for the projection of human feelings onto the natural world, something he considered a weakness of Victorian poetry and a false vision, though it has always been a device of archaic and Native poets, who share a belief that the world is alive in all its parts. Here Harjo employs it to naturalize not just her own anger but the rage of others too, especially women: "(It was the women who told me) and we understood / wordlessly / the ripe meaning of your murder." The women don't need language to understand the underlying meaning of this brutal killing.

The lines shorten as the poem comes to its conclusion — as if enacting the sense of loss while simultaneously letting go. The speaker sees past the sordidness that stopped a dedicated young woman in her prime. The poem accumulates its disparate images — the turning seasons, the whirlwind of rage, the ghost dancers — to build a final understanding. Harjo brings these images together in a single sentence expressing a new realization:

> As I understand ten years later after the slow changing
> of the seasons
> that we have just begun to touch
> the dazzling whirlwind of our anger,
> we have just begun to perceive the amazed world the ghost dancers
> entered
> crazily, beautifully.

This effervescent moment of recognition — as if it all makes sense in the end — quickly comes and goes. Anna Mae Pictou Aquash's death becomes the springboard for a cultural revitalization that is only now beginning. The speaker projects her own sense of amazement onto the world itself. The death of a single martyr is linked to the visionary trance world entered upon by the ghost dancers. That dance is unworldly, but it is also renewing and Dionysian. It is crazy and beautiful.

Joy Harjo also enters the world of the ghost dancers in this homage and memorial. She envisions a spiritual existence after death. She too has come to dance with others, to celebrate and remember the dead, to use the death of one courageous young woman as a call to action, to empower others, to wring joy out of rage and grief.

GARRETT HONGO

———

"Mendocino Rose"

(1987)

Garrett Hongo's work has always been motivated by a search for origins. A fourth-generation Japanese American, he was born in Hawai'i and raised in California. His poems are populated by people from his past. He has written with desolating accuracy about the internment of Japanese Americans during World War II, one of the most shameful episodes in American history. His poems are lush explorations, furious rescue operations, determined memorials.

Hongo's second book, *The River of Heaven* (1988), is dedicated to the memory of his father, Albert Kazuyoshi Hongo, and in memory of his grandfather, Hideo Kubota, with the inscription "ka po'e o ka 'āina me ka 'āina" ("the people of the land for the land"). He thus situates his subject — ethnically, culturally, spiritually — in a distinctly Hawaiian world. The book begins with a prologue poem, "Mendocino Rose," which originates in the traumatic aftermath of these two fundamental deaths.

Mendocino Rose

In California, north of the Golden Gate,
the vine grows almost everywhere,
       erupting out of pastureland,
from under the shade of eucalyptus
       by the side of the road,
overtaking all the ghost shacks and broken fences
       crumbling with rot
and drenched in the fresh rains.

It mimes, in its steady, cloudlike replicas,
       the shape of whatever it smothers,
a gentle greenery
       trellised up the side
of a barn or pump station
       far up the bluffs above Highway 1,
florets and blossoms,
       from the road anyway,
looking like knots and red dreadlocks,
       ephemeral and glorious,
hanging from overgrown eaves.

I'd been listening to a tape on the car stereo,
a song I'd play and rewind,
       and play again,
a ballad or a love song
       sung by my favorite tenor,
a Hawaiian man known for his poverty
       and richness of heart,
and I felt, wheeling through the vinelike curves
       of that coastal road,
sliding on the slick asphalt
       through the dips and in the S-turns,
and braking just in time,
       that it would have served as the dirge
I didn't know to sing

       when I needed to,
a song to cadence my heart
      and its tuneless stammering.

Ipo lei manu, he sang, without confusion,
    I send these garlands,
and the roses seemed everywhere around me then,
    profuse and luxurious
as the rain in its grey robes,
    undulant processionals over the land,
echoes, in snarls of extravagant color,
    of the music
and the collapsing shapes
    they seemed to triumph over.

"Mendocino Rose" is a sideways lament, an elegy that reveals itself as it goes along. This is to say that it doesn't seem to start out as an elegy, but as the record of a drive through northern California. Hongo finds his way as he proceeds, and the poem enacts a breakthrough into feeling. Indeed, he projects that feeling, a sudden release and opening out, onto a vivid western landscape, which is described with luxuriant precision. The English Romantic poets took long meandering walks in the rural countryside. As an American Romantic who also happens to be a late-modern postcolonial poet, Hongo depicts a long winding drive on an All-American Road. His speaker is on the move, leaving the city, locked in his car, an iron solitude. He takes great care to specify exactly where he is driving (in California, north of the Golden Gate Bridge, on Highway 1, up the Mendocino coast) so that we could find it on a map.

Hongo's poems have always swung between two worlds: Hawai'i and California, the one a lost utopia, the other a failed dream. Like the Romantic poets, he has a special gift for describing ruined landscapes. Here the coastal landscape and Pacific cliffsides start to remind him — they pull him back — to the Big Island where he was born. The car becomes the vehicle of a spiritual transport — and his two worlds merge.

"Mendocino Rose" spills down the page. Each stanza is a single curving sentence, the syntax mirroring the turns and twists of the road, which become the turns and twists of his own thought, his own feeling. The lines accordion in and out; the rhythmic undulations enable the speaker to observe and capture the vine "erupting out of pastureland" and the "gentle greenery / trellised up the side / of a barn or pump station." But it also gives him space to reflect upon what he is seeing.

The structural turn in the poem comes in the third stanza. The speaker is listening to a tape of ballads and love songs by his favorite tenor, the traditional slack-key guitarist and folksinger Gabby Pahinui, who is known, as Hongo puts it in an elegant formulation, "for his poverty / and richness of heart." Pahinui, who was born and raised in a poor district of Kaka'ako in Honolulu, specialized in the music of old Hawai'i, which he expressed and transformed. He is an emblematic figure of the Hawaiian Cultural Renaissance. Hongo is listening repeatedly to "Ipo Lei Manu," Pahinui's version of a nineteenth-century Hawaiian lyric, a lament written by Queen Kapi'olani in mourning for her husband, King David Kalākaua, who died far from home. The personal grief of the queen — and the grief of a people for a king who legitimized Hawaiian culture — reverberates through the landscape.

The music also opens up something inside the speaker of "Mendocino Rose," who has been lost in a raw, nameless grief. He takes the song personally and understands it as a lament for the death of his own father. It is something that might have been sung at his father's funeral. This speaks to the true power of art: a nineteenth-century dirge, reimagined as a folk song, suddenly gives the speaker a language for his feeling. It answers an inner longing. It takes his "tuneless stammering" and gives a cadence to his heart's murmurings.

In his memoir *Volcano* (1995), Hongo writes about returning for a year to the village where he was born. The last chapter, "Mendocino Rose," discusses the experience described in the poem, which he now revisits and amplifies:

> When I realized what the man was singing, true grieving rose up in me like a swelling breaker and I dove under it. I looked off from the black asphalt road winding ahead to the roses blooming around me as though they were a music too. I looked off over the cliffs across the Pacific.
>
> It was a fleeting but powerful premonition of change. The song and the rose opened me again to something I'd had when my father and Kubota grandfather were alive. It was not only a place but a resolve of purpose, I suppose, a feeling of connection not so much to any particular place, though that helps, but to the world of *feeling* and openness to it, that exchange between the human and whatever might

be the rest — the infinite, say, or the natural world of pure spirit that the nineteenth-century romantic philosophers defined as sublime. Whatever it is that is greater than the self but that, nevertheless, empowers the self, overwhelms and inspirits the self. "And who, if I cried, would hear me among the angelic orders?" wrote Rilke, skeptically, in his *Duino Elegies.* "Even if, suddenly, one of them were to grip me to his heart, I'd vanish in his overwhelming presence." Beauty is nothing but the start of a terror we can hardly bear, he concluded, a scorn so serene it could kill us. It is the Buddhist's *vajra,* the lightning bolt of pure, cosmic perception, a grieving that leads to eternity.

In the poem "Mendocino Rose" the speaker can find his own music only because a Hawaiian song delivers him back to himself. The last stanza enacts the transport. The key sentence from the song, "*Ipo lei manu,*" which means "for my beloved," actualizes the movement from language to experience. Hence:

> *I send these garlands,*
>> and the roses seemed everywhere around me then,
>>> profuse and luxurious . . .

"I send these garlands," then, is Hungo's own inner wish, evinced in his inner soul by hearing the song and witnessing the landscape. Hongo's grief is transformed by the roses growing wild in the California landscape. The music and the landscape come together. There is a kind of stateliness to the language, which puts us in the space of something larger than ourselves, a world of unantagonized feeling, something that cannot quite be articulated, something extravagant that momentarily connects us to a boundlessness within ourselves, a world outside time. That's how "Mendocino Rose" becomes a poem of spiritual regeneration, a true lyric of the American sublime.

ADRIENNE RICH

———

"(Dedications)"

(1990–91)

Adrienne Rich told Bill Moyers in an interview that her thirteen-part poem "An Atlas of the Difficult World" (1990–91) "reflects on the condition of my country, which I wrote very consciously as a citizen poet, looking at the geography, the history, the people of my country." She was trying to fathom what it meant to love her country, the so-called difficult world, in a time of crisis and war. Rich's politically engaged poem confronts American oppressions, the gap between materialism and idealism, and tries to stage an ethical intervention. The idea was to provide a book of maps or charts through a challenging democratic morass.

Here is the moving last section of the poem. We usually think of a dedication coming at the beginning of a poem, but this one comes at the end. As an epilogue, "(Dedications)" tries to reach across a great gulf to break down the final barrier between the poet and the reader, the poem and its audience. It speaks to the sociality of lyric and calls attention to itself as a poem, as something constructed and made for a potential reader. Rich insists — she *knows* — that there is an audience for poetry, especially for a poetry of witness. She treats poetry as the most intimate form of public art and reaches out to individuals in a time of need.

(Dedications)

I know you are reading this poem
late, before leaving your office
of the one intense yellow lamp-spot and the darkening window
in the lassitude of a building faded to quiet
long after rush-hour.   I know you are reading this poem
standing up in a bookstore far from the ocean
on a grey day of early spring, faint flakes driven
across the plains' enormous spaces around you.
I know you are reading this poem
in a room where too much has happened for you to bear
where the bedclothes lie in stagnant coils on the bed
and the open valise speaks of flight
but you cannot leave yet.   I know you are reading this poem
as the underground train loses momentum and before running up
     the stairs
toward a new kind of love
your life has never allowed.
I know you are reading this poem by the light
of the television screen where soundless images jerk and slide
while you wait for the newscast from the *intifada*.
I know you are reading this poem in a waiting-room
of eyes met and unmeeting, of identity with strangers.
I know you are reading this poem by fluorescent light
in the boredom and fatigue of the young who are counted out,
count themselves out, at too early an age.   I know
you are reading this poem through your failing sight, the thick
lens enlarging these letters beyond all meaning yet you read on
because even the alphabet is precious.
I know you are reading this poem as you pace beside the stove
warming milk, a crying child on your shoulder, a book in your hand
because life is short and you too are thirsty.

I know you are reading this poem which is not in your language
guessing at some words while others keep you reading
and I want to know which words they are.
I know you are reading this poem listening for something, torn between
    bitterness and hope
turning back once again to the task you cannot refuse.
I know you are reading this poem because there is nothing else left to read
there where you have landed, stripped as you are.

Rich carefully places the title in parentheses, "(Dedications)," and thus makes it seem like an explanation or afterthought. What matters is not the title, but the potential contact between the poet and her readers. The poem proceeds to catalog twelve very specific readers, each a different type and all of them lonely, isolated, and in need of connection. The list is structured. The suffering of individual readers seems to intensify as we go along, and there is a general progression down the ladder of social privilege. The irregular extra space in certain lines emphasizes the distance between separated readers — a barrier to be crossed. The anaphoric repetition — "I know you are reading" — exudes a Whitmanesque confidence that the speaker can reach out and connect to all of them. "I wanted the poem to speak to people as individuals," Rich said, "but also as individuals multiplied over and over and over and over." The people are themselves, but they also stand as representative figures, allegories of themselves. Each one is archetypal. And the poet is intent on bringing these different isolates into a distinct community.

"(Dedications)" reaches out to people who are lonely and struggling, disconnected, disenfranchised. Rich locates people wherever they are and treats reading itself as a material act. Each one is specifically placed. The gender of the individual is indeterminate. Rich's empathy has stretched from the days when she could identify only with other women. In every case here the isolated reader could be a woman or a man.

The first reader is an office worker who is still in the office late at night (the "yellow lamp-spot" and "darkening window" make one think of an Edward Hopper painting); the second is someone standing in a bookstore somewhere on the snowy plains. Rich is writing from California and thus reaches out across the country to someone she knows can't or won't buy her book. The isolation of the lone individual stands out against the vastness of the landscape. The third person is someone who has suffered from abuse, who has opened a suitcase but can't quite bear to leave yet. The fourth has escaped on an underground train and is about to run upstairs "toward a new kind of love / your life has never allowed." The implication is clear that the person is running toward some socially proscribed kind of love, probably same-sex love.

These readers don't inhabit classrooms. Rich finds a reader, probably but not necessarily a Palestinian, who has turned down the sound and is reading by the light of a television screen, waiting for news about "the *intifada*." This refers to the First Intifada, a Palestinian uprising against the Israeli occupation that lasted from 1987 to 1993. Rich's political sympathies are clear. The poem then jump-cuts to a reader in a waiting room, that bland public space where people both look and don't look at one another, thrust together as strangers at some of the most important moments of their lives. It then moves to a young person reading by a solitary light in a bedroom. There is a didactic or editorial moment when the speaker consider the young "who are counted out, / count themselves out, at too early an age." She can't resist telling the young not to discount themselves.

There's a person who is going blind and can scarcely make out the letters, a mother or father warming milk by the stove with an infant over one shoulder—this evokes Rich's own days of early motherhood—who seems to be desperately thirsty for something beyond domestic life. She finds a foreigner who can barely understand the words and wants to hear back from him or her ("and I want to know which words they are"). This imagines the poem as a conversation. She also finds someone else who is "listening for something" in the poem itself, someone "torn between bitterness and hope," like Rich herself, who was also facing a binding obligation, "the task you cannot refuse."

The last two lines send out a life raft: "I know you are reading this because there is nothing else left to read / there where you have landed, stripped as you are." The last line is multilayered. Rich told Moyers: "And then in the last line, I thought first of someone dying of AIDS. I thought of any person in an isolate situation for whom there was perhaps nothing but a book of poems to put her or him into a sense of relation with the world of other human beings, or perhaps someone in prison. But finally I was thinking of our society, stripped of so much that was hoped for and promised and given nothing in exchange but material commodities, or the hope of obtaining material commodities. And for me, that is being truly stripped."

"(Dedications)" carries with it an idea of poetry as a dialogue between strangers, a refuge or shelter for loneliness, and a consolation in time of dire need. It is like a flare sent up in the darkness. It exists for you, whoever you are, and I know you will find it.

THOM GUNN

———

"The Gas-poker"

(1991)

Thom Gunn was an Anglo-American poet with a serious formal intelligence, a warm heart, and a cool head. He loved the rigor and balance of the Elizabethan plain style, the combination of what he called "Rule and Energy." He had a wild streak tempered by a genuine sense of decorum. He was also a personal poet who disliked confessional poetry and believed in the objectifying power of lyric. His poems have a well-earned directness, a restrained nobility.

Gunn's work took a sorrowful turn with his book *The Man with Night Sweats* (1992), which contains his heart-rending elegies for friends who died in the AIDS epidemic. Equally touching but even closer to home is his elegy for his mother, "The Gas-poker," which appears in his last collection, *Boss Cupid* (2000). Gunn's mother, Charlotte Gunn, committed suicide when he was fourteen years old, but it took him nearly fifty years to write about it.

Gunn composed "The Gas-poker" in 1991 and considered calling it "The Instrument." It is a companion piece to his short poem "My Mother's Pride," which immediately precedes it in *Boss Cupid,* and closes with the line "I am unmade by her, and undone."

The Gas-poker

Forty-eight years ago
— Can it be forty-eight
Since then? — they forced the door
Which she had barricaded
With a full bureau's weight
Lest anyone find, as they did,
What she had blocked it for.

She had blocked the doorway so,
To keep the children out.
In her red dressing-gown
She wrote notes, all night busy
Pushing the things about,
Thinking till she was dizzy,
Before she had lain down.

The children went to and fro
On the harsh winter lawn
Repeating their lament,
A burden, to each other
In the December dawn,
Elder and younger brother,
Till they knew what it meant.

Knew all there was to know.
Coming back off the grass
To the room of her release,
They who had been her treasures
Knew to turn off the gas,
Take the appropriate measures,
Telephone the police.

One image from the flow
Sticks in the stubborn mind:
A sort of backwards flute.

The poker that she held up
Breathed from the holes aligned
Into her mouth till, filled up
By its music, she was mute.

The most crucial decision that Gunn made concerning "The Gas-poker" was to cast the poem in the third person. The second and third lines express his utter disbelief that so much time has passed — "Forty-eight years ago / — Can it be forty-eight / Since then?" — which is the only autobiographical clue in the poem itself. John Berryman does something parallel at the beginning of his poem "Henry's Understanding" ("He was reading late, at Richard's, down in Maine, / aged 32?"), but whereas Berryman then turns from the third to the first person ("my good wife long in bed"), Gunn does precisely the opposite and switches from the first person to the third. Once he makes that turn everything is presented as if it had happened to someone else. It objectifies the situation.

Gunn talked revealingly about "The Gas-poker" in an interview with the critic James Campbell, who asked him: "Your new book, *Boss Cupid,* contains some new poems about your mother. Is this the first time you've written about her?" Gunn mentioned "My Mother's Pride" and continued:

> The second poem about my mother is called "The Gas-poker." She killed herself, and my brother and I found the body, which was not her fault because she'd barred the doors . . . Obviously this was quite a traumatic experience; it would be in anybody's life. I wasn't able to write about it till just a few years ago. Finally I found the way to do it was really obvious: to withdraw the first-person, and to write about it in the third-person. Then it became easy, because it was no longer about myself. I don't like dramatizing myself.

In a perceptive short book about Elizabeth Bishop, Colm Tóibín connects Gunn's statement ("Obviously this was quite a traumatic experience; it would be in anybody's life") to a letter in which Bishop writes about her unhappy childhood and says, "Please don't think I dote on it." She speaks about her mother's mental illness and says, resigned, "Well, there we are."

There's something about the solitude and tact, the intense feeling mixed with a certain detachment, that leads Tóibín to Joseph Brodsky's essay "Grief and Reason," which explicates Robert Frost's poem "Home Burial." Brodsky wonders what Frost was after and declares: "He was, I think, after grief and reason, which, while poison to each other, are language's most efficient fuel — or, if you will, poetry's indelible ink." Brodsky names in Frost what Tóibín finds in Gunn and Bishop, "grief masked by reason, grief and reason battling it out."

In "The Gas-poker" reason asserts itself as a remarkably skillful lyric. The poem employs a short, punchy three-beat, or trimeter, line of six or seven syllables each. This meter, which Theodore Roethke uses so well in "My Papa's Waltz," has a brisk songlike quality that can be purposefully disconcerting in a grief-stricken poem. Gunn's lyric also consists of five seven-line stanzas. The septet has an odd extra punch, a piercing last line, which moves past the symmetry of an even-numbered stanza, and Gunn uses it to great effect. Look at the last lines. Each one simultaneously closes a sentence and a stanza:

> What she had blocked it for.

> Before she had lain down.

> Till they knew what it meant.

> Telephone the police.

> By its music, she was mute.

Gunn believed that writing in form pressed a poet to go further and further in order to explore a subject. "The Gas-poker" is one such proof. The poem is partly tied together by the way that the first lines of each stanza rhyme ("ago" / "so" / "fro" / "know" / "flow"). The rhyme scheme connects the second and fifth lines, the third and seventh lines, and the fourth and sixth lines of each stanza. This enables the poet to make some unexpected connections, such as "lament" and "meant," "treasures" and "measures." Gunn said that he probably got some help from Thomas Hardy in writing this poem, especially in the emphasis on a few awkward rhymes, such as "barricaded" and "they did."

The title of the poem, "The Gas-poker," directs our attention away from the mother to the homely object that she used to inhale the gas that killed her.

The first stanza holds back or barricades the figure of the mother's dead body. Indeed, it will be revealed only at the end of the poem. That's also where we come to understand the true significance of the gas-poker, which was normally used to ignite coal fires.

The second stanza tries to imagine what the mother did behind the blocked door:

> She wrote notes, all night busy
> Pushing the things about,
> Thinking till she was dizzy,
> Before she had lain down.

It's as if the mother was doing housework until the very end, remembering chores, trying to think of everything before she finally had to give up. The rhyme on "busy" and "dizzy" enacts what she is doing. There is metrical agitation in the lines, all that pushing and thinking, which finally relaxes at the end.

The third stanza moves the setting to a garden, which is why Clive Wilmer, the editor of Gunn's *New Selected Poems* (2018), suggests that the poem is a pastoral, though it is a counter-pastoral or doomed pastoral: the nostalgic promise of a simple peaceful life in the country comes to a crashing end on "the harsh winter lawn." At times the rhythm of this poem seems reminiscent of Hardy's lament "During Wind and Rain," especially in the following stanza:

> The children went to and fro
> On the harsh winter lawn
> Repeating their lament,
> A burden, to each other
> In the December dawn,
> Elder and younger brother,
> Till they knew what it meant.

These lines sound a bit like Hardy's "They sing their dearest songs — / He, she, all of them — yea . . ."

In the fourth line, the interpolation "A burden" breaks the rhythm, and there is a revealing pun on the word "burden." Its most familiar meaning suggests something emotionally difficult to bear. Another meaning comes from music: "a drone, as of a bagpipe," or "a chorus or refrain." Thus, the burden, the repeating lament, is a persistent theme. Gunn found a way to pity the two brothers because of how he had distanced them. He was pretending that he was writing not about himself and his brother, but about some other children. In the next stanza, the two of them act with a sort of shocked practicality:

> They who had been her treasures
> Knew to turn off the gas,
> Take the appropriate measures,
> Telephone the police.

The last stanza is the most devastating. Gunn's speaker continues to generalize — "One image from the flow / Sticks in the stubborn mind . . ." In a review of *Boss Cupid,* the scholar Langdon Hammer noted that Gunn declines to say "my" because the image itself "is alien, something from outside that has been taken in, a troubling object, and it has the effect of making the mind itself seem partially alien, objectified, its own processes open to examination."

There is a terrifying realization in the image of the poker as a "backwards flute." On one hand, it is a musical instrument, which evokes the classical tradition, since the elegy, a funeral lament, was accompanied by the flute. We recall from Anna Akhmatova's elegy for Mikhail Bulgakov how the flute is inevitably associated with the expression of grief. Like Milton in his pastoral elegy "Lycidas," Gunn rhymes "flute" with "mute." But whereas Milton begins with the word "mute" and follows it with "flute" ("Meanwhile the rural ditties were not mute; / Tempered to the oaten flute"), Gunn does precisely the opposite. For him the flute negates the possibility for expression that Milton sees in it. It has now become the perverse opposite of a musical instrument. The mother who plays the music, which is silent, becomes permanently muted by suicide. The whole poem ends on a note that is beautiful and horrible. It preserves a silence.

This is all a way of saying that in "The Gas-poker," one of Thom Gunn's most harrowing poems, grief is masked by reason, and grief and reason are forever battling it out.

HEATHER McHUGH

———

"What He Thought"

(1991)

Heather McHugh's poems have a breezy, self-reflexive, daredevil linguistic wizardry and wit. The thinking is quick and quirky, the wordplay dense and dizzying. She finds the world through words. There are dozens of smart, crackling language lessons in her first four books: *Dangers* (1977), *A World of Difference* (1981), *To the Quick* (1987), and *Shades* (1988). But the verbal dazzle and fast thinking in her work doesn't quite prepare us for "What He Thought," the first poem in *Hinge & Sign* (1994), a collection of her new and selected poems. It has a different kind of depth charge. The title of the poem refers to thought, a product of the mind, but the content shows that thinking too has its limitations.

What He Thought

for Fabio Doplicher

We were supposed to do a job in Italy
and, full of our feeling for

ourselves (our sense of being
Poets from America) we went
from Rome to Fano, met
the mayor, mulled
a couple matters over (what's
a cheap date, they asked us; what's
flat drink). Among Italian literati

we could recognize our counterparts:
the academic, the apologist,
the arrogant, the amorous,
the brazen and the glib — and there was one

administrator (the conservative), in suit
of regulation gray, who like a good tour guide
with measured pace and uninflected tone narrated
sights and histories the hired van hauled us past.
Of all, he was most politic and least poetic,
so it seemed. Our last few days in Rome
(when all but three of the New World Bards had flown)
I found a book of poems this
unprepossessing one had written: it was there
in the *pensione* room (a room he'd recommended)
where it must have been abandoned by
the German visitor (was there a bus of *them*?)
to whom he had inscribed and dated it a month before.
I couldn't read Italian, either, so I put the book
back into the wardrobe's dark. We last Americans

were due to leave tomorrow. For our parting evening then
our host chose something in a family restaurant, and there
we sat and chatted, sat and chewed,
till, sensible it was our last
big chance to be poetic, make
our mark, one of us asked
                              "What's poetry?
Is it the fruits and vegetables and

marketplace of Campo dei Fiori, or
the statue there?" Because I was

the glib one, I identified the answer
instantly, I didn't have to think — "The truth
is both, it's both," I blurted out. But that
was easy. That was easiest to say. What followed
taught me something about difficulty,
for our underestimated host spoke out,
all of a sudden, with a rising passion, and he said:

The statue represents Giordano Bruno,
brought to be burned in the public square
because of his offense against
authority, which is to say
the Church. His crime was his belief
the universe does not revolve around
the human being: God is no
fixed point or central government, but rather is
poured in waves through all things. All things
move. "If God is not the soul itself, He is
the soul of the soul of the world." Such was
his heresy. The day they brought him
forth to die, they feared he might
incite the crowd (the man was famous
for his eloquence). And so his captors
placed upon his face
an iron mask, in which

he could not speak. That's
how they burned him. That is how
he died: without a word, in front
of everyone.
                        And poetry —
                                    (we'd all
put down our forks by now, to listen to
the man in gray; he went on

softly) —

poetry is what

he thought, but did not say.

"What He Thought" is dedicated to Fabio Doplicher (1938–2003), a poet and playwright from Trieste who spent most of his life in Rome. Perhaps he's the so-called administrator referred to in the poem. This free-verse lyric is more narrative than most of McHugh's work and begins by introducing a group of American poets, who are a bit puffed up by their role, their "sense of being / Poets from America" (the capital *P* in "Poets" suggests a slight pomposity), and travel from Rome to Fano. The narrator bites down on the sound of the consonant *m* ("*m*et / the *m*ayor, *m*ulled / a couple *m*atters over"), muses over a few funny vernaculars ("what's a cheap date, they asked us, what's / flat drink"), and then introduces the American poets to their European counterparts, all of whom are recognizable types — "the academic, the apologist, / the arrogant, the amorous . . ." The assonance is characteristic of McHugh's verbal wit — she simply can't resist punning and playing with words — and here it almost seems like an instance of her self-defined glibness. That's precisely when she introduces the main character in the poem, an administrator in a gray suit, a conservative type, who serves as an unflappable tour guide. "Of all, he was most politic and least poetic, / so it seemed." The phrases "most politic" and "least poetic" are ironically wed together. The phrase "so it seemed" foreshadows something crucial in this poem. The narrator has underestimated the guide, who is going to school her in the true nature of poetry.

The public events wind down, some of the American poets go home (there's a nice enjambment on "We last Americans"), and everything closes in on a final dinner in a family restaurant in Rome ("we sat and chatted, sat and chewed"). But then, somewhat portentously, someone asks, "What's poetry?" (the question comprises a line unto itself), and then sets up a cunning duality, a parlor game: "Is it the fruits and vegetables and / marketplace of Campo dei Fiori, or / the statue there?"

Someone is surely going to answer that poetry is the daily marketplace, while someone else is going to argue that it's the statue of the philosopher, but before anyone else can speak, McHugh, who identifies herself as "the glib one," blurts out that the answer is both. She is always the quickest wit in the room, and now she has seen through the false dichotomy. But then she critiques her own speaker, her earlier self — "But that / was easy. That was easiest to say" — and acknowledges that what the dry administrator says next teaches her about difficulty and forces her to rethink her idea of poetry. This is the moment when a clever poem is transformed into an epiphany.

The Italian guide tells everyone that the statue represents the philosopher Giordano Bruno, who was burned at the stake for religious heresy by the Inquisition in Rome on Ash Wednesday, 1600. He quotes from Bruno's indictment of the church, *The Expulsion of the Triumphant Beast* ("If he is not Nature herself, he is certainly the nature of Nature, and is the soul of the Soul of the world, if he is not the soul herself," Bruno wrote) — and tells the story of how Bruno's captors put an iron mask on his face so that the eloquent philosopher could not speak. Czesław Miłosz also refers to this story in his early poem "Campo dei Fiori," where he states that Bruno "climbed to his burning" and couldn't find "in any human tongue / words for mankind." But McHugh's Italian guide tells the story with much more brutal directness:

> That's
> how they burned him. That is how
> he died: without a word, in front
> of everyone.

And then he goes on quietly to declare: "poetry is what // he thought, but did not say."

It is only at the very end that we truly understand the title of this poem: "What He Thought." As in Wisława Szymborska's "Under One Small Star," it isn't until the final two lines that we recognize that we are reading an *ars poetica,* a poem that takes the art of poetry — its own means of expression — as its explicit subject. Giordano Bruno was a Neoplatonic philosopher who persistently tried to wed philosophy to verse. But there was nothing more that he could say once he was so terribly muzzled. The Italian poet who speaks of him reminds us of the urgent need for poetry. Poetry, he suggests, is what Bruno thought at the extreme point of death but could never express.

Poets have made many attempts over the centuries to answer the question *What is poetry?* Dante conceived of it as a species of eloquence. Sir Philip Sidney called it "a speaking picture." Coleridge characterized it as "the best words in the best order." Robert Graves thought of it as "stored magic," André Breton as a "room of marvels." In our time, Joseph Brodsky described poetry as "accelerated thinking," and Seamus Heaney called it "language in orbit." And now we also know that poetry is something unsayable. Some essential part of it cannot be spoken. It is a human truth beyond words.

In "What He Thought" Heather McHugh turned away from one kind of verse, which seemed to come easily to her, and embraced another kind, something much more emotionally difficult and intellectually demanding, something grief-stricken and true.

LES MURRAY

———

"It Allows a Portrait in Line-Scan at Fifteen"

(1993)

It Allows a Portrait in Line-Scan at Fifteen" is a portrait of Les Murray's teenage son Alexander, who was diagnosed with autism as a three-year-old child. It gives us a father's perspective on the agony and joy of his son's daily life with his parents on their forty-acre farm in Bunyah, Australia. It is also a representation of his son's neurological disorder. Murray's sympathy was well earned. His biographer Peter S. Alexander recounts just how difficult it was for him to accept the full extent of his son's limitations. It also prompted Murray to recognize some of his own mildly autistic traits, which he must have intuited since he wrote a poem called "Portrait of the Autist as a New World Driver" before Alexander was born. He told an interviewer that "no father of an autistic child fails to be a bit of an autie himself" and labeled himself "a high-performing Asperger" and "a quasi-autistic child off a farm."

It Allows a Portrait in Line-Scan at Fifteen

He retains a slight "Martian" accent, from the years of single phrases,

He no longer hugs to disarm. It is gradually allowing him affection.

It does not allow proportion. Distress is absolute, shrieking, and runs him at
frantic speed through crashing doors.

He likes cyborgs. Their taciturn power, with his intonation.

It still runs him around the house, alone in the dark, cooing and laughing.

He can read about soils, populations, and New Zealand. On neutral topics
he's illiterate.

Arnie Schwarzenegger is an actor. He isn't a cyborg really, is he, Dad?

He lives on forty acres, with animals and trees, and used to draw it continu-
ally.

He knows the map of Earth's fertile soils, and can draw it freehand.

He can only lie in a panicked shout *SorrySorryIdidn'tdoit!* warding off con-
flict with others and himself.

When he ran away constantly it was to the greengrocers to worship stacked
fruit.

His favorite country was the Ukraine: it is nearly all deep fertile soil.

Giggling, he climbed all over the dim Freudian psychiatrist who told us how
autism resulted from "refrigerator" parents.

When asked to smile, he photographs a rictus-smile on his face.

It long forbade all naturalistic films. They were Adult movies.

If they (that is, he) *are bad the police will put them in hospital.*

He sometimes drew the farm amid Chinese or Balinese rice terraces.

When a runaway, he made uproar in the police station, playing at three times
adult speed.

Only animated films were proper. *Who Framed Roger Rabbit* then authorized
the rest.

Phrases spoken to him he would take as teaching, and repeat.

When he worshiped fruit, he screamed as if poisoned when it was fed to him.

A one-word first conversation: *Blane!* — *Yes! Plane, that's right baby!* —
Blane!

He has forgotten nothing, and remembers the precise quality of experiences.

It requires rulings: *Is stealing very playing up, as bad as murder?*

He counts at a glance, not looking. And he has never been lost.

When he ate only nuts and dried fruit, words were for dire emergencies.

He knows all the breeds of fowls, and the counties of Ireland.

He'd begun to talk, then returned to babble, then silence. It withdrew speech
for years.

Is that very autistic, to play video games in the day?

He is anger's mirror, and magnifies any near him, raging it down.

It still won't allow him fresh fruit, or orange juice with bits in it.

He swam in the midwinter dam at night. It had no rules about cold.

He was terrified of thunder and finally cried as if in explanation *It — angry!*

He grilled an egg he'd broken into bread. Exchanges of soil-knowledge are
called landtalking.

He lives in objectivity. I was sure Bell's palsy would leave my face only when
he said it had begun to.

Don't say word! when he was eight forbade the word "autistic" in his presence.

Bantering questions about girlfriends cause a terrified look and blocked ears.

He sometimes centred the farm in a furrowed American Midwest.

Eye contact, Mum! means he truly wants attention. It dislikes I contact,

He is equitable and kind, and only ever a little jealous. It was relief when that
little arrived.

He surfs, bowls, walks for miles. For many years he hasn't trailed his left arm
while running.

I gotta get smart! looking terrified into the years. *I gotta get smart!*

The sentences are simple, direct, repetitive, and incantatory in this one-stanza poem, which presents a catalog of long sweeping lines and operates through a buildup of parallel statements: "He retains"; "He no longer"; "It is"; "It does not." This helps to create the underlying intensity that drives the seemingly objective portrait. The lines are filled with surprises too. Parallelism is a more complex and estranging device than it might initially seem. The Russian formalist critic Viktor Shlofsky pointed out in "Art as Technique" (1917) that "the perception of disharmony in a harmonious context is important in parallelism. The purpose of parallelism, like the general purpose of imagery, is to transfer the usual perceptions of an object into the sphere of a new perception . . ."

The first thing that strikes the reader is the displacement of pronouns in this poem. The title itself turns the subject into an object. "It" refers to autism. "It" also refers to the disconcerting way that the autistic person refers to himself. Many people on the spectrum of autism find it difficult to speak about themselves in the first person. They feel more comfortable with objective facts. Murray noted that "like all autistic kids, Alexander used to refer to himself as 'they,' or 'she,' any pronoun but 'I.' The more frightening a thing was, the further the pronoun was from 'I.' If he was really scared, it was 'they.' 'If they're bad, the police will put them in hospital.' Not 'If I'm bad, the police will put me in hospital.' That would be too terrifying a thing to say. It's what you might call pronomial deflection."

Murray uses his own pronomial deflection as a sort of postmodern device to create a portrait of someone who has been completely estranged from ordinary life. Hence, "He retains a slight 'Martian' accent." But Murray's speaker also recognizes the son's development: "He no longer hugs to disarm." The shift from "he" to "it" in the second and third lines shows the gradual shift in Alexander's perspective, what "it" does and does not allow or enable him to do: "It is gradually allowing him affection. / It does not allow proportion." "It" is something fully in charge of him.

Alexander likes cyborgs because he identifies with them, because he feels that he's a bit machinelike himself. He thinks that Arnold Schwarzenegger is also a cyborg, a machine-man, who might protect him, and so he's disappointed to discover that the actor is one of the so-called regulars or ordinary folks. The poem repeatedly intersperses Alexander's impulsiveness ("It still runs him around the house, alone in the dark, cooing and laughing") with his gifts as someone with Asperger's syndrome ("He knows the map of Earth's fertile soils, and can draw it freehand"). Much of a personal story is implied ("When he ran away constantly"; "When a runaway, he made uproar in the police station"). Raising a son with autism requires constant vigilance. The poem shows how difficult it is for Alexander to make human contact ("When asked to smile, he photographs a rictus-smile on his face") and imitate ordinary feeling.

There is a quiet critique of psychotherapy here, of "the dim Freudian psychiatrist who told us how autism resulted from 'refrigerator' parents." The idea that lack of parental warmth and attachment caused autism in children had been circulating since the 1940s. Apparently, Leo Kanner's dubious and toxic term "Refrigerator Mother," which had been popularized as "Refrigerator Parents" by Bruno Bettelheim, had made its way to Australia. Murray wasn't taken in. But in his poem there is a subtle auto-critique too, a sense of how difficult it has been to raise a kid with so many arbitrary rules ("When he worshiped fruit, he screamed as if poisoned when it was fed to him") and such limited speech ("He'd begun to talk, then returned to babble, then silence. It withdrew speech for years"). The parents need to keep figuring out their own rules and rulings.

There is also a sense throughout the poem of Alexander growing up. The poem is a portrait of him in transit as a teenager: how he was then, how he is now. The poem creates this feeling by continually changing tenses: "He *counts* at a glance, not looking. And he *has* never *been* lost. / When he *ate* only nuts and dried fruit, words *were* for dire emergencies. / He *knows* all the breeds of fowls, and the counties of Ireland." The speaker retains his sense of surprise at what drives Alexander, of how he lives "in objectivity." He tries to understand Alexander's situation and suspects how hard it must be for his son to be considered a "case": "*Don't say word!* when he was eight forbade the word 'autistic' in his presence."

Murray's portrait is restrained, but emotion keeps breaking through, especially near the end of the poem. There's a moment when he allows himself a pun: "*Eye contact, Mum!* means he truly wants attention. It dislikes I contact." The father's sense of both affection and relief comes through as Alexander grows into a more sympathetic person, someone who can feel something for others: "He is equitable and kind, and only ever a little jealous. It was relief when that little arrived."

At the very end of the poem, we get a feeling for Alexander's hard-won daily activities: "He surfs, bowls, walks for miles." He is no longer so disabled: "For many years he hasn't trailed his left arm while running." And in the last line Alexander himself fittingly gets the last word, though his father's anxiety also slips through: "*I gotta get smart!* looking terrified into the years. *I gotta get smart!*"

Les Murray's portrait "It Allows a Portrait in Line-Scan at Fifteen" is a poem that tries hard to be smart about itself. It describes with uncanny precision what it's like to have a teenager with autism. It is highly self-aware, astute, and truthful.

THOMAS LUX

———

"The People of the Other Village"

(1993)

Thomas Lux started out in the 1970s as a sort of American Surrealist, an heir to the Deep Image poets, such as Robert Bly, James Wright, and W. S. Merwin, and closely akin to his contemporaries Charles Simic, James Tate, and Bill Knott, all of whom were summoning the irrational in their poems, trying to unite the conscious and unconscious mind through psychic leaps. Lux loved the antic energy of Surrealism, its commitment to strangeness, its image-centered mysteries. His early poems were disturbing portraits of what the poet Elizabeth Macklin called a "solo native . . . always strange to the world." Over the years, however, Lux moved away from disjointed images and automatic writing, the poetry of the unconscious. As he said in an interview, "I kind of drifted away from Surrealism and the arbitrariness of that. I got more interested in subjects, identifiable subjects other than my own angst or ennui or things like that . . . I paid more and more attention to the craft . . . I started looking outside of myself a lot more for subjects. I read a great deal of history, turned more outward as opposed to inward."

"The People of the Other Village" is one result of Lux's turn outward. He was also paying attention to the news, placing events in the context of history.

He wrote "The People of the Other Village" in opposition to the Gulf War (1990–91), which has also been called the Persian Gulf War, the First Gulf War, Gulf War I, the Kuwait War, and the First Iraq War. By whatever name, it was a disaster. Lux's poem takes aim at the conflict, but, unlike most protest poems, it also floats free of its occasion and speaks to the age-old and ongoing catastrophe of dehumanizing people and turning them into the Other.

The People of the Other Village

hate the people of this village
and would nail our hats
to our heads for refusing in their presence to remove them
or staple our hands to our foreheads
for refusing to salute them
if we did not hurt them first: mail them packages of rats,
mix their flour at night with broken glass.
We do this, they do that.
They peel the larynx from one of our brothers' throats.
We devein one of their sisters.
The quicksand pits they built were good.
Our amputation teams were better.
We trained some birds to steal their wheat.
They sent us exploding ambassadors of peace.
They do this, we do that.
We canceled our sheep imports.
They no longer bought our blankets.
We mocked their greatest poet
and when that had no effect
we parodied the way they dance
which did cause pain, so they, in turn, said our God
was leprous, hairless.
We do this, they do that.
Ten thousand (10,000) years, ten thousand
(10,000) brutal, beautiful years.

"The People of the Other Village" breaks the mold of the typical protest poem with its cutting wit and black humor. It is funny and upsetting at the same time. Lux strategically turns the poem of dissent and social criticism into a dark parable of tribalism: modern warfare fueled by ancient hatreds. Each example of escalating violence and revenge has a comic awfulness. There is a primal truth in the perfectly balanced refrain, which divides neatly in two: "We do this, || they do that."

Lux's poem is stichic, which means that it has an unbroken flow of lines. Like Sharon Olds's "The Race" and Les Murray's "It Allows a Portrait in Line-Scan at Fifteen," it builds a case in one determined stanza. The twenty-five free-verse lines are carefully timed, the statements poised for maximum impact. The title flows, as if naturally, into the first line, but it also contains a dramatic surprise. When we read the title, "The People of the Other Village," we expect an anthropologically oriented poem about a particular people — what they do, how they live. Maybe they have quaint ways; perhaps they're just like us, after all. Instead, the title employs an enjambment that bites down with fury. Hence the realization that "The People of the Other Village"

> *hate* the people of this village

The poem thus establishes its tragic premise.

Lux employs surreal images throughout this poem, but they operate on behalf of a crafted argument, not as ends in themselves. For example, the poet takes some minor but plausible offenses by people in occupied countries — refusing to take off a hat, failing to salute — and finds comic Dantesque punishments for them, such as nailing "our hats / to our heads" or stapling "our hands to our foreheads." There is a weirdly primitive and exaggerated cruelty to the horrors: "They peel the larynx from one of our brothers' throats. / We devein one of their sisters."

Lux knowingly put this poem in the first-person plural. It's us and them. He doesn't exempt us from responsibility. *We* do this, *they* do that. We strike the first blow, hurt them first with ugly schoolboy pranks. Notice how the poem forces us to press our lips together on the repetition of the letter *m*: "*m*ail them packages of rats, / *m*ix their flour at night with broken glass." There's a kind of grim glee in the way he keeps creatively generating attacks and counterattacks. Some of the actions and retaliations exaggerate the horror, but with a baseline of truth as to the basic primordial technology of war: "The quicksand pits they built were good. / Our amputation teams were better." So too he takes a surreal image and applies it to suicide bombers: "They sent us exploding ambassadors of peace." Other retaliations seem more realistic, even mundane, such as dumb trade wars: "We cancelled our sheep imports. / They no longer bought our blankets." With a matter-of-fact tone, Lux's poem swings wildly between realism and grotesquerie. The comical line about the unimportance of poetry ("We mocked their greatest poet / and when that had no effect") proceeds to a mockery of how people dance (note the clever enjambment in "we parodied the way they dance / which did cause pain"), and this in turn leads to everyone insulting each other's gods as "leprous, hairless." The conflict keeps escalating until there is no turning back.

Everything builds to the last two lines, a final fragment, not even a whole sentence. "We do this, they do that" continues, and it all goes on and on for "Ten thousand (10,000) years, ten thousand / (10,000) brutal, beautiful years." Spelling out numbers and then reiterating them as figures in parentheses was originally done in legal writing. Lux uses this anachronistic practice to suggest that a kind of law is operating here — as if he is clarifying a policy. He repeats the numbers twice for emphasis. The alliteration in the last line has an archaic sound and inextricably ties together the words "brutal" and "beautiful." The Gulf War may be the latest example, but this sort of conflict has been going on throughout human time. The history of every people is impure and contains violence and beauty.

Thomas Lux was a poet of the American vernacular, an existentialist with comic timing, a disabused romantic who believed in the redemptive powers of poetry. "I like to make the reader laugh — and then steal that laugh, right out of the throat," he said. "Because I think life is like that, tragedy right alongside humor." "The People of the Other Village" is a political poem with an enduring truth, a lyric that combines sad zaniness and dark wisdom to steal the laughter right out of our throats.

LINDA GREGERSON

―――

"For the Taking"

(1993)

Linda Gregerson's poem "For the Taking," which first appeared in *The At-lantic* (1993) and then in her second book, *The Woman Who Died in Her Sleep* (1996), begins without preamble, in medias res:

> *For the Taking*
>
> And always, the damp blond curls
>   on her temples
>   and bountifully down to her shoulder blades,
>
> the rich loose curls all summer mixed with sand
>   and sweat,
>   and the rare, voluptuous double
>
> curve of her nether lip — most children lose
>   that ripeness before
>   they can talk — and the solemn forehead,

which betokens thought and, alas
        for her, o-
          bedience, and the pure, unmuddied line

of the jaw, and the peeling brown shoulders —
        she was always
          a child of the sun . . . This

was his sweet piece of luck, his
        find,
          his renewable turn-on,

and my brown and golden sister at eight
        and a half
          took to hating her body and cried

in her bath, and this was years,
        my bad uncle did it
          for years, in the back of the car,

in the basement where he kept his guns,
        and we
          who could have saved her, who knew

what it was in the best of times
        to cross
          the bridge of shame, from the body un-

encumbered to the body on the
        block,
          we would be somewhere mowing the lawn

or basting the spareribs right
        outside, and — how
          many times have you heard this? — we

were deaf and blind
　　　　and have
　　ever since required of her that she

take care of us, and she has,
　　　　and here's
　　the worst, she does it for love.

The full meaning of Gregerson's title, "For the Taking," only gradually reveals itself over the course of forty-two lines. The word "taking" has several connotations in this poem. The colloquial phrase "for the taking" means "ready or available for someone to take advantage of." In the most simple and sinister way, that's what happens to the poet's sister, who, without knowing it, was there "for the taking." Most devastating, the sister becomes the one who was "taken" — seized, held, exploited — by a relative, a sexual predator, "a bad uncle," as a child might put it. He abused her, and the rest of the family was too preoccupied to notice. Over the years, the poem reveals, this sister ends up taking care of them (that is, caring for and protecting them) and — it's almost unimaginable for the poet to admit it — she does it from love.

Gregerson unequivocally implicates herself in this moral quandary. She is a key member of the "we." The interjection, which is an unacceptable excuse — "how / many times have you heard this?" — suggests that she isn't excusing herself for the family's unawareness of the cruelty inflicted on her sister. On the contrary, she is trying to confront what happened and convicting the family for its obtuseness, which had such dire consequences. The poem takes up the guilt and helplessness of not knowing. Silence, the communal act of "not seeing," is first cousin to denial, which is enablement. But instead of recognizing this, the family accepted and "took" so much from the speaker's unnamed sister. The injustice of it all seems unending.

Gregerson has said that the subject of this poem ambushed her. When she began, she thought that she was writing a poem about the loveliness of her sister as a young girl. But by the second stanza she started to feel extremely uncomfortable, even implicated, since she had strayed unwittingly into that territory where affection for children — and appreciation for a type of loveliness that is unaware of itself — becomes predation. That's when she realized that her true subject had been lying in wait behind what she had only mistaken for her subject. It was not something that she would have purposely set out to put into a poem.

There are just two sentences in this poem. The first enters with a conjunction, "And," which is followed by the word "always"; the two words establish a sense of continuity and permanence. Indeed, the entire first sentence, which runs until the fifteenth line, pictures the eternal summer of a young girl, her purity and ripeness, "a child of the sun." This part of the poem, or rather this part of the sister's life, closes with an ellipsis. It trails off into the assertion, the brutal recognition, of the second sentence, which opens with this statement: "This // was his sweet piece of luck." This sentence carries the weight of the sister's sentence, her story, the years of abuse that took away her childhood.

Gregerson uses her signature three-line stanza for this meditative poem. William Carlos Williams coined the term "variable foot" for the three-ply line that he developed in his later work. Williams claimed that the traditional fixed foot of English prosody needed to be altered to represent idiomatic American speech rhythms. He was seeking metrical relativity, a more intuitive cadence based on speech. Gregerson formalizes Williams's triadic stanza so that it emphasizes not just the character of speech but also the experience of telling a story while simultaneously thinking about it. The syntax dramatizes the unfolding of thought, a current that drives the poem forward, while the lineation creates hesitancies and interruptions, points of emphasis. The dropped three-line stanza thus enables the poet to control the pacing of the lines, which expand, contract, and then expand again.

This in turn creates a special emphasis on the foreshortened second lines, which typically consist of one metrical foot. Isolate those lines for a moment and you get a sense of the dramatic phrasing —

> on her temples,
>
> and sweat,
>
> that ripeness before,
>
> for her, o-.

The break in the word "obedience," for example, creates an exclamation, "o-," like "oh," which falls, terribly, to complete the word "obedience," the compliance that fated the eight-year-old girl.

The third line of each stanza leans back, though not all the way to the beginning, and then extends the meditation. Reread the third line of each stanza —

> his renewable turn-on,
>
> took to hating her body and cried,
>
> for years, in the back of the car,
>
> who could have saved her, who knew

and you can see how Gregerson wrings meaning out of each individual line, while keeping the flow of the poem and the subject in mind.

Gregerson tends to use this stanzaic structure for most of her poems — she once said that discovering it saved her life — but it has special purpose here. Each stanza enacts individually the overall story of the poem. It begins, it cuts off dramatically on both sides, and then it keeps going, though it cannot return to the beginning. The fullness of childhood can never be restored.

So too the stanzas unspool into each other. This gives a feeling of thought in action, time slowed and pushing forward. And it allows the poet time to emphasize certain phrases for effect. Pause for a moment over the movement that starts in the middle of the ninth stanza:

> and we
> who could have saved her, who knew
>
> what it was in the best of times
>   to cross
>   the bridge of shame, from the body un-
>
> encumbered to the body on the
>   block,

A triple break — of a word, a line, and a stanza — occurs with "un- // en-cumbered," signaling a cataclysmic loss. The prefix *un-* has a negative force field and connects to the word "encumbered," enacting how the sister could have been rescued but was instead sacrificed. So too the consonance of the letter *c* connects "could" to "cross" even as the pressure of the letter *b* connects the words "best," "bridge," "body" (which appears twice), and "block." The bridge that the family crosses turns out not to be a real bridge but a brutal abstraction, a "bridge of shame."

The weaving together of sounds, the poetic figuration, and the movement of the lines all work here in the service of the shocking revelation that a young girl lost her childhood, her innocence — she was served up — while everyone else was going on with their ordinary domestic lives ("mowing the lawn // or basting the spareribs right / outside"). It's not just that the family was "deaf and blind"; it also "ever since required of her that she // take care of us, and she has . . ." The word "required" makes this all seem painfully compulsory. The phrase "take care of us" (to keep safe, to look after) seems especially ironic and painful, and brings us back to the title. There's a ghastly family circuit of damage in operation. The poet recognizes — and the poem acknowledges — that this is shockingly unfair. The one who is most harmed is the one upon whom the others depend for absolution. And worst of all, the speaker suggests, is that she does it not from obligation but voluntarily, "for love," which everyone in the family is willing to accept, to take.

NICHOLAS CHRISTOPHER

—

"Terminus"

(1993)

Terminus

Here is a piece of required reading
at the end of our century
the end of a millennium that began with the crusades

The transcript of an interview
between a Red Cross doctor
and a Muslim girl in Bosnia
twelve years old
who described her rape by men
calling themselves soldiers
different men every night one after the other
six seven eight of them
for a week
while she was chained by the neck
to a bed in her former schoolhouse

where she saw her parents and her brothers
have their throats slit and tongues cut out
where her sister-in-law
nineteen years old and nursing her baby
was also raped night after night
until she dared to beg for water
because her milk had run dry
at which point one of the men
tore the child from her arms
and as if he were "cutting an ear of corn"
(the girl's words)
lopped off the child's head
with a hunting knife
tossed it into the mother's lap
and raped the girl again
slapping her face
smearing it with her nephew's blood
and then shot the mother
who had begun to shriek
with the head wide-eyed in her lap
shoving the gun into her mouth
and firing twice

All of this recounted to the doctor
in a monotone
a near whisper in a tent
beside an icy river
where the girl had turned up frostbitten
wearing only a soiled slip
her hair yanked out
her teeth broken

All the history you've ever read
tells you this is what men do
this is only a sliver of the reflection
of the beast
who is a fixture of human history

and the places you heard of as a boy
that were his latest stalking grounds
Auschwitz Dachau Treblinka
and the names of their dead
and their numberless dead whose names have vanished
each day now find their rolls swelled
with kindred souls
new names new numbers
from towns and villages
that have been scorched from the map

1993 may as well be 1943
and it should be clear now
that the beast in his many guises
the flags and vestments
in which he wraps himself
and the elaborate titles he assumes
can never be outrun

As that girl with the broken teeth
loaded into an ambulance
strapped down on a stretcher
so she wouldn't claw her own face
will never outrun him
no matter where she goes
solitary or lost in a crowd
the line she follows
however straight or crooked
will always lead her back to that room
like the chamber at the bottom
of Hell in the Koran
where the Zaqqūm tree grows
watered by scalding rains
"bearing fruit like devils' heads"

In not giving her name
someone has noted at the end

of the transcript that the girl herself
could not or would not recall it
and then describes her as a survivor

Which of course is from the Latin
meaning to live on
to outlive others

I would not have used that word

"Terminus" is a nerve-racking documentary poem, a dark testimonial that takes its place in a lineage of poems that tell terrifying historical truths and bring forward otherwise unheard voices. It has an eerie precision — compassionate but slightly removed, empathic but detached enough to present grueling evidence. It is a lyric with an epic heritage — think of Muriel Rukeyser's groundbreaking book-length poem *The Book of the Dead* (1938), about mine workers in West Virginia in the late 1920s and early 1930s, and Charles Reznikoff's *Holocaust* (1975), which compresses twenty-six volumes of courtroom testimony from the trials of Nazi war criminals in Nuremberg and Jerusalem. Whereas Rukeyser traveled to West Virginia to write her poem ("There are roads to take when you think of your country"), Reznikoff served as a secondary, or secondhand, witness to the grim horrors of the Shoah.

The documentary poem commits itself to testimonials, to history, to what Reznikoff called "recitatives." Christopher's poem presents the transcript of an interview between a Red Cross doctor and a twelve-year old Bosnian girl. He took the text from an official Red Cross document and condensed it. His arrangement creates some horrific points of emphasis. As in poems by Guillaume Apollinaire and W. S. Merwin, the lack of punctuation gives "Terminus" an improvisational spoken quality, a feeling of being untethered, almost lifting off the page. It enables a freer associative process than, say, the exact transcript of an interview in prose. But it works in the service of the testimony, an act of witnessing.

A terminus is a final point in time or space, the end of the line, an extremity. There is no going beyond it. The narrator of this poem, a stand-in for the poet, begins with the language of a journalist or history professor presenting evidence. "Here is a piece of required reading / at the end of our century / at the end of a millennium that began with the crusades." Christopher wrote the poem in 1993 ("1993 may as well be 1943") and reports from the end of the twentieth century, the century of mass murders, though he also recognizes that we are at the endpoint of a thousand-year history that began with religious wars.

Christopher places the girl at the very heart of his poem. We can't look away from her; we can't stop listening to her appalling testimony. She is a real person, not an abstraction of history. She tells what happened not just to her but to her parents and her brothers and her sister-in-law, who had the misfortune to be nursing a baby. By the time of her testimony, the men in her village had all been executed by Serbian militia, whom the poet sarcastically refers to as "men calling themselves soldiers." The implication is that real soldiers wouldn't act so dishonorably.

There is a moment when the narrator is so floored by the matter-of-fact way that the girl describes such unspeakable cruelty that he pauses to point out that he is using her actual words:

> at which point one of the men
> tore the child from her arms
> and as if he were "cutting an ear of corn"
> (the girl's words)
> lopped off the child's head
> with a hunting knife

There is an awful everyday quality to the monstrous cruelty.

The third stanza breaks off to describe how the girl whispers her story in a dry monotone. There is nothing theatrical or exaggerated about her report. We observe the setting and hear how she turned up frostbitten, "wearing only a soiled slip / her hair yanked out / her teeth broken." Christopher might have broken his poem off there and left us to contemplate the permanent misery of a Bosnian girl and what was inflicted upon her family.

But in the next stanza the narrator turns to address himself in the second person: "All the history you've ever read / tells you this is what men do." He puts the reader in the position of overhearing his argument, his recognition "of the beast / who is a fixture of human history." That beast is gendered as male. The narrator explicitly links what is happening in Bosnia in 1993 to what happened in Europe fifty years earlier, and he recalls the concentration camps that he heard about as a boy. Nothing changes, he insists; men continue to dehumanize other people, to wrap their cruelty in national pieties and military titles. There doesn't seem to be any end to human depravity and cruelty.

And then the story returns to the girl, as it must, and the narrator tells us how she would never escape what happened to her, how she would always be returned to that room, which he compares to "the chamber at the bottom / of Hell in the Koran." He refers to the Zaqqūm tree of the Qur'an (37:62–68), a cursed tree grown in fire, as if he is reaching for biblical language — "bearing fruit like devils' heads" — to describe the poisonous fruits of this inhumane and human earthly hell. But then he lowers the level of the language a notch. The girl won't give her name to the interviewer, he tells us, and points to a note by someone in the Red Cross who describes the girl as a "survivor."

Christopher takes an extra moment at the end of "Terminus" to provide the etymology of the word *survivor,* which he sets off as a stanza and purposely divides into three lines, the first dry and explanatory ("Which of course is from the Latin"), the next two poignant ("meaning to live on / to outlive others"). He concludes with a nearly deadpan last line, a sentence and stanza unto itself: "I would not have used that word." There really is no language to describe what this nameless Muslim girl in Bosnia has gone through, the sheer insanity of what was done to her. But the word "survivor" seems completely inadequate to define the human being at the heart of "Terminus."

MARIE HOWE

———

"What the Living Do"

(1994)

Marie Howe's younger brother John died from AIDS-related complications in 1989. He was twenty-eight years old. The two of them had always been close (she was the second oldest and he was the second youngest in a family of nine children), and he had been her dear friend and confidant ever since he was a boy. They wrote constantly to each other — sometimes two letters a week — and she showed him all her work. She was shattered by his death. It took her a few years to figure out how to write "What the Living Do," a poem in the form of a letter to him. I first read it in a magazine in 1994, and the way she has given voice to loss has stayed with me for the past twenty-five years.

What the Living Do

Johnny, the kitchen sink has been clogged for days, some utensil probably fell
    down there,
and the Drano won't work but smells dangerous, and the crusty dishes have
    piled up

waiting for the plumber I still haven't called. This is the everyday we spoke of.
It's winter again: the sky's a deep, headstrong blue, and the sunlight pours
through

the open living-room windows because the heat's on too high in here and I
can't turn it off.
For weeks now, driving, or dropping a bag of groceries in the street, the bag
breaking,

I've been thinking: This is what the living do. And yesterday, hurrying along
those
wobbly bricks in the Cambridge sidewalk, spilling my coffee down my wrist
and sleeve,

I thought it again, and again later, when buying a hairbrush: This is it.
Parking. Slamming the car door shut in the cold. What you called that
yearning.

What you finally gave up. We want the spring to come and the winter to pass.
We want
whoever to call or not call, a letter, a kiss — we want more and more and then
more of it.

But there are moments, walking, when I catch a glimpse of myself in the win-
dow glass,
say, the window of the corner video store, and I'm gripped by a cherishing so
deep

for my own blowing hair, chapped face, and unbuttoned coat that I'm
speechless:
I am living. I remember you.

Howe's grief was unlocked when she stopped trying to write a traditional
elegy for her brother and decided to write him a letter instead. She felt that
she was writing a real letter to a true friend, and the direct address released her.
She was consoling herself by sending something to him as if he could receive

it, as if he could still hear her talking to him about everyday life. She imitates the colloquial familiarity of a letter, which creates the illusion of a continuing conversation, as if the poet can still talk to her brother because he is alive inside of her. But now it is a one-sided conversation, and she must comfort herself. And, unlike an actual letter, this one is not entirely meant for its designated recipient, who is beyond reading. By figuring that letter as a poem, by shaping it into long-lined, deep-breathing couplets, she also intends it as something for us, her readers, to experience and overhear.

Howe is thus extending a tradition that began with Horace's *Epistles* (20–14 BCE), though she updates Horace's use of the imaginary letter to reflect on a larger moral or philosophical subject. Her letter is more akin to those of Richard Hugo, who brought the form closer to real letters in his book *31 Letters and 13 Dreams* (1977). And yet we never mistake the letter poem for an actual letter, which is typically intended for only one reader. Whether the letter addressed to someone who is dead is really intended for that reader is questionable. Such a letter is instead a fantasy of connection, a mode of self-consolation, a way of talking to oneself — and others.

Howe's epistolary lyric is an elegiac poem of loss that is also about the dailiness of life. Notice what she decides to confide to her dead brother — and what she doesn't tell him. This is a personal poem but not a confessional one. For example, she doesn't fill him in on what has happened to their large family over the past few years. She doesn't confess any dark secrets, as might happen in a poem by Robert Lowell or Sylvia Plath. Instead, she tells him about ordinary mishaps, the everyday, the mundane, and makes that the thematic through line of the poem.

Howe relies on the unrhymed couplet, an elemental stanzaic unit. Whereas William Meredith strongly depended on closed couplets to create an epigrammatic sense of closure at the beginning of his poem "Parents," Howe uses her first four stanzas to open up the couplet and propel the poem forward from one line and stanza to another. There is thus an emphatic change when we come to two closed, self-contained couplets:

I thought it again, and again later, when buying a hairbrush: This is it.
Parking. Slamming the car door shut in the cold. What you called that
    yearning.

What you finally gave up. We want the spring to come and the winter to pass.
   We want
whoever to call or not call, a letter, a kiss — we want more and more and then
   more of it.

The closed couplet emphasizes the short declarative sentences: "This is it. / . . . What you called that yearning." So too the poet puts considerable pressure on the enjambment: "We want / whoever to call . . ." Note how she threads the words together with the letter *w* and thus repeatedly opens our mouths in a small, tight circle: "*W*hat you finally gave up. *W*e *w*ant the spring to come and the *w*inter to pass. *W*e *w*ant / *w*hoever to call or not call, a letter, a kiss — *w*e *w*ant more . . ." She repeats the word "more" three times. The yearning or desire for love, for more life, seems to define life itself.

Howe has made the long line one of her signatures. This expansive unit pushes past the five-beat iambic pentameter line, energizing her to put things into her poems rather than take them out. Like the Whitmanesque poets Muriel Rukeyser, Galway Kinnell, Adrienne Rich, Etheridge Knight, and C. K. Williams, she shapes long lines that incline toward prose without ever turning into a prose poem. That's because each set of lines has a distinctive rhythm and maintains a kind of lyric integrity as a unit of meaning, a measure of attention.

The ten-syllable or blank-verse line has provided a kind of norm in English-language poetry. Both Wordsworth and Frost, for example, perceived that the blank-verse line could give the sensation of actual speech, of a person engaging others. The poet Allen Grossman argued that the line of more than ten syllables consequently gives a feeling of going beyond the parameters of oral utterance, or over them, beyond speech itself. The lines widen the space for reverie. "The speaker in the poem bleeds outward as in trance of sleep toward other states of himself," Grossman says. This line also radiates an oracular feeling, which is why it has so often been the line of prophetic texts, visionary poetry.

This line of argument applies to Howe's poem because its ordinary details take on a kind of sacred aura. Her speaker points out, for example, how "the sky's a deep, headstrong blue, and the sunlight pours through / the open living-room windows . . ." She is consecrating what she would later use as the title of a book: *The Kingdom of Ordinary Time* (2008). There's a bit of poetic magic in the way this conversational poem reaches beyond speech and hits a different register, a higher visionary note. The poem lands on vulnerable, sac-

ramental moments that seem to exist almost outside of time. Notice the argu-
mentative turn on the word "But":

But there are moments, walking, when I catch a glimpse of myself in the win-
     dow glass,
say, the window of the corner video store, and I'm gripped by a cherishing so
     deep

for my own blowing hair, chapped face, and unbuttoned coat that I'm
     speechless . . .

Howe is describing an intense revelatory moment, a "moment of being," to
use Virginia Woolf's phrase. It's no accident that the speaker becomes dumb-
founded and astounded at the end of the poem. It's only when she sees herself
in reflection that she is gripped by a sense of self-care, of being alive, out in the
open, exposed. She is robbed of speech and therefore concludes with a simple
living pronouncement: "I am living. I remember you."

Howe has explained in interviews how her brother's death changed her:

> After John died, the world became very clear — as if a window had
> broken — the world itself became very dear. It was the place John had
> lived, and as long as I still walked around I could catch glimpses of
> him. But more than that, when John died I felt as if I had finally en-
> tered the larger community of humans. Now I knew unbearable grief,
> and I was like other people in this world who had known this.

Howe brings her recognition of a shared community of grief to the poem,
which is pierced by a sense of mortal loss. Many people have testified to los-
ing their way after someone they love has died. They are knocked so far back
that they need to figure out how to live again. No one else can do it for them,
either. And that's precisely how this elegy becomes a poem about carrying on,
about going forward and living in the aftermath of grievous loss. The main les-
son of the poem is a simple declarative sentence: "This is what the living do."
It's almost an instruction manual too, on self-cherishing: *This is what the liv-
ing must do.* This is it. That yearning.

DUNYA MIKHAIL

"The War Works Hard"

(1994)

D unya Mikhail fled Iraq in 1996. She left because Saddam Hussein's government had questioned her. She was facing increasing threats and harassment from the Iraqi authorities for her writings after the First Gulf War, which culminated in her verse memoir *Diary of a Wave Outside the Sea*. She writes about war as a woman, mother, wife, and friend.

Mikhail lived with war in Iraq from the time she was fifteen years old. The war came with different names — the Iran-Iraq War, Desert Storm, Mother of All Battles — but it always acted with the same consistency. She has recalled that there was a room in her family house in Baghdad that her mother dubbed "the war room." It was located by the stairs and designed for security, a survival space where the family stayed during sirens and explosions. That's how she got the idea to take the war-related activities that she observed daily and make them look like any other worthwhile human endeavor.

Here is the title poem from her book *The War Works Hard*, which was written in 1994 and published in Arabic in 2000:

The War Works Hard

How magnificent the war is!
How eager
and efficient!
Early in the morning,
it wakes up the sirens
and dispatches ambulances
to various places,
swings corpses through the air,
rolls stretchers to the wounded,
summons rain
from the eyes of mothers,
digs into the earth
dislodging many things
from under the ruins . . .
Some are lifeless and glistening,
others are pale and still throbbing . . .
It produces the most questions
in the minds of children,
entertains the gods
by shooting fireworks and missiles
into the sky,
sows mines in the fields
and reaps punctures and blisters,
urges families to emigrate,
stands beside the clergymen
as they curse the devil
(poor devil, he remains
with one hand in the searing fire) . . .
The war continues working, day and night.
It inspires tyrants
to deliver long speeches,
awards medals to generals
and themes to poets.
It contributes to the industry
of artificial limbs,

provides food for flies,
adds pages to the history books,
achieves equality
between killer and killed,
teaches lovers to write letters,
accustoms young women to waiting,
fills the newspapers
with articles and pictures,
builds new houses
for the orphans,
invigorates the coffin makers,
gives grave diggers
a pat on the back
and paints a smile on the leader's face.
The war works with unparalleled diligence!
Yet no one gives it
a word of praise.

(Translated by Elizabeth Winslow)

"The War Works Hard" is a new kind of antiwar poem. It is sardonic and takes an odd, funny, reverse angle on the hateful experience of war itself. Mikhail was writing from inside a war, on the side being attacked, while American poets such as Thomas Lux and Lucia Perillo were writing against the war from the side of the attackers, the American side. Mikhail paid for her poem with experience, but the poems by all three poets are infused with a sense of bitter helplessness and irony.

"The War Works Hard" unfolds with manic energy, which is deftly enacted by the short lines. Diligent movement characterizes the stichic structure — a single stanza of fifty-three lines. The mordant personification of the war, as an industrious, indefatigable worker who has been underappreciated, gives the poem a faux-naïf quality, an understated and plaintive comedy. Personification, the attribution of human qualities to inanimate objects, animals, or ideas, has special purpose as the basis for allegory — think of those medieval morality plays in which characters are named "Lust" or "Hope." This figure of speech indicates that general ideas, and not individual people, are being dramatized.

Mikhail's personification has special ironic force: the poor war works so hard! No wonder the poem begins with two exclamatory sentences. The war gets up early in the morning—notice how emphatically the translator assonates the *e* sounds at the beginning of the poem ("How *e*ager / and *e*fficient! / *E*arly . . .")—and starts waking up sirens and dispatching ambulances. The poem is matter of fact about the everyday cruelty of the war that so industriously "swings corpses through the air, / rolls stretchers to the wounded, / summons rain / from the eyes of mothers . . ." As Robert Hayden does in "The Whipping," Mikhail conflates personal tears and rainy weather.

There is an ellipsis after the observation that "many things" have been dislodged. The poem pauses for a moment, as if to notice that some of those "things" are newly dead people ("lifeless and glistening") while others are barely alive ("pale and still throbbing"). The war dramatically marks the transition point, the thinnest of thresholds, between life and death. It turns people into objects.

The recognition behind the poem—the machinery of war never rests—is chilling. The poem enacts that recognition through its catalogs. Of course, it "produces the most questions / in the minds of children," who haven't yet learned to accept the unacceptable, and simultaneously "entertains the gods." This phrase brings to mind these lines from Shakespeare: "As flies to wanton boys are we to th' gods; / They kill us for their sport" (*King Lear,* act 4, scene 1, lines 36–37). Mikhail purposely conflates celebratory fireworks with destructive missiles: "shooting fireworks and missiles / into the sky."

The unrelenting war changes everyone's life. It puts doctors to work, "urges families to emigrate," and stands infernally next to clergymen, who see it as the work of the devil. It's typical of the strategy here for the speaker to sympathize with the "poor devil," who remains "with one hand in the searing fire." The war sweeps everyone up. It has almost too many beneficiaries—it inspires long-winded tyrants and battle-tested generals, and it even gives "themes" to poets, who find the subject inescapable and thus write poems like the very one we are reading.

Dunya Mikhail wrote "The War Works Hard" with fateful understanding of what war does to people, those who kill and those being killed—the lovers, the journalists, the newly minted orphans, the over-eager coffin makers, the hardworking gravediggers. Some people's lives are destroyed; others receive financial benefit. Everyone must be involved—no one escapes unscathed from its unending destruction. The war works so hard and yet, as the last lines ruefully conclude, "no one gives it / a word of praise." But Mikhail's poem does close on the word "praise" — the poet is the only one who suggests such recognition, in an unlikely ode, an inverted and sardonic praise poem. It approaches the subject of violent destruction with cutting wit, fierce humor, and brave humanity.

STANLEY KUNITZ

—•—

"Halley's Comet"

(1995)

Halley's Comet

Miss Murphy in first grade
wrote its name in chalk
across the board and told us
it was roaring down the stormtracks
of the Milky Way at frightful speed
and if it wandered off its course
and smashed into the earth
there'd be no school tomorrow.
A red-bearded preacher from the hills
with a wild look in his eyes
stood in the public square
at the playground's edge
proclaiming he was sent by God
to save every one of us,
even the little children.

"Repent, ye sinners!" he shouted,
waving his hand-lettered sign.
At supper I felt sad to think
that it was probably
the last meal I'd share
with my mother and my sisters;
but I felt excited too
and scarcely touched my plate.
So mother scolded me
and sent me early to my room.
The whole family's asleep
except for me. They never heard me steal
into the stairwell hall and climb
the ladder to the fresh night air.
Look for me, Father, on the roof
of the red brick building
at the foot of Green Street —
that's where we live, you know, on the top floor.
I'm the boy in the white flannel gown
sprawled on this coarse gravel bed
searching the starry sky,
waiting for the world to end.

Stanley Kunitz catapulted himself back into childhood in his poem "Halley's Comet" (1995). Kunitz was five years old on May 19, 1910, the day that Halley's Comet was scheduled to pass the earth and, if it strayed off course, crash into our planet, thus potentially blowing up the world. He was an old man when he wrote "Halley's Comet," but the language of the poem migrates back to his first-grade self. We are placed immediately in his elementary school classroom. The backdrop is the general anticipation and widespread sense of impending doom over the unusually close approach of the comet, which ended up brushing the earth with its tail.

The return of Halley's Comet in 1986 may have spurred Kunitz to engage this childhood memory from seventy-six years earlier. He kept his childhood alive in himself — he was never far from those memories of a hardscrabble life in Worcester, Massachusetts — and obsessively pursued what he called "the theme of the lost father." The poem is stichic, like Dunya Mikhail's poem, and spans the course of a single day in thirty-seven lines, one ongoing stanza. Kunitz employs an unrhymed three-beat, or trimeter, line, which is the meter Thom Gunn utilized for his elegy for his mother, "The Gas-poker," and Elizabeth Bishop marshaled to invoke her seven-year-old self in her epiphanic lyric "In the Waiting Room," also set in Worcester, where she grew up. Bishop's poem, which is about losing and finding a self, stands behind Kunitz's testimonial like a protective older sister.

The poem begins with Miss Murphy's droll observation that school would be called off if Halley's Comet hit the earth and destroyed the planet. The white chalk on the blackboard at the beginning of the poem foreshadows the "starry sky" at its end. Miss Murphy's analysis is followed immediately by the fire-and-brimstone preacher declaring the end of the world. The poem moves effortlessly from the teacher in the classroom, to the preacher on the edge of the playground, then to the family at home at suppertime. The speaker recalls not just the fear that overtook him at the roaring approach of the comet, the sadness that he felt over his final dinner with his mother and sisters, but also the excitement of the event, the thrill of something life-altering, the possibility of being hit by a cosmic snowball from afar.

Two-thirds of the way through the poem, the verb tense changes from the past to the present: "The whole family's asleep . . ." Now it is night, the boy is the only one awake, a sole consciousness, and slips up the stairwell to the roof. This is a threshold moment: he moves from inside the house, emblem of the domestic, to the outdoors, where he stands on the roof and looks searchingly into the sky. Both literally and metaphorically, he has moved from the safety of the indoors to the exposure of the outdoors. The final turn in the poem comes when he looks up to address his father.

Kunitz never knew his father, who committed suicide before he was born, but he mourned the loss all his life. His mother never forgave Solomon Kunitz for killing himself and eradicated all traces of his memory from their house. Kunitz's poem "The Portrait" tells the story of coming down from the attic with a pastel portrait of "a long-lipped stranger" and showing it to his mother, who ripped it to shreds and slapped Kunitz across the face. At sixty-four years old, he writes, "I can feel my cheek / still burning."

At the end of "Halley's Comet," there's an agitated longing in the way the speaker suddenly calls out, "Look for me, Father, on the roof . . ." He is scanning the heavens for a root connection to someone he never knew. In this bit of magical thinking, he is also letting his father know that the family has moved to a top floor of a tenement at the bottom of Green Street — how else could they find each other? That's why he must identify himself to his father:

> I'm the boy in the white flannel gown
> sprawled on this coarse gravel bed
> searching the starry sky,
> waiting for the world to end.

This is an image preserved in amber. The boy is forever locked in time, and in some sense the poet will always be that boy, wearing a white flannel night-gown on a gravel rooftop, looking up at the star-filled sky, searching the infinite spaces for his father, who never comes, and waiting for the apocalypse.

BRIGIT PEGEEN KELLY

"Song"

(1995)

B rigit Pegeen Kelly was struck by lightning when she wrote "Song," a poem
that has the rich, inexplicable strangeness of a folk tale. It is magical and
has irrational power. It seems to come from another realm of experience, a
contemporary poem with the authority of an ancient allegory. It is the title
poem of Kelly's second book and teaches us something critical about her prac-
tice. She was unflinching in the way she faced dark human truths, some of
them unspeakable, and still insisted on singing in the face of them. As the poet
Lisa Williams puts it in "The Necessity of Song," "The persistence of music (a
trope for poetry) is a task undertaken in all of Kelly's work: to continue to sing
in spite of, of even in response to, terror and fear."

Song

Listen: there was a goat's head hanging by ropes in a tree.
All night it hung there and sang. And those who heard it
Felt a hurt in their hearts and thought they were hearing
The song of a night bird. They sat up in their beds, and then

They lay back down again. In the night wind, the goat's head
Swayed back and forth, and from far off it shone faintly
The way the moonlight shone on the train track miles away
Beside which the goat's headless body lay. Some boys
Had hacked its head off. It was harder work than they had imagined.
The goat cried like a man and struggled hard. But they
Finished the job. They hung the bleeding head by the school
And then ran off into the darkness that seems to hide everything.
The head hung in the tree. The body lay by the tracks.
The head called to the body. The body to the head.
They missed each other. The missing grew large between them,
Until it pulled the heart right out of the body, until
The drawn heart flew toward the head, flew as a bird flies
Back to its cage and the familiar perch from which it trills.
Then the heart sang in the head, softly at first and then louder,
Sang long and low until the morning light came up over
The school and over the tree, and then the singing stopped. . . .
The goat had belonged to a small girl. She named
The goat Broken Thorn Sweet Blackberry, named it after
The night's bush of stars, because the goat's silky hair
Was dark as well water, because it had eyes like wild fruit.
The girl lived near a high railroad track. At night
She heard the trains passing, the sweet sound of the train's horn
Pouring softly over her bed, and each morning she woke
To give the bleating goat his pail of warm milk. She sang
Him songs about girls with ropes and cooks in boats.
She brushed him with a stiff brush. She dreamed daily
That he grew bigger, and he did. She thought her dreaming
Made it so. But one night the girl didn't hear the train's horn,
And the next morning she woke to an empty yard. The goat
Was gone. Everything looked strange. It was as if a storm
Had passed through while she slept, wind and stones, rain
Stripping the branches of fruit. She knew that someone
Had stolen the goat and that he had come to harm. She called
To him. All morning and into the afternoon, she called
And called. She walked and walked. In her chest a bad feeling
Like the feeling of the stones gouging the soft undersides

Of her bare feet. Then somebody found the goat's body
By the high tracks, the flies already filling their soft bottles
At the goat's torn neck. Then somebody found the head
Hanging in a tree by the school. They hurried to take
These things away so that girl would not see them.
They hurried to raise money to buy the girl another goat.
They hurried to find the boys who had done this, to hear
Them say it was a joke, a joke, it was nothing but a joke. . . .
But listen: here is the point. The boys thought to have
Their fun and be done with it. It was harder work than they
Had imagined, this silly sacrifice, but they finished the job,
Whistling as they washed their large hands in the dark.
What they didn't know was that the goat's head was already
Singing behind them in the tree. What they didn't know
Was that the goat's head would go on singing, just for them,
Long after the ropes were down, and that they would learn to listen,
Pail after pail, stroke after patient stroke. They would
Wake in the night thinking they heard the wind in the trees
Or a night bird, but their hearts beating harder. There
Would be a whistle, a hum, a high murmur, and, at last, a song,
The low song a lost boy sings remembering his mother's call.
Not a cruel song, no, no, not cruel at all. This song
Is sweet. It is sweet. The heart dies of this sweetness.

"Song" unfolds in a single solid block, one long sweep of lines. Like Louise Glück's "Night Song," this poem aspires to be a song, though it is a written lyric, one with characters and a plot, a story-poem. But whereas Glück addresses her sleeping lover, Kelly begins with an urgent address to the reader: "Listen." This directive recurs three-fourths of the way through the poem with even greater intensity. "But listen," the narrator declares, "here is the point." Like Coleridge's ancient mariner or Primo Levi's Holocaust survivor, the speaker is collaring us, telling us something important, a story we need to listen to, a moral we need to hear. The long lines of this poem also widen the space for reverie and help create an oracular feeling. We are not listening to a realistic short story, but a visionary or prophetic text.

"Song" narrates the story of a gang of boys who steal a little girl's pet goat, behead it, and hang its head in a tree. They do it as a joke, just for the fun of it, but the head and the body of the goat miss each other so much that the goat's heart is pulled from its body and flies like a bird to its head. That's where it sings its plaintive song. The boys have walked away, thinking they have washed their hands of their gruesome prank, but instead the slaughtered goat's head goes on singing to them for the rest of their lives.

The poem proceeds by a series of strikingly short sentences and fragments. Many are simple and direct. The repetitions create an incantatory effect. For example: "The head hung in the tree. The body lay by the tracks. / The head called to the body. The body to the head. / They missed each other. The missing grew large . . ." Note too how the sentences divide the lines neatly into two halves, lending a steady, even-handed rhetorical authority to this part of the primer.

As in Elizabeth Bishop's poem "In the Waiting Room" and Stanley Kunitz's poem "Halley's Comet," whenever Kelly's poem focuses on the little girl, the writing gravitates toward a child's vocabulary and sentence structure: "She called / To him. All morning and into the afternoon, she called / And called. She walked and walked. In her chest a bad feeling . . ." At one point it seems a school fundraising drive is being mentioned: "They hurried to raise money to buy the girl another goat." But by the end of the poem it feels as if we've entered an ancient mystery rite.

Two archaic stories stand behind this poem. One concerns Orpheus, who was given his first lyre by Apollo, the Greek god of music and poetry. Orpheus sang so sweetly that he could charm wild animals and uproot trees. He descended into the underworld to retrieve Eurydice, whom he tragically lost, and then vowed never to love another. Later, Thracian women tore him to pieces and flung his head into a river. But his severed head, with its lyre, floated along, still singing mournful songs until it reached the sea. In "Song," the goat's head is a kind of Orphic figure; its head continues singing, with a heart-wrenching sweetness, from a tree.

The goat is also a sacrificial figure, connected to classical tragedy. The word comes from the ancient Greek *tragoidia*, which derives from the words *tragos* (meaning "goat") and *ode* (meaning "song"). *Tragedy* means "goat-song." It originated in ritual hymns sung during the sacrifice of a goat at Dionysian festivals. Goats were sacred to the god Dionysus, who made them his chosen victims (Euripides, *The Bacchae,* 405 BCE). Sacrifice was a process of identification, and the goat was the embodiment of a god. Kelly updates the tragedy for our time and makes clear that the vile crime is intended as "a silly sacrifice."

The boys had committed an act of gratuitous violence. They would, however, be punished with a never-ending song of loneliness.

"Song" is a poem of suffering and music. It proceeds from a violent rupture and carries a sense of primal loss. We are told that the goat sang like a night bird and cried like a man struggling for his life. Think of the way the girl cares for her goat, feeding him "warm milk," singing him songs and brushing his body, dreaming of his growth. Like a mother, she intuitively understands when he has been harmed. So too, at the close of the poem, the song is explicitly compared to "The low song a lost boy sings remembering his mother's call." The liquid *l*'s link the "*l*ow song" to the "*l*ost boy."

The song of the goat is pervaded by a sense of homelessness that is buried inside each of us, a longing for a lost origin, a lost body. This haunting and sacred song may have originated in cruelty, a cruel separation, but it is not cruel, the narrator insists: "no, no, not cruel at all." She is emphatic about what she knows; hence the quiet drumbeat of the final three declarative sentences: "This song / Is sweet. It is sweet. The heart dies of this sweetness."

When you reread the end of the poem, notice the firm enjambment in the penultimate line ("song / is"), the triple repetition of the word "sweet," and the insistent repetition of the letters *t* and *s*, which carry the sounds from one word and sentence to another ("*This song / Is sweet. It is sweet. The heart dies of this sweetness*"). The song is not bitter, as one might expect, but ever fresh. The poet did not choose the phrase "her heart" or "their hearts"; she doesn't refer to "my heart" or "our hearts," but instead to "the heart." We have seen from poems by Langston Hughes, Charlotte Mew, and Czesław Miłosz how this usage suggests both the feelings for a loved one and the true core of a person. Instead of the usual locution "the heart breaks," the poem suggests that "the heart dies," which is more extreme and overwhelming, dire and fateful. The very human core of us dies from the pained mortal sweetness of the song.

It is just such a poignant and sorrowful sweetness that Brigit Pegeen Kelly captures in her own beautiful poem "Song."

ROSANNA WARREN

———

"Simile"

(1996)

Rosanna Warren once called writing a poem "a tightrope walk over the abyss," and that's probably what many readers felt when they read her lyric "Simile" in *The New Yorker* in April 2000. I couldn't have been the only one who opened the magazine and suddenly felt as if I were hovering over the edge of a cliff:

> *Simile*
>
> As when her friend, the crack Austrian skier, in the story
> she often told us, had to face
> his first Olympic ski jump and, from
> the starting ramp over the chute that plunged
> so vertiginously its bottom lip
> disappeared from view, gazed
> on a horizon of Alps that swam and dandled around him
> like toy boats in a bathtub, and he could not
> for all his iron determination,

training and courage
ungrip his fingers from the railings of the starting gate, so that
his teammates had to join in prying
up, finger by finger, his hands
to free him, so

facing death, my
mother gripped the bedrails but still
stared straight ahead — and
who was it, finally,
who loosened
her hands?

"Simile" has a quiet and deceptive title. We don't usually expect a poem titled after a figure of speech to take up the subject of death, let alone the death of the poet's mother. That's the plangent surprise wrapped inside this poem. The poet uses the drama of a single extended simile to get at something of critical importance. She is trying to think through and understand what happened to her mother as she was dying. The simile is the method of transport.

Warren has recalled sitting with her mother for a day, a night, and then another day as she was dying of emphysema and pneumonia. The image of the ski jump flashed into her mind at some point as she was watching her mother's hands gripping the bed railings. She felt that the observation was somehow off limits but several days later scribbled it into her notebook and tucked it away during that hallucinatory period after her mother's death, the time out of time that follows an intimate passing. It sat in her notebook (and her mind) for several months. At some point, she permitted herself to look back at the lines and fiddle with them, always troubled by a sense of violation. But the lines seemed more and more like a poem to her, and eventually she persuaded herself that the poem was not a violation but an offering.

"Simile" is a poem that stakes everything on a single comparison. It telegraphs the fact that it is explicitly going to compare one thing to another. The essence of a simile is similitude (likeness) and unlikeness, urging a comparison. It depends on a kind of heterogeneity between the elements being compared. The simile asserts a likeness between unlike things and maintains their comparability, but it also draws attention to their differences, thus affirming a state of division.

A heroic simile is one long extended comparison. It is frequently employed in epic poetry, where it intensifies the heroic nature of the subject. Warren is steeped in Homer and Virgil, the Greek and Latin classics, and for years she has taught the epics in translation to undergraduates. She harkens back to the way the epic simile lingers and digresses. The structure of comparison tends to suspend the action, opening an imaginative space. Thus, Homer compares a battle to a snowstorm and Virgil compares the ghosts of the dead on the shores of Lethe to a swarm of bees. Both comparisons are relevant here because Warren's "Simile" turns out to be a poem with a vertiginous danger at its heart. It's a short lyric with a nearly epic intention.

"Simile" stretches a single sentence across twenty lines. It consists of two asymmetrical stanzas. The poem is structured as an argument and moves from the opening word, "As" to the pivotal word, "so." It is frontloaded — most of the poem is dedicated to the woman's story of her friend, an Austrian skier facing his first Olympic trial. The poet knows this story well because she has listened to it often. Not until the end of the poem, however, do we discover that the woman who told the story time and again was the poet's mother.

The poem focuses on a hard moment of truth. Apparently nothing in the expert skier's long preparation has prepared him for this epic test. At the crucial moment, he freezes and can't summon up his many years of training to overcome his fear. Warren builds an overwhelming feeling of drama through the line breaks. Line by line we go, experiencing the story of the skier who "*had to face* / his first Olympic ski jump," who looks out from "the chute that *plunged* / so vertiginously," who "*gazed* / on a horizon of Alps." There is special intensity in giving an entire line to the phrase "training and courage." A tiny simile is buried inside the larger one: the skier gazes out at the Alps dandling around him "like toy boats in a bathtub." It all has an air of terrified unreality. But the mountains are not "toy boats," and the Alps the skier is facing are enormously real. As readers, we feel the pressure as the skier's teammates pry his hands loose finger by finger, freeing him to make the inevitable jump.

In Warren's poem, the crossing of stanzas is hazardous, a giant vault between subjects, almost like launching from a ski jump. The story of the skier is prophetic, it turns out, and foreshadows the real subject of the poem, which is the poet's mother as she faces an ultimate test, gripping the handrails on her bed, holding on, staring straight ahead into the greatest void of all. She knows that all she needs to do is to let go but can't bring herself to do it.

The poem pivots at the end into a question, which is delivered in a series of short staccato lines — "and / who was it, finally, / who loosened / her hands?" The phrase "who was it" harkens back to the skier's teammates who pried loose his hands, but it narrows the helper to a single unknown person. This isn't a ski jump but a permanent leap into death, a last letting go. That's why the word "finally" hovers fatefully at the end of a line. So too does the word "loosened." This has the feeling of an ultimate or metaphysical question, which is open-ended: At the very end, who — what unnamed force or being — took over the poet's mother and made her let go? What happens at the precise moment of death? These are questions that no one living has ever been able to answer.

———

"In Memory of Joe Brainard"

(1997)

In Memory of Joe Brainard" is a dedicatory poem for the visual artist and poet Joe Brainard, who died of AIDS-related pneumonia at the age of fifty-two. Frank Bidart has written three additional elegies for him: "The Yoke," "If I Could Mourn Like a Mourning Dove," and "A Coin for Joe, with the Image of a Horse; c. 350–325 BC." He also writes about him at the beginning of part 3 of "The Second Hour of the Night," where Brainard appears as a figure in a dream and says, "Can I borrow your body?"

There was, by all accounts, a remarkable sweetness of spirit about Joe Brainard. His imaginative visual work, though close to Pop Art, can't really be categorized. His underground classic, *I Remember,* part poem, part prose memoir, has a faux-naïf quality and charm. But it also provides an incisive portrait of an artistic kid growing up in Oklahoma in the forties and fifties, which he juxtaposes with his life as a young artist in New York in the sixties and seventies. John Ashbery called him "that recognizable American phenomenon, the odd-ball classicist." There is an openness and spontaneity about Brainard's work that Bidart has always envied, what he called "its utter directness, unadorned, unaffected candor," though his own work is weighted by a different kind of guilt-stricken consciousness. It is laboriously made and remade.

In interviews, Bidart has said that his relationship to Brainard was "more than friendship and less than a romance." They never became lovers, though for a few years they spoke every day on the phone. Bidart's poems about Brainard all have the wistfulness of something unrealized, perhaps unrealizable, what the Portuguese call *saudade,* a nostalgia not just for what was lost but also a yearning for what might have been. They are filled with longing and carry the weight of pained responsibility, which is simultaneously heavy and light. Or, as he puts it in "The Yoke," "*upon my shoulders is the yoke / that is not a yoke.*"

"In Memory of Joe Brainard" first appeared in *Desire* (1997):

> ### In Memory of Joe Brainard
>
> *the remnant of a vast, oceanic*
> *bruise (wound delivered early and long ago)*
>
> *was in you purity and*
> *sweetness self-gathered, CHOSEN*
>
> •
>
> When I tried to find words for the moral sense that unifies
> and sweetens the country voices in your collage *The Friendly Way,*
>
> you said *It's a code.*
>
> You were a code
> I yearned to decipher. —
>
> In the end, the plague that full swift runs by
> took you, broke you; —
>
> > *in the end, could not*
> > *take you, did not break you —*

you had somehow erased within you not only
meanness, but anger, the desire to punish
the universe for everything

not achieved, *not* tasted, seen again, touched — ;

. . . the undecipherable
code unbroken even as the soul

learns once again the body it loves and hates is
made of earth, and will betray it.

"In Memory of Joe Brainard" is a characteristic Bidart poem. His eccentric, highly self-conscious prosody has always served him as an expressionistic device. He treats the poem as a score to try to fasten his voice to the page. Whereas a poet like Etheridge Knight used punctuation to free his lyrics from the page, Bidart uses it to nail down his poems. The result is that a Knight poem feels oral, something to recite, while a Bidart poem feels scripted, something to read.

Here Bidart works in irregular free-verse stanzas. He uses short lines and long ones, and he moves between italic and roman type. The punctuation is notably overdetermined. There is a sentence that stops with a period and a dash; one that pauses with a semicolon, followed by a dash that further disrupts its flow forward; and one that lurches forward despite a dash, a semicolon, and an ellipsis in close succession. The result is a lyric that feels both urgent and interrupted. It continually hesitates in its determined desire to understand something that cannot be understood — or reconciled.

The poem opens with a strange statement, an italicized fragment. The italic gives the diction a certain pitch, almost like a second voice more heightened than the one in roman type. The first two-line stanza begins with a lowercase letter, as if in the middle of a sentence. The stanza contains a sort of metaphysical observation interrupted by a parenthetical comment: "*the remnant of a vast, oceanic / bruise (wound delivered early and long ago).*" This primal wound, which somehow came with our birth, occurred so long ago that we can scarcely remember it, though it has left a bruise on each of us.

The second stanza takes this observation and narrows it down in order to say something specific and psychological about Joe Brainard's triumph of character — "*was in you purity and / sweetness self-gathered, CHOSEN.*" The hyperbolic capitalization of the word "*CHOSEN*" suggests that Brainard protected, nourished, and chose to maintain his purity and sweetness. The fragment ends without a period and never concludes. Bidart has said that he was trying to find words for Brainard's "combination of wound and grace, wound and wholeness."

The second part of the poem breaks off and introduces an anecdotal element. Bidart recalls expressing admiration for Brainard's short collage-like book *The Friendly Way* (1972), which has a surreal zaniness. Blurring the boundary between the artist and his work, the speaker is left wondering about the code — not just for the collage but for its maker. There is something secret about Brainard he can't quite decipher.

The rest of the poem consists of a single run-on sentence. It moves forward by continually qualifying and arguing with itself. The speaker is all the while trying to think through his grief. The sentence begins with two stanzas in dialogue with each other. The first line refers to the "plague" of AIDS: "In the end, the plague that full swift runs by / took you, broke you . . ."

This stanza references Thomas Nashe's poem "A Litany in Time of Plague" (1600):

> All things to end are made,
>   The plague full swift goes by;
> I am sick, I must die.
>   Lord, have mercy on us!

Bidart's speaker immediately responds, in italic, with a second voice refuting the first. He can't bear the thought that the plague not only took his beloved but also *broke* him. Hence:

> *in the end, could not*
> *take you, did not break you —*

This thought breaks off to observe something hard to fathom about Brainard: how he had somehow erased in himself not just meanness but also rage and vengefulness, what the speaker calls "the desire to punish / the universe for everything . . ." The timing here is exactly calibrated. Notice the hesitation at the end of the line and stanza — "the desire to punish" — that spills over into the next phrase — "the universe for everything" — though the syntax then jumps forward to "everything // *not* achieved, *not* tasted, seen again, touched —; . . ." The phrases cannot really express the weight, the full import, of all Brainard would never manage to experience.

The poem pauses here but doesn't stop; it drives forward to its conclusion. Brainard carries his secret with him to the end.

> . . . the undecipherable
> code unbroken even as the soul
>
> learns once again the body it loves and hates is
> made of earth, and will betray it.

Bidart's own fury is palpable. The weight of negation is heavy. He repeats the prefix *un-*, meaning "not," in the words "undecipherable" and "unbroken" to refer to Brainard's mysterious code, which the poet will now never crack. In his view, the immortal soul is painfully schooled by the mortal body, which it both loves and hates. That's because the body is made of earth and thus will "betray" it by dying. How many times must the soul keep learning this lesson?

"In Memory of Joe Brainard" is a stunned remembrance, a poem that marvels at Joe Brainard's elusive purity of spirit even as it rails against the death that unfairly took him.

LUCILLE CLIFTON

—

"jasper   texas   1998"

(1998)

Lucille Clifton was an unswerving and courageous African American poet. Her audacious poem "jasper   texas   1998" appeared in a section of new work in her selected poems, *Blessing the Boats* (2000). It comes directly after one of her most enraged poems, "the photograph: a lynching." The first poem takes up a violently traumatic past that we still carry with us; the second responds to the brutal killing of a Black man in Texas near the end of the twentieth century. They are both part of what Clifton elsewhere calls "the terrible stories." "jasper   texas   1998" is also followed in *Blessing the Boats* by the poem "alabama 9/15/63," which is about the bombing of the Sixteenth Street Baptist Church, where four Black girls were killed in Birmingham, Alabama, on September 15, 1963. All three of these short poems ask large unanswerable questions. They are well-timed indictments of American society.

"jasper   texas   1998" takes its rightful place in a long line of African American poems about lynching. We have already seen how Langston Hughes helped redefine that subgenre of outraged elegies in the 1920s. At the end of the twentieth century Clifton was called upon to respond to yet another American barbarism.

jasper   texas   *1998*

for j. byrd

i am a man's head hunched in the road.
i was chosen to speak by the members
of my body.   the arm as it pulled away
pointed toward me, the hand opened once
and was gone.

why and why and why
should i call a white man brother?
who is the human in this place,
the thing that is dragged or the dragger?
what does my daughter say?

the sun is a blister overhead.
if I were alive i could not bear it.
the townsfolk sing we shall overcome
while hope bleeds slowly from my mouth
into the dirt that covers us all.
i am done with this dust.   i am done.

Clifton isolates each of the three words in the title of her poem — "jasper   texas   1998." It first appeared in *Ploughshares* (1999) with the title rendered conventionally: "Jasper, Texas, 1998." But when Clifton reprinted the poem in a book, she gave this extra weight to each word. We register the small town — "jasper" — and then the state where it is located — "texas" — and finally the date — "1998." The dedication to "j. byrd" turns this into a memorial poem. The title may initially seem bland or neutral, but when read retrospectively, every word strikes like a blow to the body. It says: this horrific thing happened, here, in this place, at this time. And it happened to this man.

The poem is based on the dragging death of forty-nine-year-old James Byrd Jr., who was dismembered as he was pulled behind a pickup truck. Three white supremacists were responsible. Clifton's poem is a radical response and a historical intervention. It's rare to find a poem that so successfully takes a contemporary event, especially one so horrific, and immediately transforms it into art. Here Clifton takes her gift for the demotic and applies it with a furious force. She is outraged and wants justice.

Clifton decided early on not to capitalize the pronoun *i,* or any proper nouns for that matter, or the first word of each sentence in her poems. The absence of capital letters is an egalitarian gesture that puts all nouns and pronouns on the same level. It was a move of radical informality right from the playbook of E. E. Cummings. She also at times has added extra space between sentences for emphasis. In other ways her punctuation tends to be somewhat regular. Here she employs her characteristic mode in sixteen lines — two stanzas with five lines and one with six.

Clifton made the radical decision to speak from the point of view of the murdered man's head. He is like Orpheus, whose severed head continued to sing as it floated down the river. But Orpheus was a mythical personage, and James Byrd Jr. was a real person who suffered unimaginable harm. The poem opens on a country road. The first line is a sentence, a blunt declaration: "i am a man's head hunched in the road." We experience the power of his voice. The second line has one of the most extraordinary enjambments in contemporary poetry: "i was chosen to speak by the members / of my body." The word "members" takes on a double meaning — it refers to parts of a body as well as the individuals composing a group. We speak, for example, of the members of a congregation. The shock comes with the realization that those individuals are body parts, which have asked the head to speak on their behalf. They have been *dismembered.* Even after death, the arm and the hand are still trying to point.

The second stanza consists of three questions. The first line is a metaphysical outcry: "why and why and why," which then coils into a more direct and specific question: "why and why and why / should i call a white man brother?" This question is rhetorical. James Byrd Jr. has been reduced to a thing dragged along a road, but he somehow retains his humanity. The racist perpetrators (the poet doesn't grant them names) have degraded themselves as something less than human. Each of them has become a "dragger." The last question, "what does my daughter say?," reminds us that the horrible sequence of events was never an abstraction. It happened to a very specific man with an actual daughter.

A feeling of hopelessness pervades the last stanza. Hope has been destroyed for the victim, who speaks from the other side of death. The sun has become a blister, which Byrd couldn't bear if he were still alive. That's because he knows what he has seen. He can't undo what he has suffered. The well-meaning townspeople may sing "we shall overcome," a gesture of hopefulness from an anthem of the civil rights movement, but hope "bleeds" from Byrd's mouth into the dust "that covers us all."

The first two stanzas of this poem create a pattern and lead us to expect a final five-line stanza. But it has an additional line, an overflow line, which provides an extra punch. The sixteenth line pairs two short declarative sentences as a single unit with a space between them. The repetition in the lines emphasizes the brutal finality for James Byrd Jr.:

> i am done with this dust.   i am done.

The colloquial phrase "I am done with" suggests that he is finished with something. He's literally done with the dust. The brutal last sentence — "i am done" — also means that he is dead. It's all over for him.

Lucille Clifton's poem speaks imaginatively for a man who will never come back, whose life is over now. It is a tribute and an elegy. It is also an indictment. And it refuses to console us.

CYNTHIA HUNTINGTON

———

"The Rapture"

(2000)

Cynthia Huntington describes and dramatizes a stupefying threshold mo-
ment in her radiant poem "The Rapture":

The Rapture

I remember standing in the kitchen, stirring bones for soup,
and in that moment, I became another person.

It was an early spring evening, the air California mild.
Outside, the eucalyptus was bowing compulsively

over the neighbor's motor home parked in the driveway.
The street was quiet for once, and all the windows were open.

Then my right arm tingled, a flutter started under the skin.
Fire charged down the nerve of my leg; my scalp exploded

in pricks of light. I shuddered and felt like laughing;
it was exhilarating as an earthquake. A city on fire

after an earthquake. Then I trembled and my legs shook,
and every muscle gripped so I fell and lay on my side,

a bolt driven down my skull into my spine. My legs were
swimming against the linoleum, and I looked up at the underside

of the stove, the dirty places where the sponge didn't reach.
Everything collapsed there in one place, one flash of time.

There in my body. In the kitchen at six in the evening, April.
A wooden spoon clutched in my hand, the smell of chicken broth.

And in that moment I knew everything that would come after:
the vision was complete as it seized me. Without diagnosis,

without history. I knew that my life was changed.
I seemed to have become entirely myself in that instant.

Not the tests, examinations in specialists' offices, not
the laboratory procedures: MRI, lumbar puncture, electrodes

pasted to my scalp, the needle scraped along the sole of my foot,
following one finger with the eyes, EEG, CAT scan, myelogram.

Not the falling down or the blindness and tremors, the stumble
and hiss in the blood, not the lying in bed in the afternoons.

Not phenobarbital, amitriptyline, prednisone, amantadine, ACTH,
cortisone, cytoxan, copolymer, baclofen, tegretol, but this:

Six o'clock in the evening in April, stirring bones for soup.
An event whose knowledge arrived whole, its meaning taking years

to open, to seem a destiny. It lasted thirty seconds, no more.
Then my muscles unlocked, the surge and shaking left my body

and I lay still beneath the white high ceiling. Then I got up
and stood there, quiet, alone, just beginning to be afraid.

The voice of the speaker is utterly trustworthy in this poem. Huntington borrows an eschatological term from evangelical Christianity — the rapture — to remember and capture the first moment when she was suddenly and violently stricken by multiple sclerosis ("For ten years I could not say the name," she confesses in another poem), though instead of being lifted up she is dropped to the floor of her own house. This epiphany moves downward.

Rapture is a form of euphoria. The sense of it as spiritual ecstasy, a state of mental transport, was first recorded around 1600. But the etymology of the noun *rapture* (meaning "the state of being transported, carried away") derives from an older usage, which comes from the medieval Latin *raptura,* meaning "seizure, rape, kidnapping," which in turn derives from the Latin *raptus,* "a carrying off, an abduction; rape." Huntington has said that she deliberately used the word *rapture* in its oldest sense, as akin to rape and abduction. She was thinking specifically of the rape of Persephone, who was grabbed into the underworld by something she didn't see coming, something that forever changed her perspective. Huntington's abduction was savage and irreversible too. At the very moment of her fall, she felt some kinship with Persephone, who was snatched up and whisked downward into Hades. Both women were rapt.

Huntington's poem unspools in eighteen long-lined, carefully shaped two-line stanzas. Formally, it resembles Marie Howe's letter to her dead brother, "What the Living Do." We have seen from a range of other poems in this book how long lines tend to create an oracular feeling and extend the voice beyond speech into something more like a prophecy. Like most epiphanic or visionary poems, this one is grounded in the quotidian world. Think of Anthony Hecht's poem "A Hill," which begins, "In Italy, where this sort of thing can occur, / I had a vision once," or James Wright's "A Blessing," which commences, "Just off the highway in Rochester, Minnesota, / Twilight bounds softly forth in the grass." Here, a woman in midlife, a poet, is standing in the kitchen on a spring night, making soup (there is something so elemental in the phrase "stirring bones") and looking out the window.

In the first two-line stanza, an intact or closed unit, this narrator immediately tells us that she is going to dramatize and recall the exact moment when she became someone else, "another person." Notice how in the second stanza the eucalyptus tree seems to be losing control of itself and "bowing compulsively // over the neighbor's motor home parked in the driveway," a presaging of the narrator's quasi-religious experience. The mobile home isn't moving. So too the street becomes unnaturally quiet. This isn't accidental — there is almost always a cessation of sound in such poetic crossings, which Wordsworth called "spots of time." The fact that "the windows were open" suggests a porousness between interior and exterior worlds. We are moving from one state of being to another. It seems to be an ordinary domestic night in the neighborhood when something extraordinary begins to happen to the narrator's body: "Then my right arm tingled . . ."

Huntington describes with great clarity the terror and exhilaration of losing control of her body. She feels a fire racing through, an explosion of light. She compares the shuddering to an earthquake and then modifies that to "A city on fire // after an earthquake." As readers, we register the double emphasis caused by a line break as well as a stanza break. We note the precision of her memory, what she sees when she falls — the underside of a stove that hasn't been cleaned, an observation that lends credibility to the leap out of time. It's as if the poet-narrator were amusing herself by imagining the quotidian view of the bottom of the stove as a figure for looking up into the world from Hades. She experiences the vision, the so-called rapture, that comes to her all at once "Without diagnosis, // without history." Once more, we register a sentence fragment, two phrases separated both by a line break and a stanza break. The moment seems to have no before or after, no chronology; it is severed from history.

"The Rapture" funnels to this flash of an instant, a prolonged moment out of time. The narrator gives us a long, detailed look into her medical future (all those tests and examinations, all those drugs). This is her self-diagnosis. It's as if she can see into the future everything that is going to happen to her. She lists these events through a series of negatives, all of them fragments: "*Not* the tests . . . , *not* / the laboratory procedures . . ."; "*Not* the falling down or the blindness and tremors . . ."; "*Not* phenobarbital . . ." A logical proposition is driving this catalog: it's not these things that seemed truly important, she argues, "*but this* . . ."

What the narrator chooses to focus on instead is the realization that this is the exact moment when she becomes herself, a different person than she used to be. The realization is so large that she feels the need to nail it down precisely, which gives it even greater credibility — "Six o'clock in the evening in April, stirring bones for soup." At that instant, she understands everything at once, "An event whose knowledge arrived whole," though it will take her years to figure it out, for it "to open, to seem a destiny." In those thirty seconds, a mere half-minute out of time, her destiny has been laid out and sealed.

Notice the logical turns at the end of the poem, which are marked by two consequential uses of the word "Then," each inaugurating a new action, a decisive next moment, a fresh realization:

> *Then* my muscles unlocked, the surge and shaking left my body
>
> and I lay still beneath the white high ceiling. *Then* I got up
> and stood there, quiet, alone, just beginning to be afraid.

The daemonic possession has left her body. For one more moment she doesn't move, lying still, trying to figure out what she has just experienced. But then she gets up and just stands there, unmoving, noticeably "quiet, alone." It's as if she is processing how she has just been returned to ordinary time. The world is restored, the exhilaration is over, and the fear has just begun to set in, a dark premonition, a first, fateful understanding of what is ahead of her, of how much she has been changed.

In "The Rapture," Cynthia Huntington insightfully tells the story and recreates the onslaught of a frightening lifelong illness. It took unusual skill, daring, and self-possession to recall and shape that moment into such a startling visionary poem.

RICHARD HOWARD

―――

"Elementary Principles at Seventy-Two"

(2001)

"Give us immedicable woes — woes that nothing can be done for — woes flat and final," Robert Frost declares in a piece about the poet Edwin Arlington Robinson. "And then to play," he continues. "The play's the thing. Play's the thing. All virtue in 'as if.'" There are immedicable woes at the core of Richard Howard's work, so much of which is elegiac, but he has resolutely deflected and transfigured those woes, those inmost losses, into other voices, which he calls *inner voices,* the reality of other lives sounded as his own, taking Hamlet's "the play's the thing" more seriously than almost any other American poet, and refashioning it to "play's the thing. All virtue in 'as if.'"

Richard Howard is among the most performance oriented of American poets. He is, in a way, helpless before his lived erudition and encyclopedic learning, the deaths he cannot abide, the lives he is sentenced to borrow, steal, and adapt, to refigure and reenact. His dependency on the work of others — abject, Borgesian — is an inescapable feature of his imagination. Since his third book of poems, *Untitled Subjects* (1969), Howard's preferred method has been a version of the dramatic monologue, the apostrophe, the letter, the conversation, the voice of the poet inhabiting another. He identifies this as "the poem of helpless trust in remembering what is there." He especially likes emblematic dialogues and meetings, "two-part inventions," what one poem labels "Close Encounters of Another Kind." His interior and dramatic monologues, which owe so much to Robert Browning, have rendered up an extraordinary cast of characters. His finest dramatic meditations and fictions, his derived terms, are almost always portraits of the artist in extremity—the artist in crisis mulling over his materials and his experience, witty, worldly, mannered, compulsively reflective, self-consciously struggling to imagine the great work into being. But in the end, all these other voices are creative ruses, vital deflections. "The poem of historical memory and of the placed person always concerns the poet's need for secrecy," Howard confesses in his essay "Sharing Secrets." The more he throws his voice and conceals, or pretends to conceal, the more it comes back as his own counter-music, what Frost deemed "counter-love, original response." Thus, the portraits of others have slowly evolved into a portrait of the poet himself. The Song of Everyone has slowly evolved into a Song of Myself.

It has also come as something of a surprise that every ten years or so Howard has written a short poem focused on taking stock. The mask drops and his voice is revealed in an objective lyric. The first of these was "At Sixty-Five," the next "Elementary Principles at Seventy-Two," the last poem in his twelfth collection, *Talking Cures* (2002). Howard's winding syntax and fluent syllabic mode (like Marianne Moore, he seeks formal interference and likes the stringency of counting), his Jamesian way of speaking across strictly charted symmetrical structures, has always been a difficult pleasure, but, as the title *Talking Cures* makes clear, it also has a curative dimension. The art and act of speaking, as they are depicted through artificial forms, become a type of necessary action, a process of making, of constructing and reconstructing a self in the face of dissolution.

Elementary Principles at Seventy-Two

When we consider the stars
(what else can we do with them?) and even
recognize among them *sidereal*

> father-figures (it was our
> *consideration* that arranged them so),
> they will always outshine us, for we change.
>
> When we behold the water
> (which cannot be held, for it keeps turning
> into itself), that is how we would move —
>
> but water overruns us.
> And when we aspire to be clad in fire
> (for who would not put on such apparel?)
>
> the flames only pass us by —
> it is a way they have of passing through.
> But earth is another matter. Ask earth
>
> to take us, the last mother —
> one womb we may reassume. Yes indeed,
> we can have the earth. Earth will have us.

"Elementary Principles at Seventy-Two" expresses our longing for transcendence while accepting our inevitable mortality. It is a poem of basic principles that also turns out to be a poem concerned with the four classical elements — indeed, as the poet runs through these elements over the course of the poem, we find out what he has come to understand as the elementary principles of mortality. Here Howard breezes through the air and begins in the ether. He subsequently takes up water and fire and then concludes, as he must, with earth. One feels the ludic pleasure he takes in this gamesmanship.

"Elementary Principles" consists of six equally balanced three-line stanzas. Each stanza commences with an emphatic, indented seven-syllable line. The subsequent two lines are each ten syllables long. The form is arbitrary, but it enables Howard to pace, qualify, and measure his thoughts, and to enact his thinking.

For example, no sooner does he begin a statement — "When we consider the stars" — than he interrupts himself with a pointed rhetorical question "(what else can we do with them?)." In fact, he interrupts himself twice in the first sentence, which unspools across the first two stanzas. It is the words themselves, some of which he italicizes, that spark his comments. Hence the verb "consider" morphs into the noun "*consideration*" and the noun "stars" transmutes into the adjective "*sidereal.*" What he is considering, and perhaps even recognizing, is how we turn the stars into constellations (something that human beings have conceptualized). These astral father-figures will "out-shine" us because they are fixed, and we alone seem to change.

The second stanza is end-stopped, but after that Howard's sentences carry across the stanzas until the very end. At every point, he self-consciously re-sponds to the language that he is using. Thus, when he states, "When we be-hold the water," he parenthetically comments "(which cannot be held . . .)." He rhymes "aspire" with "fire" and hears himself use the phrase "clad in fire," which leads him to a rhetorical question: "(for who would not put on such ap-parel?)." He seems to be at the mercy of his own linguistic play.

It is in Howard's nature to make much of words. Hence the dual use of "matter" — "But earth is another matter" — which as a noun means "physi-cal substance in general" and "subject of discussion" but as a verb means "to have importance." Earth is matter, and it also matters. He calls earth "the last mother" and immediately literalizes the metaphor and makes a kind of apho-ristic Jungian quip: "one womb we may reassume." He says rhetorically, "Yes indeed, / we can have the earth." And then, in an instance of what Greek rhet-oricians called chiasmus, he reverses and crisscrosses the sentence with a final recognition: "Earth will have us." Yes indeed. It is a beautifully balanced idea and creates a feeling of ultimate closure.

"Elementary Principles at Seventy-Two" takes great pleasure in working out an elemental idea. The play's the thing. But here that play also leads the poet to a sudden finality. The stakes are mortal. The earth will accept us, after all. In the end, it all comes down to something fateful and elementary.

EAVAN BOLAND

—

"Quarantine"

(2001)

Eavan Boland returned often in her poems to the Famine, a watershed moment in Irish history, which she called "a powerful once-and-for-all disruption of any kind of heroic history." She reenters the nineteenth century with her poem "Quarantine," which belongs with her other poems that address Irish amnesia: "The Famine Road," "The Journey," "The Achill Woman," "The Making of an Irish Goddess," and "That the Science of Cartography Is Limited." All these poems point to the suffering and defenselessness of rural people in the face of an overwhelming historical disaster. "Looking at the 19th century was the first time I began to think that writing could add to a silence rather than break it," she said. "I was interested in turning a light on the silences and erasers that we learn to tolerate in the name of history."

Quarantine

In the worst hour of the worst season
    of the worst year of a whole people

a man set out from the workhouse with his wife.
He was walking — they were both walking — north.

She was sick with famine fever and could not keep up.
     He lifted her and put her on his back.
He walked like that west and west and north.
Until at nightfall under freezing stars they arrived.

In the morning they were both found dead.
     Of cold. Of hunger. Of the toxins of a whole history.
But her feet were held against his breastbone.
The last heat of his flesh was his last gift to her.

Let no love poem ever come to this threshold.
     There is no place here for the inexact
praise of the easy graces and sensuality of the body.
There is only time for this merciless inventory:

Their death together in the winter of 1847.
     Also what they suffered. How they lived.
And what there is between a man and woman.
And in which darkness it can best be proved.

Boland's poem was triggered by an anecdote in the 1915 autobiography
Mo Scéal Féin (*My Own Story*) by An tAthair Peadar Ua Laoghaire (Peadar Ó
Laoghaire), a depiction of rural life in the Irish-speaking areas of nineteenth-
century Ireland and an especially valuable firsthand testament to the effects of
the Famine. Here is the story about a married couple, Cáit and Pádraig, who
had already lost their children and decided to slip out of quarantine and head
home:

> The cabin where they had lived before they went into the poorhouse
> was in . . . Doire Liath. So they made their way northwards . . . six
> miles to go and the night was falling. They were hungry and Cáit was
> sick with the fever. They had to walk very slowly. After a couple of
> miles they had to stop. Cáit could go no further. A neighbor . . . gave
> them something to eat and drink, but everyone was afraid to give

them shelter because they had come from the poorhouse . . . Pádraig put [Cáit] on his back and pressed on . . .

The poor man was weak . . . With the load he was carrying he had to stop often and rest . . . But . . . he carried on. He did not abandon his burden. They reached the cabin. It was empty and cold, without fire or heat.

The next morning a neighbor . . . entered the cabin. He saw the two inside. They were both dead. Pádraig had his wife's two feet against his chest as if he had been trying to warm them. It seems that he had realized that Cáit was dying and that her feet were cold so he had put them on his chest to draw the chill out . . .

"He was a good man, faithful and true," some might say, "and what he did was a noble deed."

That's true. But I will tell you this. Thousands of similar things were done all over Ireland at that time and no one looked on them as being special . . .

(Translated by Barry Tobin)

This is just one story of the catastrophic Famine that killed more than a million Irish people between 1845 and 1852. Another one and a half million emigrated.

"Quarantine" sheds light on two ordinary people trapped in a dismal situation. It views them against a large historical backdrop and tragedy. The language of the poem is spare, almost documentary in style. Boland narrates a great deal in just twenty lines, five quatrains. Each stanza operates like a paragraph. There is only one exception, the carryover from the fourth to the fifth stanza. The second line of every stanza is also marked by an indentation, a slight disruption and change. We are reading a story self-consciously made from lines.

Note the emphatic repetition of the word "worst" in the first stanza, which is one sentence long. The pentameter-based rhythm is steady and stately. The alliterative drumbeat of the letter *w*, which is repeated eleven times, weaves the words together and connects the lines:

> In the *w*orst hour of the *w*orst season
> of the *w*orst year of a *w*hole people
> a man set out from the *w*orkhouse *w*ith his *w*ife.
> He *w*as *w*alking — they *w*ere both *w*alking — north.

We seem to watch the lens of a camera moving in, finding its focus on the worst of times. Boland begins with the time frame ("the worst hour," "the worst season," "the worst year") and the great scale ("a whole people") and then narrows the view. We see a man and his wife *walking* (the word is repeated twice) north — as if that can save them.

Poetry is a form of condensation (Ezra Pound's slogan for this was a German-Latin equation: "*dicten = condensare*"). Boland's second stanza condenses the journey, the one recounted in Ua Laoghaire's memoir, into four action-packed lines:

> She was sick with famine fever and could not keep up.
>   He lifted her and put her on his back.
> He walked like that west and west and north.
> Until at nightfall under freezing stars they arrived.

Unlike lines in the first stanza, which snake across the line breaks, each line here is its own end-stopped unit. It consists of three short sentences and a final sentence fragment. Each line marks a stage in an arduous journey. The pronouns help tell the story in stages. They progress from "her" ("She was sick . . . and could not keep up") to "him" ("He lifted her . . . "; "he walked") to "them" ("Until . . . they arrived"). The first three sentences all begin with a subject and verb ("She was"; "He lifted"; "He walked"), but the fourth inverts the order, beginning with the phrase "Until at nightfall" and ending with the recognition that "they arrived."

The third or middle stanza takes the story to its wrenching conclusion, the death of the couple overnight, the way they were found in the morning. It also makes special meaning out of their journey.

> In the morning they were both found dead.
>   Of cold. Of hunger. Of the toxins of a whole history.
> But her feet were held against his breastbone.
> The last heat of his flesh was his last gift to her.

Once more each line is end-stopped. Boland breaks up the first sentence, which would normally read, "In the morning they were both found dead / Of cold, of hunger, of the toxins of a whole history," into constituent parts. She uses periods to interrupt the sentence and create full stops. Notice the progress of three phrases; each one compresses a reason why the couple die: "Of cold. Of hunger. Of the toxins of a whole history." There is a silence between each fragment. The man and woman are subject to specific hardships — cold and hunger — and also to larger historical poisons that leave them defenseless. The bitterness here is evident. But the stanza moves on to emphasize the intimacy of the couple, the most touching part of the story, the way the man presses his wife's feet up against his breastbone for warmth. It pivots on the word "But": "But her feet were held . . ." Notice the migration of *h* sounds through the stanza, as Boland presses down from "*h*unger" to "*h*istory" to "*h*er" to "*h*eld" to "*h*is" to "*h*eat" to "*h*is" (used twice) and finally to "*h*er." There is an internal rhyme on "feet" and "heat," an echo of *st* sounds in "again*st*," "brea*st*bone," and "la*st*." So too the poet repeats the word "last" for emphasis in a straightforward sentence consisting entirely of monosyllabic words: "The *last* heat of his flesh was his *last* gift to her."

"Quarantine" first appeared in a journal as a separate poem, but it is also part of a sequence called "Marriage," which appears in Boland's book *Against Love Poetry* (2001). The structural turn in the poem at the beginning of the fourth stanza ties in with that title: "Let no love poem ever come to this threshold." Boland seems alert to the fact that these deaths in Irish history stood outside the genres of love poetry and heroic action, and yet they could have had the power to clarify those genres, though they were never visible enough to do so. Here, Boland is critiquing an aspect of love poetry — its tendency to sentimentalize experience. Boland says that she wrote this poem "as a reproach to the sentimental love poem," which she characterizes here as "the inexact / praise of the easy graces and sensuality of the body." There is no place in this account, Boland argues, for such falsifications. Like Zbigniew Herbert, she dislikes what she thinks of as the corrosive history of the sublime, which inadvertently obliterated ordinary people and erased other kinds of quotidian experiences. By contrast, she takes an ethical stance toward a true love story, which is more private, more complex. Against the easy love poem, she poses a historical consciousness, her feeling that Irish people tend to forget "the levels of strength and survival and near-to-the-edge dispossession that we once had as a people." Boland returned often to the gap between the past and history, between life as it was lived and history as it was recorded, "how," she says, "one was official and articulate and the other was silent and fugitive."

Boland uses a colon to cross and connect the penultimate and the final stanza. The poem itself is warily self-conscious about how much it must inevitably leave out. It doesn't pretend to be a poem of witness. One of the central precepts of Boland's work is that we are always belated and thus helpless to capture the past or know it truly. The dead form a firmament; they are like stars, "outsiders, always." They keep their distance from us; they never entirely reveal their secrets. There's an inevitable cruelty to history as well as to poetry, which suffers from its own shorthand, its own condensations. Thus: "There is only time for this merciless inventory." Here is the shorthand list:

> Their death together in the winter of 1847.
>   Also what they suffered. How they lived.
> And what there is between a man and woman.
> And in which darkness it can best be proved.

Notice how the inventory is enacted through a series of stand-alone fragments. The adverb "Also" and the repeated conjunction "And" contribute a sense of progression. The word "what" is used as a noun and suggests the true nature of the couple's suffering and the deep connection between them. The stanza also moves from the past tense ("what they *suffered*"; "How they *lived*") to the present tense ("what there *is*"). In the final line, a modal auxiliary verb and a main verb, "can be," suggest an ongoing possibility, stretching from the past to the future, "in which darkness it can best be proved." The word "darkness" takes on additional resonance; it means not just the absence of light but also the absence of witnesses, allowing something important to remain unnoticed and fall outside of recorded history. The word "proved," with its overtones of mathematics and the law, carries a sense of validation, of a truth established. Thus, the couple has become emblematic in the way they have permanently verified their love.

In the end, "Quarantine" remembers the death of one couple in the worst season of the worst year, 1847, but it also directs our attention to what they suffered and how they lived. It memorializes them. It also illuminates a true love story, the unshakable bond between a man and a woman. Boland shines a light on a nearly anonymous couple who demonstrate their love to each other not in the light, where others may be watching, but under the cover of darkness, where it matters most.

AGI MISHOL

—

"Woman Martyr"

(2002)

A gi Mishol is a sly, subversive, empathic Israeli poet. Born in Romania to Hungarian-speaking Jewish parents who survived the Holocaust, she carries that history into her poetry. She was four years old when her family emigrated, and she writes in Hebrew. She has never thought of herself as a political poet per se, although, as she puts it, "We're not sitting in the Himalayas meditating—we're sitting here in turmoil in this mad, aggressive country and the politics percolates, seeps into my poetry."

An heir to Yehuda Amichai, with whom she studied, Mishol seems closely akin to Wisława Szymborska in the way she brings a light touch to heavy topics. Like Szymborska, whose poem "The Terrorist, He Watches" stands behind "Woman Martyr," Mishol creates poems that are unexpected interventions, sometimes on contemporary topics, and often run through all the ramifications of an idea. Here Mishol suggests that she can't get over her obsession with a young woman who has chosen to become a martyr rather than a mother, who has killed herself and mothered a great destruction. In Israeli poetry it's an extremely rare, somewhat radical move to focus on the humanity of a suicide bomber.

Woman Martyr

The evening goes blind, and you are only twenty.
Nathan Alterman, "Late Afternoon in the Market"

You are only twenty
and your first pregnancy is a bomb.
Under your broad skirt you are pregnant with dynamite
and metal shavings. This is how you walk in the market,
ticking among the people, you, Andaleeb Takatka.

Someone loosened the screws in your head
and launched you toward the city;
even though you come from Bethlehem,
the Home of Bread, you chose a bakery.
And there you pulled the trigger out of yourself,
and together with the Sabbath loaves,
sesame and poppy seed,
you flung yourself into the sky.

Together with Rebecca Fink you flew up
with Yelena Konre'ev from the Caucasus
and Nissim Cohen from Afghanistan
and Suhila Houshy from Iran
and two Chinese you swept along
to death.

Since then, other matters
have obscured your story,
about which I speak all the time
without having anything to say.

(Translated by Lisa Katz)

"Woman Martyr" tells the story of the Palestinian suicide bomber An-
daleeb Takatka, who, on April 12, 2002, blew herself up at a bus stop located at
the entrance to the Mahane Yehuda Market in Jerusalem. Mishol has said that
it was the suicide bomber's last name, Takatka, which generated the poem:
"Her name sounded like the ticking of a bomb — taka-taka like tick-tock . . ."

You might not have guessed that onomatopoeia, words that imitate sounds, triggered this troubling, tragic poem, and yet we are continually reminded that poetry, whatever else it may be, is always in some sense about language itself.

A quotation from Nathan Alterman's lyric "Late Afternoon in the Market" rhetorically launches the poem, which speaks directly to the young woman, almost as a familiar. First, Mishol addresses her as "you" and names her only at the end of the first stanza, thus turning to the third person. Mishol is both speaking to Andaleeb Takatka and talking about her, narrating in the present tense what Takatka is doing and what she has, in fact, already done. As an older woman, the poet feels connected to the younger woman, but she is also both bewildered and appalled by her. We must come to terms with a twenty-year-old woman who walks into a bakery wearing a "broad skirt" to make people think she is pregnant. In other words, pregnancy is her disguise — she is actually "pregnant with dynamite." She enters the market "ticking among the people."

The second stanza suggests that someone weaponized Takatka's psychology by loosening the screws in her head and turning her into a walking time-bomb. Mishol literalizes the colloquial phrase "having a screw loose" as a way of talking about craziness. The poet can't resist the linguistic irony of the situation. Takatka is a native of Bethlehem, which literally means "House of Bread," and yet decides to turn a bakery into a murder site. The woman and the loaves of bread, baked especially for the Sabbath, scatter together. Mishol doesn't mention that the etymology of *Bethlehem* also suggests "House of War." The poem contrasts the life-giving property of bread to the destructive act of going to war by blowing up a bakery.

The third stanza presents a roll call of helpless victims, who come from many different places. The diasporic nature of the group somehow heightens the horror. From the suicide bomber's point of view, as Israelis they are all guilty, but from Mishol's point of view as an Israeli citizen, they are all individuals who came from elsewhere, who probably left their countries because they were unsafe there. Mishol's naming of the individuals memorializes the slaughtered.

Most political or historical poems seem certain of themselves; their poets know what they think. Many such poems are undone by their own didacticism. It's therefore highly unusual for the poet herself to seem confused or bewildered. Yet Mishol concludes with a sense of profound incomprehension at an act so horrific. Others have moved on, the story has faded from the news, but the poet can't stop talking about the young woman who killed six other people and herself. It's unspeakable and yet needs to be spoken about. It's inexplicable and yet needs to be explained. That's why she can't stop obsessing over the needless sacrifice, the murderous martyrdom.

HARRYETTE MULLEN

"We Are Not Responsible"

(2002)

Harryette Mullen likes wordplay and linguistic games, puns and palin-dromes, extreme measures, what she terms "language machines." She is like an American outlier of the French avant-garde group Oulipo; though she never joined the ranks or attended the meetings, she goes on experiment-ing in her own laboratory of literary invention and serious play. Some result-ing poems, like the one that follows, have unexpected undertows that yield pointed social criticisms. Here is her prose poem "We Are Not Responsible" from her book *Sleeping with the Dictionary* (2002):

We Are Not Responsible

We are not responsible for your lost or stolen relatives. We cannot guarantee your safety if you disobey our instructions. We do not en-dorse the causes or claims of people begging for handouts. We reserve the right to refuse service to anyone. Your ticket does not guarantee that we will honor your reservations. In order to facilitate our proce-dures, please limit your carrying on. Before taking off, please extinguish all smoldering resentments. If you cannot understand English, you will be moved out of the way. In the event of a loss, you'd better look out for yourself. Your insurance was cancelled because we can no longer handle your frightful claims. Our handlers lost your luggage and are unable to find the key to your legal case. You were detained for interrogation because you fit the profile. You are not presumed to be innocent if the police have reason to suspect you are carrying a concealed wallet. It's not our fault you were born wearing a gang color. It is not our obligation to inform you of your rights. Step aside, please, while our officer inspects your bad attitude. You have no rights we are bound to respect. Please remain calm, or we can't be held responsible for what happens to you.

All of Mullen's poems are extremely alert to language. "We Are Not Responsible" borrows the language of corporations and government bureaucracies. It evokes and parodies the phrasing of rules and regulations and thereby exposes the ways that institutions attempt to disavow agency or responsibility. Thus, the first three sentences begin with disclaimers: "We are not responsible . . . ," "We cannot guarantee . . . ," "We do not endorse . . ." The fourth sentence modifies the pattern, underscoring the authority of the "we": "We reserve the right . . ." Mullen reworks this purposely bland, robotic language to expose what is behind it: racism, sexism, homophobia, and other prejudices sanctioned by the state and other powerful entities.

Mullen has commented that the poem is about the social contract:

The borrowed language in the poem runs the gamut from airline safety instructions and corporate disclaimers to the Supreme Court's ruling against Dred Scott. This was written before 9-11, when profiling was widely accepted as necessary for security. Yet, even before that terrorist attack, racial profiling targeted people of color as potential criminals, like the '99 police shooting of Amadou Diallo. We that consider ourselves law-abiding citizens have surrendered a lot of our freedoms in order to feel safe. The poem plays back the language of authority in what seems to me a logical movement from the rules and regulations we must obey as airline passengers, to the whole system of laws derived from original documents securing personal property of mostly white male owners.

There is no lyric speaker in this poem, only an institutional "we." The structure is associative, a kind of list, and employs anaphora, the repetition of the same word or phrase at the beginning of each sentence in a series. Anaphora is most engaging when each repetition includes a difference: something is reiterated, something else added or subtracted. Mullen refashions this device, so often employed in sacred or prophetic texts, to evoke a numbing set of disclaimers, rules, and laws that target and control people, especially people of color.

While "We Are Not Responsible" adopts standard bureaucratic phrasing, it also aggressively deviates from it, altering the wording to reveal the covert motives and insidious cruelty masked in officialese. This pattern begins in the very first sentence: "We are not responsible for your lost or stolen relatives." By substituting "relatives" for the expected word, "items," Mullen immediately brings race into the poem. People are treated as objects, and slavery becomes the underlying subject. So does immigration. The poet looks back to the Dred Scott case, then forward to the border policy of the Trump administration. After all, hasn't the separation of families led to a lot of "lost relatives"? Like all institutions, the government has historically hidden behind a language of neutrality — as if no one is truly responsible for losing or stealing "relatives." This poem is trying to hold it to account.

Thus, the seemingly innocuous sentence that begins "We cannot guarantee your safety" really means that you will be in danger if you don't obey orders. In the sentence "We do not endorse the causes or claims of people begging for handouts," the final phrase clarifies the true intention of a policy: a refusal to acknowledge the rights and needs of poor and disenfranchised people. Mullen changes her strategy in the fourth sentence, presenting a warning that requires no change in wording to make its point. We've all seen it thousands of times: "We reserve the right to refuse service to anyone." Here, in the poem's context of veiled threats, it evokes segregation and Jim Crow America. No wonder the critic Calvin Bedient speaks of Harryette Mullen's work as "postmodernism with a memory." That memory is historical.

Mullen uncovers the subtexts underlying bureaucratic statements and also inventively revises them to yield new meanings. For example, an airline announcement about carry-on luggage becomes an injunction against "carrying on"; it's an order to keep to one's place. She changes cigarettes into "smoldering resentments"; in a racist society, even appearing to be angry can justify retaliation. She exposes the prejudice behind the seemingly neutral ("If you cannot understand English, you will be moved out of the way"). Linguistic confusions build up in these consecutive sentences: "Your insurance was cancelled because we can no longer handle your frightful claims. Our handlers lost your luggage and are unable to find the key to your legal case." Here, the language of airline policy exposes an undercurrent of hostility toward immigrants. An innocuous word, "claims," becomes something more ominous, "frightful claims," and the "key" to the luggage implies potentially sinister legal consequences, "the key to your legal case." Throughout this poem a "we" speaks to a "you." There is always a subject; someone is always being targeted.

The poem turns to the topic of police detention: "You were detained for interrogation because you fit the profile. You are not presumed to be innocent if the police have reason to suspect you are carrying a concealed wallet. It's not our fault you were born wearing a gang color. It is not our obligation to inform you of your rights." Mullen is unearthing a set of prejudices bound up in the injustice of racial profiling. There's a clever but in the end not very funny substitution of the word "wallet" for "weapon." If you are Black and reach for your wallet when you are stopped by the police, it will be assumed that you are reaching for a weapon. The sentence "It is not our obligation . . ." speaks to the suspending of law, supposedly to protect the safety of the public. But that also means suspending the Constitution.

The last section of the poem, in which an "us" addresses a "you," is a series of directives: "Step aside, please, while our officer inspects your bad attitude. You have no rights we are bound to respect. Please remain calm, or we can't be held responsible for what happens to you." Here the voice of authority talks to victims, people whose rights have been ignored or violated. And the poem concludes with a direct threat, returning to the start of the poem, but with a difference: "We are not responsible" turns into "we can't be held responsible," expressing the absolute power of the "we." Stay calm and submit, the authorities declare, or something very bad is going to happen to you.

Harryette Mullen's social critique in "We Are Not Responsible" is scarily insightful, inspired, ominous, and unnerving. And it holds us responsible.

GALWAY KINNELL

"Shelley"

(2004)

The poems in Galway Kinnell's late books often press down on uncomfortable personal truths. They are gutsy, honest, discomfiting. The method tends to be stichic; the poems unspool in long, unbroken sections. You can feel the pressure of consciousness bearing down, a thirst that cannot be filled, a sense of time running out. My favorite of these guilt-ridden poems of reckoning is called simply "Shelley." It unfolds in a single sentence that cuts across three stanzas. It manages to encapsulate a surprising amount of information in thirty-seven lines.

> ### Shelley
>
> When I was twenty the one true
> free spirit I had heard of was Shelley,
> Shelley who wrote tracts advocating
> atheism, free love, the emancipation
> of women, and the abolition of wealth and class,
> a lively version of Plato's *Symposium,*

lyrics on the bliss and brevity
of romantic love, and complex
poems on love's difficulties, Shelley
who, I learned later — perhaps
almost too late — remarried Harriet,
then pregnant with their second child,
and a few months later ran off with Mary,
already pregnant with their first, bringing
along Mary's stepsister Claire,
who very likely also became his lover,

and in this malaise à trois, which Shelley
said would be a "paradise of exiles,"
they made their life, along with the spectres
of Harriet, who drowned herself in the Serpentine,
and of Mary's half-sister Fanny, who, fixated
on Shelley, killed herself, and with the spirits
of adored but neglected children
conceived almost incidentally
in the pursuit of Eros — Harriet's
Ianthe and Charles, denied to Shelley
and sent out to foster parents, Mary's
Clara, dead at one, her Willmouse, dead at three,
Elena, the baby in Naples, almost surely
Shelley's own, whom he "adopted" but then
left behind, dead at one and a half,
and Allegra, Claire's daughter by Byron,
whom Byron packed off to the convent
at Bagnacavallo at four, dead at five —

and in those days, before I knew
any of this, I thought I followed Shelley,
who thought he was following radiant desire.

Kinnell recalls here that when he was twenty years old the only true "free spirit" that he knew about and looked up to was the quintessential Romantic poet Percy Bysshe Shelley, the advocate of "atheism, free love, the emancipation / of women, and the abolition of wealth and class . . ." As a budding American Romantic, Kinnell was at one time obviously steeped in Shelley's work since he encapsulates here so much of Shelley's poetry and prose. The biographer Richard Holmes states that "Shelley's conception of love lies at the heart of his radical views on social justice, political liberty, and poetry itself," and that specific "conception of love" informs this poem.

Shelley's work has often spoken to young poets, and Kinnell certainly wasn't the only twenty-year-old who devoured "The Necessity of Atheism" and "The Defence of Poetry," and memorized Shelley's short poems, and studied his graceful translation of Plato's *Symposium,* and grappled with his "complex poems on love's difficulties," such as "Epipsychidion" (1821), which begins:

> My Song, I fear that thou wilt find but few
> Who fitly shall conceive thy reasoning,
> Of such hard matter dost thou entertain; . . .

Kinnell's purpose is not really to summarize Shelley's works, which kick off the poem, but what Kinnell later learned about Shelley's biography. That's even more enlightening. The speaker repeatedly invokes Shelley's name ("Shelley who . . .") and takes what he learns personally; this information has come to him "perhaps / almost too late." The line break forces us to hover over the word "perhaps" and then hesitate at the qualifying adverb "almost." The recognition seems to arrive at the latest possible moment for it to still make a difference. I read this poem when I was fifty-four years old, but I wish I had found it when I was twenty-nine, Shelley's age when he died.

In several early, somewhat strained versions of the poem, Kinnell focused on himself and "the temporariness of the liaisons / of my youth." He swiped at Freud as "the bookish / inexperienced patriarchal doctor of Vienna," guiltily referred to his mother ("I took it upon myself to say goodbye / and leave her"), and swerved to Shelley only at the end of the poem. He closed by telling a small part of Shelley's story as a way to explain his own temporary liaisons. But over the course of three or four drafts Kinnell kept expanding the part about Shelley, thus gradually reversing the focus. Shelley's biography takes over the poem and becomes the focal point, a kind of counter–instruction manual. The poet's own experience becomes a leitmotif, a touchstone to the poem, its secret mechanism.

The final poem recounts the wreckages of Shelley's life, the list of women and children that he loved and used up, discarded and destroyed, in his quest for art, his "pursuit of Eros." It's a capsule biography with a driving focus. The poem heats up in the second stanza, recounting what happened to the small clan in Italy, which Shelley called a "Paradise of Exiles," a shared sense of perfection leavened with a shared feeling of alienation. At this time and place his work reached its greatest heights. But "Paradise of Exiles" gathers ironic meaning as the poem's speaker drills down into the dire and tragic consequences for so many who were part of Shelley's circle. Kinnell coins the phrase "malaise à trois," a variation on the harmonious romantic and sexual relationship denoted by "ménage à trois" (meaning "household of three") to suggest something discomfiting and unhealthy about the relationships within Shelley's trio. But it's Kinnell's own discomfort that comes through in the list of the people left out of the magic circle, those who couldn't bear to be sacrificed, the suicides, the "spectres." The list of children's deaths makes for harrowing reading.

The poem ends not by romanticizing Shelley but by condemning him — and Kinnell's younger self. Notice the emphasis on the word "thought" in the last lines: "and in those days, before I knew / any of this, I thought I followed Shelley, / who thought he was following radiant desire." Kinnell explores the gap between what Romantically minded poets might think they are doing in the name of art and the damage they actually inflict. The gap matters. "Radiant desire" doesn't excuse personal failings; it has consequences for everyone involved.

Kinnell works through to the conclusion that it's not simply the work, but the work in tandem with the life, that matters for the creative artist. He dramatically lays out an ethic for the artist's relationship to other people. Perhaps his poem "Shelley" should be required reading for poets of all ages.

VIJAY SESHADRI

"Aphasia"

(2004)

The speaker in Vijay Seshadri's poems is a skeptic and a seeker, a wry, self-scrutinizing, keenly observant, abashed, bemused, and conflicted figure. He is prone to melancholy questions, troubled by his own thoughts, susceptible to daydreaming, determined to figure things out for himself, to sum them up, to find words for them. That gives special resonance to the poem "Aphasia."

Aphasia

His signs flick off.
His names of birds
and his beautiful words —
eleemosynary, fir, cinerarium, reckless —
skip like pearls from a snapped necklace
scattering over linoleum.

> His thinking won't
> venture out of his mouth.
> His grammar heads south.
> Pathetic his subjunctives; just as pathetic
> his mangling the emphatic enclitic
> he once was the master of.
>
> Still, all in all, he has
> his inner weather of pure meaning,
> though the wind is keening
> through his Alps and his clouds hang low
> and the forecast is "Rain mixed with snow,
> heavy at times."

"Aphasia" is a tenderhearted poem about a person with aphasia. It's clear-eyed, unsentimental, worried, and mournful. It's both sharp and affectionate about someone the speaker knows well enough to love, though Seshadri carefully conceals the identity of the person he is describing. He doesn't name him or tell us their exact relationship. Elsewhere he has commented that the poem was prompted by the incipient aphasia of an older friend whose language gifts were extraordinary. But he ended up creating a fictional character in the poem.

Aphasia, which impacts the part of the brain responsible for language, is a medical condition that, for anyone who loves language and uses it with care, seems especially cruel, and ironic. That's the case for the subject of this poem. He can't retrieve the right words; his own language has turned against him. Think of the poet Jack Spicer's extraordinary line: "My vocabulary did this to me."

Seshadri is a canny formalist. Here he has developed his own rhyme scheme — *abbccd* — in an eighteen-line poem of three symmetrical sextains, or six-line stanzas. The first and last lines of each stanza pointedly do not rhyme, and, in fact, the end-words don't seem to have any connection at all ("off" and "lino-leum," "won't" and "of," "has" and "times"). The second and third lines, however, do rhyme ("birds" and "words," "mouth" and "south," "meaning" and "keening"), and so do the fourth and fifth lines ("reckless" and "necklace," "pathetic" and "enclitic," "low" and "snow"). The inside lines link up, while the outside lines are purposely discordant. The rhyme scheme echoes and enacts the condition of the man the poem is about, who is somehow intact and keeps his "pure meaning," though he has lost his outer bearings.

The poem begins with an extremely direct short sentence: "His signs flick off." The man's brain is a machine whose signals are broken. Semiotics is the science of signs, and so there is a semiotic undertone to the word "signs." It's as if the streetlamps have gone dark. The slang meaning of the phrase "flick off," a vulgar insult, seems to apply here.

The second line starts to create a portrait of someone who cherished the names of birds and savored "beautiful words." Seshadri then gives us a list of four different kinds of words — two are exotic, two are familiar. These are words the poet seems to savor as much as his subject does, and thus each one is a sign pointing in two directions, a kind of double tell: "*eleemosynary*" (relating to or dependent on charity; charitable), "*fir*" (a kind of evergreen tree), "*cinerarium*" (a place or receptacle for depositing the ashes of cremated people), and "*reckless*" (heedless of danger or the consequences of one's actions). The reader begins piecing together the picture of a person who is charitable but would never want to depend on charity, who loves trees and is precise about naming them, who knows what it means to find a place for the cremated ashes of the dead, and who may or may not have been heedless, but is now unhappily exposed to danger. These words come to stand for all the other words that, in Seshadri's precise simile, "skip like pearls from a snapped necklace / scattering over linoleum." There is a kind of violence to the image of a "snapped necklace" and the sounds of words, precious things, scattering across the floor.

The middle stanza is the heart of the poem. The opening two lines characterize the situation. "His thinking won't / venture out of his mouth" is an apt description of aphasia. A person with this condition may be able to think his thoughts, but he can no longer say what he thinks. Words become garbled. Notice how the sentence breaks in two and thus enacts the condition it is describing. The thought pauses or hesitates on the word "won't" and then tumbles over. The speaker then details how the grammar "heads south."

There is something ruthless in the gaze of the poet; he doesn't flinch from emphasizing and using the word "pathetic" — twice: "Pathetic his subjunctives; just as pathetic / his mangling the emphatic enclitic / he once was the master of." The speaker and his subject share a world of linguistic reference, but one of them can no longer realize that knowledge. Being unable to control one's subjunctives is particularly painful. This verb mood is used to suggest something hypothetical, something wished for in the future, in contrast to what is already true. The word "enclitic" is a linguistic term for a word that is pronounced with so little emphasis that it is shortened and forms part of the preceding word (think of the *n't* in *can't*). Someone who had mastered "the emphatic enclitic" (the words mimic the meaning) is someone who subtly emphasized what is almost never emphasized. This precise verbal tactician is now rendered "pathetic," someone to be pitied, when he mangles his old linguistic trick. The sentence ends by focusing on his loss of mastery.

The third stanza, a single flexuous sentence, structurally turns and introduces the language of argumentation, as in an English Metaphysical poem: "Still, all in all . . ." The man with aphasia is still intact as a person, he has his own "inner weather of pure meaning." In his own mind he knows what he means. He is stalwart; he hasn't lost himself. But things outside are different. As a poet, Seshadri seems alert to his own phrasing, and the phrase "inner weather" triggers the closing extended metaphor, or conceit, of the poem:

> though the wind is keening
> through his Alps and his clouds hang low
> and the forecast is "Rain mixed with snow,
> heavy at times."

The poet externalizes the idea of "inner weather" and uses the language of a weather forecast to describe the extreme peril of the situation for the man exposed by his own condition — as if he is lost in a mountainous region, his own Alps, and a hard winter is coming in.

MARY SZYBIST

—

"On Wanting to Tell [ ]
About a Girl Eating Fish Eyes"

(2004)

Mary Szybist's poems often seem close to prayers. "I have always been at-
tracted to apostrophe," she told the *Paris Review*, "perhaps because of
its resemblance to prayer. A voice reaches out to something beyond itself that
cannot answer it. I find that moving in part because it enacts what is true of all
address and communication on some level — it cannot fully be heard, under-
stood, or answered. Still, some kinds of articulations can get us closer to such
connections — connections between very different consciousnesses — and I
think the linguistic ranges in poetry can enable that."

Here is "On Wanting to Tell [ ] About a Girl Eating Fish Eyes," which ap-
pears in her book *Incarnadine* (2013). It is an apostrophe, or failed apostro-
phe, because, as the title suggests, she very much wants to speak to a friend
who turns out to have died. Yet over the course of the poem she speaks to him
anyway.

"On Wanting to Tell [ ] About a Girl Eating Fish Eyes"

—how her loose curls float
above each silver fish as she leans in
to pluck its eyes —

You died just hours ago.
Not suddenly, no. You'd been dying so long
nothing looked like itself: from your window,
fishermen swirled sequins;
fishnets entangled the moon.

Now the dark rain
looks like dark rain. Only the wine
shimmers with candlelight. I refill the glasses
and we raise a toast to you
as so and so's daughter — elfin, jittery as a sparrow —
slides into another lap
to eat another pair of slippery eyes
with her soft fingers, fingers rosier each time,
for being chewed a little.

If only I could go to you, revive you.
You must be a little alive still.
I'd like to put this girl in your lap.
She's almost feverishly warm and she weighs
hardly anything. I want to show you how
she relishes each eye, to show you
her greed for them.

She is placing one on her tongue,
bright as a polished coin —

What do they taste like? I ask.
Twisting in my lap, she leans back
sleepily. They taste like eyes, she says.

"On Wanting to Tell" [ ] About a Girl Eating Fish Eyes" is an elegy that leaves out the name of the person who has died. The brackets in the title suggest that the person is now gone; a kind of blankness comes with the obliteration of death. The withholding of the name emphasizes the absence of the dead — where the deceased person ought to be, there is instead an uncomfortable space. The title marks the desire at the heart of this poem: the poet wants to tell a surprising story to a friend who is no longer there to relish it.

In the notes to *Incarnadine,* Szybist dedicates this poem to the poet Donald Justice, who died in 2004. He is the unnamed would-be addressee. The dinner that she refers to in the poem occurred on a lovely summer evening in the Northwest, which reminded her of a beautiful passage on mortality in Bede's *History of the English Church and People,* which she also includes in the notes:

> Your Majesty, when we compare the present life of man with that time of which we have no knowledge, it seems to me like the swift flight of a lone sparrow through the banqueting-hall where you sit in the winter months to dine with your thanes and counselors. Inside there is a comforting fire to warm the room; outside, the wintry storms of snow and rain are raging. This sparrow flies swiftly in through one door of the hall, and out through another. While he is inside, he is safe from wintry storms; but after a few moments of comfort, he vanishes from sight into the darkness whence he came. Similarly, man appears on earth for a little while, but we know nothing of what went before this life, and what follows.

"On Wanting to Tell" begins with a dash, in a rush, almost offhandedly, in the middle of a conversation. The speaker is so eager to tell her dead friend about the adorable young girl so gleefully trying to eat the eyes out of dead fish that she just starts speaking to him, as if he were alive, as if she were calling him on the phone immediately after the dinner with friends. Then she is immediately brought up short, cut off.

The speaker turns to address her friend directly at the beginning of the second stanza: "You died just hours ago." Perhaps she is reminding herself even as she is informing us. The friend has suffered a death so long and slow that it estranged reality, as if he had started looking at the world through a hallucinatory gauze. The images of fishermen swirling sequins and fishnets entangled in the moon refer directly to Justice's last poem, "A Chapter in the Life of Mr. Kehoe, Fisherman" (2004), which envisions Mr. Kehoe dancing on the dock in moonlight with his eyes half-shut, dreaming.

The third stanza of Szybist's poem refocuses the world in the present tense: "Now the dark rain / looks like dark rain." It's a kind of meditation on the limitations of metaphor and communication, an idea that echoes through this poem. The speaker keeps coming back to the strange truth that things are what they are; they are only themselves. This is partly sorrowful (she can't forget that her friend has just died) and partly marvelous (the young girl has a feverish liveliness). The third stanza presents the scene in which everyone toasts the friend who has just died, while the young girl — "elfin, jittery as a sparrow" — hops from place to place joyfully, taking the eyes out of each and every fish. Whereas some children might shrink back from such a spectacle, this one embraces it.

The speaker in this poem finds it hard to give up her fantasy — she so much wants to go to her friend and revive him: "You must be a little alive still," she says. She would love to put the little girl in her friend's lap, to show how greedy the young girl is for life, how fearlessly she digs out the eyes of fish. In the penultimate stanza these eyes come to resemble the coins that were put under the tongues of the dead as payment to Charon, who would ferry them to the other world: "She is placing one on her tongue, / bright as a polished coin —" Perhaps the coin for the ferryman is the last remaining sliver of the great energy and appetite that we begin with as children.

The poem closes with a three-line stanza. First, the speaker talks directly to the girl: "What do they taste like? I ask." She then describes the child: "Twisting in my lap, she leans back / sleepily." The punch line belongs to the girl: "They taste like eyes, she says." The girl simply refuses to describe the eyes as anything else but themselves. We don't normally think of tasting eyes. What would they taste like? The fearless little girl has a very clear, almost magical answer. The world tastes exactly the way it does. It is what it is. It doesn't represent something else.

MARY OLIVER

———

"Lead"

(2005)

Mary Oliver was a devotional poet — her volume of selected poems is titled *Devotions* — who paid close attention to the natural world. She was a walker who daily applied the fifteenth-century French theologian Nicolas Malebranche's maxim: "Attentiveness is the natural prayer of the soul." Or as she put it: "To pay attention, this is our endless and proper work." Oliver was a religious poet with a light, nondoctrinaire touch, and there is a solitary, sacramental element to everything she wrote. Here is her imperative poem "Lead":

> *Lead*
>
> Here is a story
> to break your heart.
> Are you willing?
> This winter
> the loons came to our harbor
> and died, one by one,
> of nothing we could see.

A friend told me
of one on the shore
that lifted its head and opened
the elegant beak and cried out
in the long, sweet savoring of its life
which, if you have heard it,
you know is a sacred thing,
and for which, if you have not heard it,
you had better hurry to where
they still sing.
And, believe me, tell no one
just where that is.
The next morning
this loon, speckled
and iridescent and with a plan
to fly home
to some hidden lake,
was dead on the shore.
I tell you this
to break your heart,
by which I mean only
that it break open and never close again
to the rest of the world.

This short poem on the death of a loon stands beside Hayden Carruth's poetic essay on the death of animals, but it also has a mythical quality that makes it kindred to Brigit Pegeen Kelly's tragic goat-song. It takes its place with Oliver's poems "The Loon" and "The Loon on Oak-Head Pond." Oliver begins her poem as a storyteller placing a moral claim upon us: "Here is a story / to break your heart." She is didactic and addresses the listener directly, one to one: "Are you willing?" The stakes are high. If you are willing to open yourself up to the story, she suggests, then you are simply going to have to have your heart broken.

The poem unfolds in one stanza, thirty short, crisp, and utterly clear lines. The two- and three-beat lines are shorter than iambic pentameter, the baseline of English prosody, and make you feel as if something has been cut or taken away. These lines isolate phrases and convey the information, piece by piece, dramatically, in time. The speaker seems calm, but the information is extremely upsetting. This is the anecdote she has come to tell you.

> This winter
> the loons came to our harbor
> and died, one by one,
> of nothing we could see.

The unexpected phrasing at the end of this sentence — we usually expect things to die for a noticeable reason — puts additional emphasis on the word "nothing." What the people on the shore cannot see is why these common loons, the so-called spirit of northern waters, are dying. Hence the title: at first it seems somewhat neutral but, in fact, ends up pointing to something toxic. In New England, lead poisoning is the leading cause of death for adult loons, who die from inadvertently ingesting lead sinkers and lead-headed jigs.

The speaker recounts a friend's story of a single loon, interpreting its poignant cry as "the long, sweet savoring of its life." She claims outright that anyone who has heard the loon knows that its cry is "a sacred thing." If you haven't heard loons, she suggests, you had better rush to the places where they still hide because their song may not exist for much longer. She cannot resist an editorial comment ("believe me, tell no one") urging readers to safeguard the places where these birds still thrive. But then she returns to the primary anecdote of the poem.

Notice how Oliver carefully breaks the next sentence into six distinct lines:

> The next morning
> this loon, speckled
> and iridescent and with a plan
> to fly home
> to some hidden lake,
> was dead on the shore.

First, she isolates the phrase "The next morning," then she presses together three stressed words, "thís lóon, spéckled," and carries over the line with two conjunctions, "speckled / *and* iridescent *and* with a plan," thus stressing both the loon's shimmering beauty and its utter practicality. She lays out the loon's intention in two succinct lines: "to fly home / to some hidden lake." But that wasn't to be. Instead, the loon ends up dead. Notice how the last two five-syllable lines are balanced for effect ("to some hidden lake, / was dead on the shore"). The words "lake" and "shore" clinch the lines and echo each other, almost act like rhyme-words.

As an environmental poem with a purpose, "Lead" is quietly accusatory about how human beings interact with nature, how we fail to protect wild and endangered things — indeed, how we endanger them ourselves. Oliver frames this poem with a commentary both at the beginning and the end, returning now to explain precisely why, like the ancient mariner, she has collared us, why she has to tell each of us this heartbreaking story:

> I tell you this
> to break your heart,
> by which I mean only
> that it break open and never close again
> to the rest of the world.

Oliver wants to break your heart, she says, not for its own sake, but for one reason only — so that it will "break open and never close again." She is asking us to be porous, not just to pay attention to the environment, which we should and must do, but to open up and expose ourselves to the suffering of other creatures, and to the suffering world itself. We have started out listening to a story about loons and ended up opening our hearts to the rest of the world.

ANYA KRUGOVOY SILVER

"Persimmon"

(2005)

Anya Krugovoy Silver considered herself a poet of witness to the experience of chronic and terminal illness. She was pregnant when she discovered that she had a particularly rare and virulent kind of inflammatory breast cancer. She gave birth to her only son, Noah, had a mastectomy, and continued to teach literature at Mercer College in Macon, Georgia. Living with metastatic breast cancer also fueled and intensified her poetry. "My poetry got better," she told an interviewer in 2010. "Nothing focuses your mind and helps you see clearly what's important quite like cancer. It made me want to explore, even more, the beauty and divinity of the ordinary world."

The rigors of treatment and a dark prognosis were two of Silver's ongoing ordeals and subjects. She was a sufferer. But she was also a poet of desperate, tenacious Christian faith. She displayed a kind of God-hunger, a Christianity born of need. The poem "Persimmon" initially appeared in *Image* (2005), a journal of art, faith, and mystery, and found a context five years later in a section of poems about cancer in her first book, *The Ninety-Third Name of God*.

Persimmon

I place you by my window so your skin can receive the setting sun,
so your flesh will yield to succulence, lush with juice,
so the saints of autumn will bless your flaming fruit.

Because cancer has left me tired.

Because when I visit God's houses, I enter and leave alone.
Not even in the melting beeswax and swinging musk of incense
has God visited me, nor when I've bowed or kneeled or sung.

Because I have found God, instead, when I've crouched in bathrooms,
lain back for the burning of my skin, covered my face and cursed.

Persimmon: votive candle at the icon of my kitchen window,
your four-petaled stem the eye of God in the Temple's dome,
tabernacle of pulp and seed,
dwelling place for my wandering prayers,

I am learning from you how to praise.

Because when your body bruises and softens, you are perfected.
Because your soul, persimmon, is sugar.

This poem fulfills Ezra Pound's Imagist axiom — that "the natural object is always the *adequate* symbol." The persimmon is a species of the genus *Diospyros,* and one folk etymology construes that Greek name as "divine fruit" or "God's pear." Silver's sixteen-line poem begins with a simple act. The speaker talks directly to the persimmon as she puts it by the window. Like Mary Szybist, Silver seems especially attracted to apostrophe because of its resemblance to prayer. Notice how she purposefully repeats the soft sound of the letters *c, s,* and *sh* to bind the words together across all three lines:

I place you by my window so your skin can receive the setting sun,
so your flesh will yield to succulence, lush with juice,
so the saints of autumn will bless your flaming fruit.

She also opens the percussive *c*'s and the two *u*'s in the word "succulence" leading into the phrase "lush with juice."

There is an argument developing and a religious vocation being implied here: "I place you . . . so your skin can receive"; "so your flesh will yield"; "so the saints of autumn will bless . . ." By deeming the simple passage of time "the saints of autumn" and characterizing the persimmon as a "flaming fruit" (a phrase that sounds as if it's been lifted from the King James Version of the Bible), the speaker loads the evidence and builds her case. The lush, orange-colored persimmon becomes the exemplum of her religious quest, the object and repository of her terror and devotion.

In the next line, which is separated out and presented as a one-line stanza, she explains why: "Because cancer has left me tired." This proposition represents an enormous leap — it's not immediately clear why you would place a persimmon by the window because cancer has left you exhausted. It is as if the body of the fruit will somehow compensate the speaker for what is happening to her own body.

The rest of the poem will try to explain that action as a leap of faith. First, she states that God does not come to her in religious sanctuaries, where one would expect this to happen. He never comes to her in prayer. This is the second proposition of the poem:

> Because when I visit God's houses, I enter and leave alone.
> Not even in the melting beeswax and swinging musk of incense
> has God visited me, nor when I've bowed or kneeled or sung.

God does not companion her in the house of worship. Note how the negatives build up — "Not even," "nor when" — and the speaker represents herself as praying here; the religious supplicant has prostrated herself in various church ceremonials, and yet she has always come away bereft.

The third stanza also begins to clarify the structure of this short poem. Like a piece by Christopher Smart, that great, eccentric, half-crazed eighteenth-century religious poet of praise, the rest of this lyric is structured around ana-phoric repetition, in this case, of the conjunction "Because." Repeating the same word at the beginning of each line in a series is one of the key devices of religious poetry, especially in the Hebrew Bible, which stands behind Silver's confessional lyric. Longinus considered it a key feature of the sublime. We have seen it used in remarkably different ways by Primo Levi, Philip Levine, and Harryette Mullen. In Silver's poem, the repetition links the observations, which might otherwise seem disconnected. Each one is a sentence fragment, a large step in a spiritual argument and journey.

The poem turns in the fourth stanza to the decidedly unexpected and unsanctified places where the speaker actually does find God. This is the third and decisive proposition.

> Because I have found God, instead, when I've crouched in bathrooms,
> lain back for the burning of my skin, covered my face and cursed.

Notice the repetition of the hard *c*'s and *r*'s ("*cr*ouched," "*c*ove*r*ed," and "*c*u*r*sed") and the doubling of *b*'s ("*b*ack," "*b*urning") in this forcefully closed couplet. It is not when she is praying but when she is physically humbled, radically reduced, that the speaker finds the God she needs. She found him not when she prayed, as one would expect, but only when she cursed — that is, said something damnable.

Now the speaker returns to address the persimmon directly again:

> Persimmon: votive candle at the icon of my kitchen window,
> your four-petaled stem the eye of God in the Temple's dome,
> tabernacle of pulp and seed,
> dwelling place for my wandering prayers,

The language in this quatrain is lush, heightened, sacred, as the poet playfully applies an extravagant religious vocabulary to the persimmon's natural color and shape ("votive candle," "the eye of God in the Temple's dome," "tabernacle of pulp and seed"), thereby characterizing it as a sacred object, "a dwelling place" for her wayward prayers.

The next line stands alone as the penultimate stanza of the poem. A simple declaration, it states the purpose of the poem, which is the education of the speaker: "I am learning from you how to praise." The final two-line stanza clenches the argument, biting down on the letter *b* and softening the mouth with the letter *s*:

> *B*ecause when your *b*ody *b*ruises and *s*often*s*, you are perfected.
> *B*ecause your *s*oul, persimmon, i*s s*ugar.

These are the final two propositions. All have been fragments. Knowledge has come to the speaker, and the poet, in a fragmented way. Everything that has happened to her in the course of her life, all that is unstated, has led her to this point. All along, by talking about the persimmon Silver has been talking about herself, her own body, her own spiritual journey. Throughout the poem, she has been teaching herself how to transform suffering into praise. At the end, she discovers and thus teaches herself that the persimmon becomes perfected only when its body "bruises and softens." The persimmon is the adequate symbol because it is astringent when it is immature but sweet when it ripens. Silver is singular, however, in the way she imparts a soul to the persimmon and invests it with meaning. Thus, the ripening fruit becomes a way to reckon with her own physical and spiritual life.

Anya Krugovoy Silver died in 2018 at the age of forty. She wrote beautifully moving testaments as a witness and survivor, and it is harrowing to close the book on her life and work.

PATRICIA SMITH

———

"Ethel's Sestina"

(2006)

E thel's Sestina" is one of the last poems that Patricia Smith wrote for *Blood Dazzler,* her gut-wrenching and enraged sequence centered on Hurricane Katrina. She has said that because of the book's subject matter — all the betrayal, the terror, the numbing loss — it was difficult for her to find a place to infuse the tragic narrative with light.

Ethel's Sestina

Ethel Freeman's body sat for days in her wheelchair outside
the New Orleans Convention Center. Her son Herbert, who
had assured his mother that help was on the way, was forced
to leave her there once she died.

Gon' be obedient in this here chair,
gon' bide my time, fanning against this sun.
I ask my boy, and all he says is *Wait.*
He wipes my brow with steam, says I should sleep.

I trust his every word. Herbert my son.
I believe him when he says help gon' come.

Been so long since all these suffrin' folks come
to this place. Now on the ground 'round my chair,
they sweat in my shade, keep asking my son
could that be a bus they see. It's the sun
foolin' them, shining much too loud for sleep,
making us hear engines, wheels. Not yet. Wait.

Lawd, some folks prayin' for rain while they wait,
forgetting what rain can do. When it come,
it smashes living flat, wakes you from sleep,
eats streets, washes you clean out of the chair
you be sittin' in. Best to praise this sun,
shinin' its dry shine. *Lawd have mercy, son,*

is it coming? Such a strong man, my son.
Can't help but believe when he tells us, *Wait.*
Wait some more. Wish some trees would block this sun.
We wait. Ain't no white men or buses come,
but look — see that there? Get me out this chair,
help me stand on up. No time for sleepin',

cause look what's rumbling this way. If you sleep
you gon' miss it. *Look there,* I tell my son.
He don't hear. I'm 'bout to get out this chair,
but the ghost in my legs tells me to wait,
wait for the salvation that's sho to come.
I see my savior's face 'longside that sun.

Nobody sees me running toward the sun.
Lawd, they think I done gone and fell asleep.
They don't hear *Come.*

Come.
Come.

Come.
Come.
Come.
Come.
Ain't but one power make me leave my son.
I can't wait, Herbert. Lawd knows I can't wait.
Don't cry, boy, I ain't in that chair no more.

Wish you coulda come on this journey, son,
seen that ol' sweet sun lift me out of sleep.
Didn't have to wait. And see my golden chair?

Patricia Smith begins this impassioned lyric with a documentary headnote that dispassionately informs us in two sentences what happened to Ethel Freeman during Hurricane Katrina. We learn the cold hard facts of the situation. This journalistic decision freed Smith to launch herself into Ethel's body, to speak from her point of view. We already know what happened to Freeman — some of us can recall turning on CNN and seeing the image of her body in a wheelchair outside the convention center in New Orleans. She was covered by a sheet. What we couldn't imagine is how she must have felt in the hours leading up to her death. This suffering is the space that Smith enters. She formalizes an empathic leap of imagination.

Smith calls her poem "Ethel's Sestina" because it is in some way meant to be Ethel's poem. It is elegiac — we know that Ethel has died — but it is not an elegy per se, or at least not a traditional one, because it takes her point of view and ventriloquizes her voice. Smith assumes a familiarity with Ethel Freeman, a person she did not know, since she refers to Ethel by her first name and infers her vernacular. She has said that Ethel reminded her of many of the elderly women she grew up with who populated the pews of Pilgrim Rest Missionary Baptist Church in Chicago, "women who sang in cracking altos with their eyes lifted to the rafters, unafraid of anything the world could do to them." These women believed in one of the basic tenets of the Baptist Church, "that there is a glorious reward in death, a heavenly life waiting just beyond this one for anyone who was patient and faithful enough."

It's also true, though, that no one speaks offhandedly in a form as elaborate as a sestina. That's why the mask slips and we inevitably feel the poet behind the speaker when we read this performative lyric. Like Anthony Hecht in "The Book of Yolek," Smith exploits the fact that the sestina is an obsessively repetitive poetic form. Whereas he treats the form as a walk, a series of compulsive returns, she picks up on the fact that people often repeat themselves when they talk, and these repetitions are fundamental to the sestina. Smith told an interviewer that she "chose the form of the sestina because it mirrored the way that elderly black women speak, returning again and again to the same idea, the same comfortable words." She calls these words "comfort spots."

Smith, who began as a spoken-word poet, displays her technical virtuosity by making this highly elaborate form sound completely natural. She chooses carefully the six decisive, meaningful words that conclude and begin each one of the six stanzas that constitute the substance of the poem. These monosyllabic words create the framework of the story: "chair," "sun," "wait," "sleep," "son," "come." Smith tightens the sounds by using a homophone ("sun" / "son"). Ethel Freeman sat in her wheelchair in the scorching sun, waiting for help, while her son kept explaining that it was going to come. All the while, she kept trying to fend off sleep, which would lead to death.

Smith skillfully utilizes a five-beat, ten-syllable line throughout the poem. I have noted elsewhere how often blank verse has been used in the history of English-language poetry — from William Shakespeare's plays to Robert Frost's dramatic monologues — to evoke the spoken word, to dramatically place a speaker in a specific situation, and that's precisely what Smith does here. She shortens many words — "going to" becomes "gon'," "suffering" becomes "suffrin'," and so on — which enables her to maintain the ten-syllable line while creating a conversational tone. She captures the local speaking voice of a woman in extremis.

There's a kind of stage management operating in the penultimate stanza, where Smith loosens and radically stretches the sestina form by repeating the word "Come" six times, on six different lines. We hear the desperation in Ethel's voice as she keeps repeating the word. Her long wait is interminable. But no one comes to rescue her. The sestina is a poem of sixes, and Ethel's repeated cry comes six times:

> *Come.*
> *Come.*
> *Come.*

Come.
Come.
Come.

The chant breaks the stanza in half and marks the definitive turning point in the poem. Ethel says one more thing, like an aside, to no one in particular: "Ain't but one power make me leave my son." After that, she speaks directly to her son at the very point of her own death. The italics are emphatic: *"I can't wait, Herbert. Lawd knows I can't wait. / Don't cry, boy, I ain't in that chair no more."*

The three-line envoi is always a send-off, but this sestina literalizes the farewell and uses the six end-words to mark a crossover into death itself. Now Ethel speaks to Herbert as if from the other side. Her speech is calmer, no longer appears in italic, and has a kind of sweet wistfulness and longing: "Wish you coulda come on this journey, son, / seen that ol' sweet sun lift me out of sleep. / Didn't have to wait. And see my golden chair?"

Ethel's wheelchair has been transformed into a throne, and the poem concludes on a triumphant note. It's as if the poet had decided that Freeman could outwit death, much like the sacrilegious Cousin Vit in Gwendolyn Brooks's sonnet "The rites for Cousin Vit." Or, as Smith has asserted, "Death wasn't going to be strong enough to end her." "Ethel's Sestina" ends with a question, which is directed to her son but overheard by all of us, believers and nonbelievers, readers who find themselves wishing that Ethel really has found herself in another realm, sitting on a beautiful golden chair in heaven.

CAROLYN CREEDON

—————

"Woman, Mined"

(2006)

Carolyn Creedon writes out of the body, out of lived experience, with no holds barred, and refuses to prettify things. Here is the poem that opens her first book, *Wet* (2012):

Woman, Mined

In the cosmetics department of Lord & Taylor
they'll take you right there, right out in the open,
plain as day, and snap you with an ultraviolet camera,
show what you've done to your skin just
by living, your face exposed suddenly like what's
really going on under a lifted-up log, the real you
you are, caught and pinned like a moth,
like a shoplifter, like a woman on a table

and the lady in the crisp white smock will expertly
flick the snapshot in front of you, laid out

like a color-coded map of conquered countries,
the purples and browns places you gave up
without a care in your twenties, to late nights
and poolside deck chairs and men, all the men
you touched, the ones who marked you, whose traces
you bear, and now you can see the archeology
of tears, their white-acid trails, and the lady
will say, sternly: *Look what you did*

and you will see the mess of it you made, and you
will see the times when you carelessly went to bed
with someone without the proper moisturizer, when you
suckled that man like a baby, and when you moved
with another like a girl on a rocker until you fell off
and lost him, and finally picked another, like the best-of-all
flower, and kept him, cried on him, made him sandwiches,
made him a baby, and you'll wear your face
with its amber earned, its amethyst, its intaglio tear-
etched diamond, and say, *I am cut that way.*

There is a Plathian virtuosity and bravado in Creedon's one-sentence poem, which carries across three stanzas and twenty-eight lines. She sweeps us along on the music of her associations, letting the literal situation yield its metaphorical power. "I guess I try to write poems the way I think," she once said, "and I 'think' a poem in long lines connected by lots of *and*s and *if*s — I kind of believe that women naturally think that way. Ends of sentences only come when we run out of time or hope."

Creedon's poems are highly gendered. In "Woman, Mined," the cosmetics counter of a department store suddenly seems like an illicit place because of what it exposes: how a woman has aged. Creedon writes about her own experience but also suggests that it is somehow representative. The title indicates an objective or objectified woman, who is confronting the cultural ideal or stereotype of flawless youth and beauty. Throughout the poem, though, the speaker always addresses the second person, as if talking to herself or some other intimate. "In the cosmetics department of Lord & Taylor / they'll take *you* right there, right out in the open . . ."

This "you" is being excavated in public, dug up and "mined" for something precious. It seems she has done something embarrassing or shameful simply by living. Now she has been "caught and pinned like a moth, / like a shoplifter, like a woman on a table ..." It's as if the cosmetician is a lepidopterist, a plainclothes policewoman, a surgeon. A woman on a table evokes the helpless image of a patient, who is put in the position of being ill, vulnerable, laid out naked for inspection. There is a dark humor and grim comedy in the situation, in the scolding by the cosmetician, who says "*Look what you did*," and the speaker's interpretation of the words as she applies them to her own experience.

What's really going on under there? At the cosmetics counter, magnification exposes how skin has been damaged over years of abuse. When the salesperson flicks a snapshot of the speaker's face, she feels "laid out / like a color-coded map of conquered countries." This triggers the memory of herself as a heedless young woman in her twenties, who gave herself up to so many unworthy men, the ones she touched, the ones who marked her so that she has been left with "the archeology / of tears." There's an echo of Allen Grossman's phrase "the fame / Of tears," now transformed into an anthropological term. Creedon returns us to the meaning of the poem's title, "Woman, Mined," to the experience of a woman whose sadness is being unearthed.

The speaker can't stop wisecracking, but there's a ruefulness to the way she numbers the memories:

> the times when you carelessly went to bed
> with someone without the proper moisturizer, when you
> suckled that man like a baby, and when you moved
> with another like a girl on a rocker until you fell off
> and lost him ...

All those crazed intimacies, infantile men, sexual escapades, lost days. But there's fulfillment in the poem as she finally finds just the right one, the keeper, her lifelong partner.

The speaker herself seems amused by the way she reels off the experiences, linking the mundane and the life-changing as if they are equivalent: "made him sandwiches, / made him a baby." There's a kind of panache in Creedon's linking of these two phrases. The phrase "made him sandwiches" has a sly eroticism and refers back to her love poem "Litany," in which she asks Tom if he will let her love him in his restaurant; he can make her a newly invented sandwich, which she will eat and call "a carolyn sandwich." Here she is reversing roles and making him "a carolyn sandwich." In "Woman, Mined," the sandwich making immediately joins up with "made him a baby." Creedon has said that she is ashamed of the line, which is there almost to placate men, since the darker truth is that she had a miscarriage. Yet there is no way of knowing that from the poem itself. In the lyric, one thing seems to lead to the other, as if naturally, as if it's a simple leap from making sandwiches to having babies.

The end of the poem seems reminiscent of Randall Jarrell's poem "The Face." In that poem, a woman registers the shock of aging and realizes that ordinary living is "dangerous," more dangerous than anything else. But whereas Jarrell projects himself across the gender divide, Creedon writes out of her own painfully earned experience as a woman. The poem crescendos in the last line, where the speaker switches from the second person to the first: "and you'll wear your face / with its amber earned, its amethyst, its intaglio tear- / etched diamond, and say, *I am cut that way*."

At the end of "Woman, Mined," Creedon's speaker takes the metaphor of mining to its determined conclusion. She understands that she has mined her life and come up with something precious, after all; that her face has earned its lines. The "archeology of tears" has been transformed into a single "intaglio tear- / etched diamond." She pauses for emphasis on "tear" and then converts it into "tear-etched." She now owns her own face. She has earned and paid for it. For the first time, she speaks in the first person with a secure boldness: "*I am cut that way*."

NATASHA TRETHEWEY

———

"Graveyard Blues"

(2006)

Natasha Trethewey is an elegiac poet. She catapults herself into the past and tries to excavate what has been obscured in memory or even obliterated from it. She investigates her own personal losses and connects them to larger historical erasures. She seeks to rectify and right the record. Her experience as a biracial Southern woman has led her to mine history for what has been overlooked or forgotten, lest it be lost. She is not a historian but a poet who dramatizes lost stories, who searches the past for what Ezra Pound called "luminous details."

Trethewey suffered a terrible personal tragedy with the death of her mother. Gwendolyn Ann Turnbough was murdered outside her Atlanta apartment by her second husband, from whom she was divorced. Their son, who was waiting for a school bus at the time, witnessed the murder. Trethewey couldn't bear to put a headstone on her mother's gravesite in Gulfport because her surname at death was the same as that of the man who shot her. It would take the dutiful daughter many years to realize that the inscription could record her mother's maiden name.

Trethewey was just nineteen, a freshman in college, when her mother was killed, but it would take her nearly two decades to figure out how to write about it. She had begun to compose the public poems that would become her third book, *Native Guard* (2006); they focus on the under-told, mostly undocumented story of Louisiana's all-Black regiment, which was called to serve in the Civil War. That's when she began to realize that she could also tell her own painful story. It too should be part of the record.

To place these elegies in context: Trethewey had just moved back to Atlanta to start a teaching position and lived down the street from the court-house where her stepfather had been sentenced. So too she was coming to the twentieth anniversary of her mother's death and approaching her own forti-eth birthday. That's how old her mother was when she died. It was a time of reckonings.

Here is "Graveyard Blues," which appears in the first section of *Native Guard*. The book is dedicated to the memory of Trethewey's mother, and one of the epigraphs it opens with comes from a poem by Charles Wright: "Memory is a cemetery / I've visited once or twice..."

Graveyard Blues

It rained the whole time we were laying her down;
Rained from church to grave when we put her down.
The suck of mud at our feet was a hollow sound.

When the preacher called out I held up my hand;
When he called for a witness I raised my hand —
Death stops the body's work, the soul's a journeyman.

The sun came out when I turned to walk away,
Glared down on me as I turned and walked away —
My back to my mother, leaving her where she lay.

The road going home was pocked with holes,
That home-going road's always full of holes;
Though we slow down, time's wheel still rolls.

I wander now among names of the dead:
My mother's name, stone pillow for my head.

Trethewey recalls that she used to jog in a graveyard where a lot of Confederate soldiers are buried. She sometimes felt that the names on the tombstones were calling out to her. Allen Tate's "Ode to the Confederate Dead" must have been hovering ironically in the background. After all, she opens her poem "Elegy for the Native Guards" with an epigraph from Tate's poem: "*Now that the salt of their blood / Stiffens the saltier oblivion of the sea.*" She thought she was going to write about those soldiers on the day that she suddenly began to pen "Graveyard Blues" and discovered what was truly on her mind.

"Graveyard Blues" has the stoic grief of a blues song. It is bereft and captures the blue note of lamentation. Rita Dove referred to a "syncopated attitude of the blues" in Trethewey's first book, *Domestic Work,* and that sense of clipped rhythm, of unexpected accents, also operates here. Trethewey expresses her own unresolved grief through a durable communal form, which gives her a way to process, express, and control her own sorrow. She employs and varies the classical twelve-bar, three-line blues stanza. She also skillfully converts it into flexible iambic pentameter lines and uses triple rhymes to bind each stanza together.

The blues stanza is basically a couplet stretched to three lines. The first line establishes the premise and scene, as in

> It rained the whole time we were laying her down;

The second line repeats the first and hammers it in. Trethewey consistently varies the second line to give it a repetitive but also emphatically different valence and meaning. Hence:

> Rained from church to grave when we put her down.

The second line drops the subject of the sentence, "It," and informally encapsulates the narrative time of a funeral. The third line then punches home the experience:

> The suck of mud at our feet was a hollow sound.

Notice the close, slightly disconcerting off-rhyme of "down" and "sound." We are right there standing in the mud with her. The poem has a stark physicality. There is a grief-stricken story being told in the most condensed way in this poem, which jumps from image to image, almost in flashes, as if the speaker is summoning back the scene in stages. In every stanza, the second line creates a different emphasis. For example, the word "witness" takes on special weight in the second line of the second stanza:

> When the preacher called out I held up my hand;
> When he called for a witness I raised my hand—

Now we know why the pastor calls out and asks for someone to respond. The first time he does so, the daughter simply holds up her hand, a somewhat passive gesture, but the second time she raises it, which is more active. She is not merely present; she is becoming a witness. The poem then quotes an invented line of scripture, a generalized statement that contrasts with the specificity of the daughter's grief:

> *Death stops the body's work, the soul's a journeyman.*

Throughout "Graveyard Blues" Trethewey uses the weather as a barometer of feeling. The rain externalizes what the speaker is going through; it emphasizes the horror. The sun comes out just as the daughter turns and walks away from her mother's grave. But it's one thing to say that the sun comes out, and it's another to emphasize that it "Glared down on me as I turned and walked away." The sun puts a glaring light on the daughter's feeling of survivor's guilt as she departs and leaves her mother in the ground: "My back to my mother, leaving her where she lay." The feeling is clinched by the triple rhymes ("away," "away," "lay").

The poem moves through the time line of a funeral, from the church to the graveyard and on to the journey home, with a chiasmus in the second line ("going home," "home-going") of the penultimate stanza:

> The road going home was pocked with holes,
> That home-going road's always full of holes;
> Though we slow down, time's wheel still rolls.

The bumpy road signals the speaker's distress. The third line has an almost allegorical feeling about time: "Though we slow down, time's wheel still rolls."

The poem concludes with a final click, a clenched, indented couplet:

> I wander now among names of the dead:
> My mother's name, stone pillow for my head.

Not until the final two lines do we understand that this blues poem is also a rhyming sonnet — indeed, it has the hard closure of the couplet that concludes a Shakespearean sonnet. The poem thus becomes a hybrid of an African American form and a European/Anglo-American one.

Rereading it as a sonnet, which here consists of four three-line stanzas and a final couplet, we can also see that structurally the volta, or turn, so characteristic of the sonnet form, comes after the sixth line: "The sun came out when I turned to walk away." The way the speaker turns away from her mother's grave is thus enacted through the form and signaled by the word "turned" itself. We recall that Wordsworth, in "Surprised by joy," his sonnet to his dead daughter, also used this word to enact the movement of turning: "I turned to share the transport . . ." But whereas Wordsworth's grief is expressed by turning toward his daughter and then discovering that she is not there, the grief of Trethewey's speaker is expressed by turning away from her mother's grave. She feels the guilt of walking off and leaving the cemetery.

As a sonnet, Trethewey's poem ends conclusively, but as a blues poem the form is not completed because the last tercet is missing a final line. Thus, we leave this blues poem with a sense of something forever left off or missing, a final absence, a permanent silence. Formally speaking, the poem comes to a ringing conclusion even as it ends in an open-ended way.

"Graveyard Blues" concludes with an image of bleak or frosty comfort. The daughter wishes to put her head down on her mother's gravestone but recognizes that it is stony and cold. Trethewey has said that she was later filled with remorse for the way that the form had led her to sacrifice the truth. That's because at the time she wrote this poem, her mother did not yet have a stone or any other grave marker. Perhaps the couplet led her to an emotional truth that was not literally true. As recompense, Trethewey decided to write another poem, "Monument," to undo the seeming falsehood of "Graveyard Blues." While doing so, she realized that she should combine, in one book, her poems dedicated to the Native Guards and the elegies for her mother. She was tending to the memories. She was trying to create for them all a lasting monument.

CAMILLE DUNGY

———

"Requiem"

(2006)

In the summer of 1998, Camille Dungy was teaching in England at a summer enrichment program for US high school students. On a field trip to Bath they witnessed a horrific accident. An Italian tourist, or a tourist who they presumed was Italian, looked the wrong way in a roundabout, stepped off the curb, and was instantly killed by a tour coach. Everyone was horrified by what they had just seen — and morbidly fascinated. "You're a poet," one of Dungy's friends and fellow teachers challenged her. "You have to write about this."

Dungy took this as a charge. She has said in interviews that she felt a great responsibility to memorialize what she had witnessed and the life that had ended in her presence. But she couldn't find a way into the poem. She looked at the accident from a variety of angles, but they all failed. Nearly a year later, in the spring of 1999, she attended a concert of Mozart's *Requiem* in Boston, where she was living at the time. One of her friends was in the choir. During the performance, a question came to her and she wrote it down on the concert program: "Will you believe me when I tell you it was beautiful, my left leg turned to uselessness and my right shoe flung some distance down the road?" It seemed a voice had spoken in her head. But the poem stalled there.

Dungy moved to Virginia and temporarily forgot about the poem. But then she received a package with a recording of the concert she had attended. She sat in her office, playing it over and over again, and that's when the poem finally took shape. She was writing to the music. Formally, Dungy decided to write her own "Requiem" in the manner she had received Mozart's *Requiem*. She divided it into five stanzas to represent the five movements of Mozart's piece. The italicized and indented three-line epigraph, which seems like a quotation from a psalm but is really a piece of her own writing, represents the "Ave Maria" that opens the mass.

There is a religious element and feeling to this poem, which relates to the sacredness of life. That feeling was released when Dungy listened to Mozart's *Requiem,* his setting of a mass for the souls of the dead, his act of remembrance. She shaped it into twenty-eight lines, a double sonnet.

Requiem

Sing the mass —
light upon me washing words
now that I am gone.

The sky was a hot, blue sheet the summer breeze fanned
out and over the town. I could have lived forever
under that sky. Forgetting where I was,
I looked left, not right, crossed into a street
and stepped in front of the bus that ended me.

Will you believe me when I tell you it was beautiful —
my left leg turned to uselessness and my right shoe flung
some distance down the road? Will you believe me
when I tell you I had never been so in love
with anyone as I was, then, with everyone I saw?

The way an age-worn man held his wife's shaking arm,
supporting the weight that seemed to sing from the heart
she clutched. Knowing her eyes embraced the pile
that was me, he guided her sacked body through the crowd.
And the way one woman began a fast the moment she looked

under the wheel. I saw her swear off decadence.
I saw her start to pray. You see, I was so beautiful
the woman sent to clean the street used words
like police tape to keep back a young boy
seconds before he rounded the grisly bumper.

The woman who cordoned the area feared my memory
would fly him through the world on pinions of passion
much as, later, the sight of my awful beauty pulled her down
to tears when she pooled my blood with water
and swiftly, swiftly washed my stains away.

Randall Jarrell's stunning little anthology piece "The Death of the Ball
Turret Gunner" is the main precursor text to Dungy's "Requiem." The close
of her poem echoes his last line: "When I died they washed me out of the tur-
ret with a hose." But whereas Jarrell's five-line poem is an allegory about the
cruelty and human waste of the government war machine ("From my moth-
er's sleep I fell into the State"), Dungy's poem is about a random, accidental
death. She is determined to make some purposeful meaning out of it, to see it
as something much more than a senseless accident.

Dungy's most fundamental decision was to speak from the point of view
of the man killed by the bus. What he sees is what she believes he might have
seen, what Dungy herself observed that day: "The sun was a hot, blue sheet the
summer breeze fanned / out and over the town." The speaker is an Italian man,
but he doesn't sound particularly Italian or male; he doesn't have a personal
history. He sounds like the poet ventriloquizing him — he presses the *s*'s and *sh*
in "*s*un," "*sh*eet," and "*s*ummer"; he repeats the hard *e*'s in "sh*ee*t" and "br*ee*ze,"
the *o*'s in "*o*ut" and "*o*ver" — which is to say that he is filled with her verbal
skills, her emotions, the beauty and the horror she feels in witnessing his death.

Dungy takes on his persona and immediately declares, "I could have lived
forever" (this sentence, or part of a sentence, hovers out there for a long time
before dropping to the next line) "under that sky." But instead of living forever,
the speaker makes a small, fatal mistake and turns the wrong way. He had for-
gotten where he was and "stepped in front of the bus that ended me."

Everything in this poem is narrated from the point of view of a dead man,
a corpse. This marks it as what the scholar Diana Fuss labels "a corpse poem,"

which embodies a curious paradox: "A dead body and a poetic discourse are mutually incompatible, two formal states each precluding the other." The speaker has a subjectivity, an interior life, which the cadaver can no longer claim. As Lucille Clifton did in her poem "jasper   texas   1998," Dungy overcomes the improbability of the situation to animate the dead body, which speaks.

Every corpse poem is undergirded by its own literal impossibility. In the second stanza, the speaker raises the issue of his own credibility by twice asking: "Will you believe me . . . ?" This is perhaps an anxiety buried in the unconscious of the poem. There is something obstinate and counterintuitive about the speaker's insistence that "it was beautiful," that he had never been so in love with anyone and everyone.

What we are meant to believe — what the speaker tells and instructs us — is that the horrifying scene is also, in some crucial way, beautiful. There is unexpected beauty in the horror. At the precise moment of his death, the speaker falls in love with the mortal world. To use Wallace Stevens's statement, "Death is the mother of beauty." Or perhaps it would be more accurate to say here that death *becomes* the mother of beauty. The poet writing this poem very much wants to believe this.

In Dungy's poem, the accidental death of a tourist puts a burden on all the people who witness it. In the third stanza, the actions of these nameless, inadvertent participants take on a harried, almost ceremonial quality, as if they have become a chorus in the lyric, which itself becomes an unlikely dirge, a service for the dead. Both the speaker and the poet who voices herself through him are outsiders to the community. We see the passersby as a stranger sees them.

As if in slow motion, we observe an old man carefully guiding his shaking wife through the crowd. She is riven and sacked by observing the speaker reduced to "the pile / that was me." The line break hovers over the lifeless word "pile." Notice how the poem moves from one person to the next and introduces a religious feeling as we cross from the fourth to the fifth stanzas: "And the way one woman began a fast the moment she looked // under the wheel. I saw her swear off decadence. / I saw her start to pray." The short declarative sentences narrate a religious conversion. Something sacred is invoked.

The poem concludes with an image of the woman who is sent to cordon the area and clean the street. She uses words sharply, "like police tape," to warn a young boy who unknowingly comes around "the grisly bumper." The last stanza is a single sinuous sentence. The language becomes heightened as the male speaker projects himself into the woman's point of view. Notice the repetition of *f*'s and *p*'s as the speaker states how she "*f*eared my memory / would *f*ly him through the world on" — the phrase seems like something out of Hopkins — "*p*inions of *p*assion." That's because she fears that he, in the future, will experience what she herself does. The poem closes with a rousing statement about that experience, from the perspective of the deceased speaker: "the sight of my awful beauty pulled her down / to tears when she pooled my blood with water / and swiftly, swiftly, washed my stains away." The line breaks pull the poem downward, like a woman kneeling, and the alliterative sounds — "*p*ulled" and "*p*ooled," "*w*ater" and "*w*ashed," "*s*wiftly" and "*s*tains" — pressure it to a fever pitch. The repetition of "swiftly" enacts the motion of doing something quickly and repetitively even as it slows the poem down.

"Requiem" concludes with the quasi-religious act of a woman kneeling in tears before an "awful beauty" and washing away the stain of death. This is the final cleansing. The poem began with a clear imperative — "*Sing the mass* — / *light upon me washing words* / *now that I am gone*" — and now the service has been concluded. The writer and the reader are bound together in this fierce and pressing chant for the dead.

"Aubade in Autumn"

(2007)

The title of Peter Everwine's poem "Aubade in Autumn" seems reminiscent of Wallace Stevens's "Auroras of Autumn." The beautiful vowel blending, or diphthong ("*Au*bade in *Au*tumn"), hits the authentic Stevensian note. There is a sense that feeling is discovering itself through sounds. Everwine's late love poem is a dawn song set in what John Keats called the "Season of mists and mellow fruitfulness" ("To Autumn"), a Romantic lyric in the season of farewells. In an aubade the speaker is usually a lover who has parted from the beloved at daybreak.

Aubade in Autumn

This morning, from under the floorboards
of the room in which I write,
Lawrence the handyman is singing the blues
in a soft falsetto as he works, the words
unclear, though surely one of them is *love*,
lugging its shadow of sadness into song.

I don't want to think about sadness;
there's never a lack of it.
I want to sit quietly for a while
and listen to my father making
a joyful sound unto his mirror
as he shaves — slap of razor
against the strop, the familiar rasp of his voice
singing his favorite hymn, but faint now,
coming from so far back in time:
Oh, come to the church in the wildwood . . .
my father, who had no faith, but loved
how the long, ascending syllable of *wild*
echoed from the walls in celebration
as the morning opened around him . . .
as now it opens around me, the light shifting
in the leaf-fall of the pear tree and across
the bedraggled backyard roses
that I have been careless of
but brighten the air, nevertheless.
Who am I, if not one who listens
for words to stir from the silences they keep?
Love is the ground note; we cannot do
without it or the sorrow of its changes.
Come to the wildwood, love,
Oh, to the wiiildwood as the morning deepens,
and from a branch in the cedar tree a small bird
quickens his song into the blue reaches of heaven —
hey sweetie sweetie hey.

Everwine's speaker is sitting quietly at his desk. He is not so much writing as listening. Coming from underneath the floorboards, as if from underground, the handyman, Lawrence, is singing the blues. The speaker can't make out the words, "though surely one of them is *love,* / lugging its shadow of sadness into song." That's a good characterization of the blues feeling on a fall day in the early morning, especially for someone who has parted from his lover.

But here the poem turns, as if naturally, away from sadness, which, Everwine understands, will always shadow us. Instead the speaker summons the memory of his father singing. Thus, he self-consciously breaks from the bluesy sound to hit a more joyful note lifted out of memory. He is listening hard so that he can pick up the distant sound of his father singing as he shaved in the early morning. In a note about writing "Aubade," Everwine said that everything shifted when his father suddenly entered the poem: "I had a countersong where I could listen to his hymn and the undercurrent of blues in the same moment of time." The speaker lets us hear, as he is also hearing, the intimate "slap of razor / against the strop" and "the familiar rasp of his voice / singing his favorite hymn, but faint now, / coming from so far back in time."

The speaker is intentionally joining two different kinds of song, the hymn and the blues, and listening to them simultaneously. Both are his birthright. And he makes clear that the joy coming from the hymn is a secular joy; it has nothing to do with his father's religious belief, though the song is called "The Church in the Wildwood." The speaker is re-creating the sound of the words that are blasting out of memory:

> *Oh, come to the church in the wildwood . . .*
> my father, who had no faith, but loved
> how the long, ascending syllable of *wild*
> echoed from the walls in celebration
> as the morning opened around him . . .

The ellipsis marks the way that the aubade breaks from the past and turns to the present. Attention to the sound of the words themselves shuttles the speaker back to the autumn day spreading out before him. The Wordsworthian memory alerts him to the present morning, which now opens around him in the garden:

> the light shifting
> in the leaf-fall of the pear tree and across
> the bedraggled backyard roses
> that I have been careless of
> but brighten the air, nevertheless.

The *l* sounds lilt ("light," "leaf-fall"), and the *b*'s connect "bedraggled" and "backyard" to the words "but brighten." The phrase in the last line, "brighten the air," recalls the marvelous line from Thomas Nash's seventeenth-century poem "A Litany in Time of Plague": "Brightness falls from the air." As in Richard Howard's poem "Elementary Principles at Seventy-Two" and Vijay Seshadri's lyric "Aphasia," the sounds of words themselves trigger the poet's thought. For a moment, "Aubade in Autumn" becomes an *ars poetica,* a statement of the poetics that had been driving Everwine from his first two books of pure poetry, *Collecting the Animals* (1973) and *Keeping the Darkness* (1977): "Who am I, if not one who listens / for words to stir from the silences they keep?"

The poem identifies itself as an aubade because love is "the ground note." Its speaker recognizes, with a wisdom derived from experience, that we cannot manage without love and must also suffer "the sorrow of its changes." Thus, the hymn morphs into a secular love poem, but one that brings with it the joy of a father's hymn. The word "love" is now added to the line from that hymn, and the long *i* is drawn out in the repetition of the word "wildwood" ("*wiiild-wood*"), thus emphasizing the uncontrollable wildness of love.

> *Come to the wildwood, love,*
> *Oh, to the wiiildwood* as the morning deepens,
> and from a branch in the cedar tree a small bird
> quickens his song into the blue reaches of heaven —
> *hey sweetie sweetie hey.*

Though Everwine's poem is a lyric of simple clarity, many songs come together in it: there is the song of the poet, an aubade; the song of the handyman, the blues; the song of the father, a hymn; and the song of the bird, a natural music. The poem is about singing. And all the songs unite in an informal sweetness and intimacy to form a contemporary pastoral lyric, which looks to nature for solace. It closes with what the poet takes to be the lovely vernacular sound of a small bird calling to its lost lover: "*hey sweetie sweetie hey.*"

TONY HOAGLAND

———

"Barton Springs"

(2007)

O for a life of Sensations rather than of Thoughts!" John Keats exclaimed
in a letter to his friend Benjamin Bailey (November 22, 1817) — and that's
what came to mind when I read Tony Hoagland's poem "Barton Springs" in
Poetry magazine in July 2007. Hoagland tended to be a poet of thoughts rather
than sensations, a postmodern ironist, a sassy, insightful social critic alert to
the changing mores of late-twentieth-century American capitalism, and a tac-
tician of the vernacular. Hidden depths of feeling underlay his poems, but his
clever sendups of contemporary reality often obscured them. Veering between
comedy and outrage, his edgy poems took aim at the omnipotence and ines-
capability of mass culture, which surrounds us everywhere, like a sea.

Hoagland never lost his cutting-edge humorous skepticism, but over time
a drift toward more expressive feeling became apparent in his poems. This was
heightened as he grappled more and more openly with cancer. Great grief en-
ters his poems about dealing with this disease, along with an increasing sense
of gratitude for the fleeting temporal world. This poem, which puts me in
mind of Maxine Kumin's poem "To Swim, to Believe," discovers an almost re-
ligious element in the act of immersion, the work of swimming itself.

Barton Springs

Oh life, how I loved your cold spring mornings
of putting my stuff in the green gym-bag
and crossing wet grass to the southeast gate
to push my crumpled dollar through the slot.

When I get my allotted case of cancer,
let me swim ten more times at Barton Springs,
in the outdoor pool at 6 AM, in the cold water
with the geezers and the jocks.

With my head bald from radiation
and my chemotherapeutic weight loss
I will be sleek as a cheetah
— and I will not complain about life's

pedestrian hypocrisies,
I will not consider death a contractual violation.
Let my cancer be the slow-growing kind
so I will have all the time I need

to backstroke over the rocks and little fishes,
looking upwards through my bronze-tinted goggles
into the vaults and rafters of the oaks,
as the crows exchange their morning gossip

in the pale mutations of early light.
It was worth death to see you through these optic nerves,
to feel breeze through the fur on my arms
to be chilled and stirred in your mortal martini.

In documents elsewhere I have already recorded
my complaints in some painstaking detail.
Now, because all things are joyful near water,
there just might be time to catch up on praise.

Barton Springs Pool, which extends over a full three acres, is part of Zilker Metropolitan Park in Austin, Texas. It is fed from underground springs, and you can swim in it year-round. When I first read "Barton Springs," I assumed it was a lyric about Hoagland's experience of cancer, but in fact he wrote it a full decade before receiving his diagnosis. The imaginative impulse for the poem arose because his friend, the poet Jason Shinder, was sick with two different kinds of cancer. In 2006, Hoagland and his wife took Shinder for a swim at Barton Springs. The poem was born afterward.

"Barton Springs" consists of seven even-keeled quatrains. It's odd to start a postmodern poem with an apostrophe to life, in the manner of an eighteenth-century allegory. Hoagland's poem starts in the grand manner — "Oh life, how I loved your cold spring mornings" — but then the speaker brings it down to the quotidian, to dumping his stuff in a gym-bag and crossing the wet grass to the southeast gate, where he pushes a crumpled dollar through a slot. This sweet, funny scene has the texture of authentic daily life. That's why it takes a moment for the past tense to register: "Oh life, how I *loved* your cold spring mornings . . ." At the literal level, the speaker is remembering a time when he went swimming every day. But the memory also suggests a sense of finality.

This finality is confirmed in the second stanza. There is a chilling inevitability to the line "*When* I get my allotted case of cancer . . ." Rainer Maria Rilke's poem "Slumbersong" makes the same move: "*When* I lose you, someday . . ." But whereas Rilke wonders about his lover ("How will you sleep without me"), Hoagland lowers the temperature with a specific concrete wish: "let me swim ten more times at Barton Springs." This quiet poise, this almost Zen-like quality of calmness — and the notable absence of hysteria — reveals a certain attitude about the future. The speaker knows the forecast is bleak, the darkest clouds are gathering, but nonetheless he wants to get in some swimming. Each of the first two stanzas consists of a single winding sentence and moves along steadily, like a swimmer doing a couple of laps.

Beginning with the third stanza, the sentences become jumpier and crisscross stanzas. Typically jokey, Hoagland lets his speaker comment jauntily on his future cancer, his bald head and "chemotherapeutic" weight loss; he seems determined not to complain. Notice the comic timing in the double pause (line break and stanza break) separating a possessive noun and its object in "and I will not complain about life's // pedestrian hypocrisies." The language becomes weirdly distanced as he jokes about "a contractual violation," as if he had thought about taking death to court in a civil suit. But a subtle prayer is implicit in the lines "Let my cancer be the slow-growing kind / so I will have all the time I need . . ."

Hoagland captures the sensuousness of swimming in Barton Springs Pool. His discursiveness has always been image laden. We're with the swimmer as he gazes upward through his goggles "into the vaults and rafters of the oaks" and moves through the water in the early morning light. Notice the push and pull in the language, the way the poem immerses us in the vital experience of swimming and then upends it with the witty image of being "chilled and stirred in your mortal martini." The speaker's cleverness here seems like a defense against what he is feeling.

The final stanza consists of two balanced sentences. First, the speaker pulls the language even further back to announce: "In documents elsewhere I have already recorded / my complaints in some painstaking detail." That's a deft, amusing way to describe earlier poems that complain about the unfairness of life. "Oh life!" Hoagland exclaims in his poem "Personal": "Can you blame me / for making a scene?"

But as a poem "Barton Springs" takes one final turn. It comes down with fervent immediacy to the present moment: "*Now* . . ." There is also an argument developing here — "*Now, because* . . ." — which becomes an assertion of unadorned feeling, of joy: "Now, because all things are joyful near water . . ." This sounds almost like a religious axiom, suggesting baptism, purification by water. And then, with a full sense of the transitory nature of life, the speaker turns to praise: "there just might be time to catch up on praise."

In the end, Tony Hoagland's poem about swimming turns into a praise poem, a kind of lyric that restores us to the world again, to our good luck in being here. W. H. Auden once said that "every poem is rooted in imaginative awe." "Barton Springs" is a poem of thoughts overcome and sensations realized. It carries its dark subject lightly, even buoyantly. And it was written just in the nick of time.

PHILIP SCHULTZ

———

"Failure"

(2007)

There is something unflinching and remorseless, something almost help-
less about the way that Philip Schultz keeps returning to the subject of
his father's funeral, one of the darkest moments in his past. He was eighteen
when his father died in poverty. It seems he has never been able to shake his
family's immigrant story, his father's complete inability to make a go of it in
America. Schultz has said elsewhere that Samuel Schultz's bankruptcy essen-
tially killed him and rendered his wife and son destitute, financially and emo-
tionally.

Schultz's earlier elegy "For My Father" appeared in *Poetry* magazine in the
late seventies. It had a *Death of a Salesman* quality, presenting the portrait of a
man who was always tired at night, whose "vending machines turned peanuts
into pennies," and whose schemes never seemed to pan out. As the poet recalls
it, "The morning his heart stopped I borrowed money to bury him / & his
eyes still look at me out of mirrors." Schultz was thirty-three when he wrote
"For My Father"; he was sixty-two when he returned to his father's funeral in
"Failure," a poem that took him three years to complete. This poem adds a hu-

miliating fact: the son not only had to borrow money for the funeral but had
to get it from the very people that his father was still indebted to.

Failure

To pay for my father's funeral
I borrowed money from people
he already owed money to.
One called him a nobody.
No, I said, he was a failure.
You can't remember
a nobody's name, that's why
they're called nobodies.
Failures are unforgettable.
The rabbi who read a stock eulogy
about a man who didn't belong to
or believe in anything
was both a failure and a nobody.
He failed to imagine the son
and wife of the dead man
being shamed by each word.
To understand that not
believing in or belonging to
anything demanded a kind
of faith and buoyancy.
An uncle, counting on his fingers
my father's business failures —
a parking lot that raised geese,
a motel that raffled honeymoons,
a bowling alley with roving mariachis —
failed to love and honor his brother,
who showed him how to whistle
under covers, steal apples
with his right or left hand. Indeed,
my father was comical.
His watches pinched, he tripped

on his pant cuffs and snored
loudly in movies, where
his weariness overcame him
finally. He didn't believe in:
savings insurance newspapers
vegetables good or evil human
frailty history or God.
Our family avoided us,
fearing boils. I left town
but failed to get away.

"Failure" is an unswerving poem. In one determined stanza, it takes up a subject that's practically off limits in a culture obsessed with wealth and success. The poem progresses by a series of declarative statements. It compresses a story. There is a sort of grim merriment in the distinction between "a nobody" and "a failure." It's almost a Yiddish joke. It's worth pausing over the timing of the short, mostly three-beat lines and the understated emphasis on the line breaks. Each line creates its own quietly pronounced statement. Hence:

You can't remember
a nobody's name, that's why
they're called nobodies.
Failures are unforgettable.

Where the line and the sentence coincide, it seems like the punch line to a joke. "Failures are unforgettable" is an eternal truth disguised as a wisecrack, which, as the critic Peter Schjeldahl quips, is "the American form of Montaigne-style aphorism."

The speaker levels a sarcastic fury at the rabbi, who delivers "a stock eulogy" — he calls him "both a failure and a nobody." The clergyman has failed to take into account the feelings of the bereaved mother and son dying from shame in the front row. The speaker in "Failure," unlike the one in "For My Father," now seems to understand the faith and even the buoyancy that his father had to summon up in order to sustain himself, to keep going. It's exhausting not to believe in anything. The speaker still can't quite forgive his uncle, who counts out on his fingers his brother's lame and unlikely business ventures but can't recall the savvy older brother who taught him things as a kid. The list of ways in which the father was "comical" does not read as comedy. Rather, the father's perpetual weariness is what stands out.

We typically think of a poetic catalog as a gesture of affirmation. The cataloging impulse almost always expresses, in Richard Wilbur's words, "a longing to possess the whole world, and to praise it." That's why Schultz's list of all the things that his father *didn't* believe in is amusing in a glum, bleak way. It's a catalog of negativities. Think of it as a colliding series of subjects that most certainly don't rhyme: "savings insurance newspapers / vegetables good or evil human / frailty history or God." Some items are equivalent to reasons why the family is left destitute (savings, insurance), some show the father's lack of interest in the larger world (newspapers), and some reveal his provincial background (vegetables). The fact that he didn't believe in (presumably eating) vegetables is paired with the much more significant truth that he didn't distinguish between good or evil, or believe in human weakness, history, or God. We vault from "savings" to "God" in one short list, which captures the extent of the father's bankruptcy; he was not only financially broke but also exhausted and lost, physically unhealthy, spiritually bereft.

Funerals are supposed to bring families together. Not this one. The larger family apparently fears contagion and treats the two chief mourners accordingly. The effect is like a medieval shunning. In the end, the speaker is left alone, first with his mother, and then with his own feelings: "I left town / but failed to get away." The poem concludes not on the father's failure, which has been the subject all along, but on the son's. He may leave town, but he never gets away, metaphorically speaking. Failure is his inheritance, his legacy.

The conclusion to the poem circles back to the writing of it. The poet is so obsessed by his father's failure, as well as his own inability to escape from it, that he now needs to write a poem about it. This is a lonely, obsessive project. That's lucky for us, though, because Philip Schulz has written a wonderfully successful poem about one of the great neglected subjects in American life: *failure*.

MICHAEL COLLIER

———

"An Individual History"

(2007)

Michael Collier's poems are so smoothly and cannily made that it's possible to overlook their undercurrents, the way they find a seam in experience and plunge into the unknown, the mysterious. In "An Individual History," the title poem of his sixth book, he unflinchingly enters the past to remember and reimagine one particular life. The poet has also turned this sparely noted life into a representative story. This unique history also illuminates the unwritten histories of thousands of others, "the detained and unparoled," the marginal and misfortunate ones, the scarcely remembered and troubled "mentally ill."

An Individual History

This was before the time of lithium and Zoloft

before mood stabilizers and anxiolytics

and almost all the psychotropic drugs, but not before Thorazine, which the suicide O'Laughlin called "handcuffs for the mind."

It was before, during, and after the time of atomic fallout,

Auschwitz, the Nakba, DDT, and you could take the water cures,

find solace in quarantines, participate in shunnings,

or stand at Lourdes among the canes and crutches.

It was when the March of Time kept taking off its boots.

Fridays when families prayed the Living Rosary

to neutralize communists with prayer.

When electroshock was electrocution

and hammers recognized the purpose of a nail.

And so, if you were as crazy as my maternal grandmother was then

you might make the pilgrimage she did through the wards

of state and private institutions,

and make of your own body a nail for pounding, its head

sunk past quagmires, coups d'etat, and disappearances

and in this way find a place in history

among the detained and unparoled, an individual like her,

though hidden by an epoch of lean notation — "Marked

Parkinsonian tremor," "Chronic paranoid type" —

a time when the animal slowed by its fate

was excited to catch a glimpse of its tail

or feel through her skin the dulled-over joy

when for a moment her hands were still.

Collier has written a short note explaining the origin of "An Individual History." At first, he started a poem based on transcriptions of his grandmother's medical records, which one of his sisters had come upon in a roundabout way. He was moved by the bare notations — "Placed on iron and thorazine (50 mg, 4X a day). Up in a wheel chair. No weight on fractured leg" — and statements recording her cryptic delusional pronouncements — "There was a heritage invasion" or "I changed my skin, my hair, and my weight all in one year." But he could never find a framework for the found poem that he imagined he would write.

Years later, he read an essay about the history of psychotropic drugs and found himself responding viscerally to the names of the drugs. Their etymologies started to spark figurative possibilities. That's how his long-dead college roommate Jimmy O'Laughlin came into the poem, calling Thorazine "handcuffs for the mind." That designation, by the way, breaks Ezra Pound's modernist credo by mixing a concrete noun and an abstraction ("don't say 'dim lands of peace'") and is a vivid capsule description of how Thorazine manacles the mind of someone who takes it. It sounds like a phrase from an asylum poem by Theodore Roethke. Along the way, Collier also realized that he had found an avenue to tell his grandmother's story, which, as he says, "might also speak to certain paranoid and delusional characteristics of our culture."

One striking thing about the final version of this poem is that the grandmother doesn't enter until the second half. That's when it all becomes personal. "An Individual History" operates like a long, evenly distributed sonnet. It begins with a declaration seemingly out of a legend ("This was before the time of lithium and Zoloft"). It then takes thirteen lines to get to the turn, or volta, at line 14 ("And so, if you were as crazy as my maternal grandmother was then") and then thirteen more lines to the finish. The lines are lengthy enough to carry both images and historical information. As the poem progresses, the individual lines keep stretching out and getting curbed back, especially toward the end, to a quasi-pentameter line of nine to twelve syllables. This creates a useful tension between the feeling and the facts. The extra spaces between the lines also give each one a greater emphasis, a longer pause between, and this provides the reader with more time to savor and process the myriad images and the information.

The poem begins with a statement about a period when almost no drugs existed to help people with psychoses. The second pronouncement considerably enlarges upon the situation: "It was before, during, and after the time of atomic fallout, / Auschwitz, the Nakba, DDT ..." Here, in quick succession, the speaker catalogs four twentieth-century cataclysms: the fallout from nuclear weapons, the Holocaust, the 1948 Palestinian exodus, the Vietnam War. This was also an era when, he suggests, "you could take the water cures, find solace in quarantines, participate in shunnings, / or stand at Lourdes among the canes and crutches." The twentieth century, in other words, was actually somewhat primitive in that people still tried to comfort themselves by means of magical thinking, escaping somewhere soothing, shutting others away, participating in social rejections (which he calls "shunnings"), or making a religious pilgrimage to a small town in the Pyrenees, as Catholics have been doing since the mid-nineteenth century. In other words, as he cleverly states, "It was when the March of Time kept taking off its boots." Ancient rituals continue, but now with markedly twentieth-century goals: "Fridays when families prayed the Living Rosary / to neutralize communists with prayer." The first section concludes in concise, fateful brutality: "When electroshock was electrocution / and hammers recognized the purpose of a nail." The repetition of the prefix *electro-* darkly, inevitably, and fatally equates "electroshock" with "electrocution." Also, hammers have been endowed with consciousness.

In the second section, the poem brings a single representative individual into focus. The grandmother's journey from institution to institution is called a "pilgrimage," giving it a religious or sacred dimension, and the hammer recognizing the function of the nail takes on special force as the woman makes of her body "a nail for pounding." This is a hidden story, an unreported history, and thus this grandmother takes her place with those who have been sacrificed, who are "hidden by an epoch of lean notation." Those scanty details from Collier's grandmother's medical records now find their proper place:

"Marked Parkinsonian tremor," "Chronic paranoid type." A whole person and unnamed generations of people are being thus described. This is all that remains of them. But the poem ends not on the diagnosis, but on the animal life, the moment of vitality, something inside each of them:

> a time when the animal slowed by its fate
>
> was excited to catch a glimpse of its tail
>
> or feel through her skin the dulled-over joy
>
> when for a moment her hands were still.

By a leap of imaginative sympathy, Michael Collier has memorialized his grandmother, who was fated to live at a time before psychotropic drugs could help her. He also enlarges her story and sheds a bright light on our various paranoias, aspects of our painfully violent and delusional culture. A disquieting individual history points to a larger cultural story of magical religious thinking and murderous human impulses.

LUCIA PERILLO

——

"The Second Slaughter"

(2008)

The assumption that animals are without rights and the illusion that our treatment of them has no moral significance is a positively outrageous example of Western crudity and barbarity," Arthur Schopenhauer wrote in *On the Basis of Morality* (1840). "Universal compassion is the only guarantee of morality." Lucia Perillo shows the same sense of moral outrage in her cunning and furious anti-war poem "The Second Slaughter."

The Second Slaughter

Achilles slays the man who slew his friend, pierces the corpse
behind the heels and drags it
behind his chariot like the cans that trail
a bride and groom. Then he lays out
a banquet for his men, oxen and goats
and pigs and sheep; the soldiers eat
until a greasy moonbeam lights their beards.

The first slaughter is for victory, but the second slaughter is for grief —
in the morning more animals must be killed
for burning with the body of the friend. But Achilles finds
no consolation in the hiss and crackle of their fat;
not even heaving four stallions on the pyre
can lift the ballast of his sorrow.

And here I turn my back on the epic hero — the one who slits
the throats of his friend's dogs,
killing what the loved one loved
to reverse the polarity of grief. Let him repent
by vanishing from my concern
after he throws the dogs onto the fire.
The singed fur makes the air too difficult to breathe.

When the oil wells of Persia burned I did not weep
until I heard about the birds, the long-legged ones especially
which I imagined to be scarlet, with crests like egrets
and tails like peacocks, covered in tar
weighting the feathers they dragged through black shallows
at the rim of the marsh. But once

I told this to a man who said I was inhuman, for giving animals
my first lament. So now I guard
my inhumanity like the jackal
who appears behind the army base at dusk,
come there for scraps with his head lowered
in a posture that looks like appeasement
though it is not.

Perillo told an interviewer that she wrote the fourth stanza of this poem in 1991, during the First Gulf War. The poem had started out as an anecdote — "When the oil wells of Persia burned I did not weep / until I heard about the birds." She continued with the image of long-legged birds

which I imagined to be scarlet, with crests like egrets
and tails like peacocks, covered in tar

weighting the feathers they dragged through black shallows
at the rim of the marsh.

This is a precise image of the natural cost of industrial warfare. "By juxtaposing the birds' vibrant colors with the dark hue of spilled oil," the poet John James has noted, "Perillo emphasizes the damage inflicted by human carelessness."

It took Perillo another seventeen years to find a place for this anecdote in a larger war poem triggered by the *Iliad,* an epic poem that was itself triggered by the vengeful wrath of Achilles ("Rage, O Goddess, sing the fury of Peleus's son Achilles"). Perillo's first stanza recalls how Achilles, devastated by the death of his friend Patroclus, savagely slaughtered and humiliated their enemy, Hector. Perillo quickly condenses the story from Book 22. She needs the anecdote to kick off her poem, but her real interest lies elsewhere. Her style is nonchalant, mordant, utterly contemporary:

Achilles slays the man who slew his friend, pierces the corpse
behind the heels and drags it
beyond the chariot like the cans that trail
a bride and groom.

The simile — dragging a corpse behind a chariot like a string of cans behind a wedding car — is purposely anachronistic and discordant. The tone is jaunty — everyone sits down to feast at a banquet, and the grief hasn't really set in.

The second stanza turns to the second slaughter, the true subject of the poem: "The first slaughter is for victory, but the second slaughter is for grief." The entire stanza is one sentence long. It takes up the sacrifice of animals, a sacrifice that cannot appease or comfort Achilles, who is blinded by his own feelings. The speaker of this poem is first of all a reader, though in a recitation of the poem Perillo offhandedly mentioned that she was reading the *Iliad* for the first time. She was thus coming fresh to the twenty-third, penultimate book of the epic. Achilles, who is still out of his mind with grief, has heaped the flayed carcasses of sheep and cattle on the funeral pyre for Patroclus. He has set two-handled jars of honey and oil beside the bier "and then with wild zeal / slung the bodies of four massive stallions onto the pyre." The image of the four horses heaved into the fire seems to shock Perillo out of the text she is reading. This leads to the structural turning point in her poem.

Formally, the first stanza of "The Second Slaughter" has seven lines, and the second six, as if something has been quietly cut off, foreshortened. It isn't until the third stanza that we begin to see a pattern emerge: alternating seven- and six-line stanzas. This creates a kind of symmetry that is also slightly off balance. We can feel the rhythm caused by something imperceptibly being taken away, then added. The stanzas jump from one subject to the next, but the narratives accrue into the perpetual story of human cruelty to animals.

Like Natasha Trethewey in "Graveyard Blues," Perillo signals the volta, or turn, in her poem by using the word "turn" itself: "And here I *turn* my back on the epic hero . . ." The speaker is closing the book in disgust because of its murderous, unappeasable hero. It fits with the subject of the poem that Perillo focuses on how Achilles slit the throats of two of Patroclus's dogs but doesn't mention the twelve "brave sons / of the proud Trojans he hacked to pieces with his bronze." Perillo's speaker intentionally mixes up the action of the *Iliad* with her experience of reading it. She banishes the hero from her presence with a certain arch formality: "Let him repent / by vanishing from my concern / after he throws the dogs onto the fire." Achilles's actions have become so real and repugnant to her that she can no longer bear to be in his presence: "The singed fur makes the air too difficult to breathe." She closes the *Iliad* for good and turns to the subject of two recent American wars.

The epic poem narrates a legend ("Whatever else the epic may have been," the scholar M. L. Finley declares, "it was *not history*"), but the American interventions are unfortunately historical. Perillo had now found a place for her stanza related to the invasion of Iraq. The speaker of the poem is well aware that the larger, more newsworthy story about the burning of the oil fields does not affect her so much as the tale of the birds, which triggers her mournful imagination. It's hard to shake the image of those birds "covered in tar," the image that triggers one more conclusive turn in the poem.

The stanzas in Perillo's poem tend to operate as paragraphs — they are all intact — except for this last one, which proceeds with an informal argumentative tone: "*But once //* I told this to a man who said I was inhuman, for giving animals / my first lament. *So now* . . ." But the speaker doesn't back down from her argument. Instead, she takes it underground. There is a highly self-conscious awareness in this poem that the first slaughter, the first lament, is usually reserved for human beings. Some people, like the man in Perillo's last stanza (one can't help but notice how definitively she specifies his gender), consider it "inhuman" to lament for animals before one grieves for other human beings. But Perillo sneakily, ironically, decides to "guard" her "inhumanity," which she doesn't believe is inhumane at all, by comparing herself to a jackal, who somewhat magically "appears behind the army base at dusk, / come there for scraps with his head lowered / in a posture that looks like appeasement / though it is not."

Perillo told an interviewer that the jackal in the poem is based on a real one, from Jonathan Trouern-Trend's book *Birding Babylon,* a soldier's field notes and online journal from his two tours of duty in Iraq. What she picks up from the golden jackal is an attitude, a deceptive way of being, a posture. She too seems to be making concessions to a larger dictatorial power, an enforced morality. But she is not sorry; no, she is not at all sorry. Her resistance is evident. She is grief-stricken, clear-eyed, and empathic. And she memorializes the slaughter of the animals.

MICHAEL WATERS

"Old School"

(2010)

Michael Waters took the title for his tenth book, *Celestial Joyride*, from his poem "Old School." The title puts together two words that make an unlikely match: "celestial," a Latinate word with a sense of the divine, and "joyride," a slang word with connotations of recklessness, of driving around dangerously. It has a jolt of lawlessness. The oxymoron of a divine joyride fits the character of the poem — and the book.

Old School

Seth wrestled the Camaro with one fist & popped
Handfuls of pills while the pistol rode my thigh.
I shouted *Is it loaded?* over Grandmaster Flash.
Amateur thug, he slipped the piece into his boot
& swaggered like a bouncer into the funeral home.

Sunglass'd still & jittery, he scanned the room,
Swept past uncles to the open coffin, knelt there,

Then wedged the gun between our father's thumbs,
Insurance for the celestial joyride, & tattooed,
Pierced, & fucked up, bowed his shaven skull and wept.

"Old School" is a poem of reckoning. The title suggests an old-fashioned way of doing things, at one time considered the best and right way, which has now lapsed. How is that idea going to manifest itself here? One feature of this short poem is its tactical release of information, which heightens the drama. It unfolds quickly but carefully over the course of two five-line stanzas, presenting a terrifically compressed story in just ten lines. The capital letter at the beginning of each line, the poised free verse, a near iambic pentameter, and the well-conceived symmetrical structure all give the poem a feeling of formality. But the pacing, the jittery vernacular, and even the ampersands create a contrary feeling of haste and informality. As the two impulses jostle, they create a dynamic and purposeful tension.

"Old School" unfolds in the past tense and thus seems positioned as a memory. It starts off with what we may think of as a somewhat typical "joyride." You could almost film the scene. It all happens fast, and we're immediately thrust into the situation: there's an out-of-control driver named Seth who "wrestled the Camaro with one fist." The Camaro is a symbol of old school American muscle power. With his other hand, Seth is popping pills. At the same time, the speaker is nervously pressing Seth's pistol under his thigh and shouting "*Is it loaded?*" over the blasting music of Grandmaster Flash, that pioneer of old school hip-hop who made "scratching" popular in DJ-ing. The situation appears to be dangerous — a sketchy character zipping around with a skittish friend in what could be a stolen car. But at the end of the stanza we learn that this so-called thug, who, after all, is only just an "amateur" — in other words, not a true or professional thug — is entering an extremely unlikely place, a funeral home. That's not where this joyride had seemed to be taking them, or us.

The next and final stanza consists of a single twisting sentence. The second line suggests that the two of them are going to the funeral of a relative, though it's not until the end of the third line that we discover the surprising fact that the protagonists of the poem are brothers; the person who has died is their father. We also learn that one brother is putting the gun in their father's hands for "insurance" on his ride into the next world. It's an unlikely gesture. He is doing what he can for their father, who, he believes, just might need firepower for the journey after death. After all, he might be meeting up with some unsavory characters on the other side.

It's not until the conclusion of the poem that we feel the genuine grief of a son, "tattooed, / Pierced, & fucked up," over the death of his father, the parent he cannot really help but somehow still wants to protect by arming him. The unexpected way that Seth, seemingly so tough, suddenly breaks down catches us off guard and floods us too. A father has died, but this poem is not so much an elegy for him as a touching portrait of a screwed-up brother lost in sorrow. The grief of both brothers is unexpected and genuine. The outright expression of such grief is truly "old school."

"Old School" is a dramatic monologue. It is so emotionally convincing that I initially took it as a straightforward if possibly exaggerated autobiographical story. But that was naive. Later, I discovered through an interview that Michael Waters is an only child. He got the idea for the poem from a time when his cousin, a prison guard in Ossining, who had been drinking, brought a gun to his own father's funeral. Waters's father, a former detective, figured out what was going on and got him to hasten his cousin out of the funeral home. That was in 1990. It lodged in the poet's mind and eventually became the genesis of "Old School."

Michael Waters has said that in the poem the speaker and his brother, Seth, seem like two versions of himself, a person who is somehow both reckless and responsible. He was split in two and still trying to figure out how to mourn his father, who died in 1993, when he wrote this poem seventeen years later.

LUCIE BROCK-BROIDO

—

"Infinite Riches in the Smallest Room"

(2013)

Infinite Riches in the Smallest Room" is the lead poem in Lucie Brock-Broido's last book, *Stay, Illusion* (2013). It first appeared in *The New Yorker* under the title "The Noctuary." The archaic word *noctuary* suggests a nightly journal, or a journal of nocturnal incidents, and this meaning continues to carry into the poem, which, in some sense, consists of a series of singular night statements, each an entry unto itself. But the revised title also has a richer, more Dickinsonian flair and suggests the majestic possibilities of an imagination that cannot be confined by a tiny space. It also has an overtone of the limitless imagination roaming free in the confined space of the body.

Infinite Riches in the Smallest Room

Silk spool of the recluse as she confects her eventual mythomania.

If it is written down, you can't rescind it.

Spoon and pottage bowl. You *are* starving. Come closer now.

What if I were gone and the wind still reeks of hyacinth, what then.

Who will I be: a gaudy arrangement of nuclei, an apple-size gray circle

On the tunic of a Jew, preventing more bad biological accidents

                                      From breeding-in. I have not bred-

In. Each child still has one lantern inside lit. May the Mother not

Blow her children out. She says her hair is thinning, thin.

The flowerbed is black, sumptuous in emptiness.

Blue-footed mushrooms line the walkway to my door. I would as soon

Die as serve them in a salad to the man I love. We lie down

In the shape of a gondola. Venice is gorgeous cold. 3 December,

Unspeakable anxiety about locked-in syndrome, about a fourth world.

I cannot promise to say. The violin spider, she

Has six good eyes, arranged in threes.

                                    The rims of wounds have wounds

   as well.

Sphinx, small print, you are inscrutable.

                                    On the roads, blue thistles, barely

Visible by night, and, by these, you may yet find your way home.

   Brock-Broido followed a circuitous route in her poems, and each line in this mysterious summary is like a station stop on a secret journey. As in Michael Collier's "An Individual History," there is extra space between the lines, a strategy of lineation she probably borrowed from her friend the poet Henri Cole, who has made it one of his signatures. Here, the lines are almost all end-stopped, single sentences, or fragments of sentences. This gives each one the feeling of a solo journal entry. Yet taken together, these entries are also connected by an inner logic, an allusive set of associations that are not immediately clear. The poem establishes its own method and accrues meaning as it proceeds.

The first line marks the terrain of Brock-Broido's baroque lexicon and strategic imagination: "Silk spool of the recluse as she confects her eventual mythomania." This refers to the "silk spool," or elegant spiderweb, of a solitary as she "confects" or creates something elaborate, an exaggerated, perhaps even pathological story. This fragment points not just to the poem we are reading, but to the entire body of work that is being created by the recluse in her small room, a miniaturist's space. She is weaving a story about herself that will eventually seem legendary. The word *mythomania,* which derives from the Greek *mythos* ("myth") and the Late Latin *mania* ("insanity, madness"), feels ancient though it derives from the early twentieth century. So too Brock-Broido's work can feel archaic while being utterly new.

The second line establishes the method of the poem and jumps from the third to the second person: "If it is written down, you can't rescind it." The speaker is talking to herself, positing and acknowledging that what is inscribed cannot be taken back. The implication is that she would continue to "rescind it," whatever "it" is, if it were not written down. She is an endless procrastinator, a reviser, who continually rethinks what she has just said. The writing of the lines is thus a firm commitment.

As "Infinite Riches" continues, we come to understand it as a cryptic and elliptical self-portrait. Hence the third line where the speaker refers to herself, in a sort of nineteenth-century way, as someone who is perpetually hungry: "Spoon and pottage bowl. You *are* starving. Come closer now." The italicized word emphasizes that the speaker is hungry *right now* — even as she writes this. Like a figure out of Dickens, she is alone with her "spoon and pottage bowl." She may be anorexic, but she is also starving in a variety of ways, which includes being starved for company. After all, whom is she asking to "come closer now"? She seems to be talking to herself, but also to some unseen listener. The address creates a greater feeling of intimacy. The reader leans in.

This intimacy is intensified by the next question: "What if I were gone and the wind still reeks of hyacinth, what then." The fact that this beautiful line ends not with a question mark, but a period, makes it seem rhetorical. The speaker is talking about her own mortality. The reference to hyacinth, an especially fragrant flower, brings to mind the figure in T. S. Eliot's "Waste Land": "You gave me hyacinths first a year ago; / They called me the hyacinth girl." It seems relevant to invoke a woman speaking and remembering a long-ago time when someone gave her hyacinth flowers. Eliot's disjunctive, collage-like method stands distantly behind Brock-Broido's more personal lyric form. Here she seems to be asking what will happen if (and when) the fragrance of hyacinth outlasts her.

Now she wonders what will persist of her self after death: "Who will I be: a gaudy arrangement of nuclei, an apple-size gray circle." She still retains some part of her gaudy self even as she has been reduced to an arrangement of "nuclei," nothing more than a circle of ashes no larger than an apple. This leads to an association with her Jewish ancestry and a kind of joke about biology. We note too that these are the first lines in the poem that carry over to the next:

... an apple-size gray circle

On the tunic of a Jew, preventing more bad biological accidents

From breeding-in. I have not bred-

In. Each child still has one lantern inside lit. May the Mother not

Blow her children out. She says her hair is thinning, thin.

The comic thought about biblical clothing and ancestral "breeding" leads the speaker to make a more vexed statement about her own childlessness. Notice how she breaks up the line: "I have not bred- / In." Associating more rapidly now, the speaker makes a large, quite marvelous statement about the unique light inside every young person: "Each child still has one lantern inside lit." The word "still" suggests that children may once have had more than one source of light. No matter how many others have been extinguished, a single lantern, an old-fashioned type of light, continues to burn for each one. The sentence twists in such a way that it ends on the word "lit." And this in turn is followed by a sort of prayer. There is a special emphasis on the injunction, the word "not": "May the Mother not / Blow her children out." The lantern has become a metonym for the spirit of the children. The speaker shows an awareness that the Mother is aging: "She says her hair is thinning, thin." The speaker purposely capitalizes the word "Mother." She also doesn't say "my Mother" but "the Mother," a larger, more representative or allegorical figure.

The poem continues to utilize a disjunctive method and moves to the garden outside: "The flowerbed is black, sumptuous in emptiness." The scene is bleak, a black flowerbed, but the speaker characterizes the emptiness of a garden in winter as "sumptuous." She keeps finding words — "gaudy," "sumptuous" — for her own method of finding "infinite riches" in an otherwise empty space.

Hence the gill-capped mushrooms with spores that create a path from the garden to the speaker's room: "Blue-footed mushrooms line the walkway to my door." They seem to rise out of the emptiness. These mushrooms are potentially edible, but the speaker declares, with her usual extravagance, "I would as soon / Die as serve them in a salad to the man I love."

The poem introduces a lover and declares outright, "We lie down / In the shape of a gondola." The speaker hasn't left her small room, and so this is a either a memory or a fantasy, which is presumably presented in the present tense because it is entirely present to her. The two lovers lying down in "the shape of a gondola" create a unique elongated form. This in turn leads to a statement about Venice in winter: "Venice is gorgeous cold." But the specific date — "3 December" — leads her back to her own room, her sense of isolation, her fear of being locked in, locked out: "Unspeakable anxiety about locked-in syndrome, about a fourth world." Two extremes of isolation are bound together: the individual who cannot move or communicate and the subpopulation of people socially excluded from global society. The speaker is terrified of both exclusions.

This recluse confesses: "I cannot promise to say." She may not be able to speak her "unspeakable anxiety," but she does note that her figure for herself, the "violin spider," "Has six good eyes, arranged in threes." She is hyper-observant. The next statement is indented for emphasis:

> The rims of wounds have wounds
as well.

This oracular declaration suggests that wounds continue to enlarge; even the outermost parts of wounds have wounds. What is implied, but not stated, is that the speaker's psychological wounds have continued to ramify. They have grown "rims," and the "rims" are also wounded. The injury is far-reaching.

There is an unspoken trauma or anguish underlying all this, which the speaker acknowledges: "Sphinx, small print, you are inscrutable." She links the sphinx, that enigmatic mythical creature with the head of a human and the body of a lion, with the small print in a formal agreement, the part that is binding but might be overlooked. There are things she cannot understand — some monstrous, some miniature — and they are also part of herself.

The poem closes as if in the midst of a journey:

> On the roads, blue thistles, barely
>
> Visible by night, and, by these, you may yet find your way home.

This suggests that the speaker, who once again refers to herself in the second person, has gotten lost in the dark. Like a figure in a fairy tale, she has found herself wandering on dark roads at night. But she also sees blue thistles, spiny perennials, which are scarcely visible. What can be dimly or duskily perceived may yet let her find her way home, the place where she started out. The phrase "may yet" is delicate and suggests that, though not inevitable, it is still possible for her to find her way back.

Brock-Broido's quirky, enigmatic lyric reveals and releases its secrets in stages, one by one. It may never give up all of them. But it does present an extraordinary portrait of a poet thinking about the end of her life. We know something deep and true about what she was like. How she thought, who she was. "Infinite Riches in the Smallest Room" is a sumptuous self-portrait of a poet in extremis, a precise enactment of her extravagant imagination.

YUSEF KOMUNYAKAA

"The African Burial Ground"

(2014)

Yusef Komunyakaa's poem "The African Burial Ground" is a remembrance and an awakening. It has a quiet, insistent drumbeat that brings back the spirit of a forgotten people. The poem names and invokes a sacred space in lower Manhattan where the remains of enslaved and free Africans who lived and died in New York are now buried.

The African Burial Ground

They came as Congo, Guinea, & Angola,
    feet tuned to rhythms of a thumb piano.
        They came to work fields of barley & flax,

livestock, stone & slab, brick & mortar,
    to make wooden barrels, some going
        from slave to servant & half-freeman.

They built tongue & groove — wedged
    into their place in New Amsterdam.
        Decades of seasons changed the city

from Dutch to York, & dream-footed
    hard work rattled their bones.
        They danced Ashanti. They lived

& died. Shrouded in cloth, in cedar
    & pine coffins, Trinity Church
        owned them in six & a half acres

of sloping soil. Before speculators
    arrived grass & weeds overtook
        what was most easily forgotten,

& tannery shops drained there.
    Did descendants & newcomers
        shoulder rock & heave loose gravel

into the landfill before building crews
    came, their guitars & harmonicas
        chasing away ghosts at lunch break?

Soon, footsteps of lower Manhattan
    strutted overhead, back & forth
        between old denials & new arrivals,

going from major to minor pieties,
    always on the go. The click of heels
        the tap of a drum awaking the dead.

Komunyakaa's memorial poem employs a form that he has often used be-
fore — a vernacular triadic or three-step stanza, which unfolds into three de-
scending and indented parts. It was invented by William Carlos Williams to
address the problem of freedom and form in modern poetry. But whereas Wil-
liams conceived of "the variable foot" as the three stages of a single long line,

Komunyakaa works it as a downward ladder of three interconnected lines. Here he employs it with great rhythmic flexibility and pulse to shape his experience.

Komunyakaa skillfully varies end-stopped and enjambed lines within his three-step stanza. As you reread the poem, pay special attention to the extra pause and emphasis at the ends of lines that carry over. Some of them seem to leap over an abyss, such as "some going / from slave to servant . . ." or "Trinity Church / owned them . . ." The word "wedged" at the top of the third stanza creates a feeling of how these people were hemmed in, "wedged / into their place . . ." The people who strut overhead go "back & forth / between old denials & new arrivals." Sometimes the poet creates an extra emphasis by varying longer sentences with shorter ones, such as the declaration, which takes up just half a line, that "They danced Ashanti." Syncopation often occurs between the sentence and the line. Notice, for example, the line break and stanza break falling within one short sentence, the gulf that opens in "They lived // & died."

It's worth pausing to say something about Komunyakaa's use of the ampersand. This shorthand symbol for the conjunction "and" is something that he borrowed from his predecessors John Berryman, Etheridge Knight, and Larry Levis, and it adds an element of colloquial or jazzy informality and casual intimacy to his poems, which nod to the spoken even as they are written. Here that informality jostles a little with the formality of a visit to sacred ground.

"The African Burial Ground" begins by remembering the people themselves: "They came as Congo, Guinea, & Angola." The speaker pointedly does not say "They came *from* the Congo, Guinea, & Angola." These people are not so much from those African countries as they are embodiments of them. The second line — "feet tuned to rhythms of a thumb piano" — recalls how they came with their own music inside them. The reference to the thumb piano, an African percussion instrument, shows the people moving from one continent to the other, carrying their own rhythm. These Africans may have been used to dancing, but they were brought to the New World in order to work. And they had been brought from three of the sites where the buying and selling of people took place.

The poem focuses on the daily lives of these Africans in the New World, the backbreaking work they were forced to do, how they persevered. It doesn't concentrate on the cruelty inflicted upon them, though that hovers in the background. After all, much of the poem compresses, encapsulates, and dramatizes a history of slavery in New York City, which marks the progress of people "from slave to servant & half-freeman." The speaker focuses on Black people and their experience, though he also recognizes the horrifying reality of slavery as part of the larger history of New York itself, the transformation of New Amsterdam, the name of the seventeenth-century Dutch settlement established at the southern tip of what is now known as Manhattan.

The Dutch slave trade started in 1626 when the Dutch West India Company imported eleven African slaves. The first slave auction was held in 1655. The British expanded slavery in New York so much that by the early eighteenth century more than 40 percent of white households held slaves, often as domestic servants and laborers. Slavery in New York officially ended in 1827, though many Africans were forced to stay on as bound servants. The poem aptly calls them "half-free." This is a part of our history that most white people would prefer to forget.

There has been a tendency to think of slavery, that so-called peculiar institution, as a nineteenth-century cruelty rooted in the South. This has been the primary focus of many poems about slavery too. But Komunyakaa forces us to recall that it was also part of life in the North, part of the colonial history of our most cosmopolitan metropolis. It happened during the time when the city was changing from Dutch to British. He memorializes those people who lived in African dreams and North American realities, who were "dream-footed" even as "hard work rattled their bones." "They danced Ashanti" — they kept alive and "danced" the traditional culture they had brought with them from the Gold Coast of Africa, what is now central Ghana.

There is a transition in the poem where the speaker pauses to summarize: "They lived // & died." He describes how they were buried ("Shrouded in cloth, in cedar / & pine coffins") and where ("Trinity Church / owned them in six & a half acres // of sloping soil"). The word "owned" has poisonous power. The speaker's bitterness about this history has thus far been kept at bay, but it breaks through as he describes how the land lapsed and the people were forgotten until "speculators" arrived:

> Did descendants & newcomers
>   shoulder rock & heave loose gravel
>
> into the landfill before building crews
>   came, their guitars & harmonicas
>   chasing away ghosts at lunch break?

These are ghostly, hallowed grounds, and he wonders whether modern workers, or "building crews," used music to chase away "ghosts."

The poem encapsulates a second history. In 1991, the city of New York began construction on a thirty-four-story federal office tower and adjoining four-story pavilion on lower Broadway. But workers stumbled upon intact human skeletal remains thirty feet under street level. A federally mandated archaeological dig subsequently uncovered a six-and-one-half-acre burial ground, which had been subsumed under decades of urban development and landfill. The African community in New York had created its own burial ground far from the city's main one. This sacred space dates from the mid-1630s to 1795. Some fifteen thousand people are buried there.

What ensued was a furious quarrel over this burial ground. As Spencer P. M. Harrington writes, "African-American outrage over the handling of the excavation stemmed from a perception that the black community had no control over the fate of its heritage — that decisions about the burial ground were being made by white bureaucrats with little insight into African-American history and spiritual sensitivities." The site is now a national monument. It has been studied to give us a much fuller sense of African life — and death — in New York and elsewhere.

The last lines of the poem are both telling and troubling:

> Soon, footsteps of lower Manhattan
> strutted overhead, back & forth
> between old denials & new arrivals,
>
> going from major to minor pieties,
> always on the go. The click of heels
> the tap of a drum awaking the dead.

It didn't take long — "Soon" — for the modern city to return to business as usual. People are passing by this burial ground, rushing overhead without any awareness that they are treading on the graves of Africans. We think of people going "back & forth" between places, but Komunyakaa pairs the words "old" and "new" to suggest that they are passing to and fro in constant movement between "old denials & new arrivals." The phrase "old denials" resonates with the long-standing American pattern of refusing to come to terms with the hard truths about slavery, the people brought to America against their will. Newcomers and others in the modern city are blissfully unaware of where they are treading. The speaker sardonically characterizes their daily lives, "going from major to minor pieties, / always on the go." In their supercharged busy days, they rush unthinking through life.

There is no comma at the end of the penultimate line; imagine an equal sign there. The passing by of pedestrians, "the click of heels," is equated to "the tap of a drum awaking the dead." People are literally walking above the burial ground, and Komunyakaa connects this to the tapping of a drum. He is referencing and summoning up the key place of the drum in traditional African communities, how it acts as a heartbeat, how it is used to communicate and make music, to contact the other world. Here the click of heels awakens the dead who have been sleeping for centuries in the ground below.

KATE DANIELS

———

"The Addict's Mother: Birth Story"

(2014–15)

In her fifth book, *In the Months of My Son's Recovery,* Kate Daniels writes about heroin addiction not from the point of view of a recovering addict but from the position of the addict's mother. In other words, she situates herself in maternal relationship to addiction and recovery. She is well aware that the primary drama is not something that is happening to her — she is not her son — but she feels the collateral damage. She also feels somehow responsible — painfully close, helpless, guilt-ridden. She too is suffering — at one remove.

The second section of the book is called "The Addict's Mother." Here is its second poem:

> ### The Addict's Mother: Birth Story
>
> She wasn't watching when they cut him
> Out. C-section, you know. Green drape
> Obscuring the mound of ripened belly
> They extracted him from. He spilled
> Out squalling, already starving. Still

Stitching her up, they fastened him
To her breast so he could feed. There
He rooted for the milk, so lustful
In his sucking that weeping roses
Grew from the edges of her nipples.
For weeks, they festered there,
Blooming bloody trails anew each
And every time he made a meal of her.
I know what you're thinking.
But he was her child.
She had to let him
Do that to her.

Daniels has always been a self-scrutinizing poet. Influenced by Sharon Olds, she is like Olds a personal poet, and she sometimes takes extra precautions to distance herself from the speaker of her poems. Hence the disclaimer to her book: "These poems are narrated by a character similar, but not identical, to myself . . ." This may be helpful psychologically to the poet and a useful reminder to the reader that the speaker in a poem is in some sense what Emily Dickinson called "a supposed person." And yet Daniels does also give us a first-hand account of her family's experience. She writes from the inside of the opioid epidemic. That's not a fiction.

"The Addict's Mother" came out of Daniels's own experience. She has verified that her son weighed 10.5 pounds at birth though he was born by C-section two weeks early, and he was such a voracious feeder that he wounded her just by trying to get a sip of milk. The poem began long after he had grown up, starting with a hunch about the commingling of maternal love and bodily violence. Just as Thom Gunn decided to write about his mother's suicide from a third-person point of view, so Daniels's most consequential decision in this poem was to dramatize in the third person her own experience of giving birth. She almost treats it as something that has happened to someone else. There's a certain alienation in the experience; the mother can't see her child being pulled out of her.

Formally speaking, this short free-verse poem consists of a single stanza of seventeen lines. The diction is informal and somewhat colloquial, but by capitalizing the first letter of each line Daniels also adds a certain quiet formality. As you reread the poem, notice how many sentences end just after the line itself ends and breaks. A single word (or words) hangs out there by itself at the line's end. There is something unnerving in these slightly arrhythmic line breaks, which enact the discomfort of the experience the poet is describing. This jolt is heightened by the fact that each line begins with a touch of the formal.

The poem starts with a declaration and a violent line break at the end of the first line: "She wasn't watching when they cut him / Out." The second line halts abruptly after that first word, and then picks up again in an oddly offhanded manner, as if the poet — or the speaker — is talking intimately to the reader: "C-section, you know." The green drape cuts her off from seeing herself giving birth.

The next lines turn the poem into a sort of parable. Notice the hissing *s* sounds that tie the words together: "He *s*pilled / Out *s*qualling, already *s*tarving." The push of the line enacts the feeling of the baby spilling out from his mother. The phrase "already starving" is the first hint of the baby's need, the son's future addiction. The *s*'s continue and now alliteratively blend with the letter *t*. The sound is especially aggressive in the sound of the letters *sti* in the crossover of "*Sti*ll" to "*Sti*tching." Listen again to get the full effect of a sentence that holds off the subject and verb: "*Sti*ll / *Sti*tching her up, they fa*s*tened him / *T*o her brea*s*t *s*o he could feed." It all happens so quickly. She is still being stitched back together from her C-section when he is already fixed on her.

The next lines are the heart of the poem: "There / He rooted for the milk, so lustful / In his sucking that weeping roses / Grew from the edges of her nipples." Here Daniels turns a baby's natural lust for the mother's breast into a sign of future addiction. He sucks and bites so hard on her nipples that they fester into wounds. The baby is draining his mother, making a meal of her, sustaining himself by feeding on her. She provides the substance that triggers his overwhelming hunger. But what she understood at the time to be natural appetite she has now begun to intuit was really something else, something closer to craving, or at least some form of pre-craving, an overwhelming neediness that may tend toward substance abuse.

There is a striking moment when the speaker directly addresses the reader again, as if making a confession. For the first time, the sentence and the line coincide, forming an intact unit: "I know what you're thinking." And what are we thinking? Only what the speaker has led us to think, which is that the mother has let the infant suck her dry. She projects the idea onto the reader, onto you and me, that she has let him take too much out of her. She feels marked or singled out as an addict's mother and puts the reader in the position of judging her a failure, although, really, she is the one who is judging herself. She says, "I know what you're thinking" precisely because she knows what she herself is thinking.

That's when the poem takes an argumentative turn, as in the conclusion to a sonnet, with another one-sentence line: "But he was her child." The last two lines thus explain or rationalize the situation. As readers, we register the aggressive enjambment that divides this simple sentence into two equal parts: "She had to let him / Do that to her." The guilt here is overwhelming. The speaker realizes that she has somehow enabled her son's addiction, but she throws up her hands, as if in bewilderment: What else was she to do? He was her child. She couldn't help herself. She had to sacrifice herself for him.

It is strange and troubling that "The Addict's Mother: Birth Story" reads addiction back into childbirth and breastfeeding. A mother and son become locked in a mutual, near-death struggle. The poet creates a poem from her own experience as a mother. But she has also split herself off from the situation in order to understand the bond that she has created with her son. She is overwhelmed by the way that she has unwittingly enabled his addiction. And she also wonders if either of them could have done anything else. Maybe they were doomed from the start.

AFAA MICHAEL WEAVER

——

"Spirit Boxing"

(2015)

Spirit Boxing" is one of Afaa Michael Weaver's most representative poems because it combines the brutality of his early experience working in a factory with his later spiritual interest in Chinese martial arts and healing. Weaver has spoken of working-class "interiority" as "a very solid tool of resistance against working-class oppression." Here he brings that interiority together with something that he has gleaned from his long practice in the art of Taiji, or tai chi.

Weaver spent fifteen years as a factory worker in his native Baltimore. He worked first at Bethlehem Steel and then at Procter & Gamble, scribbling lines of poetry during coffee breaks and writing after his shift. "In the warehouse, it was thousands of boxes circling around — every day the same thing," he recalls. "You felt like you were being pounded into anonymity. Holding on to the poetry was a way of keeping myself alive."

Here is the testimonial that he wrote forty years after starting work in the warehouse:

Spirit Boxing

It is the tightness in the gut when the load
is heavy enough to knock me over backwards,
turn me back on my heel until my ankle cracks

and I holler out Jesus, this Jesus of Joe Gans
setting up for the next punch while taking in
one that just made his soul wobble, the grunt

I make when the shift is young, my body
a heavy meat on bones, conveyors not wired
for compassion, trucks on deadlines, uncaring

pressure of a nation waiting to be washed, made
clean, me looking into the eye of something like
death, and I look up, throwing fifty-pound boxes,

Jesus now John Henry pounding visions of what
work is, the wish for black life to crumble, snap
under all it is given, these three souls of spirit,

hands like hammers, a hammer like the word
made holy, word echoing a scripture from inside
the wise mind that knows men cannot be makers,

that in making we want to break each other,
ache moving us to refuse to surrender in time
in factories, catacombs feeding on the spirit.

"Spirit Boxing" has a vigorous kinetic energy. It drives you forward as it winds one long sentence across seven three-line stanzas. It doesn't take time to linger over any one of its myriad references. The movement enacts the experience, which takes place in the present tense: "It *is* the tightness in the gut when the load / *is* heavy enough . . ." This all seems to be happening now. But the poet who is writing this is catapulting himself back into the past. The combination gives Weaver a canny perspective, the ability to re-create an experience in the present while summoning up a range of references. He is working on the floor in a factory, but he is also placing that experience in a larger perspective.

"Spirit Boxing" is a poem of great velocity, but we need to slow it down to talk about how it works. It's as if the speaker has just entered the ring. The workload is a fighter who immediately knocks him back on his heels. The boxes are so heavy that they've got him staggering on the ropes. He has been hit so hard that he cries out "Jesus," which sets off a trail of associations. Weaver seems especially alert to his own phrasing and often builds on it. The exclamation leads him to "Jesus of Joe Gans / setting up for the next punch while taking in / one that just made his soul wobble."

By making up a new name, "Jesus of Joe Gans," Weaver references one of the greatest American boxers, the Black fighter Joe Gans, who came from Weaver's side of town, the East End of Baltimore. Gans won the world lightweight title in 1902 and thus became the first African American to win a world championship in any sport. He was dubbed "The Old Master" and known for his slick technique, his ability to knock out an opponent with either hand. Yet the fights were sometimes rigged against him. He also lost an eye and kept on fighting. H. L. Mencken called him "the most gentlemanly pugilist on earth," and Weaver goes one step further by linking him to the Christian savior, though in a sort of curse. This is a savior who must take one soul-wobbling punch while setting up another. Like the fighter, the speaker grunts, and the poem quickly continues.

"Spirit Boxing" captures the hard physicality of factory work, but it also manages to build a subtle critique of capitalism, and its dehumanizing force, through a series of rapid associations.

> my body
> a heavy meat on bones, conveyors not wired
> for compassion, trucks on deadlines, uncaring
>
> pressure of a nation waiting to be washed, made
> clean, me looking into the eye of something like
> death, and I look up, throwing fifty-pound boxes, . . .

The worker is reduced to animal status, his body "a heavy meat on bones," though the conveyor belts don't care; they move relentlessly forward, like the trucks pulling out of the warehouse to make their deadlines, to fulfill the needs of consumers, the "uncaring / [*pause for the line break*] pressure of a nation waiting to be washed, made / [*pause for the line break*] clean." Notice the consonance of the letter *c* that threads "conveyors" to "compassion" and then "compassion" to "uncaring" and "clean." The speaker is working in a factory that produces soaps and detergents. At P & G, Weaver often stacked boxes of soap by hand. He recalls how they came like soldiers around the curves on conveyor belts. The heaviest were boxes of one hundred giant bars of Ivory hand soap. Weaver uses the boxes of soap as a metaphor for what the country wants, something that will cleanse it of its sins. In the meantime, the worker is practically killing himself with hard labor, looking straight into the eye not of a person but of something that feels very much like death, looking back up to "throw" fifty-pound boxes onto skids or trucks.

This action makes the speaker think of an African American folk hero — "Jesus now John Henry" — the legendary "steel-driving man" who boasted that no machine could ever break him down:

> Before I let that steel drill beat me down
> I'll die with this hammer in my hand
> I'll die with this hammer in my hand

John Henry famously won a race against a steam-powered rock-drilling machine to cut through a mountain, but he died with a hammer in his hand. The hammer is the object of transference here; the experience of being hammered connects boxing, John Henry, and the Christian savior.

The poem takes another associative punch when it asserts that "Jesus now John Henry pounding visions of what / work is . . ." There is a nod to Philip Levine in the phrase "what work is," the title poem of Levine's 1992 collection. Weaver's phrasing is a way of tipping his hat to one of his few older contemporaries who placed work and working people at the center of his poetry. Weaver uses a line break to divide Levine's phrase into "what / work is" and thus emphasizes the "whatness," or materiality, of manual labor.

Joe Gans and John Henry were both heroes of African American life. Race is relevant here, and the poem moves on to a series of associations about a system that wants "black life to crumble, snap / under all it is given . . ." But the Black poet refuses to buckle and instead sweeps up three figures connected by hammers and hammering, all more than just fighters, "these three souls of spirit."

The notion of "spirit boxing" is coming into focus. These three souls of spirit are also fighting for the spirit with their "hands like hammers, a hammer like the word / made holy, word echoing a scripture from inside / the wise mind that knows men cannot be makers . . ." The hammer is compared to the word (or the Word), which is sacred, which in turn echoes a spirit from "inside the wise mind . . ." That wise mind seems to refer to God, "Creator of heaven and earth." Weaver seems to be arguing that human beings cannot be God or gods, who create life, because we have destructive impulses that lead us to destroy one another ("that in making we want to break each other . . .").

Particular sounds start to pile up at the conclusion of this poem. Listen to how three words are tied together by the *m* sounds in the line "the wise *m*ind that knows *m*en cannot be *m*akers." So too these sounds echo as rhyme emerges in the words "makers," "making," "break," and "ache." It is almost as if the sounds of the words are driving the thought, the spirit of resistance, the rising against oppression: "ache moving us to refuse to surrender in time / in factories, catacombs feeding on the spirit." Factory work is spirit killing — as if factories have been specifically designed to crush Black life — and working in a factory is a form of spirit boxing. But the three great spirits invoked in the poem — Jesus, Joe Gans, and John Henry — refuse to surrender. They won't crumple or give up.

This leads us back to the title of the poem: "Spirit Boxing." Weaver has literalized this martial arts term in a specific way by applying it to factory work. As a spiritual discipline, spirit boxing aims to utilize and also transcend the mechanics, techniques, and physical aspects of boxing. Its definition is "to look within and gather one's true essence and inner strength, directing the will, thereby activating the power of the mind and harnessing the 'Chi.'" That is called the Tao of Spirit Boxing.

Afaa Michael Weaver has found his own Tao, his own path or way, in this hard-won and exacting poem.

VICTORIA CHANG

—◆—

"Obit [The Blue Dress]"

(2016)

After a long illness, Victoria Chang's mother died on August 6, 2015, of pulmonary fibrosis. Her mother's death made the poet feel as if almost everything around her had also died. She was surprised by grief and wrote an entire series of obituary poems over a two-week period of somewhat crazed mourning; she then revised them over the next year.

Each of Chang's grief-stricken poems for her mother is spaced on the page in a way that makes it look objective and impersonal, like a newspaper obituary. The visual display is reminiscent of Renaissance figure poems, in which words are arranged to form a perceivable design that mimics the subject. Chang's poems create a tension between highly subjective content, which includes a series of quirky questions, and the coldness of print, which imparts its own kind of finality. But these are anything but official obituaries. "Obit," after all, is an informal word for "obituary."

Obit [The Blue Dress]

The Blue Dress — died on August 6, 2015, along with the little blue
flowers, all silent. Once the petals looked up. Now small pieces of
dust. I wonder whether they burned the dress or just the body? I won-
der who lifted her up into the fire? I wonder if her hair brushed his
cheek before it grew into a bonfire? I wonder what sound the body
made as it burned? They dyed her hair for the funeral, too black. She
looked like a comic character. I waited for the next comic panel, to see
the speech bubble and what she might say. But her words never came
and we were left with the stillness of blown glass. The irreversibility of
rain. And millions of little blue flowers. Imagination is having to live
in a dead person's future. Grief is wearing a dead person's dress forever.

One of the moving things about this poem is the way it metonymically dis-
places the obituary for the poet's mother into an obituary for the mother's out-
fit (The Blue Dress). We learn about the mother by reading about her dress.
In this way, it is a sideways or angular elegy. It reminds me of the prose poem
"Night Singer" by the Argentine poet Alejandra Pizarnik, which begins, "She
who died of her blue dress is singing . . . Inside her song there is a blue dress."

"Obit" drills down on a set of questions about what happens to the pretty
dress with small blue flowers, which the family has picked for the mother to
wear in her coffin. The flowers themselves seem to flame into life momentarily
("Once the petals looked up") but then are snuffed out ("Now small pieces of
dust"). Since the mother can no longer choose an appropriate outfit — how
she dressed had obviously mattered to her — the family chooses one that re-
minds them of her. They want her to look pretty. This is one of the many small
countless rituals involved in preparing for a funeral. In one sense, selecting the
right dress is not exactly a pressing concern — after all, the mother is dead and
the dress is simply something to be worn in the coffin — but it also mimics the
way certain details loom large after a death. Sometimes in the shock of grief,
the mind fixes on odd, seemingly irrelevant items. For example, as the speaker
broods about her mother's cremation, she comes up with a strange question:
"I wonder whether they burned the dress or just the body?"

The speaker can't help but comment on the way that her mother's hair has
been dyed. It's too black, much blacker than she had worn it, which makes her
look comical. This kind of disconcerting observation, which many of us have

made while looking into the coffin of a loved one, never appears in a newspaper obituary. The speaker appreciates her own wit — "I waited for the next comic panel, to see the speech bubble and what she might say." But then she is brought back to the stark reality of the situation — "But her words never came and we were left with the stillness of blown glass." Since blown glass is shaped by forcing air into a ball of molten glass, there is something eerie and appropriate in linking it to the mother's absence of breath, the silence or stillness after death. From this silence, the speaker makes an associative leap to "The irreversibility of rain." Like death, rain is a natural phenomenon that humans cannot intervene in. Indeed, the blue flowers on the dress now somehow morph into millions of little blue flowers, the beauty and impersonality of nature.

In this elegy, subjective questions about a mother keep bumping up against the objective reality of her death. There is a moment where Chang adapts and darkens Richard Siken's line "I live in someone else's future" (from "The Worm King's Lullaby") into "Imagination is having to live in a dead person's future." She imagines, objectifies, and generalizes grief into the experience of "wearing a dead person's dress forever." Grief is personified and characterized here. The mother is gone and so is her blue dress. And yet somehow this poet — this elegy and obituary — will inhabit it forever.

TOI DERRICOTTE

"Pantoum for the Broken"

(2017)

Toi Derricotte had already written "Beds" (2011), a series of difficult, harrowing, essayistic prose poems about her father's violence during her childhood ("He'd explain how he had studied hard so he knew where to hit me and not leave a single mark") when she turned to the traditional form of the pantoum to confront another unspeakable subject: what it's like for young girls to be violated, molested, and harmed, sometimes by an unknown perpetrator, sometimes by a person who is all too well known. In this shocking poem Derricotte deploys the pantoum form to dramatize sexual abuse, capturing an experience that is extremely difficult to write or talk about. In just five stanzas, twenty lines, she unmasks a horrific brutality and somehow connects to a community of survivors.

Pantoum for the Broken

How many of us were fingered?
A soft thing with a hole in it,

a thing that won't tell, that can't.
I forget how many times I was broken,

a soft thing with a hole in it.
Some remember, grateful it wasn't worse;
I forget how many times I was broken.
Someone faceless rolled on me like a horse.

Some remember, grateful it wasn't worse.
Some forget but their bodies do inexplicable things.
Someone faceless rolled on me like a horse.
Sleepwalking, I go back to where it happens.

Some forget but their bodies do inexplicable things.
We don't know when or why or who broke in.
Sleepwalking, we go back to where it happens.
Not wanting to go back, we make it happen.

If we escaped, will we escape again?
I leapt from my body like a burning thing.
Not wanting to go back, I make it happen
until I hold the broken one, hold her and sing.

The pantoum originated as an oral Malayan form — it first entered written literature in the fifteenth century — and Derricotte retains something of its original spoken quality. The form is highly, perhaps even obsessively repetitive. It consists of interweaving quatrains of indeterminate length. The second and fourth lines of each stanza repeat as the first and third lines of the following stanza. Every stanza takes four steps forward and two steps back — and thus, as a form, it keeps looking back over its shoulder. The fact that it turns back while moving forward makes it well suited to poems of loss, such as Donald Justice's "Pantoum of the Great Depression," and poems of departure, such as Louis MacNeice's "Leaving Barra." But these poems are gentle compared to "Pantoum for the Broken." Also, the pantoum started out as a disjunctive form (the first two lines had no apparent connection to the second set of lines), and here Derricotte employs disjunctive memory in her poem of severe brokenness.

"How many of us were fingered?" — is there a more appalled or appalling opening line in the history of the pantoum? The word "fingered" does double service here: its primary meaning points to a horrifying sexual violation. But the word also means "targeted," and the sense of being fingered by sexual predators also comes into play.

Each end-stopped line in a pantoum tends to present a statement, and Derricotte shocks the reader by showing how young girls have been reduced to objects: "A soft thing with a hole in it, / a thing that won't tell, that can't." The partial rhyme that connects the small but crucial words "it" and "can't" reinforces the feeling of helplessness. The pronouns related to these girls switch from the third-person plural — "How many of *us* were fingered" — to the first-person singular: "*I* forget how many times *I* was broken." The words "fingered" and "broken" emphatically do not rhyme, another disjunction. The first stanza ends not with a period, but a comma, and the double pause of line break and punctuation emphasizes the connection to the beginning of the second stanza: "I forget how many times I was broken, // a soft thing with a hole in it."

In a strong pantoum, every time a line repeats, it accrues a different or additional meaning. The first time Derricotte evokes "a soft thing with a hole in it," she is referring to the vagina of a young girl. But the second time, because the line comes after the horrifying confession "I forget how many times I was broken," the image comes also to stand for the speaker's whole self. The wound has grown. She has been broken so many times that she has been hollowed out.

For the rest of the poem, Derricotte moves fluently between the plural and the singular to reflect on memories of sexual abuse: "Some remember, grateful it wasn't worse; / I forget how many times I was broken." Some may be grateful that the violence wasn't even worse, a documented perspective among some survivors of trauma, but the speaker evidently isn't one of them. Derricotte has said that the next image came to her from a recurring childhood dream: "Someone faceless rolled on me like a horse. / Sleepwalking, I go back to where it happens." Each successive statement comes at us like a blow, reenacting the horror as the speaker keeps going back to it, in memory. Thus, the pantoum enacts a series of compulsive returns.

It is purposeful to reduce the abuser, in this case an unnamed man, to "someone faceless." The face is the center of human recognition. If the human face "orders and ordains" us, as the philosopher Emmanuel Lévinas declares, the abuser has been reduced here to something less than human, the animal body and nothing more; hence the simile "Someone faceless rolled on me like a horse." The comparison seems to add on to the action, doubling it, repeating it, worsening it. The mention of the horse also harkens back to the speaker's sense of being broken. To break a horse is to stamp out its spirit and conquer it. That's precisely what the sexual predator is doing to the young girl. The horror is reinforced by the dissonant near rhyme of the words "worse" and "horse," which emphatically reoccurs in the next stanza.

Derricotte's speaker summarizes how the experience of abuse shapes different people, sometimes through remembering, sometimes through forgetting:

> Some remember, grateful it wasn't worse.
> Some forget but their bodies do inexplicable things.
> Someone faceless rolled on me like a horse.
> Sleepwalking, I go back to where it happens.

The word "faceless" also evokes the idea of facing or not facing up to something. Nonetheless, whether one remembers or forgets, confronting or avoiding the past, the return is inescapable. It turns some women into "sleepwalkers," others into people who go through life doing things that they can't understand.

It's worth pausing a moment to focus on the rhyming of this pantoum. In every stanza, Derricotte reinforces connections with a single close or near rhyme. Two lines rhyme, but two others do not. Recall the words "it" and "can't" (stanza 1), "worse" and "horse" (stanzas 2 and 3), "in" and "happen" (stanza 4). Throughout the poem, the lines that rhyme reinforce a sense of connectedness; the lines that don't rhyme reinforce a feeling of brokenness. This pattern also fortifies the poem's dialogue between remembering and forgetting.

There is a turn, or change in sound, in the penultimate stanza. Here the lines that don't rhyme are brought into closer relation with the words "things" and "happen." You hear the jangling repetition of the letter *n* in all four words: "things," "in," "happen," "happens." Something is happening—and the thing that is happening is enacted in the sound.

This sound carries forward into the final stanza, where all four end-words are also connected. But now, for the first time, the entire stanza rhymes in a simple alternation, *abab:*

> If we escaped, will we escape *again*?
> I leapt from my body like a burning *thing*.
> Not wanting to go back, I make it *happen*
> until I hold the broken one, hold her and *sing*.

The rhyming doesn't just strengthen the meaning; it enacts a movement from one form of speech to another. The speaker is transforming herself — and other victims of sexual abuse — from objects into subjects. She is reclaiming their personhood. They are becoming singers, and the language is lifting off.

The last stanza opens with a question — "If we escaped, will we escape again?" It is followed by a recollection of how the speaker herself once responded: "I leapt from my body like a burning thing." The consonant *b* presses the word "body" toward the word "burning," and the analogy captures the urgency. The "thing that won't tell" had become a "burning thing" that needed to vault away from the speaker's own body — as if she were jumping out of a burning building. In the last two lines, Derricotte dramatizes a fear that is faced and conquered: "Not wanting to go back, I make it happen / until I hold the broken one, hold her and sing." Note the change from "we" in the penultimate stanza to "I" in the last stanza — this is the single crucial transformation of the pantoum form. Derricotte has carefully saved it for the final two lines. The speaker does not want to return to the past, and thus she must return in order to transfigure it. She is the only one who can make that happen.

The last line transports this poem from speech into song, and into determined action. The speaker has created a split and a coming together: the part of the self that survives is holding and consoling the part of the self that was victimized. She is holding and consoling her younger self, the broken part of her. The speaker is being transformed. Something has been completed; something is being sung. "Pantoum for the Broken" has become a poem not just of brokenness but also of healing.

MEENA ALEXANDER

———

"Krishna, 3:29 A.M."

(2018)

Meena Alexander was a poet of dislocation and exile, of what she termed "fault lines." She wrote "Krishna, 3:29 A.M." when she was deep in the midst of a doomed fight against cancer. It is a dark-night-of-the-soul poem, a summing up. In the end, it turns into an *ars poetica*. In this way, it is like Wisława Szymborska's "Under One Small Star" and Heather McHugh's "What He Thought," though it has a much more pressing personal reality, since Alexander was facing her own death when she wrote it. She is the "you" in the poem, the memories are hers, and this may suggest that she wasn't quite ready to let go.

Krishna, 3:29 A.M.

In a crumpled shirt (so casual for a god)

Bow tucked loosely under an arm still jittery from battle

He balanced himself on a flat boat painted black.

Each wave as I kneel closer a migrant flag

A tongue with syllables no script can catch.

The many births you have passed through, try to remember them as I do mine

Memory is all you have.

Still, how much can you bear on your back?

You've lost one language, gained another, lost a third.

There's nothing you'll inherit, neither per stirpes nor per capita

No plot by the riverbank in your father's village of Kozencheri

Or by the burning ghat in Varanasi.

All you have is a writing hand smeared with ink and little bits of paper

Swirling in a violent wind.

I am a blue-black child cheeks swollen with a butter ball

I stole from mama's kitchen

Stones and sky and stars melt in my mouth

Wooden spoon in hand she chased me

Round and round the tamarind tree.

I am musk in the wings of the koel which nests in that tree —

You heard its cry in the jolting bus from Santa Monica to Malibu

After the Ferris wheel, the lovers with their wind slashed hair

Toxic foam on the drifts of the ocean

Come the dry cactus lands

The child who crosses the border water bottle in hand

Fallen asleep in the aisle where backpacks and sodden baskets are stashed.

Out of her soiled pink skirt whirl these blood-scratched skies

And all the singing rifts of story.

The speaker is reading the Bhagavad Gita, the Song of God, in the middle of the night. The title yokes the boundless vision of Krishna, the eighth incarnation of Lord Vishnu, to the specificity of the hour (3:29 A.M.), which is calculated down to the minute. We are very precisely located at a moment in time. Alexander's last poem follows the format that Michael Collier employed in "An Individual History" and Lucie Brock-Broido used in her summary poem "Infinite Riches in the Smallest Room"; it consists of a series of single lines, each isolated on the page. It takes an extra leap to get from one line to the next, as if to suggest that thinking comes in fragments at this hour of the night, this late moment in life.

Things get disjointed, and the thinking is not linear, but associative. The first line shows us Krishna in human form, though the speaker is wryly aware that the text (or the translator) is going a little far in picturing him wearing a crumpled shirt. Hence the parenthetical joke ("so casual for a god"). The first three lines present Krishna, who has taken human form, returning from battle with his celestial bow, or Sharanga, and balancing on a boat. The reference here is not only to Krishna in the Bhagavad Gita but also, perhaps even more so, to Krishna in the tenth book of the Bhagavata Purana (The Beautiful Legend of God), which Alexander especially loved. This text presents the stories of Krishna first as a mischievous child, then as an adolescent who lollygagged with young cow-herding girls, and always as a miracle worker. Alexander often returned to one of her favorite stories, the sly tale of Krishna stealing butter to feed to the monkeys.

The next verses of the poem ("Each wave as I kneel closer a migrant flag / A tongue with syllables no script can catch") show the speaker leaning into the text, looking down into the water that surrounds Krishna's boat, reading between the lines. The image of the waves provides a portal to her own past. That's why each wave becomes "a migrant flag," a symbolic banner of displacement, of moving into exile. It is a "tongue with syllables" that could never be captured by a "script." It will always evade the written word.

The sea evoked strong feelings in Alexander. She was born in Allahabad, India, though when she was five years old her father, a meteorologist for the Indian government, took a post in Sudan, a newly independent country in northeast Africa. She celebrated her birthday on an ocean liner headed for Khartoum. "The sea cast me loose," she recalled in *Poetics of Dislocation*. "The sea tore away from me all that I had." It encouraged a subterranean inner life, she thought, but at great cost.

That interior life operates in "Krishna, 3:29 A.M.," and so does the sense of its cost. The poem is triggered by what the poet is reading, what she is listening for in and even imposing on the text. That's why it turns to a *shloka,* or metered passage, in the Gita: "*The many births you have passed through, try to remember them as I do mine / Memory is all you have.*" This reference modifies chapter 4, verse 5, where Krishna says, "You and I have passed through many births, Arjuna. You have forgotten, but I remember them all."

Alexander takes Krishna's words and wrenches them into "*Memory is all you have,*" which is the true trigger of the poem, the place where it turns to the speaker's own past with a vast nostalgia and longing: we survive many lives. An argument implicitly develops here. Memory may be an imperative, "all you have": "*Still,* how much can you bear . . . ?" The next lines express a powerful sense of loss, of dislocation and disinheritance. This is not the universal "you"; the speaker is talking to herself in the second person:

You've lost one language, gained another, lost a third.

There's nothing you'll inherit, neither per stirpes nor per capita

No plot by the riverbank in your father's village of Kozencheri

Or by the burning ghat in Varanasi.

Alexander is remembering her own migration, what she has lost. She is also thinking about her inheritance and uses discordant legal terms for the two ways that parents can leave their estates to their children: per stirpes and per capita. In the case of per stirpes: the grantor intends that the beneficiary's share of the inheritance will go to his or her heir. According to per capita: the grantor intends that no one except the named beneficiary will receive that share of the estate. She knows the legal terms, but neither one is operative if there is nothing left to leave or inherit.

The speaker then considers something more intimate that she will also not inherit. Notice the change in diction. Facing her own death, Alexander is thinking not only about what she might leave as an inheritance, but also, perhaps even more, about the inheritance that was lost to her, first by her leaving India and more recently by the sale and destruction of her family home in Kerala. That's why she refers first to her father's village in South India, on the banks of the river Pampa, and then to the burning ghat, or Manikarnika Ghat. Ghats are riverfront steps leading down to the banks of the Ganges. A few are used as cremation sites. The burning ghat is where most of the dead are cremated in Varanasi. It is a place, Hindus believe, that will liberate them from the cycle of death and rebirth.

The speaker believes that she has been left with nothing but her memories and a way of writing them down: "All you have is a writing hand smeared with ink and little bits of paper / Swirling in a violent wind." This image speaks to the inherent fragility of handwritten text. What does the writer have but markings on a blank page to summon up her world? This is reminiscent of an image created by the Florentine poet Guido Cavalcanti, who writes, "We are the poor bewildered quills, / The little scissors and the grieving penknife." While Cavalcanti projects his own feelings of inadequacy onto the writer's tools, quills and the knives to sharpen them, Alexander thinks of her actual writing hand leaving marks on tiny bits of paper "Swirling in a violent wind." What chance do these scratches have of surviving?

Nonetheless, Alexander is catapulted by memory back into the past. Notice how the pronoun changes from the second to the first person. That's because she is no longer speaking *to* herself but *as* herself. A fragment of memory comes flying back to her, and she inhabits her younger undivided self, who takes on a vivid presence:

I am a blue-black child cheeks swollen with a butter ball

I stole from mama's kitchen

Stones and sky and stars melt in my mouth

Wooden spoon in hand she chased me

Round and round the tamarind tree.

I am musk in the wings of the koel which nests in that tree —

The language shuttles between the vernacular ("I stole from mama's kitchen") and the high Romantic ("Stones and sky and stars melt in my mouth"). For a moment Alexander's speaker is back in the past, inside the memory of circling the tamarind tree. That leads her from a child's statement to a poet's line — "I am musk in the wings of the koel which nests in that tree" — and the cuckoo moves her back into a memory of adulthood. The signal of the change is marked by a pronoun shift back to the second person:

You heard its cry in the jolting bus from Santa Monica to Malibu

After the Ferris wheel, the lovers with their wind slashed hair

Toxic foam on the drifts of the ocean

Come the dry cactus lands

Alexander has moved from the positive mischief of Krishna, child and lover, to the Santa Monica vision of lovers. The memory of hearing the koel on a "jolting bus" in California transports her from her childhood to her adulthood and then back to childhood. Time collapses quickly here as associations carry her from the ocean to the dry cactus lands, from the memory of her own settled home to the vision of a child, who, holding a water bottle, is crossing the border on a bus. Alexander had seen the terrible photo of a dead child on the Mexican American border. That child is now viewed, as through a camera, and described in the third person:

The child who crosses the border water bottle in hand

Fallen asleep in the aisle where backpacks and sodden baskets are stashed.

Out of her soiled pink skirt whirl these blood-scratched skies

And all the singing rifts of story.

The memory of a bus ride has led Alexander to the image of a girl, some version of herself, who has become a refugee traveling from one unnamed place to another. She is caught in a liminal space, asleep in the aisle of a moving vehicle. The suggestion is that an entire world comes out of her dreaming, that the small "soiled pink skirt" contains the entire "blood-scratched skies." She will inherit and invent and transform "the singing rifts of story," which is to say that she will make poetry out of the gaps and fissures, the holes and cracks in narrative, in the past.

In the end, "Krishna, 3:29 A.M." becomes a poem that marks a vocation. It sings itself into being and offers a condensed road map to how Meena Alexander wrote poetry and turned herself into a Romantic postcolonial poet of diaspora.

ACKNOWLEDGMENTS

My debt to my great love Lauren Watel is incalculable. She scrupulously inter-rogated, revised, enriched, and rewrote the first twenty-one pieces. She knows Spanish (I do not) and retranslated poems by Alfonsina Storni and Julia de Burgos. She brought her own ferocious reading skills to interpreting all the poems and found things that I had under-read or missed. I talked about each of these hundred poems with her, and I am indebted to her on every page.

Grateful acknowledgment to the editors of the various magazines and books where these pieces, or parts of them, initially appeared. I have also writ-ten about some of these poets in other books, especially *Poet's Choice,* and there is invariably some overlap. I tend to cannibalize my own work. All of the following pieces have been substantially revised for this book:

John Keats, "This living hand": website for the Poetry Society of America.

Constantine Cavafy, "The God Abandons Antony": . . . *what these Ithakas mean: Readings in Cavafy* (Hellenic Literary and Historical Archive, 2002).

Edna St. Vincent Millay, "What lips my lips have kissed, and where, and why": The section about the five female lyricists is lifted from my overview, "Helmet of Fire: American Poetry in the 1920s," in *A Profile of Twentieth-Cen-*

tury American Poetry, edited by Jack Myers and David Wojahn (Southern Illinois University Press, 1991).

Miklós Radnóti, "The Fifth Eclogue": *World Literature Today* (Fall 2019).

Czesław Miłosz, "Café": The first section is repurposed from my review "Czeslaw Milosz's Invincible Reason," *The New Republic* (June 30, 2017).

Nâzım Hikmet, "On Living": The opening appeared in the foreword to Nâzım Hikmet, *Human Landscapes from My Country,* translated by Randy Blasing and Mutlu Konuk (Persea Books, 2009).

Stevie Smith, "Not Waving but Drowning": The opening appeared in my essay "Stevie: The Movie," in *Writers at the Movies,* edited by Jim Shepard (HarperCollins, 2000).

Tadeusz Różewicz, "In the Midst of Life": The opening appeared in the foreword to *Sobbing Superpower: Selected Poems of Tadeusz Rozewicz,* translated by Joanna Trzeciak (W. W. Norton and Co., 2011).

L. E. Sissman, "A Deathplace": Part of this piece appeared as the foreword to L. E. Sissman, *Night Music,* edited by Peter Davison (Houghton Mifflin, 1999).

Philip Levine, "They Feed They Lion": *Field* (Fall 2009).

Stephen Berg, "On This Side of the River": Part of this piece appeared in my memorial essay "'Being Here, Like This': The Poetry of Stephen Berg," *American Poetry Review* (43, no. 5, 2014).

Zbigniew Herbert, "Mr Cogito and the Imagination": Published in Polish as "Chlust zimnej wody," translated by Magda Heydel, in *Poeci czytają Herberta* (a5, 2009).

Louise Glück, "Night Song": Part of this piece appeared in "The Watcher," *American Poetry Review* (November/December, 1986).

Gerald Stern, "The Dancing": Parts of this piece appeared in "Guide for the Perplexed," in *Insane Devotion: On the Writing of Gerald Stern,"* edited by Mihaela Moscaliuc (Trinity University Press, 2016).

Carolyn Creedon, "Woman, Mined": Part of this piece appeared as the foreword to Carolyn Creedon, *Wet* (Kent State University Press, 2016).

My dear friend André Bernard, who has encouraged and edited each of my prose books, has once more brought out his blue pencil, virtually speaking, and made this a stronger book. I am lucky to be able to count on my exceptional agent and friend, Liz Darhansoff. Special thanks to everyone at Houghton Mifflin Harcourt, especially the exemplary poetry editor Jenny Xu, who guided this book with so much certainty in such uncertain times.

Special thanks for their help on individual pieces to my friends Joanna Trzeciak (Anna Akhmatova), Charles Baxter (Weldon Kees, Louise Glück), Bobbi Bristol (Galway Kinnell), Kathleen Lee (Tony Hoagland), Rabbi Ellen Lippmann (Kadya Molodowsky, Primo Levi), David Lelyveld (Meena Alexander), Alberto Manguel (Jorge Luis Borges), and Mari Pack (Agi Mishol).

For generously answering questions about their poems, special thanks to the late Eavan Boland, whom I am still mourning, and to Victoria Chang, Nicholas Christopher, Michael Collier, Carolyn Creedon, Kate Daniels, Toi Derricotte, Camille Dungy, Linda Gregerson, Joy Harjo, Garrett Hongo, Marie Howe, Cynthia Huntington, Dunya Mikhail, Naomi Shihab Nye, Sharon Olds, Philip Schultz, Vijay Seshadri, Patricia Smith, Mary Szybist, Rosanna Warren, Michael Waters, and Afaa Michael Weaver. I have incorporated some of their responses into my essays.

CREDITS

appeared in *The New Yorker.* Copyright © 1983 by Louise Glück. Used by permission of HarperCollins Publishers LLC.

"The Race" from *The Father* by Sharon Olds. First appeared in *The New Yorker.* Copyright © 1983 by Sharon Olds. Used by permission of Alfred A. Knopf, an imprint of the Knopf Doubleday Publishing Group, a division of Penguin Random House LLC.

"In Memory of the Unknown Poet, Robert Boardman Vaughn" from *The Sunset Maker* by Donald Justice. First appeared in *Antaeus.* Copyright © 1984 by Donald Justice. Used by permission of Alfred A. Knopf, an imprint of the Knopf Doubleday Publishing Group, a division of Penguin Random House LLC.

"The Dancing" from *Early Collected Poems: 1965–1992* by Gerald Stern. Copyright © 1984 by Gerald Stern. Used by permission of W. W. Norton & Company, Inc.

"For Anna Mae Pictou Aquash, Whose Spirit Is Present Here and in the Dappled Stars (for we remember the story and must tell it again so we may all live)" from *In Mad Love and War* by Joy Harjo. First appeared in the collection *And the Ground Spoke* (Guadalupe Cultural Arts Center). Copyright © 1986 by Joy Harjo. Reprinted by permission of Wesleyan University Press.

"Mendocino Rose" from *River of Heaven* by Garrett Hongo. First appeared in *Crazyhorse.* Copyright © 1987 by Garrett Hongo. Used by permission of Alfred A. Knopf, an imprint of the Knopf Doubleday Publishing Group, a division of Penguin Random House LLC.

"Part XII (Dedications)" from "An Atlas of the Difficult World" from *Collected Poems: 1950–2012* by Adrienne Rich. First appeared in *Bridges: A Journal for Jewish Feminists and Our Friends.* Copyright © 1991 by Adrienne Rich. Used by permission of W. W. Norton & Company, Inc.

"The Gas-poker" from *New Selected Poems* by Thom Gunn, edited by Clive Wilmer. First appeared in the *Threepenny Review.* Copyright © 1992 by Thom Gunn. Reprinted by permission of Farrar, Straus and Giroux and The Estate of Thom Gunn.

"What He Thought" from *Hinge & Sign: Poems, 1968–1993* by Heather McHugh. First appeared in *Tikkun.* Copyright © 1991 by Heather McHugh. Reprinted by permission of Wesleyan University Press.

"It Allows a Portrait in Line-Scan at Fifteen" from *Subhuman Redneck Poems* by Les Murray. First appeared in the *Times Literary Supplement.* Copy-